COMMON LAW IN SOUTHERN AFRICA

Recent Titles in
Contributions in Legal Studies

Death by Installments: The Ordeal of Willie Francis
Arthur S. Miller and Jeffrey H. Bowman

Truman's Court: A Study in Judicial Restraint
Frances Howell Rudko

The Gladsome Light of Jurisprudence: Learning the Law in England and the United States in the 18th and 19th Centuries
Michael H. Hoeflich, editor and compiler

James Madison on the Constitution and the Bill of Rights
Robert J. Morgan

Lawyers, Courts, and Professionalism: The Agenda for Reform
Rudolph J. Gerber

John Marshall's Achievement: Law, Politics, and Constitutional Interpretations
Thomas C. Shevory, editor

Affirmative Action and Principles of Justice
Kathanne W. Greene

Unfounded Fears: Myths and Realities of a Constitutional Convention
Paul J. Weber and Barbara Perry

Protecting Constitutional Freedoms: A Role for Federal Courts
Daan Braveman

The Employment Relationship in Anglo-American Law: A Historical Perspective
Marc Linder

The Aristocracy of the Long Robe
J. M. Sosin

Equal Separation: Understanding the Religion Clauses of the First Amendment
Paul J. Weber, editor

COMMON LAW IN SOUTHERN AFRICA

Conflict of Laws and Torts Precedents

PETER B KUTNER

CONTRIBUTIONS IN LEGAL STUDIES, NUMBER 47

GREENWOOD PRESS
New York • Westport, Connecticut • London

Library of Congress Cataloging-in-Publication Data

Kutner, Peter B
Common law in Southern Africa : conflict of laws and torts precedents / Peter B Kutner.
p. cm. — (Contributions in legal studies, ISSN 0147-1074 ; no. 47)
Bibliography: p.
Includes index.
ISBN 0-313-26275-6 (lib. bdg. : alk. paper)
1. Conflict of laws—Africa, Southern. 2. Torts—Africa, Southern. I. Title. II. Series.
LAW
340.9'0968—dc19 88-10242

British Library Cataloguing in Publication Data is available.

Library of Congress Catalog Card Number: 88-10242
ISBN: 0-313-26275-6
ISSN: 0147-1074

First published in 1990

Greenwood Press, 88 Post Road West, Westport, CT 06881
An imprint of Greenwood Publishing Group, Inc.

Printed in the United States of America

The paper used in this book complies with the Permanent Paper Standard issued by the National Information Standards Organization (Z39.48-1984).

10 9 8 7 6 5 4 3 2 1

CONTENTS

PART II: SOUTHERN AFRICAN PRECEDENTS FOR THE LAW OF TORTS

PREFACE

The sole responsibility for the contents of this book is mine, but writing the book would have been neither feasible nor rewarding without the assistance and encouragement of numerous individuals and institutions.

My principal acknowledgement must be to the University of Cape Town Faculty of Law. I am very grateful not only for the Faculty's generosity in providing office, secretarial and library facilities to an overseas visitor for eleven months, but also for the assistance and friendship extended to me by the academic and non-academic staff. I valued the opportunity to be a *de facto* colleague of the able academics in the Faculty of Law and learned much from them. (Inevitably some passages in this book will show that there are things about Southern African law that I should have learned but did not. No one at U.C.T. is responsible for this.)

Also:

The University of Oklahoma College of Law, which granted the sabbatical during which much of the book was written.

The Faculties of Law of Monash University and the University of Edinburgh, which generously provided office and library facilities and thus assisted my research for several projects, including this one.

The librarians and library staff members--particularly at the law libraries of the University of Cape Town, Monash University, the University of Oklahoma and the Bodleian Library, Oxford--who were tremendously helpful in enabling me to use the collections of their libraries and to locate and obtain materials from other libraries.

Denise Greyling, who while a student in the University of Cape Town Faculty of Law served ably as my research assistant and translated judgments published in Afrikaans.

Student research assistants at the University of Oklahoma--particularly Brad Campbell, Jeff Lim and Joy Lim--who proofread and made suggestions for the manuscripts.

My colleagues at the University of Oklahoma, Mark Gillett, Mac Reynolds and Mickie Voges, whose advice and encouragement were much appreciated, and Michal Gray, whose commitment to this book was a *sine qua non* of its publication.

The secretarial staff of the University of Oklahoma College of Law and the University of Cape Town Faculty of Law, who prepared manuscripts of the book. Particular mention is due Debbie Case and Sheryl Waters of the University of Oklahoma and Maureen Fleming of the University of Cape Town. The index was first put into type by Jan Jay of Monash University.

This is a book on Southern African law, but it is written for use outside Southern Africa--by persons concerned with the law in countries whose legal systems are founded on English common law, *i.e.* the United States and most nations of the Commonwealth. For this reason, the text does not conform to some conventions of legal writing in Southern Africa, such as identifying the judge who delivered a judgment agreed to by the entire court. (Another convention not followed is referring to judgments "with respect". It should be assumed that all references to the judiciary are respectful, unless otherwise specified.) Furthermore, since the book's purpose is to identify and analyse judgments and statutes in light of their significance to common law jurisdictions, not to serve as a collection of edited judgments and statutes, there is less precision of quotation than generally found in Southern African legal writing and material in judgments that is not consistent with common law is mentioned only when necessary for explanation. Conversely, material consistent with common law is drawn upon even though Southern African lawyers would regard it as derived from principles of Roman-Dutch law. The cases, statutes, law reports and secondary sources cited in the book are listed in the bibliographic note, table of principal works cited and abbreviations, table of cases and table of statues.

Although aimed at a readership outside Southern Africa, I believe that lawyers within the region also can derive some benefit from the presentation of Southern African law and commentary found in this book. I hope they will be tolerant of what they may regard as undue liberties with the expressions of Southern African jurists or an excess of zeal in finding common law therein.

INTRODUCTION

This book results from the author's studies of Conflict of Laws (Private International Law) and the law of Delict (Tort) in the countries of Southern Africa that adopted Roman-Dutch law as the basis of their substantive law. These comprise South Africa, Zimbabwe (formerly Southern Rhodesia and then Rhodesia), Botswana (Bechuanaland), Lesotho (Basutoland), Swaziland, South West Africa, and the states granted independence by South Africa: Transkei, Bophuthatswana, Venda and Ciskei.[1] With the exception of South West Africa (now also known as Namibia), a former German colony administered by South Africa since World War I, the entire region consisted of British colonies and protectorates prior to the establishment of the Union of South Africa in 1910. English law has had a great influence, direct and indirect, upon the development of law in Southern Africa.[2] Many judgments in Southern African courts

1 The terms "Southern Africa" and "Southern African" will be used to refer collectively to the African countries with Roman-Dutch legal systems. This excludes Angola and Moçambique, which received Portuguese law, and Malaŵi and Zambia, which received English law. For those countries whose names were changed upon independence, the pre-independence name will be used when referring to events that occurred and judgments that were delivered before independence.

2 See Schreiner, The Contribution of English Law to South African Law; and the Rule of Law in South Africa (1967); Beinart, *The English Legal Contribution in South Africa: the Interaction of Civil and Common Law*, 1981 Acta Juridica 7; Boberg, *Oak Tree or Acorn?--Conflicting Approaches to our Law of Delict*, (1966) 83 S.A.L.J. 150. The adoption of Roman-Dutch law stems from its retention in the Cape Colony after the Cape's occupation by

proceed along lines consistent with jurisprudence in common law jurisdictions, states whose law was derived from English common law.

These judgments have made substantial contributions to the body of common law, yet they are little-known in England and other common law countries. Common lawyers rarely survey them--for understandable reasons: the substantial differences between Roman-Dutch law and common law, an increasing language barrier,[3] and the immense volume of published judgments from common law jurisdictions, which discourages further research. In contrast, references to British and Commonwealth authorities (both cases and literature) are commonplace in Southern African courts, and American authorities appear to carry more weight in South Africa than in any other foreign country.

The principal purpose of this book is to identify and describe judgments in Southern African courts[4] that are significant for their treatment of conflicts and tort issues and can serve as authorities or models in common law jurisdictions. They can so serve because their selection of legal principles or approach to the case is the same as or similar to that which might be found in a common law court. The most important legislative reforms in related subjects are also described. The text thus will provide lawyers in common law countries with access to the Southern African cases and statutes most pertinent to questions of Conflict of Laws and Torts that arise in common law jurisdictions.

The judgments surveyed are those published in the South African Law Reports, which commenced in 1947, and the official law

the British early in the nineteenth century.

3 A growing proportion of the judgments in the South African Law Reports is published in Afrikaans. English translations of Afrikaans material in the law reports ceased after the 1980 volume. Prior to the commencement of the translations in 1969, most judgments were published in English.

4 References to the "Appellate Division" are to the Appellate Division of the Supreme Court of South Africa. The name of the country is included in references to other appellate divisions, such as that of the High Court of Rhodesia. The Federal Supreme Court is the Supreme Court of the former Federation of Rhodesia and Nyasaland. Lower courts are identified only in the citation to the report of the court's judgment. Every judgment is attributed to the court, rather than to the judge who delivered it, unless the judgment represents the view of less than a majority of the court.

reports of other Southern African countries from 1947 to the present.[5] All the material is thus of fairly recent vintage. There are extensive quotations from some cases, but the intention is to give the gist or import rather than the *ipsissima verba* of the judgments. The implications as well as the expressions of the judgments are drawn upon. Helpful English-language commentaries on cases and statutes discussed in the text are cited in the notes.

This book does not purport to describe the Southern African law of Delict or Conflict of Laws as a whole. It encompasses only modern judgments which should be regarded as within the body of common law, as well as Roman-Dutch law, and legislation that should be of interest to common law countries.[6] The statutes can serve as models (to be followed, modified or shunned) in those countries as well as in Southern Africa. In order to avoid presenting a work of undue length, I have not undertaken systematic criticism of all the cases and statutes or comparison of common law precedents with decisions of Southern African courts. I have noted criticisms published in Southern African literature and added my own comments when warranted. The comments on cases are intended to indicate whether the decision should be followed in common law jurisdictions rather than whether the court's exposition of the law of South Africa or another Southern African nation was accurate.

In evaluating the authority which a Southern African case should carry in common law countries, one must of course keep in mind the extent to which the decision may have depended upon principles of Roman-Dutch law that are distinctly different from principles of common law. The influence of Roman-Dutch authorities may be present but unexpressed. A court's application of Roman-Dutch law does not necessarily mean that its judgment does not form part of the

5 The volumes covered are 1947-1986 South African Law Reports (S.A.), 1947-1955 Southern Rhodesia Law Reports (S.R.), 1947-1955 Rhodesia and Nyasaland Court of Appeal Decisions (R. & N.C.A.), 1956-1964 Rhodesia and Nyasaland Law Reports (R. & N.), 1964-1979 Rhodesian Law Reports (R.L.R.), 1980-1983 Zimbabwe Law Reports (Z.L.R.), 1947-1966 High Commission Territories Law Reports (H.C.T.L.R.), 1964-1982 Botswana Law Reports (B.L.R.), 1967-1977 and 1980-1981 Lesotho Law Reports (L.L.R.), 1963-1981 Swaziland Law Reports (S.L.R.), and 1977-1981 Bophuthatswana Law Reports (B.S.C.). There is several years' delay in the publication of reports other than the South African Law Reports.

6 Comprehensive treatments of Southern African law are found in South African texts. The principal work in English on Private International Law is Forsyth. For Delict (Tort), see the works by Boberg, McKerron and van der Walt.

common law. That depends upon whether the court's approach to the case and its application of legal principles are consistent with common law doctrine and tradition.

Southern African case law is substantial in many areas of Conflict of Laws, including jurisdiction, recognition of foreign judgments, choice of law in contract, validity of marriage and child custody. No treatment of domicile or matrimonial property matters from a common law perspective could be complete without reference to Southern African decisions on those subjects. Outside the field of jurisdiction, the law reflected in modern Southern African cases is largely similar to the law in common law countries other than the United States. When different rules are applied--as for the essential validity of a marriage--this is readily discernible. The similarity may be explained not only by the influence of English law in Southern Africa but also by the influence of Roman-Dutch writers upon the development of English and American Private International Law.[7]

A lawyer familiar with the place of tort choice of law in common law countries, especially the United States, would expect it to be prominent in litigation elsewhere, but in Southern Africa there is a total absence of definitive decisions on the subject. There are only two cases on the actionability of foreign delicts.[8] Neither established any choice of law principles. A leading Conflicts text introduces its discussion of delictual choice of law with the question, "Is there South African law on choice of law in delict?"[9] If such law exists, it is contained in texts, journals and foreign judicial decisions, not in Southern African law reports.[10] Judicial pronouncements on choice of law concerning property and succession are not as rare, but outside cases involving matrimonial property, there is little of precedential value to be found in the judgments of the last four

7 See Cheshire & North, 22-23, 32-33; Forsyth, 30-36, 46; Scoles & Hay, 8-13.

8 Mackay v. Philip, (1830) 1 Menzies 455; Rogaly v. General Imports (Pty.) Ltd., 1948 (1) S.A. 1216 (C), discussed in Pollak, *Conflict of Laws*, 1948 Ann. Surv. S. Afr. L. 203, 209-10. In Guggenheim v. Rosenbaum (2), 1961 (4) S.A. 21 (W), discussed pp. 75-77, *infra*, the court awarded delictual damages for breach of promise of marriage but did not consider application of delictual choice of law principles. It applied the "proper law" of the "contract" (the agreement to marry).

9 Forsyth, 279.

10 See *ibid.*, 278-86, and literature cited therein, for discussion of choice of law principles that a Southern African court might apply.

decades.

There is more Southern African case law on Delict than on Conflict of Laws, but it diverges more from its common law counterpart, Tort. In size, Southern Africa's greatest contribution to tort law has been to the law of negligence. In relative terms, the greatest contribution has been to the law of defamation.[11] Southern African developments in economic torts and apportionment of damages are particularly noteworthy. The cases on assessment of damages merit attention in common law jurisdictions, and Southern African cases on vicarious liability form a significant part of the common law on the subject. Largely absent from this book are cases concerned with dignitary wrongs, ownership and possession of property, interference with family relations and doctrines of strict liability, in which there are marked differences between common law and the law of Southern Africa.

Of the cases discussed in the book, the great majority are from South Africa. (All but a few of the others are from Southern Rhodesia/Zimbabwe.) Most of the cases are of a type that could have arisen as easily in one of the "First World" common law countries as in Southern Africa. Some, however, are distinctly South African. Major issues of South African politics underly a number of the defamation cases.[12] Racial politics are reflected in several of these cases,[13] but none directly presented issues of race or the effects of race laws. The few cases that did present such issues are *Radebe v. Hough*,[14] *Ex parte Cathrall*,[15] *Winters v. Winters*[16] and *Amod v.*

11 Defamation cases constitute an unusually high proportion of the reported decisions on the law of Delict--forty per cent in the period prior to Union (1910). See Boberg, *Oak Tree or Acorn?--Conflicting Approaches to our Law of Delict*, (1966) 83 S.A.L.J. 150, 158-59.

12 See especially de Klerk v. Union Government (pp. 314, 338-39) and the cases cited in note 13, *infra*.

13 See Golding v. Torch Printing & Publishing Co. (Pty.), Ltd. (p. 317); Vermaas v. Pelser (pp. 322-23); Pienaar v. Argus Printing and Publishing Co. Ltd. (pp. 325-26); and the ostensibly non-political cases Gayre v. S.A. Associated Newspapers Ltd. (pp. 314-16) and South Africa Associated Newspapers Ltd. v. Estate Pelser (pp. 323-25).

14 Pp. 229-31.

15 Pp. 113, 128-29.

16 Pp. 116-17, 129.

Andrews Bakery (Pty.) Ltd.[17]

In the *Radebe* case, the Appellate Division emphatically rejected race as a factor in the assessment of damages for pain and suffering. In *Cathrall*, a South African court found itself obliged to hold an interracial marriage void if it fell under the provisions of the Prohibition of Mixed Marriages Act.[18] In *Winters*, however, a Swaziland court treated such a marriage as valid and thereby offered a party to it the satisfaction of a divorce instead of an annulment. *Amod* holds that a person illegally residing in an area reserved for whites cannot maintain an action for nuisance. This reflects judicial unwillingness to afford legal remedies to persons engaged in illegal activities, which is also found in the cases on injuries causing loss of illegally-derived income.[19] Valid criticisms can be made of decisions in these and other private law cases in which race was an element, but it should be accepted that the South African higher judiciary generally has given such cases a "straight" treatment and delivered judgments that can be cited outside South Africa without embarrassment. It might also be observed that on the sensitive subject of police assaults and unlawful arrests, every Appellate Division decision discussed in the text favours the victim.[20]

South Africa's position on the Rhodesian unilateral declaration of independence ("U.D.I.") is addressed in *Ocean Commodities Inc. v. Standard Bank of S.A. Ltd.*,[21] in which it is laid down in *dictum* that the courts do not recognise the laws of an unrecognised state. Whether the enactments of unilaterally-independent Rhodesia constituted "laws", whether the judgments of Rhodesian courts bound the parties and whether Rhodesian judgments were "precedents" have become academic questions. (The laws and judgments were validated by Britain in its arrangements for the establishment of Zimbabwe in 1980.) However, similar questions exist concerning South West Africa/Namibia and the "national states" granted independence by

17 P. 252.

18 No. 55 of 1949, repealed, Immorality and Prohibition of Mixed Marriages Amendment Act, No. 72 of 1985, s. 7 (S. Afr.).

19 Pp. 240-44.

20 See pp. 161-62, 213-16, 220-26.

21 Pp. 87-92.

South Africa.[22] Transkei, Bophuthatswana, Venda and Ciskei are not internationally recognised as independent entities and *de jure* recognition has been withdrawn from South Africa's administration of South West Africa.

Lack of international recognition is not a sound reason for regarding the laws or judgments of the national states as invalid. If the states are not independent, they are entities of South Africa, and their governments and courts exercise powers conferred upon them by the recognised government of South Africa.[23] Judgments handed down in the supposedly-independent national states should, therefore, be accorded the status of precedent, leaving only judgments in cases from South West Africa in the disputed category. With the exception of its brief consideration in the *Ocean Commodities* case, non-recognition of governments plays no part in the decisions discussed in the text. What can be seen is the creation of choice of law and foreign judgment questions by the separation of the national states from South Africa.[24]

Caution in transplanting principles and precedents from one legal system to another has been advised,[25] but what is undertaken here is not to transplant from Southern African law to common law but to draw upon the many Southern African authorities which are within the body of common law, concurrently with the Roman-Dutch law of Southern Africa. In general, there is no less reason to draw upon Southern African cases or statutes in developing common law jurisprudence than to draw upon cases and statutes from common law countries overseas. Common law countries can only benefit from recognition and appropriate use of Southern Africa's contributions to the common law.

22 See generally Leslie, *Unrecognised Governments in the Conflict of Laws: Lord Denning's Contribution*, (1981) 14 C.I.L.S.A. 165.

23 See Gur Corporation v. Trust Bank of Africa Ltd., [1986] 3 W.L.R. 583 (C.A.).

24 See *e.g.* Viljoen v. Venter, N.O. (pp. 109-10); Abrahams v. Abrahams (pp. 148-50).

25 See Watson, Legal Transplants (1974).

I

SOUTHERN AFRICAN PRECEDENTS FOR THE CONFLICT OF LAWS

1

DOMICILE

GEOGRAPHIC UNIT

One of the most fundamental questions not only of domicile but of Conflict of Laws generally is one of the least decided: to what geographic entity should a court refer when applying Conflict of Laws principles? For example, does South Africa, a country with a single Supreme Court, divided into provincial divisions, and relatively few remaining provincial variations in private law, consist of four "law units" (the four provinces) or one for purposes of Conflict of Laws? Should a nation whose states or provinces are usually treated as separate "law units" be treated as a single unit when a law of nation-wide application is involved? Can a person be domiciled for some purposes in Australia, Canada, South Africa, the United Kingdom, the United States, etc., without being domiciled in one of the nation's constituent parts?[1]

This question arose in *Smith v. Smith*,[2] an action for divorce commenced in Rhodesia. The defendant, Smith, claimed that the court lacked jurisdiction because he was domiciled in Australia, not Rhodesia. No evidence that Smith was domiciled in any particular state or territory of Australia was presented. He claimed to be domiciled in Australia as a whole. One of the bases of this claim

1 See 1 Castel, 103-06; Cheshire & North, 163-64; Forsyth, 97-99; Kahn, Domicile, 5-11.

2 1969 (2) R.L.R. 476 (G.D.), 1970 (1) S.A. 146 (R). See Hackwill, *Domicil in Federated States*, 1971 Rhod. L.J. 5; Kahn, *Conflict of Laws*, 1970 Ann. Surv. S. Afr. L. 419, 420-24.

was that the national legislation governing divorce proceedings in Australia, the Matrimonial Causes Act, 1959,[3] had the effect of creating a matrimonial domicile in Australia for purposes of divorce. Jurisdiction in divorce actions brought in Australia now depended upon whether a party was domiciled in Australia. However, Smith failed to establish that it was possible under the Australian legislation to be domiciled in Australia without at the same time being domiciled in a particular state or territory. Furthermore, assuming this was possible, he failed to persuade the court that he had the *animus manendi* (intent to remain) necessary to establish an Australian domicile of choice. Consequently, the objection to the court's jurisdiction failed.

It is likely that the result would have been the same even if Smith proved that for purposes of a divorce action in Australia he had established an Australian domicile. The court accepted without qualification that at common law a person could not be domiciled in a country such as Australia as a whole. One could have a domicile only in a particular state of Australia because each had its own autonomous government, courts and system of laws. The same applied to the United States and Canada. Thus, the common law position was that Smith retained his Rhodesian domicile unless he established a domicile in a particular Australian state. There was no evidence that he had.

The court stressed that legislation in a foreign country concerning domicile in that country could not modify the forum's rules on the determination of domicile. If a foreign country provided by legislation that matrimonial domicile was acquired upon residence in that country for thirty days, it could enable a person domiciled in Rhodesia to obtain a decree of divorce in that country. But that would not necessarily replace his domicile in Rhodesia or oust the jurisdiction of the Rhodesian court. It follows that the court would not have been persuaded by proof of an Australian domicile under the Australian legislation that Smith had relinquished his Rhodesian domicile and that a Rhodesian court could no longer divorce him from his wife. It was, however, stated that "A different approach may be justified if the court was concerned with the validity of a divorce granted on the basis of a rule of municipal law of a foreign

3 Matrimonial Causes Act, 1959, No. 104, repealed, Family Law Act, 1975, No. 53, s. 3 (Aust.).

country."[4]

It does seem undesirable that a person who has permanently settled in one nation should be regarded as domiciled in another nation and therefore subject to the jurisdiction of its courts (or governed by its laws). But it would have been wrong for the court to decide that a person who settles in a nation is domiciled there without regard to state or provincial boundaries. This could result in the person's not being accepted as a domiciliary in either country. There might be no court willing to exercise jurisdiction in cases, such as divorce proceedings, in which jurisdiction depends upon domicile. An alternative is to decide that a person can acquire a domicile in a foreign nation, as distinct from its constituent states or provinces, when this is possible under the law of that nation. It is true that a court must consider the foreign nation's law in order to determine whether the nation consists of one "law unit" or several.[5] But when a court's jurisdiction depends upon whether a party is domiciled within the forum state, the court should follow the usual rule that domicile is identified according to the forum's own legal principles.[6]

A court has jurisdiction when certain connections between the forum state and the litigation or parties are present. The relevant connecting factors, such as domicile, are established by the law of the forum, which deems them appropriate bases for the exercise of jurisdiction. They should be identified in accordance with the forum's law. The presence of such a connecting factor should not be regarded as dependent upon whether the law of another country identifies the same connection between the country and the parties or the litigation and confers jurisdiction upon its courts accordingly. If the courts of another country will exercise jurisdiction, that is an appropriate basis for a decision to dismiss or stay an action on the ground of *forum non conveniens*, but not for a decision to dismiss for want of jurisdiction. For these reasons, the court's apparent determination in *Smith v. Smith* to identify domicile without regard to Australian law was sound.

It was also sound for the court to leave the door open to a "different approach" in the case of a foreign divorce. If an Australian court grants a divorce (valid throughout Australia) on the basis that

4 Smith v. Smith, 1969 (2) R.L.R. 476, 481 (G.D.), 1970 (1) S.A. 146, 150 (R).

5 See Kahn, Domicile, 10.

6 See Forsyth, 99-100; Kahn, Domicile, 11-12; Sykes & Pryles, 195-96.

the parties have a domicile in Australia, without regard to state boundaries, a court outside Australia should not insist upon identifying domicile on a state-by-state basis and refuse recognition when the parties to the divorce were not domiciled in any particular state.[7]

CHOICE OF LAW

Smith v. Smith can be viewed as a case on choice of law principles in identifying domicile. It involved the question of whether domicile is ascertained solely by reference to the domicile rules of the *lex fori* or also by reference to the domicile rules of a foreign state. This question was presented more directly in *Ex parte Jones*.[8] Mrs. Jones sought to divorce her husband in South Africa, where she lived. The court's jurisdiction depended upon whether Mrs. Jones was domiciled in South Africa. According to the principles usually applied in that country Mrs. Jones, as a married woman, was domiciled in England because that was where her husband was domiciled. English law provided that a married woman's domicile was independent of her husband's; Mrs. Jones was regarded as having a domicile in South Africa.[9] She submitted that for this reason she should be treated as having a South African domicile for purposes of the divorce action.

The court disagreed, holding that domicile was to be determined in accordance with the *lex fori* (South African law). Mrs. Jones, therefore, was not domiciled in South Africa and the court was without jurisdiction on the facts put into evidence. The court's judgment supports the argument made above that a court's jurisdiction depends upon the existence of connecting factors established by the forum's law and the connecting factors should be identified in accordance with the forum's law.

7 See Graveson, 185-87. The court had another situation in mind: that in which the divorce court, in exercising jurisdiction, applied a concept of domicile different from that of the forum but in which a court of the forum state would have had jurisdiction over an analogous case. Robinson-Scott v. Robinson-Scott, [1958] P. 71, was cited in this regard.

8 1984 (4) S.A. 725 (W). See Kahn, *Domicile: As Connecting and Jurisdictional Factor; Choice of Law*, (1985) 102 S.A.L.J. 407.

9 Domicile and Matrimonial Proceedings Act, 1973, c. 45, s. 1 (U.K.).

> It is to be remembered that we are here concerned with the interpretation of the South African Divorce Act,[10] s 2(1)(*b*)(i) of which refers to a wife who ". . . is domiciled in the Republic . . .". Those words, in my view, refer to a domicile determined in accordance with the law of the Republic.[11]

The court was not persuaded that capacity to acquire a domicile of choice should be determined by the law of the domicile to be relinquished.

ACQUISITION OF DOMICILE OF CHOICE

Courts in Southern Africa, like courts elsewhere, have often been required to decide whether a person had established a domicile of choice in a particular place. Many of the cases do little more than decide whether acquisition of a domicile of choice would be inferred from the evidence presented. Judgments in the following cases address the general requirements for acquisition and proof of a domicile of choice.

In *O'Mant v. O'Mant*,[12] Mrs. O'Mant applied in South Africa for a temporary interdict against her husband pending an action for judicial separation. Her husband claimed to have acquired a domicile of choice in Southern Rhodesia, so that the court was without jurisdiction. He was in fact residing and employed in Southern

10 No. 70 of 1979.

11 Ex parte Jones, 1984 (4) S.A. 725, 728 (W). It is unlikely that Parliament intended to confer the privilege of obtaining a divorce upon women settled in South Africa whose husbands were domiciled in countries which granted married women capacity to acquire an independent domicile, while withholding divorce from women whose husbands were domiciled in other countries. However, if Parliament retained domicile as a requirement of jurisdiction in order to avoid the grant of divorces which would not be recognised in other countries, the divorce courts could well be opened to women in Mrs. Jones' position. If the state in which the husband is domiciled accepts that the wife has a domicile in a second state, the state of the husband's domicile and, likely, other states will recognise a divorce granted by the second state. See Armitage v. Attorney-General, [1906] P. 135; Guggenheim v. Rosenbaum (2), 1961 (4) S.A. 21 (W), discussed pp. 144-45, *infra*.

12 1947 (1) S.A. 26 (W).

Rhodesia. Whether Mr. O'Mant was domiciled there depended upon his intention.

The court accepted that "the intention necessary to acquire a domicile of choice excludes all contemplation of any event on the occurrence of which the residence would cease".[13] It then found that Mr. O'Mant did not have this intention--essentially because at all times he had the "mental reservation" that he would leave Southern Rhodesia if Mrs. O'Mant came there. There was evidence of Mr. O'Mant's desire to leave should Mrs. O'Mant follow him and of his efforts to avoid her. Mr. O'Mant's intention to live forever in Southern Rhodesia was subject to the qualification that his wife must be nowhere near him. Always at the back of his mind he had the intention that if she did follow him he would be prepared to leave any country to which he had gone. For these reasons, Mr. O'Mant was found not to have established a domicile of choice in Southern Rhodesia, and the court proceeded on the assumption that it had jurisdiction.

Ley v. Ley's Executors[14] presented a very different set of circumstances. A young stone mason, Ley, emigrated from England to the Cape Colony, worked in various places in the Cape Colony and the Orange River Colony, returned to England to marry his fiancée, came back to South Africa alone, and eventually settled in the Transvaal with his wife. Forty years later, when Ley died, there arose the question of whether he and his wife had been married in community of property. They were married without community of property if Ley was domiciled in England at the time of the marriage, but within community of property if he was domiciled in the Cape Colony.[15] Clearly Ley intended to abandon England and settle in South Africa permanently when he originally emigrated. Whether he formed the requisite intention to acquire a domicile of choice in the Cape was in issue.

The trial court reluctantly concluded that the necessary intention had not been proved. The intention deemed necessary was the same as that stated in *O'Mant v. O'Mant*: an intention which excluded all contemplation of any event on the occurrence of which residence in a place would cease. While Ley had resided in the Cape Colony and

13 Lewis v. Lewis, 1939 W.L.D. 140, following Johnson v. Johnson, 1931 A.D. 391, 398, and Westlake, Private International Law, s. 264 (7th ed. 1925).

14 1951 (3) S.A. 186 (A.D.).

15 See pp. 94-97, *infra*.

intended to live in South Africa permanently, it had not been shown that he had excluded as his home one of the other South African colonies. If his best opportunity was in another colony he would have gone there, as he eventually did.

Upon Mrs. Ley's appeal to the Appellate Division, that court first addressed the applicable burden of proof. It laid down that the standard of proof was no higher than in other civil cases. The *onus* of proving the establishment of a domicile of choice was discharged on the same "preponderance of probability" standard applicable to other matters in civil cases. It was not necessary to prove the requisite intention "with perfect clearness and satisfaction".[16]

The Appellate Division then addressed the intention requirement. In its opinion, it was erroneous to include in the requirement exclusion from the person's mind of all possibility that he might in the future emigrate to another country. If the trial court meant to do this, it had erred. Westlake's statement that the necessary intention "excludes all contemplation of any event on the occurrence of which the residence would cease"[17] was interpreted to mean:

> if the state of mind of the *de cujus* is something like this, "I may settle here permanently, and anyhow I'll stay for a time; but perhaps I'll move to another country" the intention required to establish a domicile is not present. But if his state of mind is like this, "I shall settle here", that is enough, even though it is not proved that if he had been asked, "Will you never move elsewhere?" he might not have said something like, "Well, never is a long day. Who knows? I might move if I change my mind or if circumstances were to change."[18]

Any doubt actually present in the person's mind concerning whether he will move would exclude the intention to settle permanently, but the possibility that, if the idea of a move in the future had been suggested to him, he might not at once have "scouted" it did not amount to contemplation of an event on which the residence would cease. It was only the former that had to be disproved by a person

16 Winans v. Attorney-General, [1904] A.C. 287, 291 (H.L.) (Lord Macnaghten), quoted with apparent disapproval.

17 See note 13, *supra*, and accompanying text.

18 Ley v. Ley's Executors, 1951 (3) S.A. 186, 195 (A.D.).

alleging a change of domicile.

The court found it to have been proved, on the balance of probabilities, that Ley intended to settle in the Cape Colony before his return to England. Consequently, he became domiciled there, he was married in community of property, and his widow could claim half of the joint estate.

The Appellate Division returned to this subject in *Eilon v. Eilon*,[19] an action for divorce, custody of children and other relief. Jurisdiction depended upon the husband's domicile. Different views were expressed concerning the test of intention to be applied. According to the majority, the *onus* of proving a domicile of choice was discharged upon proof of physical presence and proof that the *de cujus* had at the relevant time a fixed and deliberate intention to abandon his previous domicile and settle permanently in the country of choice. Contemplation of any certain or foreseeable future event on the occurrence of which residence in that country would cease excluded such an intention. If the *de cujus* entertained any doubt as to whether he would remain or not, intention to settle permanently was likewise excluded. On the other hand, the contingency of an unforeseeable event would not prevent the existence of the required intention. "Excludes all contemplation"[20] could not mean and was never intended to mean that the *de cujus* had excluded from his mind all possibility that in the future he might leave the country.

Williamson, J.A., rejected the "unrealistic" "strict and rigid" approach found in such English cases as *Moorhouse v. Lord*[21] and *Winans v. Attorney-General*.[22] Domicile required a "present intention to reside permanently . . . an intention unlimited in period but not irrevocable in character".[23] The question in the present case was whether, on a balance of probabilities, Eilon had at the time the action was commenced a present intention to reside permanently in South Africa "in the sense that he had no intention of limiting the period of his residence". The enquiry did not involve "a scrupulous

19 1965 (1) S.A. 703 (A.D.). See Kahn, *A Gloss on Animus Manendi*, (1965) 82 S.A.L.J. 152.

20 See p. 16, *supra*.

21 (1863) 10 H.L. Cas. 272.

22 [1904] A.C. 287 (H.L.).

23 Eilon v. Eilon, 1965 (1) S.A. 703, 708-09 (A.D.) (Williamson, J.A.), quoting Gulbenkian v. Gulbenkian, [1937] 4 All E.R. 618, 627 (P.D.).

and solicitous investigation as to whether perhaps in the future he might not in certain circumstances decide to remove his permanent home". Rumpff, J.A., agreed with Williamson, J.A., and added that an intention to live in a new country indefinitely need not be accompanied by a desire to turn one's back on the country of origin, to sever all connections with that country, or never to return there. The views of Williamson and Rumpff, JJ.A., were influenced to a substantial degree by Roman-Dutch authorities, and differences between those authorities and English authorities were emphasised.

The majority ultimately decided that Eilon had not become domiciled in South Africa. Williamson and Rumpff, JJ.A., decided that a South African domicile had been proved. This division appears to have stemmed less from the judges' disagreement concerning the legal tests to be applied than from their different conclusions on the basic question of whether Eilon had decided to settle in South Africa.

The test formulated by Williamson, J.A., seems preferable to the test formulated by the majority. The former is more likely than the latter to identify as a person's domicile the state with which he has the most substantial associations and the state which should, in preference to others, exercise jurisdiction over his affairs. The majority's emphasis upon foreseeability may be misplaced. A person should not be prevented from establishing a domicile of choice in the place where he lives simply because he foresees an unlikely event which would cause or persuade him to move.[24]

FOREIGN SERVICEMEN AND OFFICIALS

While Southern African courts could be demanding with respect to the intention requirement of domicile of choice, they were willing to decide that a person's status as a foreign serviceman, official or immigrant did not prevent him from forming the required intention or otherwise exclude the establishment of a domicile of choice.

In *Ex parte Glass*,[25] Glass, a Scotsman serving in the British Army, was sent to South Africa for convalescence. He was advised that he was no longer required for military service and would be discharged at the conclusion of his convalescence. He desired to

24 See Anton, 178; Cheshire & North, 157-62; Kahn, Domicile, 49-51.

25 1948 (4) S.A. 379 (W).

settle in South Africa and successfully applied for demobilisation in that country. He was also permitted to take civilian employment. While so employed, before his discharge from the Army, he married. Whether the marriage was in community of property depended upon whether Glass had established a domicile of choice in South Africa at that time.

The court was bound by an earlier case, *McMillan v. McMillan*,[26] in which it was held that a person in military service could not acquire a domicile of choice in the place where he was stationed. The rationale of that decision was that

> there is a clear distinction between accepting this intention [to settle in South Africa] and giving effect thereto during the period of the plaintiff's service; the accepted intention remains in abeyance during such period and only becomes operative as one of the factors establishing acquisition of a domicile of choice, when the plaintiff is discharged and is no longer under disability as regards his freedom of action. The authorities are clear, I think, that a mere intention to reside permanently at the proposed domicile effects no change of domicile until such intention is carried into effect by actual assumption of residence. If so, it seems to me that it is only when the plaintiff resides in the Union as a free agent, that is, after he has been freed by his discharge from the constant liability to immediate transfer, that the two elements necessary for the establishment of a domicile of choice concur.[27]

The court distinguished *McMillan* from the case before it on the ground that the military authorities not only undertook to demobilise Glass in South Africa, but also permitted him to accept employment there and "intimated" that he would not, pending his discharge, be transferred elsewhere. Glass was, therefore, not under any disability in his freedom of action. He was in a position to exercise his intention to remain permanently in South Africa, independent of the control of any authority. For these reasons, held the court, Glass was free to establish a domicile in South Africa and had done so by the time of his marriage.

26 1943 T.P.D. 345.

27 *Ibid.*, 353-54.

Nicol v. Nicol[28] involved the more usual circumstance of a person who continued in active service prior to his discharge from the armed forces. Nicol, a marine in the Royal Navy, had been stationed in the Cape Province for almost six years. Not long after his arrival he married a South African, who now sought to divorce him. The court had jurisdiction if Nicol was domiciled in the Cape Province. Nicol allegedly had assured his wife that he intended to make the Cape his permanent home. This was supported by evidence that he unsuccessfully applied for transfer to the South African Navy, applied for discharge from the Royal Navy in South Africa, and had arranged for civilian employment in Cape Town after his discharge. His application for discharge in South Africa was not likely to be refused, but it had not been granted.

The court was not bound by older South African decisions (which were in conflict) on the question of whether a serving soldier or sailor could acquire a domicile of choice. Being free to express and apply its own opinion, the court reasoned as follows: A man might acquire a domicile of choice in a new country "by establishing his actual residence in that country with the intention of making it his permanent home".[29] It was obvious that mere corporeal presence in a country pursuant to service orders did not by itself establish domicile within that country. "Service residence" was to be distinguished from the "actual residence" required for acquisition of a domicile of choice. This was so whether the *de cujus* resided in barracks, in a warship, or in his own private home. Should, however, the intention to make that country his permanent home (the *animus manendi*) supervene, and should such intention be satisfactorily proved, there was not in principle any reason why a serviceman should not be able to acquire a domicile during his period of service. The circumstance that his residence was liable to be terminated as the result of service orders to proceed elsewhere was not necessarily fatal. Pending any such order, the serviceman intended to remain. Should an order have been given, he *ex hypothesi* intended to return.

In the court's opinion, Westlake's statement that "the intention necessary for acquiring a domicile of choice excludes all contemplation of any event on the occurrence of which the residence would cease"[30] was to be restricted to contemplation of cessation of

28 1948 (2) S.A. 613 (C).

29 *Ibid.*, 617, quoting from Webber v. Webber, 1915 A.D. 239, 242 (Innes, C.J.).

30 See p. 16, *supra.*

residence by voluntary action. Otherwise, it was impossible to reconcile the statement with such cases as *Boldrini v. Boldrini*,[31] where the circumstance of being at all material times subject to the risk of deportation from a country was held to be not incompatible with acquisition of a domicile within that country. The cases which denied the possibility of a serviceman's obtaining a domicile in the country where he was serving did not directly rest upon the principle enunciated by Westlake. Rather, they accepted the contention that because a serviceman was not a free agent, he lacked the ability to make a choice during his period of service, even when the court was satisfied as to what his intention in fact was. This meant that, despite the presence of *animus manendi*, "service residence" could never become "actual residence". The court could not accept this. If the circumstances of the case showed that, because of the *animus manendi*, what commenced as mere "service residence" had now become "something more", there was no insuperable legal obstacle to holding that there was a sufficient combination of residence (the fact of actual residence) and intention (*animus manendi*) to constitute domicile.

On this view, the court had to be satisfied concerning Nicol's intention and residence. In this type of case, residence was *prima facie* "service residence" only. That was in itself no evidence of domicile. A serviceman's mere inclination to settle, after termination of service, in the country where he was stationed was not equivalent to the "present exercise of the choice of a permanent home in that country". "Something more", reflecting a voluntary choice of permanent residence, had to be shown. However, the acquisition of a private home was not indispensable. The court found a sufficient showing in the evidence of Nicol's actions and intention placed before it. Accordingly, it held that Nicol had acquired a domicile of choice in the Cape and the court had jurisdiction.[32]

In *Naville v. Naville*,[33] once again the court's jurisdiction in a matrimonial cause depended upon whether the husband had established a domicile of choice in the Cape Province. Naville, a career official of the Swiss government, had been the Swiss consul

31 [1932] P. 9 (C.A.).

32 See also Hibbs v. Wynne, 1949 (2) S.A. 10 (C), and Ex parte Readings, 1958 (4) S.A. 432 (C), in which the judgment in Nicol v. Nicol was approved and applied.

33 1957 (1) S.A. 280 (C).

in Cape Town for six years. He was near retirement and intended to make his home in Cape Town thereafter. The question arose whether a person in the consular service of a foreign government could establish a domicile in the place where he was posted.

The court drew upon the precedents involving servicemen. It followed cases such as *Nicol v. Nicol* in which it was decided that a serviceman was not incapable of establishing a domicile of choice where he was stationed. Accordingly, Naville could and did establish a domicile of choice in the Cape. The court could have drawn an analogy between the case before it and *Ex parte Glass*[34] because the Swiss government had undertaken to not transfer Naville from Cape Town and to discharge him from service there. Thus Naville, like Glass, had the freedom from transfer which most persons in the military and the consular and diplomatic services lacked.

IMMIGRANTS WITHOUT PERMANENT ADMISSION

Another category of person who may not be free to remain in a place of chosen residence is the immigrant who has not been admitted to permanent residence. He may be summarily required to leave the country to which he has emigrated. Can he nevertheless acquire a domicile of choice in that country?

In *Gwambe v. Gwambe*,[35] an action for divorce, the plaintiff had lived in South Africa for thirty years and intended to remain there for the rest of his life. His passport entitled him to enter the country, but he was a foreign national ineligible for naturalisation and his right to stay in South Africa could be terminated at any time by the authorities. The court held that this did not prevent him from acquiring a domicile of choice there. It relied principally upon the decision of the English Court of Appeal in *Boldrini v. Boldrini*,[36] in which the alien concerned was eligible for naturalisation. The cases pertaining to a member of the forces' ability to acquire a domicile of choice were thought "clearly not in point".

In *Van Rensburg v. Ballinger*,[37] the person whose domicile was

34 1948 (4) S.A. 379 (W). See pp. 19-21, *supra*.

35 1950 (2) S.A. 643 (T).

36 [1932] P. 9 (C.A.).

37 1950 (4) S.A. 427 (T).

in question had been elected a Senator in the South African Parliament. A petition was brought to declare Ballinger's election invalid on the ground that he was not a Union (South African) national. Whether Ballinger was a Union national depended upon whether he was domiciled in South Africa. He had emigrated from Scotland over twenty years earlier. Fearing that Ballinger's activities in South Africa might be undesirable, the Minister of the Interior issued before Ballinger's arrival an order deeming him to be an undesirable inhabitant of or visitor to South Africa. As a result of the deeming order, Ballinger became a "prohibited immigrant". He was, however, granted a temporary entry permit for three months. After representations were made on Ballinger's behalf, the Minister decided to grant a temporary residence permit of unlimited duration. The deeming order was not withdrawn. In effect, Ballinger was "on probation", with successive Ministers of the Interior retaining the power to deport him if his behaviour warranted this. The position remained unchanged until the election petition was instituted. Neither the government nor Ballinger took any steps to alter his status, although it had been reviewed by the Minister of the Interior a few years before the case arose. In the years since his arrival, Ballinger had resided in South Africa, acquired a South African passport and returned to South Africa after trips abroad.

The court held that Ballinger was domiciled in South Africa; his election as Senator was valid. Murray, J., believed that in principle

> the power of a higher authority to terminate a person's residence in a particular area cannot *per se* affect the question whether that person intended to make his permanent abode there. If the power of termination is actually exercised, then naturally with the disappearance of physical residence the domicile thus acquired is brought to an end. Until such termination the only effect of the possibility of that power of deportation being exercised by a higher authority is that the person may (I do not say he must) be taken to realise the precarious character of his residence and consequently may not be held to have formed the intention of making his permanent home in such area.[38]

38 *Ibid.*, 441.

Ballinger had the required intention as well as the required actual residence. Revocation of his residence permit was a remote possibility and he believed that it would not occur. In cases such as the present, while higher authority could terminate permission to reside in the country, the alien was "master of his own destiny". He could decide to have his home in the particular place and carry that decision into effect. Ballinger's liability to deportation did not prevent him from becoming domiciled in South Africa.

De Villiers, J., was of the opinion that a domicile of choice could not be acquired if there was an obstacle in the way of one of the two requirements--presence and intention to remain permanently. The obstacle could be physical (as in the case of an internee) or legal. There would be a legal obstacle if a person was denied the right to stay in his chosen country and thus knew that he could not get permanent residence there. But here the Minister of the Interior had removed the obstacle when he granted an unlimited residence permit in lieu of the three months permit. Ballinger could stay permanently provided he behaved himself. Westlake had laid down that "the intention necessary to acquire a domicile of choice excludes all contemplation of any event on the occurrence of which the residence would cease",[39] but the event referred to was voluntary termination of residence--the interpretation made in *Nicol v. Nicol.*[40] It was one which would be accepted by the person himself and motivate him to leave the country. The alien who wished to settle in the country, probably would not be disturbed and believed he would not be could acquire a domicile of choice there.[41]

In *Smith v. Smith*,[42] another matrimonial action in which the husband's domicile was in issue, the Federal Supreme Court accepted that an alien liable to deportation could establish a domicile of choice. But in the case before it, unlike previous cases, the alien's initial entry and residence in the country were unlawful at all times. Smith entered Southern Rhodesia under a false name and concealed his criminal record. His illegal residence had not been condoned by the authorities.

The trial court held that, were it not for the illegal nature of

39 Westlake, Private International Law, s. 264 (7th ed. 1925).

40 1948 (2) S.A. 613, 617 (C). See pp. 21-22, *supra*.

41 Van Rensburg v. Ballinger, 1950 (4) S.A. 427, 443-44 (T) (de Villiers, J.).

42 1962 R. & N. 469 (F.S.C.), 1962 (3) S.A. 930 (F.S.C.).

his residence, Smith would have established a domicile in Southern Rhodesia; but an illegal resident could not acquire a domicile of choice.

> It is fundamental principle of our law that legal rights may not be acquired by unlawful means. Although the acquisition of a domicile of choice is not normally regarded as the acquisition of a privilege conferring rights and benefits under the law it does in my view have this effect. The acquisition confers among other rights the right now under consideration--the right to sue in this court. Such a right can only be acquired by lawful means.[43]

The Federal Supreme Court agreed with the trial court's conclusion and reasons, adding,

> A person acquiring a domicile of choice must . . . be deemed to have in mind the rights and obligations which will spring from it. He must be taken to intend the natural consequences of his acts, and so to have an intention to obtain the rights to which the learned judge refers.[44]

It is submitted that the trial court's reasons are not a satisfactory basis for the conclusion that an illegal resident cannot establish a domicile and the Federal Supreme Court's addendum is even less satisfactory. Any person who seeks to have a legal matter resolved in his favour on the premiss that he is domiciled in a state can be said to be seeking to acquire a benefit from his domicile, but it goes too far to assert that an illegal resident seeks to acquire legal rights by unlawful means. Any "intention" to obtain legal rights by illegal residence would be purely fictional in most cases. Acquisition of the legal rights (and obligations) pertinent to the case would be but a side effect of residence taken up for other reasons. In *Smith v. Smith*, Smith came to Africa as a fugitive to escape criminal prosecution in England, not to institute or avoid matrimonial litigation.

The no-acquisition-of-rights-by-unlawful-means rationale is especially unsatisfactory when the user of unlawful means is not

43 *Ibid.*, 474-75, 935.

44 *Ibid.*, 475, 936.

basing a claim or defence on his acquisition of a domicile of choice. The Federal Supreme Court evidently intended its decision to apply to such cases, for the result of *Smith v. Smith* was that Smith's wife, who was the plaintiff, could not obtain the annulment she sought--a Southern Rhodesian court had no jurisdiction. Thus it was the wrongdoer who prevailed! If legal policy requires that the person whose entry and residence in the country was illegal be incapable of establishing a domicile there, this is not because his conduct was unlawful, but because his connection with the country is likely to be so tenuous and temporary that his rights, obligations and status should not be governed by that country's laws or adjudicated by its courts.[45]

A more satisfactory basis for the conclusion that a domicile of choice could not be acquired in the circumstances of the case can be found in the following passage of the Federal Supreme Court's judgment:

> Fears that the worst may happen do not necessarily preclude a sufficient animus. But knowledge that one is residing only in defiance of the law, and will so continue indefinitely, makes it impossible to have an animus manendi of the requisite quality . . . . The animus manendi, though it does not require an absolute intention to reside permanently, must at least be an unconditional intention to reside for an indefinite period. It would not be enough if a chronic invalid were to come to this country and say, "I will settle here if the climate suits my health", if he died a few days later. There would at least have to be a trial period, after which the unconditional intention might come into existence. In this case the intention of the appellant, putting it at the highest, can only have been, "I will stay in Rhodesia if I can escape the attention of the authorities, whose statutory duty is to deport me, and who will at once do so if they learn the true facts about me". I think a conditional or provisional intention of this kind cannot in law amount to the animus manendi necessary to establish a domicile of choice.[46]

45 See also the criticisms discussed in Spiro, *Domicile of Illegal Immigrant*, (1963) 12 I.C.L.Q. 680. But see Kahn, Domicile, 62-64.

46 Smith v. Smith, 1962 R. & N. 469, 475 (F.S.C.), 1962 (3) S.A. 930, 936 (F.S.C.).

This appears to mean that a person does not in fact have the *animus manendi* necessary to establish a domicile when he realises that he will be required to leave should the authorities discover that he is in the country illegally.

The plaintiff in *Drakensbergpers Bpk. v. Sharpe*,[47] an immigrant from Britain, did acquire a domicile of choice in South Africa. The issue was whether he had lost this domicile when he was deported. If so, it was necessary to him to give security for the costs of a defamation action he had instituted. The plaintiff averred that he intended to return to South Africa as soon as he was able to. As a deportee he was a prohibited immigrant unless the government granted him authority to return, which it had not done. It appears that re-entry without such authority would be illegal.

The court held that a person loses his domicile of choice when he is deported pursuant to the applicable provision of South African immigration law, which authorised deportation of persons sentenced to imprisonment.[48] The court referred with apparent approval to a passage in Dicey[49] which distinguished deportees whose re-entry would not be illegal from deportees who could not legally re-enter the country, but it did not adopt this distinction. It is submitted that if a deportee is to lose his domicile of choice upon deportation, this should be because in the circumstances he really does not have *animus revertendi* or his intention to return is so unrealistic that it should be disregarded, not because his presence in the country would be unlawful.[50]

47 1963 (4) S.A. 615 (N).

48 Admission of Persons to the Union Regulation Act, No. 22 of 1913, s. 22, repealed, Admission of Persons to the Republic Regulation Act, No. 59 of 1972 (S. Afr.).

49 Dicey, Conflict of Laws 106 (7th ed. 1958).

50 Dicey discussed deportation in the context of determining whether a person had the requisite intent to acquire or retain a domicile. The decision in Drakensbergpers Bpk. v. Sharpe is not necessarily authority for the proposition that if the deportee had *animus revertendi* at the time of the deportation, he nevertheless lost his domicile of choice because re-entry would be illegal. But see Forsyth, 110-12; Kahn, *Conflict of Laws*, 1963 Ann. Surv. S. Afr. L. 542, 543-44; Spiro, *Deportation and Domicile*, (1964) 81 S.A.L.J. 173, 176-78.

CHILDREN

One of the disputed questions of the law of domicile has been how the domicile of a child whose parents have separated is to be determined. Three Southern African cases touching upon this question should be mentioned.

In *Favard v. Favard*,[51] in order to identify the defendant's domicile at the time of his marriage, the court considered whether his domicile had been changed when he was a child. The defendant's domicile of origin was in England. His parents separated and were divorced. Thereafter he was in the custody of his mother, who came to South Africa when the defendant was about twelve years of age. The plaintiff submitted that the defendant's mother changed her domicile to South Africa and this had the effect of changing her son's domicile. The court responded:

> any question of a change of status is essentially of a nature in which the decision rests with the guardian rather than the custodian. The effect of a change of domicile in a minor as a result of action by the parent is to attribute to the minor a decision on the part of the parent to change his or her permanent residence, and a decision on such a point seems to me to be a matter ordinarily within the powers of the guardian.[52]

Whether a child's domicile changed therefore depended upon the intention of its guardian rather than the intention of its custodian, when guardianship and custody were separated. In the absence of proof that the defendant's mother changed her domicile to South Africa and of any evidence that she had become the defendant's legal guardian, the court would not find that the defendant had become domiciled in South Africa during his minority.

The views expressed in *Favard v. Favard* leave open the possibility that a child becomes domiciled with its mother when the father (its guardian) has agreed to the mother having custody of the child. Such agreement could be taken to reflect the intention of the guardian concerning the child's domicile. But the court in *Martine*

51 1951 S.R. 97, 1953 (3) S.A. 656 (S.R.).

52 *Ibid.*, 97, 657.

v. Large,[53] in which divorced spouses agreed that the mother should have custody, denied that the children had assumed their mother's domicile. Even if a father could allow his children to acquire a domicile other than his own, it would be wrong to assume that he had done so by allowing them to be in the custody of their mother. *Favard v. Favard* was interpreted to mean that the domicile of the father, as guardian, should be the domicile of the minor children.

Littauer v. Littauer[54] confirms that if the child's mother has become the guardian, the child's domicile is that of the mother. A court in Denmark, which was then the domicile of the parents, had awarded custody of the child to the mother when the parents' marriage was dissolved. Danish law made no distinction between the custody and guardianship of minors. While the court's order referred only to custody, the mother was in effect also awarded guardianship. The domicile of a minor, the court stated, was dependent upon the domicile of the guardian parent. Therefore, when the mother established a domicile in Switzerland, her son became domiciled in Switzerland.

There is merit in the proposition that the domicile of a child should not change whenever custody changes, but it is submitted that the preferable position is that a minor child takes the domicile of the custodial parent.[55] This is more likely to locate the child's domicile in the state most closely associated with the child and avoids giving a change in the non-custodial parent's domicile the effect of changing the child's domicile.

53 1952 (4) S.A. 31 (W).

54 1973 (4) S.A. 290 (W).

55 See Forsyth, 124; Kahn, Domicile, 87-93.

2

JURISDICTION

Much of the law of jurisdiction in Southern Africa is quite foreign to common law jurisprudence. There is, however, a body of decisions on matters found in both the law of Southern Africa and common law.[1]

SUBMISSION TO COURT'S JURISDICTION

Subject to some exceptions not found in common law systems, a party's consent or other submission to a court's jurisdiction is recognised in Southern Africa as a basis for the court's exercise of jurisdiction in an action against that party.[2] The issue of submission may arise when a party denies that the court in which an action against him is instituted has jurisdiction or denies that a foreign court, upon whose judgment an opposing party relies, had jurisdiction.

When submission to a court's jurisdiction is in issue, the matter frequently "boils down" to the question of whether a party's conduct (before or after the litigation commenced) constituted submission. For example, it was decided in *Beverley Building Society v. de Courcy*[3] that the defendants' choice in a deed of suretyship of *domicilium citandi et executandi* (a "domicile" for the purpose of serving a

1 Jurisdiction in family matters is considered pp. 111-25, *infra*.

2 See Forsyth, 164-67, 177-79, 327-32; Silberberg, 11-19.

3 1963 R. & N. 208 (S.R.), 1964 (4) S.A. 264 (S.R.).

summons and levying execution) at a Southern Rhodesian address constituted consent to the jurisdiction of a Southern Rhodesian court. In *Standard Bank Ltd. v. Butlin*,[4] a contrary decision was made. The effect of the first decision was that a Southern Rhodesian court exercised jurisdiction over an action for amounts owed under the deed of suretyship. The effect of the second decision was that a South African court refused to recognise a Rhodesian judgment in an action on the deed.

In *Beverley Building Society v. de Courcy*, the defendants had not been resident or domiciled in Southern Rhodesia at the time the deed was entered and did not have any property there. Also, under the deed the plaintiff could claim from the defendants instalments of interest as they came due without claiming capital. It therefore appeared to the court that the intention of the choice of a *domicilium citandi et executandi* was to submit to the jurisdiction of the Southern Rhodesian court and thereby enable the plaintiff to bring suit there, not merely to facilitate service of process (by providing a local address) when another basis of jurisdiction could be found. In *Standard Bank Ltd. v. Butlin*, the defendant had been domiciled and resident in Rhodesia when he executed the deed. A Rhodesian court would have had jurisdiction over him in any event. This led the South African court to distinguish *Beverley Building Society v. de Courcy* and infer that the choice of *domicilium citandi et executandi* in the case before it was not a consent to jurisdiction, only a means of facilitating service of process by specifying a fixed address.

Although the court in *Standard Bank Ltd. v. Butlin* concluded that there had been no consent to jurisdiction, it was of the opinion that submission to a court's jurisdiction could be implied in a contractual agreement. A portion of the judgment is devoted to criticising the English rule that to be considered effective, a contractual submission to jurisdiction must be expressed.[5] However, it takes the position that submission is never to be inferred solely from selection of a *domicilium citandi et executandi*. Another significant element of *Standard Bank Ltd. v. Butlin* is its decision that the defendant did not submit to the Rhodesian court's jurisdiction when, after the judgment against him was entered, he agreed to the plaintiff's suggestion that it sell his shares in a Rhodesian company (which were about to be attached in execution of the judgment) and

4 1981 (4) S.A. 158 (D).

5 Vogel v. R. and A. Kohnstamm Ltd., [1973] Q.B. 133. See Cheshire & North, 83-84, 635-37; Dicey & Morris, 1050-52.

keep the proceeds, thus reducing the judgment debt.[6]

Different contractual provisions were involved in *Reiss Engineering Co. Ltd. v. Insamcor (Pty.) Ltd.*[7] The parties had agreed in a written contract that, "This agreement shall be subject to the laws of the United Kingdom of Great Britain." This was interpreted as an agreement that the law of Great Britain (probably intended to mean the law of England) be the proper law of the contract. The court held that this was not to be taken as an implied agreement to submit disputes arising out of the contract to the English courts. Agreements on choice of law and agreements on jurisdiction were to be differentiated. In consequence, an English default judgment against the defendant could not be enforced. The court rejected the argument that because English law gave English courts jurisdiction over actions concerning contracts governed by English law,[8] the parties impliedly agreed that the English courts would have jurisdiction when they provided that their agreement would be subject to British (*i.e.* English) law.

JURISDICTION OF *SITUS* OF LAND

The presence of land within the court's area of jurisdiction may provide a basis for the exercise of jurisdiction in certain instances. In *Sonia (Pty.) Ltd. v. Wheeler*,[9] a domiciliary of the Orange Free State there entered a contract for the purchase of land in the Eastern Cape Province from the defendant, which was domiciled in the Transvaal. The purchaser brought suit in the Eastern Cape for cancellation of the contract, refund of the purchase price with interest, and costs of suit. The purchaser alleged that the contract was induced by the seller's fraudulent misrepresentations.

6 See also du Preez v. Philip-King, 1963 (1) S.A. 801 (W), in which it was held that various steps taken by the defendant's attorneys in response to an action for damages, including pleading to the merits of the plaintiff's claim, did not constitute submission to the jurisdiction of the court in which the action was commenced. The court applied the test that an act was not submission to jurisdiction unless it was consistent only with acquiescence to jurisdiction, *i.e.* necessarily inconsistent with his objection to jurisdiction.

7 1983 (1) S.A. 1033 (W).

8 Rules of the Supreme Court, 1965, O. 11, r. 1(1)(*f*)(iii) (Eng.).

9 1958 (1) S.A. 555 (A.D.).

The Appellate Division held that the court of the Eastern Cape, as *situs* of the land involved, had jurisdiction to grant all the relief claimed. On grounds of "principle, convenience and common sense" the Appellate Division approved the old case of *Palm v. Simpson,*[10] which was said to hold that

> a claim to rescind a contract for the sale of immovable property can be effectively dealt with by the Courts of the State in which the property is situate. Such State has complete control over the property and can therefore effectively release a person from his obligation to transfer or to take transfer of the property. It follows that in an action in which a judgment rescinding a contract to transfer immovable property is claimed it is a sufficient basis for jurisdiction that the property is situate within the State in whose Court the action is brought.[11]

The Appellate Division stated that the court of the area in which property is situate can control the transfer of, or any interference with, the property--through the Register of Deeds of that area and by other means. If a buyer repudiated a sale of land after he paid the price, the seller might create "an awkward and complicated position" by transferring the property to the buyer and he might file transfer documents to effect this purpose. A court could control the Registrar of Deeds by issuing an interdict. The *situs* court was the only court that could do this. It could deal with attempts to register servitudes over the property or to cancel existing servitudes against or in favour of the property. All property was exposed to interference by third parties, both as regards claims to ownership or other rights over the property, and as regards physical acts such as acts of trespass. Property which was the subject of a sale was not exempt from those kinds of interference and only the court of the *situs* had jurisdiction to deal with such matters. *Palm v. Simpson* had recognised the "patent fact" that the court of the *situs* is the court best equipped to deal with matters relating to land situated within its territorial jurisdiction.

The court in *Palm v. Simpson* had held that it had no jurisdiction over a money claim (for an overdue portion of the price

10 (1848) 3 Menzies 565.

11 Sonia (Pty.) Ltd. v. Wheeler, 1958 (1) S.A. 555, 561 (A.D.).

of the land sold) brought with the claim for rescission of the contract. In *Sonia (Pty.) Ltd. v. Wheeler*, however, it was held that the *situs* court had jurisdiction over the purchaser's money claims because the court's judgment would be enforceable (by attachment of the defendant's property situate in the Eastern Cape and execution of the judgment in other parts of South Africa) and because, if it had jurisdiction to decree cancellation of the sale contract, "every consideration of convenience and common sense" would suggest that it had jurisdiction in respect of any consequential claims, such as a claim for return of the purchase price and costs. It would be "monstrous" if the plaintiff were entitled to sue in the Eastern Cape for cancellation of the sale but the law obliged him to sue for consequential money claims in some other province, especially when the Eastern Cape court was able to give an effective judgment which it could enforce in respect of the money claims. "The frustration goes even further" if the plaintiff would have to go to some other court in order to get a judgment for his costs. "The modern world is indeed a world of many frustrations, and it would be grievous pity to add this frustration to those which already exist."[12]

The Appellate Division's decision with respect to the money claims has been criticised by South African commentators[13] and is unlikely to be followed in common law jurisdictions. There, the relationship between money and property claims and considerations of convenience and enforceability cannot support jurisdiction in an action for money when the court lacks jurisdiction over the defendant. The decision with respect to cancellation, however, can be followed as an appropriate exercise of jurisdiction over the land, inasmuch as its effect is to decide that ownership of the land will not be transferred from the seller to the buyer.[14]

Ex parte Maschwitz[15] presented to a Transvaal court an application by a widow to approve the sale and transfer of her minor son's interest in Transvaal land. The widow applied as guardian of her son. Both were resident and domiciled in the United States. The

12 *Ibid.*, 564.

13 Kahn, *Jurisdiction in Action for Rescission of Sale, Refund of Price and Costs: the Law as Logic and Experience*, (1958) 75 S.A.L.J. 141; Pollak, *Conflict of Laws*, 1958 Ann. Surv. S. Afr. L. 245, 245-46.

14 See Scoles & Hay, 220-21.

15 1965 (4) S.A. 356 (T).

court held that it did not, as the court of the *situs* of the land, have jurisdiction to approve the sale and transfer. It was necessary first to obtain an appropriate order from the court of the minor's domicile, which could then be recognised by the court of the *situs*. A possible exception, left open by the court, was when it had been shown that the domicile did not require the minor's guardian to obtain approval from a court or other tribunal.

The court distinguished cases in which a court had been asked to determine the title to immovable property or in which a plaintiff sought transfer or possession of such property:

> in such matters the Court of the area in which the property is situate would undoubtedly have jurisdiction and probably sole jurisdiction. What we are here concerned with is the want of capacity in the guardian to dispose of assets of the ward, a want that can be supplemented by the Court which is the upper guardian of all minors within its jurisdiction . . . . In principle then, if the Transvaal Provincial Division of the Supreme Court is not the upper guardian, no initial jurisdiction to decide the matter can reside in it. I say "initial" because it may be that the Registrar of Deeds will not be disposed to act upon an order of Court from outside the Province without some form of confirmation from this Division.[16]

If the court where the property lies was not the upper guardian, mere *locus sitae* could not give it jurisdiction to determine a question outside its competence, on which the upper guardian might take a different view.

Ex parte Maschwitz was followed in *In re Estate Swart*.[17] The land was in Botswana and the minor's domicile in South Africa. In holding that it was without jurisdiction to give leave for the sale of the land, the Botswana court referred with apparent approval to a passage in Dicey and Morris[18] which treats a person's capacity to alienate an immovable as a matter of choice of law. There it was submitted that capacity is generally governed by the *lex situs*, but the

16 *Ibid.*, 357.

17 1974 (1) B.L.R. 88 (H.C.).

18 Dicey & Morris, Conflict of Laws 521 (8th ed. 1967). See also Morris, 347-49.

situs' law may be interpreted as inapplicable to persons domiciled outside the *situs*. If this is so, it may follow (a) that the *situs* should apply the domicile's law on capacity to alienate an immovable, and (b) that the courts of the *situs* should not entertain an application for approval in the circumstances of *Ex parte Maschwitz* and *In re Estate Swart*--not because the court lacks jurisdiction, but because it has not been shown (through a court order from the domicile or otherwise) that the minor's guardian has power under the domicile's law to transfer the immovable.[19]

CASES INVOLVING FOREIGN LAND

It is accepted in Southern Africa, as elsewhere, that a court cannot or will not exercise jurisdiction in certain cases involving immovables situated in a foreign state. A court will not, for example, determine title to foreign land or authorise a foreign registrar to transfer title.[20] It can, however, entertain certain actions relating to foreign land. For example, *Ex parte Maschwitz* and *In re Estate Swart* contemplate that when a guardian wishes to sell land owned by a minor, approval be sought from the court of the minor's domicile. This procedure was followed in *Ex parte Erasmus*.[21] In what actions, then, can a court exercise jurisdiction, when foreign

19 But see In re the Golding Trust, 1964 R.L.R. 249 (G.D.), 1964 (4) S.A. 239 (S.R.). A minor resident and domiciled in England was one of the beneficiaries of a trust created in Southern Rhodesia. The donor and the other beneficiaries were also resident and domiciled in the United Kingdom. The trust fund consisted primarily of immovable property in Southern Rhodesia. A Southern Rhodesian court was asked by all parties interested to approve an amendment to the trust deed. The amendment concerned the appropriation of income from the trust. There had been no order by an English court. The Southern Rhodesian court assumed jurisdiction to approve the amendment on behalf of the minor. Its decision is criticised in Ex parte Maschwitz.

20 See Forsyth, 181-87.

21 1950 (3) S.A. 59 (T). The court held that while it could and would approve the transfer of foreign land and confirm the deed of sale, it could not authorise the foreign registrar of deeds to transfer title, free of certain servitudes. Compare Ex parte Bothma, 1979 (2) S.A. 1177 (N.C.), in which it was held that a court did not have jurisdiction to grant leave to sell foreign immovables burdened with a *fideicommissum* when a minor fideicommissary heir and his guardian were domiciled in the court's area of jurisdiction.

immovables are involved?

In *C.M. Asbestos Co. (Pty.) Ltd. v. King Chrysotyle Asbestos Mines (Pty.) Ltd.*,[22] the first defendant entered an agreement for the sale of base metal claims to the plaintiff. Fearing that the first defendant was about to transfer these claims to the second defendant, the plaintiff sought an order restraining the first defendant from transferring the claims to the second defendant and restraining the second defendant from registering such a transfer. The jurisdiction in which the application was brought was the residence of the defendants but not the *situs* of the claims. The plaintiff intended that the restraining order operate pending an action in the *situs* for specific performance of the sale agreement and transfer of the claims. This action had not yet been instituted.

The defendants contended that the court lacked jurisdiction in the matter because the claims were immovable property situated outside the court's area of jurisdiction. The court held that it had jurisdiction. The general rule was that a court could forbid a person within its jurisdiction from taking action in a foreign state. This rule extended to prohibition of the conveyance of foreign land. Such an order did not infringe the sovereignty of the foreign state.[23]

Whether foreign immovable property was involved at all in *South Atlantic Islands Development Corporation Ltd. v. Buchan*[24] is debatable. The plaintiff had been granted exclusive rights to fish in the territorial waters of Tristan da Cunha and other islands in the South Atlantic Ocean. When the St. Helena government first granted

22 1953 (3) S.A. 431 (W).

23 The court distinguished prohibitory interdicts from mandatory interdicts. The plaintiff conceded that the action for specific performance of the sale agreement and transfer of the claims would have to be brought in the court of the *situs*. However, it was arguable that because the first defendant resided in its area of jurisdiction, the court had the power to order the defendant to perform the agreement and execute the transfer documents, although it could not have transferred ownership directly. See Forsyth, 182-83; Wessels v. Hugo, 1985 (4) S.A. 262 (O). In that case, a divorce order incorporated an agreement providing that the wife would purchase a house with funds furnished by the husband and register the house in the names of the children. A house in another province allegedly was purchased and registered in the name of the wife as well as the children. It was decided that the court which granted the divorce had jurisdiction over the husband's petition for an order requiring the wife to effect registration in the names of the children only.

24 1971 (1) S.A. 234 (C).

this concession, the territorial waters extended for a distance of three miles from the islands' low water mark. A St. Helena ordinance subsequently extended the territorial waters, insofar as fishing was concerned, to twelve miles. Learning that the defendant was about to sail from Cape Town to fish in those waters, the plaintiff sought an order from the court of the Cape Provincial Division prohibiting the defendant from doing so. The plaintiff originally asked for an order restraining the defendant from sailing from Cape Town with the purpose of fishing in Tristan da Cunha waters from his vessel, but an order which simply prohibited the defendant from fishing in those waters was also suggested. The defendant denied that the court had jurisdiction and also denied the validity of the St. Helena ordinance extending the fishing limits from three miles to twelve.

The court held that it was without jurisdiction even if the defendant was temporarily resident in Cape Town. Its decision rested on two rationales. One was that its judgment would not be effective. The court could not enforce an interdict if the defendant chose to ignore it. Why an interdict could not be enforced by contempt proceedings was not explained. The other rationale was found in the leading English case on jurisdiction in cases involving foreign immovables, *British South Africa Company v. Companhia de Moçambique*.[25] There, the plaintiffs had claimed damages for trespass to land outside England. It had been conceded that an English court could not grant an injunction to restrain trespass abroad. The House of Lords would not accept that an English court had jurisdiction in a money claim. It would become "necessary for the Court to adjudicate upon the conflicting claims of the parties to real estate".[26] The court in the *South Atlantic Islands* case believed it would be faced with the same issue if it exercised jurisdiction. It was not for a court in the Cape to determine who was entitled to fish in the waters of Tristan da Cunha.

25 [1893] A.C. 602 (H.L.).

26 *Ibid.*, 624 (Lord Herschell, L.C.).

3

RECOGNITION OF FOREIGN MONEY JUDGMENTS

JURISDICTION OF FOREIGN COURT

The approach taken to recognition of foreign money judgments in modern Southern African cases is similar to the approach found in common law countries. The critical requirement of recognition is that the foreign court have had jurisdiction to render the judgment concerned. As held in *De Naamloze Vennootschap Alintex v. Von Gerlach*,[1] this means not jurisdiction under the law of the state from which the judgment originated but jurisdiction under the principles of Private International Law in the state where recognition is sought. In that case, the judgment debtor conceded that the *onus* lay on him to establish that the judgment was unenforceable, but in later cases it was held that the party seeking to enforce the judgment had the *onus* of showing that the foreign court had jurisdiction.[2]

In *De Naamloze Vennootschap Alintex v. Von Gerlach*, a judgment had been given in the Netherlands in favour of a company registered there. The defendant had not appeared in the foreign court, had not submitted to its jurisdiction, and had never been in the Netherlands. The cause of action (for breach of contract) arose elsewhere. The court decided that the judgment was unenforceable. It considered the grounds on which a foreign court would be regarded as having jurisdiction over the judgment debtor but did not reach a

1 1958 (1) S.A. 13 (T).

2 Coluflandres Ltd. v. Scandia Industrial Products Ltd., 1969 (2) R.L.R. 431 (G.D.), 1969 (3) S.A. 551 (R), appeal refused, 1969 (2) R.L.R. 413 (G.D.); Reiss Engineering Co. Ltd. v. Insamcor (Pty.) Ltd., 1983 (1) S.A. 1033 (W).

definite conclusion on this point.

Coluflandres Ltd. v. Scandia Industrial Products Ltd.[3] is an analogous case. A Belgian company sought to enforce in Rhodesia a Belgian judgment given against a Rhodesian company *in absentia*. The plaintiff relied upon an alleged contractual submission by the defendant to the jurisdiction of the Belgian court. The Rhodesian court agreed that submission to the jurisdiction of a foreign court was a ground of jurisdiction for purposes of recognising a foreign judgment but held that the plaintiff, upon whom the *onus* of proof lay, had failed to prove contractual submission by the defendant.

Whether the defendant submitted to the Belgian court's jurisdiction depended upon whether the defendant was a party to the contract on which the plaintiff sued and whether the contract contained a provision for submission. The plaintiff apparently contended that these matters went to the merits of the claim presented in the Belgian court and could not be examined by the Rhodesian court, for in proceedings to enforce a foreign judgment the defendant could not attack the judgment on its merits. The court applied the principle that a court called upon to enforce a foreign judgment is entitled to make its own findings concerning the relevant "jurisdictional facts". In other words, the court can decide for itself whether the facts upon which the jurisdiction of the foreign court was founded really existed.[4] It therefore was open to the Rhodesian court to make its own findings on whether the defendant was a party to the contract and whether the contract provided for submission to the jurisdiction which the Belgian court exercised. Evidence on these points was admissible even if it also was fundamental to the merits of the plaintiff's claim. In so deciding, the court assumed that the Belgian court had found that the defendant was a party and had submitted in the contract to its jurisdiction.[5] Thus it was decided that in order to obtain recognition of the judgment, the plaintiff had to prove contested "jurisdictional facts" which the foreign court had

3 1969 (2) R.L.R. 431 (G.D.), 1969 (3) S.A. 551 (R), appeal refused, 1969 (2) R.L.R. 413 (G.D.).

4 See Forsyth, 364; Silberberg, 28-31.

5 No reason for this assumption was stated. Whether it should have been made and whether it was accurate is open to question. The Belgian court may have refrained from making such findings, because the defendant did not appear, or found that it had jurisdiction on another ground.

previously found in its favour.[6]

When an American bank sought to enforce a six million dollar default judgment in the courts of Rhodesia, the defendant used the fact that he was a fugitive from justice as an argument for refusing enforcement. He claimed that he was denied natural justice in the American proceedings because he had fled from the United States.[7] Instead, the Rhodesian Appellate Division, in *Steinberg v. Cosmopolitan National Bank of Chicago*,[8] decided that the defendant's flight was reason to enforce a judgment which otherwise would have been unenforceable for lack of jurisdiction.

The claim on which the bank obtained the judgment was for an amount that the defendant allegedly had "fraudulently embezzled" from the bank. The judgment was granted by a state court in Illinois. The bank's cause of action was treated by judges in the Rhodesian Appellate Division as one for a tort committed in Illinois. The defendant seems to have been domiciled and resident in Illinois when the embezzlement occurred, but he left the United States and established residence in Rhodesia before the bank commenced its action against him. The Rhodesian court assigned pending criminal proceedings arising from the embezzlement as the reason for the defendant's departure from the United States.

Had the defendant been served with process in Illinois, the Illinois court would have had the jurisdiction necessary for enforcement of its judgment in Rhodesia, but he could not be served in Illinois (nor did he retain a domicile or residence there) because he had fled the United States.[9] The defendant was served in

6 See also Moresby-White v. Moresby-White, 1972 (1) R.L.R. 199 (A.D.), 1972 (3) S.A. 222 (R.A.D.), discussed p. 143, *infra*. It must be emphasised that while the defendant denied the court's jurisdiction when it replied to notice of the Belgian action, it did not present arguments to the Belgian court. It is doubtful that the "jurisdictional facts" could have been re-examined in Rhodesia if the defendant had contested them in Belgium. See Hackwill, *The Enforcement of Foreign Judgment*, 1970 Rhod. L.J. 8. Standard Bank Ltd. v. Butlin, 1981 (4) S.A. 158 (D), and Reiss Engineering Co. Ltd. v. Insamcor (Pty.) Ltd., 1983 (1) S.A. 1033 (W), discussed pp. 32-33, *supra*, are other cases in which a judgment creditor unsuccessfully attempted to have a foreign default judgment enforced on the ground that the debtor had submitted in a contract to the jurisdiction of the foreign court.

7 This point is discussed pp. 47-48, *infra*.

8 1973 (2) R.L.R. 128 (A.D.), 1973 (4) S.A. 564 (R.A.D.).

9 Beadle, C.J., and *sub silentio* the other judges of the Rhodesian Appellate

Rhodesia by the Rhodesian sheriff. The court held that the judgment was nevertheless entitled to enforcement; a foreign judgment would not be denied recognition when the defendant had fled the jurisdiction of the foreign court to escape prosecution for the conduct which gave rise to the plaintiff's cause of action and thereby prevented the foreign court from acquiring jurisdiction that it would otherwise have had.

Beadle, C.J., reached this result on the basis of a legal fiction--that the defendant was in Illinois at the time process in the Illinois proceedings was served and that he was duly served with process there.[10] He thought it necessary as a matter of public policy to employ this fiction so that a person who fled a country to "evade the criminal law and to avoid the civil law consequences of his criminal conduct" could not "take advantage of his own inequity". Applying the fiction, the Illinois court had jurisdiction to grant the judgment the bank was attempting to enforce.

Macdonald, J.P., agreed that it was against public policy to refuse to recognise the Illinois judgment but disagreed with the use of a legal fiction. In his opinion, natural justice was a criterion for recognition of foreign judgments and it was contrary to natural justice to refuse recognition when the defendant had left the United States and come to Rhodesia to obtain refuge from the criminal proceedings pending in the United States.

Lewis, J.A., took the position that

> If one has to come to the conclusion that the law is that the appellant's residence in the foreign country at the time of the commencement of action there is an essential prerequisite to such recognition, despite the fact that the appellant has committed the delict there, has subsequently fled from criminal justice there arising out of the same transaction and has subsequently been served personally with process in this country where he has taken refuge,

Division assumed for the purposes of the case that the defendant had established a domicile in Rhodesia when the Illinois action was brought or, alternatively, that domicile in Illinois alone was insufficient for recognition of an Illinois judgment.

10 His judgment refers to the defendant's absence from "America" and employs the fiction that he was served in "America", but one may assume that Beadle, C.J., and the other judges appreciated that the relevant legal unit for jurisdictional purposes was the state of Illinois.

> then I agree that he cannot be allowed to defeat the respondent's just claim by setting up his own wrongful act and he must be treated as though he had not fled from criminal justice but had remained in Illinois to receive service there.[11]

Lewis, J.A., found both the legal fiction and natural justice approaches "supportable" but leaned more toward the views of Macdonald, J.P.

The decision in *Steinberg v. Cosmopolitan National Bank of Chicago* has rightly attracted criticism on the ground that a judgment of a court that lacks jurisdiction cannot be made enforceable by a legal fiction or considerations of natural justice.

> The requisite that in the case of a foreign judgment sounding in money the defendant at the time of the commencement of the proceedings resided within the jurisdiction of the court which gave the judgment is clearly based upon the power of such court over the defendant. What matters is thus a factual relationship between the court of the foreign country and the defendant at the relevant time. It either existed or did not exist, and the relationship between the defendant and the plaintiff as such is of no importance. It is not possible to deal with the defendant who at the relevant time was not resident in the foreign country as if he had been. Such fiction is wholly incapable of creating the requisite power of the court of that country over the defendant. Whether or not the defendant was a fugitive from justice in the foreign country is not in point at all nor does it affect the public policy of the country where the enforcement of the judgment is sought . . . .
>
> . . . [The plaintiff] should not have sued in Illinois in the first instance. He knew (or could have ascertained from his lawyer) before he instituted those proceedings that the defendant had settled in Rhodesia where in fact he effected service of process and that in the premises a judgment of the court in Illinois would not be recognized and enforced in Rhodesia. In this respect he did not

11 Steinberg v. Cosmopolitan National Bank of Chicago, 1973 (2) R.L.R. 128, 144-45 (A.D.), 1973 (4) S.A. 564, 578 (R.A.D.) (Lewis, J.A.).

> deserve any sympathy from any court. In those circumstances it cannot be seen how it violates "natural justice" if the plaintiff has to sue afresh in Rhodesia if so advised.[12]

The clearest recent statement by a Southern African court on the bases of jurisdiction "in the international sense" is to be found in *Reiss Engineering Co. Ltd. v. Insamcor (Pty.) Ltd.*:[13]

> A foreign court has jurisdiction to entertain an action for a judgment sounding in money against a defendant who is a natural person in the following cases:
>
> 1. If at the time of the commencement of the action the defendant is physically present within the state to which the court belongs;
> 2. If at the time of the commencement of the action the defendant, although not physically present within such state, is either (*a*) domiciled, or (*b*) resident within such state;
> 3. If the defendant has submitted to the jurisdiction of the court.
>
> There are no other grounds of jurisdiction.[14]

The court also made it clear, as had the court in *De Naamloze Vennootschap Alintex v. Von Gerlach*,[15] that the fact that the foreign court had jurisdiction under its own law did not mean that it had

12 Spiro, *Enforcement of a Foreign Judgment Sounding in Money Against a Fugitive From Justice*, (1974) 7 C.I.L.S.A. 339, 342-43. See also Forsyth, 335-37. An additional criticism is that the defendant had not been convicted. Without a conviction, it could not be assumed that to refuse to enforce the Illinois judgment would allow the defendant to escape the civil consequences of criminal misconduct. But see Kahn, *Conflict of Laws*, 1973 Ann. Surv. S. Afr. L. 428, 437 (if personal service within foreign court's territory is ground of jurisdiction, result of case is to be welcomed).

13 1983 (1) S.A. 1033 (W).

14 *Ibid.*, 1037-38, quoting from Pollak, The South African Law of Jurisdiction 219 (1937). The court acknowledged the absence of South African judicial authority on whether temporary presence without domicile or residence is a basis of jurisdiction. On the bases of jurisdiction, see Forsyth, 326-39; Silberberg, 8-19.

15 1958 (1) S.A. 13 (T), discussed pp. 41-42, *supra*.

jurisdiction for purposes of recognition of its judgment in another country.[16] The court declined to enforce the foreign judgment that had been presented to it, the plaintiff having failed to establish that the foreign court had jurisdiction on any of the bases specified.

NATURAL JUSTICE

A failure of "natural justice" in the foreign proceedings is a recognised but seldom successful ground for refusing recognition to a foreign judgment.[17] As stated earlier, the defendant in *Steinberg v. Cosmopolitan National Bank of Chicago*[18] contended that he had been denied natural justice in the American proceedings because he was a fugitive from justice. He claimed that because he was a fugitive, no attorney would act for him. He therefore would not be allowed to enter an appearance to defend the action in Illinois or take any appeal--a denial of natural justice under the *audi alteram partem* rule. This defence was no more successful than the defence of want of jurisdiction. The trial court, whose decision Beadle, C.J., approved, found no failure of natural justice because it had not been established that the defendant would have been denied an attorney's services or an audience in the court if he returned to the United States.[19] The court commented,

16 This point had also been made by Beadle, C.J., in Steinberg v. Cosmopolitan National Bank of Chicago, 1973 (2) R.L.R. 128, 138 (A.D.), 1973 (4) S.A. 564, 573 (R.A.D.). He added that this was true even if the court where recognition was sought would have exercised jurisdiction in similar circumstances. See Forsyth, 326. In Duarte v. Lissack, 1973 (3) S.A. 615 (D), rev'd, 1974 (4) S.A. 560 (N), it was held that a foreign judgment was not enforceable in South Africa insofar as it granted damages for a delict which occurred in a third country, but it was enforceable insofar as it granted damages for breach of contract in the country in which the judgment was rendered because this was consistent with South African principles of domestic jurisdiction. Forsyth, 335, and Kahn, *Conflict of Laws*, 1973 Ann. Surv. S. Afr. L. 428, 437-39, contend that the court erred in its decision that the foreign court had jurisdiction over the contract claim.

17 See Forsyth, 359-61; Silberberg, 36-39.

18 1973 (2) R.L.R. 128 (A.D.), 1973 (4) S.A. 564 (R.A.D.).

19 Cosmopolitan National Bank of Chicago v. Steinberg, 1973 (1) R.L.R. 23 (G.D.), 1973 (4) S.A. 579 (R), aff'd, 1973 (2) R.L.R. 128 (A.D.), 1973 (4) S.A. 564 (R.A.D.).

> The fact that he prefers to remain out of the United States because the authorities of that country regard him as a fugitive from justice, can hardly be laid at the door of the [plaintiff], nor can it fairly be suggested that the [plaintiff] took advantage of the situation by instituting action in the foreign court. Not only was process of the court served on him personally but he was later appraised of the judgment and invited to take steps to challenge it in Illinois if he thought ground existed for doing so.[20]

The defendant failed to convince the court that natural justice had been denied in this instance, but the defence succeeded in another action between the same two parties. Long before he left the United States, the defendant and other officers of a company had guaranteed loans the plaintiff bank extended to the company. The guarantee document provided for "confession of judgment" in the bank's favour when any of the signatories failed to honour their guarantee. It authorised any attorney of a court of record to appear for the signatories, confess judgment for the amount unpaid on the guarantee, "waive and release all errors which may intervene in the proceedings" and consent to immediate execution on the judgment. Service of process was waived. According to an Illinois attorney whose affidavit was entered in the case, it was normal in Illinois for the signatories to both promissory notes and guarantees to waive service and authorise an attorney to confess judgment for amounts unpaid.

After the defendant's company defaulted on a promissory note, the bank obtained, by means of the confession of judgment in the guarantee, an Illinois court's judgment against the defendant for almost half a million dollars. The defendant was not served with process or otherwise notified of the proceedings. The bank appointed an attorney to confess judgment on the defendant's behalf. By this time, the defendant had left the United States for Rhodesia. The bank brought an action in Rhodesia to enforce the Illinois judgment.

The defendant contended that the judgment was unenforceable for want of natural justice because it had been obtained without notice and without affording him an opportunity to be heard in the Illinois court. Alternatively, the judgment was unenforceable as oppressive and contrary to public policy because it was based upon

20 *Ibid.*, 31 [not included in 1973 (4) S.A. 579 (R)]. *Quaere* whether a defence of denial of natural justice should be rejected on the ground that the judgment creditor was not responsible for the denial.

a contract that provided for judicial proceedings without notice to the defendant. The trial court rejected these arguments and enforced the Illinois judgment, believing that the agreement which the defendant had made with the bank--apparently a normal agreement in Illinois--was not unconscionable or oppressive and that it was not contrary to natural justice to apply the waiver of notice and confession of judgment the defendant had agreed to.[21]

The defendant successfully appealed to the Rhodesian Appellate Division.[22] That court, after discussing the uncertain validity of confession of judgment (*cognovit*) proceedings in American law, stated that it was a cornerstone of its legal system that a person was entitled to notice of legal proceedings instituted against him. In this case, the judgment had become final without notice to the defendant of the proceedings, without him being afforded an opportunity of a hearing, and without notice, within a time which would permit an appeal, that judgment had been entered against him. It followed "of necessity" that the proceedings were contrary to natural justice. Consequently, the Illinois judgment was not enforceable.

The court quoted Pollak's statement that a defendant sued on a foreign judgment may set up the defence that he "was not given such notice as was reasonably calculated to give him knowledge of the proceedings"[23] and the statement in *Robinson v. Fenner*[24] that a foreign judgment imposes an enforceable obligation upon parties "who have been duly and in accordance with our idea of natural justice summoned to that foreign Court, that is to say have been so summoned as to have had a hearing or an opportunity of having a hearing". The failure of natural justice lay in the defendant's lack of knowledge of the foreign proceedings, not the absence of service of process as such.[25]

21 Cosmopolitan National Bank of Chicago v. Steinberg, 1972 (2) R.L.R. 534 (G.D.), rev'd, 1973 (1) R.L.R. 265 (A.D.), 1973 (3) S.A. 885 (R.A.D.).

22 Steinberg v. Cosmopolitan National Bank of Chicago, 1973 (1) R.L.R. 265 (A.D.), 1973 (3) S.A. 885 (R.A.D.).

23 Pollak, The South African Law of Jurisdiction 229 (1937).

24 [1913] 3 K.B. 835, 844.

25 The court pointed out that the present case did not involve constructive notice (substituted service) under the rules of the foreign court. There was no occasion for this because the plaintiff's American attorney was aware of the defendant's presence and address in Rhodesia. Substituted service should be

A curious application of the natural justice principle is to be found in *Corona v. Zimbabwe Iron & Steel Co. Ltd.*[26] The case arose from an alleged agreement by the defendant to sell motor vehicles to the plaintiff. The vehicles were not delivered and the plaintiff sought to recover the sums it had paid the defendant. The plaintiff proceeded in a Zimbabwe court against Air Halers (Pvt.) Ltd., for whom the defendant allegedly acted in the transaction. The plaintiff obtained a default judgment, which was never satisfied. Soon thereafter, in a separate action, the plaintiff was granted a default judgment against the defendant. The allegations and relief claimed in the action against the defendant were the same as in the action against Air Halers. The plaintiff now sought to enforce the second judgment in Transkei.

The Transkei Appellate Division held that the judgment could not be enforced; the proceedings in which it was granted were in conflict with the principles of natural justice. The denial of natural justice was in granting a judgment against the defendant when a judgment had been obtained against Air Halers on the same grounds and for the same sum, in circumstances in which only one party could have been liable. (In Zimbabwe, the plaintiff had alleged in the alternative that the defendant acted on his own behalf, on behalf of Air Halers, or on behalf of an undisclosed principal now known to be Air Halers. The plaintiff claimed judgment "the one paying, the other to be absolved". According to the Transkei court, if the defendant received the plaintiff's money on behalf of Air Halers, he was not liable; if the defendant received the money in his personal capacity, Air Halers was not liable.)

The court asserted that the Zimbabwe judge who granted the judgment against the defendant would not have done so if he had been aware of the judgment against Air Halers. Accepting that the plaintiff was not entitled to the second judgment, it is difficult to appreciate how its grant (or its enforcement in Transkei) could amount to a denial of natural justice. There seems to have been no more than the type of legal error that does not impair the enforceability of a foreign judgment.[27] There was no suggestion that the plaintiff oppressed the defendant by obtaining the judgment. The

effective when personal service cannot be effected. See Graveson, 633-34; McLeod, 617-19; Silberberg, 36-37.

26 1985 (2) S.A. 423 (Tk. A.D.).

27 See 1 Castel, 464-71; Dicey & Morris, 1072-77; Graveson, 628-30.

court specified that "the plaintiff innocently but incorrectly adopted this procedure" because it was not certain whether Air Halers or the defendant was liable and it could not obtain satisfaction of the judgment against Air Halers.

Entry of judgment against a defendant after an earlier judgment on the same claim had been *satisfied* might amount to a denial of natural justice in some circumstances, but there is no reference to this in the Transkei court's judgment. Enforcement of the Zimbabwe judgment in Transkei would not have enabled the plaintiff to obtain a double recovery. There is every reason to suppose that if the judgment against the defendant was satisfied by its enforcement in Transkei,[28] the judgment against Air Halers would cease to be enforceable.

It is very unlikely that a failure of natural justice will be found when the judgment debtor received and responded to notice of the foreign proceedings.[29] But the defendant in *Duarte v. Lissack*[30] ultimately prevailed in these circumstances. He had gone on holiday from South Africa to Lourenço Marques, Moçambique, and hired a motor car there. The car was damaged beyond repair in an accident. The defendant's father and, later, the defendant received letters demanding damages arising from the accident. Correspondence passed between the attorneys of the defendant and the plaintiff (the proprietor of the firm that let the car). The plaintiff's attorneys then wrote that they had been instructed to pursue the matter in the Lourenço Marques court. The defendant subsequently received several documents in Portuguese in registered mail from Lourenço Marques. One of the documents was translated into English--a "summons letter" for a suit brought in Lourenço Marques against the defendant. This letter was less than clear but indicated that the addressee (the defendant) could refute or contest the suit through the "Unique Register Office" of the Lourenço Marques court. The absence of refutation or contestation would result in confession of the facts "paragraphed" by the plaintiff. The document containing the plaintiff's statement of claim was not translated.

28 See 1 Castel, 523-24; Scoles & Hay, 958-59.

29 See Coluflandres Ltd. v. Scandia Industrial Products Ltd., 1969 (2) R.L.R. 431 (G.D.), 1969 (3) S.A. 551 (R), appeal refused, 1969 (2) R.L.R. 413 (G.D.) (defendant responded to notice by writing letter denying jurisdiction of court; foreign court granted default judgment without further notice).

30 1973 (3) S.A. 615 (D), rev'd, 1974 (4) S.A. 560 (N).

The defendant responded by personally writing a letter to the Unique Register Office:

> I have received, by registered post, what appears to be a summons issued against me by one Vitorino Pareira Duarte. With what appears to be the summons, was a covering letter translated into the English language. The translation is, however, not entirely comprehensible and I am completely uncertain as to what precisely is required of me.
>
> What I assume to be the summons is in what is to me a foreign language (I imagine Portuguese) which I do not understand, and is not accompanied by a translation. In the circumstances, I am totally unaware of what allegations have been made against me.
>
> Mr. Vitorino Pareira Duarte is unknown to me and I can conceive of no reason why he should allege that I am indebted to him. I accordingly refute or contest all the facts paragraphed by the plaintiff.

The defendant received no reply to or acknowledgement of his letter. Three months later the plaintiff's attorneys wrote to inform the defendant that the Lourenço Marques court had given a default judgment against him. The judgment recited that "Having been personally notified, the defendant did not contest, so that . . . the facts alleged by the plaintiff have been considered as proved." The defendant's letter to the court was ineffective as a denial of the plaintiff's allegations because the law of Moçambique (Portuguese law) required that each of the facts in the plaintiff's statement be traversed (a "defence of general issue" was not accepted) and that contestation of the facts be set forth in a statement drawn by an advocate.

The plaintiff brought an action in South Africa to enforce the judgment. The defendant claimed that there had been a failure of natural justice on the ground that he was not properly informed of the proceedings in the Lourenço Marques court and was not afforded a proper opportunity of presenting his case. After contesting (in his letter) the facts "paragraphed" by the plaintiff, as the "summons letter" apparently called for, a default judgment was granted without further notice. The trial court rejected this argument and held that the judgment was enforceable.

The defendant had been given notice that the plaintiff had instituted action against him. He was told of the forum. This was contained in a formal document emanating from the Lourenço Marques court itself. The defendant was told that "refute" or "contestation" within fifty days was necessary. It was true that the document which apparently gave information of the cause of action and the amount claimed was not translated. It was also true that the "summons letter" did not tell the defendant that a general denial was insufficient and that his refute would have to be by means of a document prepared with the assistance of an advocate. It should, however, have been clear to any reasonably prudent person that there might be formalities prescribed by the Lourenço Marques courts which would render invalid any informal refute.

> While it might have been desirable that the defendant be given more information in the documents with which he was served by registered post, it certainly cannot be said that the failure to give that information was unconscionable by the tenets of any civilised society. He was told of the action and he was given an opportunity of defending it. By an ill-advised step and a failure to obtain informed advice he was deprived of that opportunity.[31]

The defendant must have known that the action was that foreshadowed in the letter from the plaintiff's attorneys. The defendant had attorneys acting for him in the correspondence that preceded the action and through them could have obtained advice and representation in Lourenço Marques.

The trial court evidently regarded the defendant as himself to blame for his predicament because he failed to take legal advice when he replied to the summons letter. The appellate court (the Natal Provincial Division)[32] did not agree. It believed that this approach would mean that there would never be a failure of natural justice when a person sued in a foreign country failed to seek legal advice in that country. The court would not adopt so "extreme" a view. Failure to seek legal advice was only one of the relevant circumstances. The defendant had every intention of defending the action.[33] If his version of the accident was correct, he had a good

31 *Ibid.*, 622-23.

32 Lissack v. Duarte, 1974 (4) S.A. 560 (N).

33 The court distinguished Coluflandres Ltd. v. Scandia Industrial Products Ltd., note 29, *supra*, on this ground.

defence. The trial court paid insufficient regard to "the real burden of the defendant's complaint". It was not that the defendant was given insufficient information in the documents he received, but that judgment was granted against him despite the fact that he had done precisely what the summons letter required him to do--refute or contest the facts "paragraphed" by the plaintiff.

Nowhere in the summons letter was there any indication that this had to be done in a particular manner or with the assistance of an advocate. The defendant could not be expected to traverse the individual allegations in the plaintiff's statement inasmuch as no translation of it was provided. The defendant was reasonably entitled to assume that he had complied with the instructions he had received and was not required to take further steps. In light of the information the defendant had been given and his response thereto, fundamental principles of fairness required the Lourenço Marques court to apprise him of the correct procedure after it received his letter. Failing to do so, its grant of a default judgment denied natural justice. The defendant was unfairly deprived of the opportunity of presenting "his side of the case". Therefore, the judgment could not be enforced against him.

ENFORCEMENT OF FOREIGN REVENUE LAWS

Commissioner of Taxes, Federation of Rhodesia v. McFarland[34] applies the widely-followed rule that a court will not enforce a foreign revenue law, either directly or by enforcing a foreign judgment.[35] The court (in South Africa) held that it had no jurisdiction to enforce a Southern Rhodesian judgment for unpaid taxes.[36] The case is notable less for the court's adoption of the rule than for its analysis of the rationale for the rule.

The court did not accept that considerations of comity and public policy required it to refrain from enforcing a foreign revenue judgment. It believed that the basis of recognition of foreign

34 1965 (1) S.A. 470 (W). See Spiro, *Enforcement of the Revenue Laws of Another State*, (1965) 14 I.C.L.Q. 987.

35 See Forsyth, 87-88, 362.

36 Properly speaking, the court did not lack jurisdiction. A rule of Private International Law required it not to enforce the judgment. Kahn, *Conflict of Laws*, 1965 Ann. Surv. S. Afr. L. 475, 486.

judgments was not the comity of nations but recognition of rights acquired under the law of a foreign country. As for public policy, "One would have thought that it is public policy that persons should pay their taxes and not evade such payment by escaping the country which imposed them."[37] Foreign revenue laws were distinct from foreign penal laws, which also could not be enforced, because "A penal law is punitive in nature, while a revenue law defines the extent of the citizen's pecuniary obligation to the State, and provides a remedy for its collection."[38] The rule's origins might have been "interwoven with questions of freedom of trade" but that was no more than an accident of birth.

There was, however, one explanation for the foreign revenue law rule which the court believed "fundamental and unexceptionable":

> that enforcement of a claim for taxes is but an extension of the sovereign power which imposed the taxes and that an assertion of authority by one State within the territory of another, as distinct from a patrimonial claim by a foreign Sovereign is (treaty or convention apart) contrary to all concepts of independent sovereignties.[39]

One state could not carry out acts of sovereignty in the territory of another state. Fiscal power was an attribute of sovereignty. To allow a foreign state to obtain a judgment for taxes imposed upon persons who in its eyes shared in the economic or social life of the state, in the courts of another country, would be "a judicial intervention in direct derogation of that country's territorial supremacy". On this basis an analogy could be drawn between penal and revenue laws. Just as one state could not send its police force into another state, so also it could not send its tax-gatherers. If it was desirable that the tax-gatherer be permitted to pursue his claims "beyond the domestic confines", this had to be achieved by conventions and treaties between the governments concerned.

37 Commissioner of Taxes, Federation of Rhodesia v. McFarland, 1965 (1) S.A. 470, 473 (W).

38 *Ibid.*, quoting from State of Oklahoma, ex rel. The Oklahoma Tax Commission v. Rodgers, 238 Mo. App. 1115, 1126, 193 S.W.2d 919, 926 (1946).

39 *Ibid.*, quoting from Government of India, Ministry of Finance (Revenue Division) v. Taylor, [1955] A.C. 491, 511 (H.L.) (Lord Keith of Avonholm).

RECIPROCITY OF RECOGNITION

The reciprocity rule of *Hilton v. Guyot*[40] has never found favour outside the United States. Except in those American states which still follow *Hilton v. Guyot*, recognition of a foreign judgment at common law does not depend upon whether courts in the state from which the judgment originated would recognise as conclusive a judgment granted in similar circumstances by the court in which recognition is sought.[41]

Reciprocity of recognition was considered by the lower courts in both of the *Steinberg* cases,[42] discussed earlier in connection with jurisdiction of the foreign court and natural justice.[43] The defendant submitted that the American judgments granted in the plaintiff's favour should not be recognised because there was no "comity" between the United States and Rhodesia; the judgment of a Rhodesian court would not be recognised by an American court. This argument was based upon the apparently unsupported supposition that an American court would not recognise a post-"U.D.I." Rhodesian judgment because the United States did not recognise the *de facto* government of Rhodesia.

Both courts gave short shrift to this argument. The first court to consider it quoted Pollak to the effect that the basis of enforcement of a foreign judgment was enforcement of the right created by the judgment, not comity, and South African law did not include a requirement of reciprocity.[44] As far as comity was concerned, the court was in no position to state whether there was comity between Rhodesia and the United States, and it was disposed to extend comity to the judgments of a country which "is a product

40 159 U.S. 113 (1895).

41 See 1 Castel, 412-13; Silberberg, 2-3.

42 Cosmopolitan National Bank of Chicago v. Steinberg, 1972 (2) R.L.R. 534 (G.D.), rev'd, 1973 (1) R.L.R. 265 (A.D.), 1973 (3) S.A. 885 (R.A.D.); Cosmopolitan National Bank of Chicago v. Steinberg, 1973 (1) R.L.R. 23 (G.D.), 1973 (4) S.A. 579 (R), aff'd, 1973 (2) R.L.R. 128 (A.D.), 1973 (4) S.A. 564 (R.A.D.).

43 See pp. 43-46, 47-49, *supra*.

44 Pollak, The South African Law of Jurisdiction 204-05 (1937).

of Western civilization and based upon common law".[45] The second court, also finding that it was not in a position to decide whether Rhodesian judgments were recognised in the United States, endorsed Pollak's statement.[46] The Rhodesian Appellate Division did not believe the reciprocity argument merited comment in addressing the defendant's appeals.[47]

That reciprocity was not accepted as a requirement of recognition is to be welcomed. Whether reciprocity should be required (or absence of reciprocity made a barrier to recognition) is a political judgment best made by the government of the country. The government is in a better position than the courts to predict the international effects of reciprocity (or its absence) and decide upon the course which best furthers the interests of its citizens.[48]

In rejecting reciprocity, the courts in the *Steinberg* cases relied more upon authority than upon their own analyses of the question. The authorities referred to did not address the special circumstances of Rhodesia as a country with an unrecognised government. Perhaps the courts in the *Steinberg* cases can be criticised for not evaluating reciprocity independently in the light of those special circumstances.

LEGISLATION

In Southern Africa, as elsewhere, legislation has been enacted to establish reciprocal enforcement of money judgments generally and of orders for payment of maintenance. Soon after the United Kingdom enacted the Administration of Justice Act, 1920,[49] Southern Rhodesia

45 Cosmopolitan National Bank of Chicago v. Steinberg, 1972 (2) R.L.R. 534, 546-47 (G.D.).

46 Cosmopolitan National Bank of Chicago v. Steinberg, 1973 (1) R.L.R. 23, 31-32 (G.D.) [not included in 1973 (4) S.A. 579 (R)].

47 In the first case, the defendant prevailed on the ground of failure of natural justice. In the second case, the reciprocity argument appears to have been disposed of by the decision of Beadle, C.J., that a foreign judgment for a tort or delict committed within the foreign state was entitled to recognition if the defendant was served with process in the foreign state. Steinberg v. Cosmopolitan National Bank of Chicago, 1973 (2) R.L.R. 128, 137-40 (A.D.), 1973 (4) S.A. 564, 572-75 (R.A.D.).

48 See Scoles & Hay, 962-63.

49 10 & 11 Geo. 5, c. 81 (U.K.).

adopted legislation modelled on it--the Reciprocal Enforcement of Judgments Act.[50] Much later, South Africa enacted the Reciprocal Enforcement of Civil Judgments Act,[51] which was modelled on the British Foreign Judgments (Reciprocal Enforcement) Act, 1933.[52] The 1933 British act bars the common law action on a foreign judgment when the judgment is registerable under the act.[53] The South African act, in contrast, provides:

> Notwithstanding anything to the contrary in any law or the common law contained, no judgment given by any court of law of competent jurisdiction outside the Republic shall be enforceable by any court, including a magistrate's court, in the Republic otherwise than in accordance with the provisions of this Act.[54]

This could mean that the common law action is entirely excluded and only judgments from countries proclaimed for purposes of the act can be enforced in South Africa.[55] This ambiguous provision may be one of the reasons why, two decades after its enactment, the South African act has never been brought into force.

Legislation facilitating the enforcement of foreign maintenance orders, on a reciprocal basis, has been intended to both reduce the practical difficulties of enforcement and overcome the principal legal obstacle to enforcement at common law: the rule that non-final

50 C. 51 (1974) (Rhod.).

51 No. 9 of 1966. See Spiro, Law of Parent and Child 548-51 (4th ed. 1985); Kahn, *Conflict of Laws*, 1966 Ann. Surv. S. Afr. L. 431, 431-35.

52 22 & 23 Geo. 5, c. 13 (U.K.).

53 S. 6. See Dicey & Morris, 1097-98, 1110.

54 Reciprocal Enforcement of Civil Judgments Act, No. 9 of 1966, s. 8 (S. Afr.).

55 The act was intended to encourage enforcement of South African judgments in other countries. See Kahn, *Conflict of Laws*, 1966 Ann. Surv. S. Afr. L. 431, 431. Withdrawal of common law enforcement would provide such encouragement. However, Kahn interprets the provision to apply only to proclaimed countries; the common law continues to apply to judgments from unproclaimed countries. *Ibid.*, 435. The act does not prevent a South African court from recognising, under common law principles, a foreign judgment "as conclusive of any matter of law or of fact decided in such judgment". S. 9.

foreign judgments are not enforceable.[56] Zimbabwe has a Maintenance Orders (Facilities for Enforcement) Act,[57] which originally was copied from the British act of the same name.[58] Also, its Maintenance Act authorises the Minister of Justice to make regulations providing for recognition and enforcement of maintenance orders of countries in which Zimbabwean maintenance orders are recognised and enforced.[59] The governing legislation in South Africa is now the Reciprocal Enforcement of Maintenance Orders Act.[60]

South Africa's Protection of Businesses Act[61] serves not to facilitate but to prevent the enforcement of foreign judgments and orders. It originally was a legislative response to extraterritorial application of American antitrust laws. Later it was extended in order to prevent enforcement in South Africa of judgments for multiple and punitive damages given in American products liability cases.[62] The act's terms are very broad and much is left to ministerial discretion. Section 1(1)(*b*) provides that without the permission of the Minister of Economic Affairs, "no person shall in compliance with any order, direction or letters of request issued or

56 See Estate H. v. Estate H., 1952 (4) S.A. 168 (C) (foreign order for periodic alimony not enforceable in respect of alimony in arrears, as to which order was modifiable); Hirschowitz v. Hirschowitz, 1965 (3) S.A. 407 (W) (foreign maintenance order subject to variation could not be sued upon); Coluflandres Ltd. v. Scandia Industrial Products Ltd., 1969 (2) R.L.R. 431 (G.D.), 1969 (3) S.A. 551 (R), appeal refused, 1969 (2) R.L.R. 413 (G.D.) (finality requirement applied to judgment for breach of contract; judgment's finality concerning damages not affected by lack of finality concerning costs of action). See generally Dicey & Morris, 1092-97; Forsyth, 357-59; McLeod, 622-27; Silberberg, 32-34.

57 C. 36 (1974) (Rhod.). See Thompson, *Commentary on the Maintenance Orders (Facilities for Enforcement) Act*, 1964 Rhod. L.J. 133.

58 Maintenance Orders (Facilities for Enforcement) Act, 1920, 10 & 11 Geo. 5, c. 33 (Eng. & N.I.).

59 Maintenance Act, c. 35, s. 28 (1974) (Rhod.).

60 No. 80 of 1963. See Forsyth, 352-53; Spiro, Law of Parent and Child 545-48 (4th ed. 1985). Like its Zimbabwe counterpart, the South African act excludes affiliation orders from its operation. S. 1.

61 No. 99 of 1978. See Forsyth, 362-63.

62 Protection of Businesses Amendment Act, No. 71 of 1984 (S. Afr.). See Kahn, *Conflict of Laws*, 1984 Ann. Surv. S. Afr. L. 566, 566-67.

emanating from outside the Republic, furnish any information as to any business whether carried on in or outside the Republic". Section 2 makes violation of this provision a criminal offence. The remainder of the act applies to judgments, orders, etc. arising from "any act or transaction . . . connected with the production, importation, exportation, refinement, possession, [use, sale or ownership of] any matter or material, of whatever nature, whether within, outside, into or from the Republic".[63] Section 1(1)(*a*) directs that no foreign judgment, order, direction, arbitration award or letter of request arising from such an act or transaction be enforced in South Africa without ministerial permission.

Section 1A provides that a foreign judgment that directs the payment of multiple or punitive damages (defined as damages which exceed compensation of actual damage or loss) shall not be recognised or enforced. This section could be interpreted to permit enforcement of the judgment to the extent it awards compensatory damages. Section 1B provides for recovery back of multiple or punitive damages paid in compliance with the judgment of a foreign court. When the plaintiff in the judgment was a company, the multiple or punitive damages can be recovered back from a company which it controls, a company which controls it, or another company controlled by its controlling company. In general, persons who at the time the foreign proceedings were instituted were domiciled, ordinarily resident, incorporated or carrying on business in South Africa can avail themselves of the recovery back provisions; but persons who were ordinarily resident outside South Africa and juristic persons who had their principal place of business outside South Africa cannot. There is an exception for judgments in foreign proceedings which related to activities exclusively carried on outside South Africa in connection with business conducted outside South Africa.

63 Protection of Businesses Act, No. 99 of 1978, s. 1(3) (S. Afr.).

4

CHOICE OF LAW

PROOF OF FOREIGN LAW

A litigant who intends to base a claim or defence on foreign law must establish the content of the appropriate law in a proper manner. Southern Africa's adoption of English law as the common law of evidence brought with it the rule that the content of foreign law is a question of fact and must be proved--usually by the evidence of an expert.[1]

Whatever the merits of this rule as a general proposition, a requirement of formal proof is unjustified, it is submitted, in the case of a law from a country whose legal system shares a common origin with the court's own system and whose contents can readily be understood and interpreted by judges and counsel. Foreign cases, statutes and texts are frequently used in common law countries and Southern Africa for the purpose of deciding a point of domestic law, without any question of formal proof or expert evidence. One might propose that courts in common law jurisdictions be free to refer directly to the law of another common law jurisdiction and interpret it independently, when a question of foreign law arises, and that courts in Southern Africa have a similar freedom with respect to the law of other Southern African countries.

Perhaps Southern Africa should also apply this approach to the law of common law countries, especially England, which is familiar to Southern African lawyers and which has given Southern Africa

1 See Forsyth, 76-81; van der Merwe, Morkel, Paizes & Skeen, Evidence 360-61 (1983).

many of the elements of its contemporary legal system.[2] The court in *Anderson v. The Master,*[3] however, held that the question of whether Scottish law gave a widow a right to her late husband's movable property was a question of fact. It had to be "proved in the ordinary way"--that is, through the evidence of experts--"apart possibly from consent where minors are not concerned".[4] The judgment indicates that the same requirement would apply to the law of the principal Commonwealth countries, such as Australia and Canada.

Where English law was concerned, the usual practice was to dispense with formal proof by experts or otherwise. When it was necessary to ascertain English law, counsel and courts would refer directly to English cases and statutes.[5] This practice appears to have been brought to an end in South Africa--absent the consent of the parties--by a statement of the Appellate Division in *Schlesinger v. Commissioner for Inland Revenue:*[6] "Inasmuch as English law is foreign law, our Courts cannot take judicial notice of it. Foreign law is a question of fact and must be proved."[7]

The parties in *Schlesinger* had freely referred to English statutes, rules of court and cases in the lower court. The Appellate Division took this as a tacit agreement that the court "should have regard to the laws referred to by them, and to laws referred to in such laws and the aforesaid reports, as they appear in the generally accepted publications, without further proof".[8] The Appellate Division then proceeded to make its own analysis of English law. This apparently signifies that while the foreign-law-as-fact rule was to apply to

2 See Forsyth, 81-83; Kahn, *Proving the Laws of Our Friends and Neighbours,* (1965) 82 S.A.L.J. 133.

3 1949 (4) S.A. 660 (E).

4 *Ibid.*, 671.

5 See Kahn, *Proving the Laws of Our Friends and Neighbours,* (1965) 82 S.A.L.J. 133.

6 1964 (3) S.A. 389 (A.D.).

7 *Ibid.*, 396. The question of English law was whether alimony was payable under an English order for judicial separation, in which case the paying spouse's taxable income was reduced for purposes of South African income tax by the amount payable.

8 *Ibid.*, 397.

English law, the rule could be dispensed with on the basis of a "tacit" agreement, as well as express consent, when any foreign law--not only English law--was in issue.

G. & P. Ltd. v. Commissioner of Taxes,[9] a Southern Rhodesian case, strongly supports the view that formal proof of the law of England and Southern African countries should not be required. Whether a company could obtain a depletion allowance under the Rhodesian federal income tax law depended upon whether British tax legislation afforded a similar allowance for purposes of British income tax and whether it provided that the company's income from Rhodesian mining operations was taxable in the United Kingdom. The court refused to receive an expert's evidence on the interpretation of the relevant British statutes. Instead, it referred directly to the statutes and made its own interpretation.

The court's ruling was based upon the established practice of deciding points of English law without hearing expert evidence ("*cursus curiae lex curiae*") and the court's familiarity with English law and English principles of statutory construction. Those principles and other elements of English law, such as the law of evidence and companies legislation, had been adopted locally. The same was true of South African law.

> When a local court gives a ruling in accordance with the English rules of evidence, it is in principle doing no more than we are doing in the present case, namely coming to a conclusion as to the effect of certain legislation having force in the U.K. Strictly speaking, there should be evidence by an expert in English law as to what the relevant rules of evidence are every time a point for decision arises in any of our courts. Such a situation would be utterly ridiculous and impracticable and the juristic basis for dispensing with such evidence is the practice of all our courts not to hear it.
>
> The reason for the rule requiring evidence to prove Foreign law is the lack of familiarity of a local court with the Foreign law. The more familiar the local court is with the relevant topic of the Foreign law, so the need for evidence diminishes in inverse ratio. If the present Appellant had been a South African instead of a British company, the South African Income Tax legislation would

9 1960 R. & N. 596 (S.R.), 1960 (4) S.A. 163 (S.R.).

> have been the subject of our consideration. This legislation is almost as familiar to us as the Federal legislation. The principles upon which tax is levied are the same. Numerous sections are *verbatim* the same. Our law reports bristle with cases in which South African cases have been held to be conclusive of the point at issue. In such a case it would be ridiculous to suppose that this court would be prepared to hear evidence of experts as to its proper meaning.[10]

The court believed that if expert evidence were admitted, it would have been "no more than a forensic argument given under oath". The expert's reasoning would have been based upon principles of construction already known to the court. The expert would have been concerned only with the meaning of English words in their ordinary usage in United Kingdom statutes. The court was free to disregard the expert's evidence and reach a different conclusion based upon its own reasoning. An expert's familiarity with British tax legislation as a whole would enable him to resolve obscurities that would confront a court lacking this familiarity, but such obscurities could be dispelled by counsel having the assistance of an expert.

On the basis of this decision, the court in *Grauman v. Pers*[11] decided that it could interpret South African Rules of Court without hearing the evidence of expert witnesses. Whether a South African judgment was enforceable in Rhodesia depended upon whether it was final. The court reached the conclusion that the judgment was final on the basis of its reading of the South African Rules of Court and interpretation of the rules in a South African text. Perhaps the court would have hesitated to do this if the *Schlesinger* case had been cited to it. Nevertheless, its judgment provides some additional authority for direct reference by the court to the sources of foreign law and authorities interpreting it.

DAMAGES IN FOREIGN CURRENCY

In *Voest Alpine Intertrading Gesellschaft M.B.H. v. Burwill and*

10 *Ibid.*, 603-04, 168-69.

11 1970 (1) R.L.R. 130 (G.D.).

Co. S.A. (Pty.) (Ltd.),[12] the defendant repudiated its contractual undertaking to sell ferrochrome to the plaintiff. The plaintiff was required to purchase ferrochrome from another source at a higher price. In claiming damages, the plaintiff quantified its loss--the difference between the contract price and the price paid to obtain ferrochrome--in United States dollars, the currency in which the contract price was expressed. The court believed it was required to grant judgment in local currency--South African rand. The rand's value had declined substantially since the defendant's repudiation of the contract. The plaintiff therefore argued that its loss in dollars should be converted into rand according to the exchange rate prevailing when judgment was given.

The court held that the conversion date was the date the contract was breached, *i.e.* the date of repudiation. In South African law, when the price of goods was expressed in a foreign currency, payment might be made in the currency of the place of payment. The applicable exchange rate would be the rate on the date payment was due. By analogy, damages in the present case were payable in United States dollars (because the ferrochrome was priced in dollars) and payment might be made in the currency of the place of payment (South Africa) at the rate of exchange of the date payment was due. Though only quantified by judgment, damages were payable and assessed when breach of contract (repudiation) occurred. Accordingly, the defendant's liability in rand was to be determined at the time of repudiation. Subsequent fluctuations in the value of the currency were to be ignored.

The court referred with approval to *Cosmopolitan National Bank of Chicago v. Steinberg.*[13] There it was held that in proceedings to enforce an American judgment in Rhodesia, judgment was to be given in Rhodesian currency at the exchange rate for United States currency on the date of the American judgment, not the date on which the plaintiff commenced the enforcement proceedings. "To adopt any other date would be tantamount to altering the *quantum* of the debt according to when the [judgment creditor] seeks to exact it."[14] The court in the *Voest Alpine* case left open the possibility that

12 1985 (2) S.A. 149 (W). See Kerr, *Date for Determining Loss Through Breach of Contract; Fluctuating Exchange Rates*, (1986) 103 S.A.L.J. 339.

13 1973 (1) R.L.R. 23 (G.D.), 1973 (4) S.A. 579 (R), aff'd, 1973 (2) R.L.R. 128 (A.D.), 1973 (4) S.A. 564 (R.A.D.).

14 *Ibid.*, 33, 581. The court in Cosmopolitan National Bank of Chicago v.

loss incurred as a result of fluctuation in currency values could be claimed as "a further head of damages" flowing from the defendant's refusal to pay damages when due. This could not, however, justify taking "the quite fortuitous and often delayed" date of judgment as the relevant date for conversion of a dollar liability to rand. In England, there might be conversion as of the date judgment was given or enforced, but this depended upon an English court's power to give judgment in a foreign currency.[15] A South African court had no such power. Therefore, the English cases in point, while "attractive and persuasive" in their reasoning, could not be applied.

In *Murata Machinery Ltd. v. Capelon Yarns (Pty.) Ltd.*,[16] a Japanese company sued for enforcement of a contract under which it was to sell machinery to the defendant. Payment was to be effected by a letter of credit for ¥14,490,000. The plaintiff applied to amend its pleadings in order to seek, in the alternative, an order requiring the defendant to furnish a letter of credit for ¥14,490,000, an order requiring payment of ¥14,490,000, or an order requiring payment of the rand equivalent of ¥14,490,000 at the exchange rate of the date of payment.

The court granted the application. Whilst acknowledging that if damages were sought a South African court probably would award them in rand, converted at breach, the court distinguished a foreign creditor's action to obtain performance of a contract stipulating payment in foreign currency from a damages claim. It denied that there was a rule barring South African courts from giving judgments framed in foreign currency and it would not accept that the conversion date must be the date on which payment fell due. In the court's opinion, the currency conversion should be made at the time of payment, with the foreign creditor receiving the money stipulated in the contract. Otherwise, a debtor could profit from his default. (The tardy debtor disadvantaged by adverse exchange rates on payment would have himself to blame for the loss.) *Cosmopolitan National Bank of Chicago v. Steinberg* was wrong or distinguishable because the defendant in that case lacked knowledge of the *quantum* and existence of the debt that was to be exacted.

Steinberg, 1972 (2) R.L.R. 534 (G.D.), rev'd, 1973 (1) R.L.R. 265 (A.D.), 1973 (3) S.A. 885 (R.A.D.), made the same decision.

15 Miliangos v. George Frank (Textiles) Ltd., [1976] A.C. 443 (H.L.).

16 1986 (4) S.A. 671 (C).

LIMITATION OF ACTIONS

Kuhne & Nagel A.G. Zurich v. A.P.A. Distributors (Pty.) Ltd.[17] is a recent example of the orthodox approach to statutes of limitations (or prescription) in Conflict of Laws. When the *lex causae* of the cause of action sued upon is foreign, the relevant statutes of limitations of the *lex causae* and the *lex fori* are characterised as "substantive" or "procedural". A statute which extinguishes the plaintiff's right of action is treated as substantive. A statute which merely bars the remedy is considered procedural. Matters of substance are governed by the *lex causae*, whereas matters of procedure are governed by the *lex fori*. Therefore, a statute of limitations is applicable if substantive and part of the *lex causae* or procedural and part of the *lex fori*.[18]

In the *Kuhne & Nagel* case, a Swiss forwarding agent sought to recover amounts allegedly due for the shipment of a crane from Germany to the defendant in South Africa. The parties agreed that the proper law of the contract was the law of Switzerland. Under the Swiss Code, the plaintiff's claim had not become prescribed, but the South African Prescription Act[19] provided that such claims prescribed in three years, which had already elapsed. The question before the court was whether the South African act applied to the action. If so, the plaintiff could not succeed. This depended upon whether the relevant provisions of the statute were substantive or procedural.

The court held that these provisions were substantive because the statute provided that a debt would be "extinguished" upon the lapse of the prescription period.[20] The statute was therefore inapplicable. It was contrasted with the previous Prescription Act, which had defined "extinctive prescription" as "the rendering unenforceable of a right by the lapse of time".[21] This was procedural. That the present act required that prescription be pleaded--a

17 1981 (3) S.A. 536 (W). See Forsyth, *Extinctive Prescription and the Lex Fori: A New Direction?*, (1982) 99 S.A.L.J. 16; Kahn, *Conflict of Laws*, 1981 Ann. Surv. S. Afr. L. 562, 575-78.

18 See 1 Castel, 608-11; Dicey & Morris, 1179-82; McLeod, 215-16.

19 No. 68 of 1969, ss. 11(*d*), 12(1).

20 S. 10(1).

21 Prescription Act, No. 18 of 1943, s. 3(1), repealed, Prescription Act, No. 68 of 1969, s. 22 (S. Afr.).

requirement usually not applied to matters of substantive law--did not persuade the court that its provisions were procedural. Inasmuch as the present South African Prescription Act did not bar the plaintiff's action, it was necessary to characterise the relevant provisions of the Swiss Code--a step postponed to a future date.

The plaintiff had contended that the South African and Swiss statutes were both substantive. An otherwise clear judgment became murky when the court considered this--not a surprising development in view of the court's reference to the inexplicable conclusion by Dicey and Morris[22] that, in these circumstances, the *lex fori* would probably be applied if its limitation period was shorter than that of the *lex causae*. If the statutes of *lex fori* and *lex causae* are both substantive, it should be clear (under the orthodox approach) that the *lex causae*'s statute applies and the *lex fori*'s statute does not.[23] This was the result the court reached--a conclusion buttressed by academic opinion favouring the protection of rights still in existence under the *lex causae*.[24]

Kuhne & Nagel was followed in *Laconian Maritime Enterprises Ltd. v. Agromar Lineas Ltd.*[25] The plaintiff had obtained in London an arbitration award against the defendant. The plaintiff applied to have the award made an order of court, as provided in South Africa's Recognition and Enforcement of Foreign Arbitral Awards Act.[26] The plaintiff had earlier applied to an American court for confirmation of the award. This action was dismissed because it was commenced after the expiry of the three-year period provided by the American federal statute governing such proceedings. According to an expert on American law, the three-year statute of limitation was a substantive provision that extinguished the plaintiff's cause of action, and the dismissal operated as a substantive adjudication on the merits that would prevent the plaintiff from maintaining in any American

22 Dicey & Morris, Conflict of Laws 1105 (9th ed. 1973).

23 See McLeod, 215-16.

24 The court was unaware of any reported case dealing with this situation and believed it unlikely to arise in an English or American court. It is, however, a common occurrence in fatal accident cases. Many common law jurisdictions have fatal accident legislation with a "substantive" limitation provision. See Leflar, 350-51; Morris, 454.

25 1986 (3) S.A. 509, 522-24, 530-31 (D).

26 No. 40 of 1977. See pp. 79-80, *infra*.

court another action to enforce the arbitration award. Counsel agreed that the rules of American law were substantive. The South African Prescription Act, as decided in *Kuhne & Nagel*, was substantive because it extinguished the plaintiff's right; it did not merely bar the remedy. It followed that the plaintiff's claim was prescribed by the provisions of American law if the *lex causae* was American.

The court, however, identified the *lex causae* as English. Counsel had agreed that the time-limitation rules of English law were procedural. To apply the general choice of law rule for limitations would mean that neither the *lex causae* (being procedural) nor the *lex fori* (being substantive) would apply. While "strict logic" might advise this result, the court would not accept it. Instead, it would apply the forum's law. The court was influenced "to some extent" by Ehrenzweig's "scepticism and preference for the residual *lex fori* approach". Ehrenzweig had advised that forum law rationally remains the starting point,[27] and "if I am not enjoined by my own law to apply foreign law, I am enjoined by my oath to apply my country's law".[28] Under the Prescription Act, the plaintiff's claim was not prescribed because the defendant had been outside South Africa. There being no other impediment to making the arbitration award an order of court, the plaintiff's application was granted.

In time-limitation cases generally, the court's approach would be beneficial if the time periods of both the *lex fori* and the *lex causae* had run out. The plaintiff could not avoid the common prescription by establishing that the *lex fori*'s statute was substantive and the *lex causae*'s procedural. But in the *Laconian Maritime* case the plaintiff's claim to enforcement of the arbitration award was not prescribed by English law, so there was no need for the court to adopt the "residual *lex fori* approach" in order to resolve the matter before it. It could simply have noted the absence of conflict between the *lex causae* and the *lex fori* concerning prescription. The court stated that if the arbitration award had become prescribed or "superannuated" in terms of English law, it might apply by analogy the rule that a foreign judgment superannuated in the country in which it was given would not be recognised.[29]

27 Ehrenzweig, Private International Law 125 (1967).

28 Laconian Maritime Enterprises Ltd. v. Agromar Lineas Ltd., 1986 (3) S.A. 509, 524 (D).

29 The court rejected not only the defence of prescription but also the defendant's plea of *res judicata*, based on the dismissal of the American

CONTRACTS

That the validity and interpretation of a contract is governed by its "proper law" appears to be as fundamental in Southern Africa as it is in common law countries (the United States excepted).[30] Explications of the proper law doctrine are found in *Pretorius v. Natal South Sea Investment Trust Ltd.*[31] and *Improvair (Cape) (Pty.) Ltd. v. Establissements Neu.*[32]

The applicants in the first case contended that agreements to purchase shares in a South African company should be set aside because of the directors' failure to disclose the existence of a certain contract. Disclosure of the contract was required by Rhodesian law. A provision of the Companies Act forbade any person from issuing in Rhodesia an application for shares in a foreign company without furnishing a prospectus that satisfied various requirements, including the disclosure of such matters as the contract in question. Arguably, South African common law required a similar disclosure for purposes of the share purchase.

action to enforce the arbitration award. *Ibid.*, 521-23. The ground of this decision was that the subject-matter of the action in the United States was different from the subject-matter of the action in South Africa. The former was a proceeding under an American statute to have the arbitration award enforced in Alabama. The latter was a proceeding under the South African statute, which did not have the three-year limitation of the American statute, to have the award enforced in South Africa. It is submitted that the subject-matter of the two proceedings was very much the same. Both were actions to obtain judicial recognition and enforcement of the one arbitration award given the plaintiff. Both were brought pursuant to national legislation giving effect to the New York Convention on the Recognition and Enforcement of Foreign Arbitral Awards. If the award had been fully enforced in the United States, no action would have been commenced in South Africa. The court, reasoning that the rules relating to *res judicata* were procedural and therefore governed by the *lex fori*, appears to have simply applied domestic (South African) principles of *res judicata* instead of addressing the effects of foreign judgments specifically. The plea of *res judicata* could have been rejected on the ground that a court's dismissal of an action by reason of the forum's statute of limitations does not bar an action in a second country, even if the dismissal operates to bar in the first country the action commenced in the second. See Dicey & Morris, 1117-20; Leflar, 245-46; Silberberg, 40-43.

30 See Forsyth, 257-78.

31 1965 (3) S.A. 410 (W).

32 1983 (2) S.A. 138 (C).

The court stated that "The question now to be determined is whether the Rhodesian law is to be considered the proper law of the contract for the purchase of shares at least in regard to whether or not it was obligatory to disclose the matter under consideration."[33] It then quoted from the judgment of de Villiers, J.A., in *Standard Bank of South Africa, Ltd. v. Efroiken*,[34] a judgment which illustrates the confusion that has plagued contractual choice of law.

> The rule to be applied is that the *lex loci contractus* governs the nature, the obligations and the interpretation of the contract; the *locus contractus* being the place where the contract was entered into, except where the contract is to be performed elsewhere, in which case the latter place is considered to be the *locus contractus*. That is, broadly speaking, the rule as it has been adopted. At the same time it must not be forgotten that the intention of the parties to the contract is the true criterion to determine by what law its interpretation and effect are to be governed . . . . But that also must not be taken too literally, for, where parties did not give the matter a thought, courts of law have of necessity to fall back upon what ought, reading the contract by the light of the subject-matter and of the surrounding circumstances, to be presumed to have been the intention of the parties.[35]

The court in the *Pretorius* case interpreted this as a direction to endeavour to find the intention of the parties to the share purchase agreements, the parties not having expressly chosen the applicable law. Their intention was to be discovered in the "nature and terms of the contract and general circumstances".[36] In the present case, a

33 Pretorius v. Natal South Sea Investment Trust Ltd., 1965 (3) S.A. 410, 417 (W).

34 1924 A.D. 171.

35 *Ibid.*, 185.

36 An alternative interpretation is that unless the parties can be shown to have intended otherwise, the proper law is presumed to be the *lex loci contractus* when the contract is to be performed in the state where it was concluded and the *lex loci solutionis* when the contract is to be performed elsewhere. See Forsyth, 267-72; Guggenheim v. Rosenbaum (2), 1961 (4) S.A. 21, 31 (W), discussed pp. 75-77, *infra*.

director of the company approached the applicants in Rhodesia and induced them to buy shares in the company. The documents constituting and accompanying the offers were made in Rhodesia and returned to the applicants there endorsed with the company's purported acceptance. Had this been a valid acceptance the agreement would have been concluded in Rhodesia. That apparently was what the directors had in mind. (The acceptance was not valid because it was made by one director only, without the authority of the board of directors.)

> It is irrelevant that it is difficult now to establish the *locus contractus*. The above circumstances . . . lead to the conclusion that it must be presumed that the Rhodesian law was the proper law for the determination of the requirements of the proposed contract.[37]

As the proper law was Rhodesian, disclosure of the prior contract was required under the provisions of the Rhodesian Companies Act. It was also, the court found, required by South African common law. No other relevant distinction between Rhodesian law and South African law is mentioned in the judgment, so it appears that no choice of law was necessary.

In *Improvair (Cape) (Pty.) Ltd. v. Establissements Neu*,[38] a South African company and a French company entered a written agreement establishing an association between them. The association's purpose was to submit tenders for and if successful provide air-conditioning and ventilation equipment for a nuclear power station in South Africa. The agreement provided for arbitration of disagreements concerning the interpretation or execution of the contract. The South African company nevertheless brought suit against the French company in South Africa. The only issue before the court was whether the contract was governed by French law or by South African law. This required the court to ascertain the contract's proper law. If French, the parties' dispute would go to arbitration. If South African, the action would proceed. The defendant did not wish to have arbitration if the contract was governed by South African law.

The parties had not made an express agreement on the law

37 Pretorius v. Natal South Sea Investment Trust Ltd., 1965 (3) S.A. 410, 417 (W).

38 1983 (2) S.A. 138 (C). See Kahn, *Conflict of Laws*, 1983 Ann. Surv. S. Afr. L. 489, 496-502.

governing their relationship, nor was there any pertinent "tacit term" necessary to give "business efficacy" to the contract. The court believed that such tacit agreements would rarely be found. Requirements of business efficacy might require that some law be designated to govern the contract, but they would seldom dictate that the governing law should be system A rather than system B. (This could occur when the contract dealt with concepts peculiar to a particular legal system.)[39]

In the absence of an express or tacit agreement, the traditional means of identifying a contract's proper law--reflected in such cases as *Standard Bank of South Africa, Ltd. v. Efroiken*[40]--was to impute an intention to the parties. This position had been abandoned in England in favour of an "objective" approach. Under the objective approach, when no actual intention was expressed or could be inferred, the proper law was that of the legal system with which the transaction had its closest and most real connection.[41] The court preferred this to the presumed intention approach, but believed it was probably bound by the latter's adoption in *Standard Bank of South Africa, Ltd. v. Efroiken.* This did not matter because the result would be the same under either formula. "From a practical point of view the different formulations would . . . seldom, if ever, lead to different conclusions."[42]

The court made the following observations on "subsidiary points":

> An indivisible contract laying down reciprocal rights and obligations can, as a matter of logic, not be governed by more than one proper law. I exclude contracts where the parties expressly agreed otherwise, or possibly some other exceptional cases. But in the ordinary contract which forms an organic whole the parties' rights and obligations

39 The use of expressions or principles peculiar to a particular legal system reflects a tacit choice of that system's law as the law governing the agreement. See Dicey & Morris, 762-63; Forsyth, 264-67.

40 1924 A.D. 171. See p. 71, *supra.*

41 See Cheshire & North, 195-98; Graveson, 404-09; Morris, 268-70.

42 Laconian Maritime Enterprises Ltd. v. Agromar Lineas Ltd., 1986 (3) S.A. 509, 525-30 (D), is comparable in this respect. The court preferred the objective to the presumed intention approach, believed itself bound to apply the latter, and concluded that both led to the same result.

> would be distorted if some were to be governed by one system of law and others by another. The same logic applies in a temporal sense--the proper law which is assigned to a contract at the time of its formation should continue to apply until all rights and obligations thereunder are extinguished.
>
> The rule that a contract is normally subject to a single proper law has, however, one exception, or apparent exception. Although the substantive obligations of the parties should be governed, and should continue to be governed, by a single system of law, the manner of performance may differ according to the *lex loci solutionis*.[43]

The court disagreed with suggestions that a single contract might be governed by different proper laws merely because there is more than one *locus solutionis*.[44]

Returning to the case before it, the court decided that French law was the proper law of the parties' agreement. French law had the closest and most real connection with the transaction and the parties were taken to have intended it to apply. The contract and disputes arising under it were therefore governed by French law. Numerous details of the parties' relationship were analysed for purposes of this decision. Of significant force in favour of South African law were the facts that South Africa was the domicile of the

43 Improvair (Cape) (Pty.) Ltd. v. Establissements Neu, 1983 (2) S.A. 138, 147 (C).

44 The court found these suggestions in Standard Bank of South Africa, Ltd. v. Efroiken and Shacklock v. Shacklock, 1948 (2) S.A. 40, 51 (W), rev'd, 1949 (1) S.A. 91 (A.D.). What was stated in the *Shacklock* case is

> where a contract is entered into in one country and is to be performed in another, the parties are presumed, in the absence of indications to the contrary, to have intended that the law of the latter country shall apply to questions of performance; that country is therefore the *locus contractus*, and its laws govern the nature, the obligations and the interpretation of the contract. . . . [E]ven where part only of a contract is to be performed in a certain country, the law of that country applies to that portion which is to be performed within it . . . .

See also Laconian Maritime Enterprises Ltd. v. Agromar Lineas Ltd., 1986 (3) S.A. 509, 524-25, 528-29 (D).

plaintiff and the country where the income-producing activity was to be performed.

The court decided in favour of French law principally because the parties' agreement was separate from contracts for performance of the work at the power station, it regulated the basis of their joint venture, there was no certainty that their tenders would be accepted (in which case no part of the contract would be performed in South Africa except limited work in preparing the tender documents), and the main administration of the joint enterprise was conducted in France by the French company. The French company was the dominant member of the association, at least before the tenders were awarded. Before that time, the parties' connection with work to be done in South Africa was either "a matter of future uncertainty or one of unrealized hope". It was too tenuous to justify a conclusion that the proper law was South African. If the proper law was French at that stage, it did not change merely because tenders were awarded to the parties.

Guggenheim v. Rosenbaum (2)[45] is another case in which the proper law principle was applied to choice of law. The proper law was defined as "the law of the country which the parties have agreed or intended or are presumed to have intended shall govern it".[46] The distinct feature of *Guggenheim v. Rosenbaum* is that the contract in question was a marriage contract. The action was for breach of promise of marriage. The court saw no reason not to apply the proper law principle to contracts of marriage. Given that a promise of marriage is no ordinary contract and that delictual damages can be awarded for its breach, the court's unhesitant application of choice of law principles for "ordinary contracts" should be questioned.[47] The court did award delictual damages, in addition to contractual damages, but this did not lead it to consider application of delictual (tort) principles of choice of law.

The defendant, a South African stockbroker, met the plaintiff in New York, where the plaintiff lived and worked. Several years later, during a short visit by the defendant to New York, they met again. The court found that the plaintiff and the defendant agreed to be married at this time. The plaintiff would follow the defendant back

45 1961 (4) S.A. 21 (W). See Hahlo & Kahn, *A Matter of Breach of Promise*, (1961) 78 S.A.L.J. 355; Spiro, *Breach of Promise*, (1962) 11 I.C.L.Q. 260.

46 Guggenheim v. Rosenbaum (2), 1961 (4) S.A. 21, 31 (W).

47 See Graveson, 240-41. The court's approach is supported in Forsyth, 229-30.

to South Africa and marry him there. South Africa would be their permanent home. The plaintiff "uprooted herself" from New York and came to South Africa, but the marriage never took place. Under New York law (unlike South African law), no damages for breach of promise could be recovered. Consequently, a choice of law was necessary.

The court decided that the proper law was South African, so the action could be maintained. The parties had agreed to marry in South Africa. In the case of a contract concluded in one country to be performed in another, it could be presumed that the proper law was the law of the latter, absent an express term or "any other indication to the contrary". Furthermore, the parties had intended to make their permanent home in South Africa, where the defendant was domiciled and had his business, and uncertainty about the effect of New York law upon matrimonial property rights was one of the reasons why the marriage did not take place in New York. The parties could not have intended New York law to apply to their relationship. The "irresistible inference" was that both intended South African law to apply.

A different set of choice law principles applied in the judgment determined the validity of the contract to marry according to either the plaintiff's capacity to contract or the plaintiff's status at the time the contract was entered. The plaintiff's capacity was governed by the law of either her domicile or the place where the contract was made. Her status was governed by the law of her domicile. The plaintiff's domicile and the place of contracting were both in New York.

Although the court did not say so, these principles were not apt to resolve the choice of law issue arising from New York's abolition of breach of promise actions. They were applied to resolve a second issue, which arose from the plaintiff's prior divorce. The plaintiff had obtained the divorce in Nevada, but her husband was domiciled in New York. In South Africa's eyes the plaintiff, as a married woman, was domiciled where her husband was domiciled. If the divorce was invalid, because not granted in the matrimonial domicile, the plaintiff did not have the requisite capacity or status to enter a contract to marry. She would still be married. New York law (which applied to her capacity or status, on the principles stated above) recognised the divorce as valid. It therefore regarded the plaintiff as unmarried and qualified to enter the contract for whose breach she sought damages. If South African law, as the proper law of the contract, applied to this issue, the validity of the contract depended upon whether South Africa would recognise the Nevada divorce. It would, held the court, because the divorce was recognised in the matrimonial domicile, New York.[48]

ARBITRATION

The effect of an arbitration agreement has frequently depended upon judicial choice of law. *Improvair (Cape) (Pty.) Ltd. v. Establissements Neu*, discussed above,[49] is an atypical example of this. It is more common for choice of law to affect whether a dispute can be litigated in court, despite the parties' agreement to arbitrate disputes, or whether an arbitration award can be enforced. The choice of law may be indirect, or an implicit rather than explicit application of "proper law" or other choice principles.

In *Yorigami Maritime Construction Co. Ltd. v. Nissho-Iwai Co. Ltd.*[50] the respondent, for the purpose of claiming damages from the applicant in a South African court, obtained an order attaching a tug belonging to the applicant. The tug was in Cape Town at the time. The damage claim arose from the wrecking near Cape Town of two of the respondent's tankers while under tow by the tug. Both parties were Japanese companies. The applicant sought to set aside the attachment order on the ground, *inter alia*, that the towage charter provided that disputes arising under the charter would be arbitrated in Japan. The charter explicitly provided that the agreement was to be construed and its performance determined by Japanese law. The applicant presented an affidavit stating that under Japanese law the arbitration clause exluded the jurisdiction of a court to hear the dispute; the arbitration clause had to be given effect.

The court did not accept the affidavit as proof of Japanese law. In the absence of proof, it was presumed that Japanese law was the same as South African law. In South African law an arbitration clause did not oust the court's jurisdiction. A court could hear the action or, in its discretion, stay the proceedings pending the arbitrator's decision. The court decided that the proceedings in the present case should not be stayed and that the attachment should not be set aside.

48 See pp. 144-45, *infra*. See Forsyth, 272-76, concerning the choice of law principles which may be applied to questions of contractual capacity generally.

49 See pp. 72-75, *supra*.

50 1977 (4) S.A. 682 (C), aff'd, 1978 (2) S.A. 391 (C).

Benidai Trading Co. Ltd. v. Gouws & Gouws (Pty.) Ltd.[51] is a more significant case. Through brokers in the United States and Canada, a Japanese company entered contracts with a South African company for the purchase of grass seed. The seed was to be sent from South Africa to Japan, where it would be paid for in United States dollars. The South African company failed to supply the seed. The contracts contained the notation "Rules: F.I.S. Arbitration: F.I.S., London". This meant that disputes would be arbitrated in London under the rules of the F.I.S., a body concerned with international transactions between seed suppliers and purchasers. The purchaser took the matter to arbitration in London. The arbitrators awarded the purchaser a sum to compensate it for the seller's failure to supply the seed. The seller then brought suit in South Africa to enforce the award--that is, recover from the seller the amount the arbitrators decided the purchaser should receive.

The principal question before the court was whether the parties' agreement contemplated that the arbitration award would be immediately enforceable in South Africa. The defendant contended that the agreement did not provide for this; an award could only be enforced in the courts of England, the venue of the arbitration. There would then be an English judgment which a party could move to have enforced in South Africa (or Japan). A secondary question was whether in any event a foreign arbitration award provided a cause of action maintainable in a South African court. If the parties' agreement did not implicitly provide for enforcement of an arbitration award in South Africa (the seller's place of business) or if the award was not enforceable for another reason, the action had to be dismissed.

The lower court's interpretation of the contract was that it did not provide for immediate enforcement of the award in South Africa. Among its premisses were that the parties intended in the arbitration provision to submit to the jurisdiction of the English courts, which would enforce an arbitration award, and to have English law apply. The appellate court (the Transvaal Provincial Division) rejected these premisses and the conclusion. A provision for arbitration in London was neither a submission to the jurisdiction of the English courts nor a selection of English law as the proper law of the agreement. The court quoted at length from *Compagnie d'Armement Maritime S.A. v.*

51 1977 (3) S.A. 1020 (T).

Compagnie Tunisienne de Navigation S.A.,[52] in which it was held that foreign parties' selection of London as the place of arbitration did not make English law the contract's proper law.

The court attributed the practice of selecting London as the seat of arbitration to considerations of convenience, London being an important commercial centre, and to the expertise of London arbitrators. It did not believe that parties to international mercantile transactions necessarily had confidence in English law. The transaction in the present case had no real connection with England apart from its provision for arbitration in London. F.I.S. had its own procedural rules, so the "curial" (procedural) law of England could have only limited application in any event. F.I.S. rules did not require enforcement of an award in the country where arbitration was held. The parties must have intended that the contract be enforceable. The only proper course in the present case was for the purchaser to seek recognition of the award in the court to which the seller was amenable, that is, the court which had jurisdiction over the seller.

No choice of law question concerning the details of the seed contract or damages arose. The seller had not appealed the award, as permitted by F.I.S. rules. Failure to appeal appears to have had the effect of foreclosing any defence against the award except those which could be raised against foreign judgments: failure of natural justice, fraud in obtaining the award, and repugnance to the public policy of the forum. No such defence was raised. Damages had been calculated in a matter consistent with South African law.

The only remaining issue was whether a South African court had power to enforce a foreign arbitral award. It was not addressed as a choice of law question, but the enforceability of a foreign arbitration award should be considered a matter of choice of law unless a statute gives the award the status of a court judgment. The court in *Benidai Trading* was required to decide whether a contractual obligation to comply with the arbitrators' award, enforceable under its proper law, was enforceable in the forum. The court held that a foreign arbitral award was enforceable in South Africa and granted the purchaser the amount awarded by the London arbitrators.

South Africa has enacted a Recognition and Enforcement of Foreign Arbitral Awards Act.[53] It provides that, upon application, a

52 [1971] A.C. 572 (H.L.).

53 No. 40 of 1977. See Kahn, *Conflict of Laws*, 1977 Ann. Surv. S. Afr. L. 564, 565-73. It gives legislative effect to the New York Convention on the

foreign arbitral award may be made an "order of court" in South Africa, which then can be enforced in the same manner as a judgment or court order. The currency exchange rate on the date of the award is applicable.[54] An application may be refused if (1) a reference to arbitration is not permissible in South Africa in respect of the subject matter of the dispute; (2) enforcement of the award would be contrary to South African public policy; (3) the parties to the arbitration agreement had, under the law applicable to them, no capacity to contract; (4) the agreement is invalid under the "law to which the parties have subjected it" or the law of the country in which the award was made; (5) the party against whom enforcement is sought did not receive the required notice of the appointment of the arbitrator or of the arbitration proceedings or otherwise was not able to present his case; (6) the award deals with a dispute not falling within or contemplated by the reference to arbitration or decides matters beyond the scope of the reference (the part of the award deciding matters which were referred to arbitration can be made an order of court, if severable); (7) the arbitration tribunal or proceedings was or were not in accordance with the relevant arbitration agreement or the law of the country in which the arbitration took place; (8) the award has not become binding on the parties; or (9) the award has been suspended or set aside by a "competent authority" of the country in which, or under the law of which, the award was made.[55]

GAMBLING CONTRACTS

It is trite law that a foreign law will not be applied when its application would be contrary to the public policy of the forum state.[56] A principal application of this rule has been to actions to enforce an obligation assumed in a gambling transaction.

In *Timms v. Nicol*,[57] a resident of Zambia had become indebted to a turf accountant. The debt arose from betting transactions in

Recognition and Enforcement of Foreign Arbital Awards of 1958.

54 S. 2.

55 S. 4.

56 See Forsyth, 85-86.

57 1967 R.L.R. 386 (G.D.), 1968 (1) S.A. 299 (R).

Zambia, where the turf accountant conducted business. The debt was enforceable in Zambia. Under the law of Rhodesia, where suit was brought to recover the debt, the contract was not illegal but not enforceable. The court held that the plaintiff could not recover. The rule of Roman-Dutch law that gambling debts were not recoverable was of an "overriding nature" and based upon a fundamental principle of public policy. Therefore, it was applicable in all actions. No good reason existed for the contention that it should not apply to contracts entered in another country.

No specific reason was given why Rhodesian public policy would be offended by recovery of a gambling debt entirely connected to a country where gambling debts were legal and enforceable. It would have been reasonable to conclude that while enforcement of local gambling contracts was contrary to public policy, enforcement of foreign gambling contracts was not. But this could have opened the door to actions on foreign gambling debts incurred by Rhodesians, which might be thought undesirable.

An additional reason given for refusing to enforce the debt was that the local rule that betting transactions were unenforceable was "a rule of procedure adopted in this court". A right to recover or the remedy available to a person to recover his claim by action was a matter of procedure and therefore governed by the *lex fori*. While there was precedent for this position and it could be supported by reference to the "unenforceability"--as distinct from "invalidity"--of the contract, it is submitted that the rule of unenforceability of gambling debts was not procedural. As a rule totally barring an action on the debt, rather than one regulating the circumstances in which an action could be initiated and prosecuted, it was substantive. It did not regulate the remedy; it eliminated the possibility of a remedy. If the rule properly applied to contracts whose proper law was foreign, it was because the rule embodied public policy, not because it was procedural and therefore applicable as part of the *lex fori*.[58]

Bishop v. Conrath[59] is also a gambling contract case but very different from *Timms v. Nicol*. Several persons agreed in the Transvaal that, on behalf of all of them, one Conrath would purchase (in his own name) tickets in the Rhodesian State Lottery. If any of the tickets was successful, the prize money would be collected in

58 Both the "public policy" and "procedural" grounds of the court's decision are criticised in Hackwill, *The Enforceability of Foreign Gambling Debts*, 1967 Rhod. L.J. 20.

59 1947 (2) S.A. 800 (T).

Southern Rhodesia and then transmitted to the Transvaal, where it would be shared among the participants in the pool. Conrath, a Transvaal resident, obtained the tickets in the Transvaal by correspondence with Southern Rhodesia. One ticket won the first prize in the lottery. The prize money was transmitted to a Transvaal bank. The other members of the pool sued Conrath's executrix and the bank in a Transvaal court to recover their agreed shares of the prize money.

The lottery was lawfully conducted by the Southern Rhodesian government, so far as the law of Southern Rhodesia was concerned, but under the law of the Transvaal a criminal offence was committed by any person who "sells or disposes of any ticket in a lottery or offers to sell or dispose of or takes or purchases or has any share therein". The defendants claimed that this rendered the contract sued upon illegal.

The court rejected this contention. The judgments of the two judges are devoted principally to establishing that the Transvaal statute did not reach the parties' agreement and conduct. The statute did not have an extraterritorial effect so as to reach arrangements in the Transvaal for the purchase of lottery tickets in Southern Rhodesia or mere ownership in the Transvaal of shares of Rhodesian lottery tickets. Acquisition of a ticket was an offence only if it occurred in the Transvaal. Here it occurred in Southern Rhodesia. There was, therefore, no illegality. Agreeing in the Transvaal to purchase tickets in Southern Rhodesia was lawful.

Malan, J., apparently accepted that the legality of a contract is determined by the law of the place where the contract is entered into. However, his judgment seems to formulate a special rule for a contract to enter a second contract: a contract unlawful where it is entered into is nevertheless lawful if it is a contract to make a second contract which is lawful under the law of the place where it is to be made and performed. Under this rule, the lottery pool contract made in the Transvaal was lawful because in essence it was an agreement to purchase lottery tickets in Southern Rhodesia and it was lawful under Southern Rhodesian law to enter and perform a ticket purchase contract.

This is an awkward approach and some confusion between the entries into the two contracts (the lottery pool arrangement and the purchase of the lottery tickets) is to be found in the judgment of Malan, J. But the instinct is sound. A court should not rigidly apply the law of the place where the contract was made (which may well be its proper law) when the contract provides for a foreign transaction which is lawful in the place where it will occur. However, it is hardly likely that Malan, J., would have upheld the lottery pool contract if its making or performance had been found to be an offence under Transvaal law.

REVENUE LAWS AND EXCHANGE CONTROL

The rule that a court will not enforce foreign revenue laws was applied to bar enforcement of a foreign judgment in *Commissioner of Taxes, Federation of Rhodesia v. McFarland,*[60] which was discussed earlier.[61] The rule also applies to bar enforcement of a cause of action created by a foreign revenue law.[62] The reasoning of the *McFarland* case applies equally to an action to enforce a judgment for a tax liability and an action to enforce the tax liability itself. The court refused to accept a distinction between the two.

McFarland supports the proposition that a court is not to enforce a foreign revenue law "directly or indirectly",[63] but the court in *Priestley v. Clegg*[64] gave an order that had the effect of making assets available to satisfy a foreign income tax debt. Priestley had been appointed in England as trustee of Clegg's estate after Clegg was adjudged insolvent. Clegg, it seems, had substantial assets in South Africa. Priestley desired to take possession of these assets, realise them, and distribute the proceeds among Clegg's creditors. He therefore sought recognition in South Africa as trustee, with power to administer Clegg's South African assets. Clegg resisted the application on the ground that the British Commissioner of Inland Revenue was "mainly the moving force" in the events leading to the English receiving and bankruptcy orders, ninety-four per cent of the debts received for proof consisted of a claim for income tax by the Commissioner, and liability for the other six per cent was denied; the application was thus in substance an attempt to enforce a British tax commitment.

60 1965 (1) S.A. 470 (W).

61 See pp. 54-55, *supra.*

62 See Forsyth, 87-88.

63 Commissioner of Taxes, Federation of Rhodesia v. McFarland, 1965 (1) S.A. 470, 474 (W).

64 1985 (3) S.A. 955 (T).

The court decided that Priestley was not in substance seeking to enforce the British revenue laws and that his application should be granted. Priestley was not the representative of the British *fiscus.* His function was to take possession of the insolvent's assets, wherever located, to administer them, and if needed to realise them. The Commissioner of Inland Revenue was the creditor with the largest claim, but the trustee had to take account of the interests of other creditors. Clegg had not given a reason for doubting the validity of claims other than the Commissioner's, so Priestly was bound to accept these claims as genuine.

The court adopted reasoning found in *Ayres v. Evans*,[65] in which the official assignee of a New Zealand bankrupt, more than sixty per cent of whose debts were New Zealand revenue claims, was permitted to obtain control of the bankrupt's Australian assets. Fox, J., had stated:

> The rule [against enforcement of foreign revenue laws] applies to cases where the revenue authority, or some person acting in its interest or on its behalf, seeks to enforce the revenue liability as such. A liquidator, or an official receiver or assignee, does not act to enforce the revenue claim, but to obtain property which is to be dealt with in a due course of administration. In his own country he will doubtless meet revenue claims where these are payable out of the property coming to his hands, but in the foreign country he is simply seeking to get in property under a title recognized in that country . . . .
>
> I am of the opinion that the rule does not apply where a liquidator or an official assignee seeks to get in property which will in a due course of administration benefit ordinary creditors as well as the revenue . . . . Doubtless, if there were a bankruptcy administration here, the official receiver or trustee would quite properly refuse to pay a claim by the New Zealand revenue authority, but I do not see how the local executor can refuse to transfer the [bankrupt's] interest to the official assignee overseas, once he is shown to be the person having title to it.[66]

65 (1981) 56 F.L.R. 235 (F.C.), aff'g Re Ayres; Ex parte Evans, (1981) 51 F.L.R. 395 (G.D.).

66 *Ibid.*, 237-39.

The last sentence serves to distinguish *Priestley v. Clegg* from the earlier case of *Jones, N.O. v. Borland S.S.C.*,[67] which was not cited in *Priestley*. A domiciliary of Scotland had left two wills, one concerned with her property in the United Kingdom and one concerned with her property in South Africa. Because of a subsequent change in British law, her United Kingdom assets were insufficient to pay all of the British estate duty. Her South African estate showed a substantial surplus. The executors of the South African estate sought a declaratory order on the question of whether the surplus should be distributed direct to the testamentary beneficiaries, ignoring the estate duty, or partially transferred to the Scottish executors for payment of the remaining estate duty.

The court held that there was to be no transfer of assets to discharge the British estate duty; the South African estate was to be distributed without regard to the duty. One ground of its decision was that the testatrix intended the surplus of the South African estate to be distributed to the testamentary beneficiaries, without any transfer to the Scottish executors. A second ground was that under the foreign revenue law rule, the claim for the payment of estate duty was not provable against the South African estate. The claim was unenforceable in a South African court and because it was unenforceable it was not provable. Because the claim was not provable, the South African executors were not obliged or entitled to pay it or provide for its payment by transfer of the estate's surplus.

What the result would have been had the testatrix definitely directed transfer of South African assets to Britain is not clear. Under the judgment of Fox, J., in *Ayres v. Evans*,[68] approved by the court in *Priestley v. Clegg*, a local executor is to transfer property in a decedent's estate to the person having a valid claim to the property even though some amount is owed to foreign revenue authorities. Otherwise, beneficiaries would be prevented from participating in the estate, and the rule would "rebound" against local persons who were creditors or beneficiaries in an overseas estate.

The principle that a court will not enforce foreign revenue laws may be applied to foreign exchange control regulations, with the result that the validity of a claim or defence is not affected by such a regulation. The same result may be reached by deciding that a regulation is not applicable under general principles for choice of

67 1969 (4) S.A. 29 (W).

68 (1981) 56 F.L.R. 235, 238-39 (F.C.).

law in contract or property. Both approaches are found in South African judgments.

Cargo Motor Corporation Ltd. v. Tofalos Transport Ltd.[69] arose from the sale of lorries and trailers by a South African company to a Zambian concern. Purchase funds were transmitted by the Zambian company's bank to another branch of the same bank in South Africa, but the seller was not paid when the vehicles were delivered. The seller obtained attachment of the funds. It then reached a settlement with the purchaser, which provided for payment of the attached funds to the seller and its attorneys. The bank applied for an order under which the attachment would continue pending the vehicles' entry into Zambia. Zambian exchange control regulations conditioned transfer of funds for purchase of the lorries and trailers upon their importation into Zambia. If the vehicles were not imported, the Zambian authorities might countermand the transfer. In making the transfer to the South African branch, the Zambian branch of the bank had stated that it would authorise release of the money upon production of customs bills of entry and invoices and receipts for the vehicles. Under the settlement, the seller would receive the funds without arrival of the vehicles in Zambia.

The bank's application presented the question whether the court would prevent performance of a settlement that violated foreign exchange control regulations. The court held that the settlement was enforceable and refused the application. The basis of its decision was that South African law was the proper law of the settlement contract and the *lex loci solutionis*. The settlement was concluded in South Africa, in disposal of litigation conducted in South Africa, with reference to a debt which the seller claimed in South Africa and sought to enforce under South African law. Under the settlement, all payments and deliveries were to be effected in South Africa.

According to English authorities, which the court followed, the enforceability of a contract depended upon the laws of the *locus solutionis* (the place of performance). A court would not enforce a contract if the *locus solutionis* was in a foreign country and the contract or its performance would be illegal under the laws of that country. But if the performance was not illegal under the *lex loci solutionis* and the contract's proper law, illegality under some other law, such as the law of the place where a contracting party resided, was not a bar to enforcement of the contract. These principles

69 1972 (1) S.A. 186 (W). See Hackwill, *Foreign Exchange Control Regulations and the Conflict of Laws*, 1972 Rhod. L.J. 24.

applied to foreign exchange control legislation. Thus, a contract valid under its proper law and the *lex loci solutionis* was enforceable even if performance was illegal under the law of the place where a party resided, carried on business, or of which he was a national. Here, the settlement agreement was enforceable under the law of South Africa--the country whose law governed the settlement and where it was to be performed. Consequently, the possible violation of Zambian exchange control regulations did not affect the settlement's enforceability. The bank was not entitled to protection against being put in violation of the regulations itself by release of the funds to the seller.

Ocean Commodities Inc. v. Standard Bank of S.A. Ltd.[70] involved Rhodesian exchange control regulations governing transactions in "external securities": securities quoted on a stock exchange outside Rhodesia or on a register maintained outside Rhodesia. Initially, the regulations permitted Rhodesian residents to acquire and transfer foreign currency for purchase of external securities, provided payments were made through an "authorised dealer" (a Rhodesian bank) and the scrip was registered in the name of a "specified nominee" (the nominee company of a Rhodesian bank or stockbroker). After "U.D.I." acquisition of external securities in this manner was no longer permitted. Only external securities previously owned by Rhodesian residents were available for purchase, subject to the requirements of acquisition of funds through an "authorised dealer" and registration in the name of a "specified nominee". These requirements ensured that Rhodesian residents and emigrants could receive only Rhodesian currency payable in Rhodesia for the sale of external securities purchased with Rhodesian funds.

Two brothers (the Harris brothers) who were citizens and permanent residents of Rhodesia conducted in partnership the business of trading in stocks and shares. Among these were shares and debentures purchased on the Johannesburg Stock Exchange. The Harris brothers were customers of a branch of the Standard Bank Ltd. in Bulawayo. This branch acted as authorised dealer in the brothers' external securities transactions. The Rhodesian exchange control authorities eventually granted a "dispensation" under which the brothers were permitted to have a South African nominee for their shares. This was the nominee company (Standard Bank Nominees) of the South African bank (Standard Bank of South Africa) affiliated

70 1978 (2) S.A. 367 (W), rev'd, 1980 (2) S.A. 175 (T), aff'd, 1983 (1) S.A. 276 (A.D.).

with the bank in Bulawayo. The securities were registered in the name of the nominee company, which held them to the order of a branch of the South African bank. The scrip was lodged with and kept in the custody of this branch to the order of the bank in Bulawayo. The Bulawayo bank and the Harris brothers themselves gave instructions to a South African stockbroker for the sale of external securities and the purchase of other securities with the proceeds.

In 1975, the brothers were granted "emigrant status" by the Rhodesian exchange control authorities. This meant that they would be considered non-residents of Rhodesia for purposes of the regulations after that date. Shortly thereafter, they established permanent residence in South Africa and sold all their external securities to a Panamanian company managed in Switzerland, Ocean Commodities. The securities remained registered in the name of the South African nominee company and the scrip remained in the custody of the South African bank branch to the order of the Bulawayo bank. Dividends were remitted to the Harris brothers in South Africa. They deposited the dividends to a bank account in the name of Ocean Commodities, which had appointed them as its representatives in South Africa. Securities were traded in the same manner as before the sale, on orders from the Harris brothers in their own names.

In 1976 the Bulawayo bank, at the instance of the Rhodesian exchange control authorities, requested delivery to it of the shares and debentures held by the South African bank branch. Learning of this, Ocean Commodities called upon the South African bank not to part with the securities. The bank replied that it held the securities to the direct order of the Bulawayo bank and therefore had to observe the mandate from that bank. Ocean Commodities thereupon sought court orders to the South African bank and its nominee company (a) restraining them from dealing with or parting with possession of the shares and debentures and (b) requiring them to deliver the securities to Ocean Commodities with signed transfer documents.[71]

The case first came before the Witwatersrand Local Division.[72] This court held that the sale of the securities to Ocean Commodities

71 This statement of facts is taken from the judgment in the Appellate Division, Standard Bank of South Africa Ltd. v. Ocean Commodities Inc., 1983 (1) S.A. 276 (A.D.).

72 Ocean Commodities Inc. v. Standard Bank of S.A. Ltd., 1978 (2) S.A. 367 (W).

was invalid. The Harris brothers remained the beneficial owners. They had intervened in the proceedings and sought orders similar to those Ocean Commodities had sought. The court characterised the relationship between the brothers and the Bulawayo bank as one of bailor and bailee. The contract of bailment was governed by Rhodesian law, including the Rhodesian exchange control regulations. The bank, as bailee, was not only subject to the common law provisions concerning a bailee but also had the right and obligation to comply with the regulations. The bank therefore was entitled to retain the share certificates held to its order in South Africa until the Rhodesian authorities gave consent for delivery of the shares to the brothers. For these reasons, the court would not order that the securities be handed over to the Harris brothers. *Kahler v. Midland Bank Ltd.*[73] was the principal authority supporting this decision.

Given these reasons, one would have expected the court to refuse to restrain the South African bank and nominee from returning the shares to the Bulawayo bank, to whose order the shares were held. There is no mention of any contractual or proprietary right possessed by the Harris brothers against the South African parties. Instead, the court granted the restraining order on the ground of "the rule against enforcing foreign fiscal legislation". Its reasoning was that "currency legislation", such as that involved in the present case, fell under the rule against enforcing foreign fiscal laws, which more typically applied to tax legislation. While currency restrictions could generally be "recognised and applied" when they formed part of the *lex loci contractus*, "it is a different question whether such currency legislation should be enforced by a foreign Court". An application by the Rhodesian authorities for return of the securities would be refused. The South African bank was acting at the request of the Bulawayo bank, which was an "active instrument" in administering the Rhodesian currency control regulations. The court could not be "an instrument by which that foreign Government exercises its sovereign power".[74] Consequently, the South African bank and nominee would not be permitted to return the securities to the Bulawayo bank against the wishes of their beneficial owners.

Both sides appealed to the Transvaal Provincial Division.[75] A

73 [1950] A.C. 24 (H.L.).

74 Ocean Commodities Inc. v. Standard Bank of S.A. Ltd., 1978 (2) S.A. 367, 375-76 (W).

75 Standard Bank of S.A. Ltd. v. Ocean Commodities Inc., 1980 (2) S.A. 175

majority of the court held that the Harris brothers' sale of the securities to Ocean Commodities was valid. It was also held that as beneficial owner of the securities, Ocean Commodities was *prima facie* entitled to possession of them. In South African law, ownership gave a *prima facie* right to possession. The parties' rights to the securities were governed by South African law because the matter was one of property rights, property rights were governed by the *lex situs*, and the *situs* of the shares was South Africa as the location of the share registers. The Rhodesian currency regulations were inapplicable as not part of the *lex situs*. They could not affect the disposition of property in South Africa. *Kahler v. Midland Bank Ltd.* would not be followed because it ignored the applicability of the *lex situs*.

The *onus* was on the South African bank and nominee to establish that they had a contractual right to possession of the share certificates over and above the rights of the owner. This *onus* had not been discharged for a number of reasons, including failure to prove provisions of the Rhodesian exchange control regulations that allegedly were terms of the arrangement between the Harris brothers and the Bulawayo bank and the absence of evidence to suggest that the arrangement was irrevocable. The shares were beneficially owned by the brothers. The bank was subject to their instructions and there was nothing to indicate that the brothers could not revoke the instruction and give a mandate to another authorised dealer in Rhodesia. Also, the "dispensation" enabling them to have their shares registered in the name of a South African nominee was never revoked. The brothers, therefore, were entitled to have the shares retained by the nominee, not sent to Rhodesia.

Additional grounds given by the majority for not applying the Rhodesian currency control regulations were that the regulations could not be accepted as binding upon non-citizens of Rhodesia, as the Harris brothers had become, and that "A court will not permit a foreign State to exercise its sovereignty in the country in which the court sits."[76] This was based upon the reasoning in *Commissioner of Taxes, Federation of Rhodesia v. McFarland*,[77] which endorsed the rule that foreign revenue laws are unenforceable. A court would refuse not only to assist in enforcing foreign exchange regulations,

(T).

76 *Ibid.*, 184.

77 1965 (1) S.A. 470 (W).

but also to permit the enforcement of foreign government regulations over local property of a local resident. Property within the court's jurisdiction could not be removed against the owner's will for the benefit of a foreign state. These principles applied to indirect as well as direct enforcement of foreign regulations, whether as a "weapon of attack" or a "shield of defence". Here, the Bulawayo bank was acting as a tool of the Rhodesian government. Return of the shares to that bank would enable the government to recover possession of the shares. This would not be permitted.[78]

Finding no contractual or regulatory bar to the Harris brothers' exercise of their right of ownership, the majority held that the brothers and now, as buyer, Ocean Commodities were entitled to instruct the nominee to sign the necessary transfer documents and deliver the share certificates. An order to this effect was granted to Ocean Commodities, thus reversing the Witwatersrand Local Division in part.

De Villiers, J., dissenting, believed that under the agreement between the Bulawayo bank and the Harris brothers, the brothers had no right to prevent the shares from being returned to Rhodesia. The agreement was governed by the terms of the "dispensation" granted by the Rhodesian authorities. It permitted the Bulawayo bank at any stage to terminate the agreement and arrange for the shares to be returned to Rhodesia. This was not affected by the Harris brothers' departure from Rhodesia. If the sale was valid, Ocean Commodities could not obtain greater rights to the shares than the brothers had. It was wholly inconceivable that the Bulawayo bank would be party to an agreement which did not make provision for effective control over the shares after the Harris brothers left Rhodesia, thus making the whole exercise of having the shares registered in the name of a specific nominee of no force and effect and thereby nullifying the very basis on which the "dispensation" was granted. The judgment of de Villiers, J., is, it is submitted, the most persuasive of the four judgments delivered in this case.

The South African bank and its nominee company brought a further appeal to the Appellate Division.[79] The Appellate Division

78 An additional factor was that there was no evidence that the then government of Rhodesia was recognised by South Africa. "[O]ur Courts will not recognise the laws of an unrecognised State." Standard Bank of S.A. Ltd. v. Ocean Commodities Inc., 1980 (2) S.A. 175, 181 (T), criticised in Forsyth, 15-16.

79 Standard Bank of South Africa Ltd. v. Ocean Commodities Inc., 1983 (1) S.A. 276 (A.D.).

characterised the claim against the appellants as one by the beneficial owners for delivery of shares which were in the appellants' possession. It was not a claim for the enforcement of contractual rights against the Bulawayo bank. There was "much to be said" for characterisation of the cause of action as one analogous to the *rei vindicatio* in respect of property. In that event, the *lex causae* would be the *lex situs*, *i.e.* South African law. If the claim was characterised as contractual and the proper law of the contract was Rhodesian, the relevant elements of that law--the exchange control regulations and instructions--had not been properly proved. (Counsel had conceded that the regulations could not be given extraterritorial operation in South Africa--a concession the court endorsed as correct--but contended that they applied as part of the contract's proper law.) Also, it had not been proved that the Harris brothers expressly or tacitly agreed that the mandate to the Bulawayo bank could not be terminated unilaterally or that their external securities would be held subect to exchange control restrictions even after their emigration from Rhodesia. The Appellate Division, like the majority in the Transvaal Provincial Division, found no contractual or other bar to Ocean Commodities' claim, as beneficial owner of the shares, for delivery of the share certificates with signed transfer documents. The lower court's order was therefore confirmed.

TRUSTS

Fattorini v. Johannesburg Board of Executors & Trust Co. Ltd.[80] is a leading case on choice of law for matters pertaining to trusts. Fattorini (the settlor) created a trust for the purpose of "safeguarding his future and of making some provision for any future wife and/or child or children or remoter issue". In terms of the deed of settlement, the trustees were obliged to pay the settlor the income of the trust fund and in certain circumstances a portion of the capital. After his death the income was to be paid to his wife, children, remoter heirs or other beneficiaries as directed by deed or will, failing which it would go to his heirs on intestacy. The deed empowered the settlor to appoint new trustees. Also, the trustees were required to comply with a request by the settlor to transfer the trust's assets to any country selected by him and invest in specified investments located there.

80 1948 (4) S.A. 806 (W).

The trust was created in England, where the settlor was domiciled. Its trustees and assets were also English. Nine years later the settlor, who remained unmarried, emigrated to South Africa. The investments of the trust fund were transferred to South Africa and the settlor appointed a South African company as trustee in substitution for the English trustees. He wished to obtain the capital of the trust fund in order to establish a business in South Africa. With the new trustee he entered into a deed providing for the cancellation of the trust (revocation of the deed of settlement). The court was required to decide whether this was valid. Under English law, there was no right to cancel. Under South African law, cancellation was effective if it occurred before "acceptance of benefits by any person who might be entitled thereto".

The settlor contended that South African law was applicable; it had become the proper law of the deed of settlement because the deed contemplated a change in the *situs* and the law of the trust through a change of trustees and removal of the funds, which had come about. Representatives of those who would receive income from the trust if it were irrevocable (intestate heirs and the possible future wife and children) contended that the proper law of the deed could not change. It remained English, so there could be no cancellation.

The court resolved this issue by development of the principle that the proper law of the trust (or trust deed) depended upon the intention of the settlor. This was analogous to the principle that the proper law of a contract depended upon the intention of the contracting parties. The intention to be looked to was that of the creator of the trust because the trustees were "only concerned to carry out his wishes at his request". The court did not endorse the view that the proper law of a trust was forever fixed. Assuming a change in the proper law was possible, this had to be found in the intention of the settlor at the time the trust was created. Unless a contrary intention was established, the same law would apply to the "endurance" of a trust deed as applied to its validity.

The applicable law at the time of the trust's creation undoubtedly was the law of England--the only country then connected to the trust and the settlor. In view of the deed's provisions for change of trustees and transfer of trust assets, the court found "much to be said" for the view that the settlor intended that new trustees governing the assets in a new country should do so in accordance with the law of that country. But no further intention to change the governing law was found. Consequently, the governing law remained English law and the trust could not be cancelled. This conclusion was based primarily upon the facts that the settlor created the trust in England, where trusts were irrevocable, and made no provision for revocation. It followed, in the court's opinion, that he did not contemplate that the deed should ever be subject to a law that allowed revocation.

The court adopted an alternative approach leading to the same result. If South African law applied, its requirement that a beneficiary must perform an act (acceptance of benefits) in order to prevent cancellation of the trust did not apply when it was not necessary to perform such an act under the law which governed at the time of the trust deed's execution. That law--the law of England--did not require a beneficiary to perform any act to secure the benefits of the trust. In these circumstances, South African law would not permit cancellation without the beneficiary's consent, despite the beneficiary's inaction.[81]

MATRIMONIAL PROPERTY AND CONTRACTS

Southern Africa took from Roman-Dutch law the rule of "community of property" in marriage. As a general rule, marriages are in community of property unless an ante-nuptial contract provides otherwise, which is often the case.[82] The volume of immigration from common law countries, where community of property did not prevail, required courts in Southern Africa to formulate choice of law principles for cases in which the validity of a claim to property or enforcement of a contract depended upon whether a community property regime applied.

The courts adopted as their fundamental rule that the

81 Compare Kalshoven v. Kalshoven, 1966 R.L.R. 216 (G.D.), 1966 (3) S.A. 466 (R), in which a trust created by an English will fell to be administered in accordance with Rhodesian law because it was intended that the trust funds be administered in Rhodesia. This was in accord with English conflicts principles. The case may be interpreted as an example of *renvoi*. See Kahn, *Conflict of Laws*, 1966 Ann. Surv. S. Afr. L. 431, 436-38.

82 See Olivier, Barnard & Cronjé, The South African Law of Persons and Family Law 231-69 (2d ed. 1980). The Matrimonial Property Act, No. 88 of 1984 (S. Afr.), establishes a new type of marriage: marriage out of community subject to an accrual system (a deferred community of gains). See Hahlo, The South African Law of Husband and Wife 153-55 (5th ed. 1985). A Southern Rhodesian statute reversed the position in that country so that marriages would be out of community unless an ante-nuptial contract provided otherwise. Married Persons Property Act, c. 38 (1974) (Rhod.).

matrimonial regime is governed by the law of the husband's domicile at the time of the marriage. Once established as being in or out of community of property, a marriage was not affected in this respect by a subsequent change of domicile. The litigation usually concerned the property rights of a spouse or heirs of a deceased spouse, but the law of the *situs* of the property, even immovable property, or of the deceased spouse's last domicile was not applicable.[83]

This position was reaffirmed in *Frankel's Estate v. The Master*[84] and *Sperling v. Sperling*.[85] The specific question posed in the *Frankel* case was whether the marriage was in community when at the time of the marriage the husband was domiciled in a state whose law provided for no community but the spouses intended to settle permanently in a community property state and soon did so. The husband had been domiciled in Germany and the wife in Czechoslovakia at the time of their marriage, which was celebrated in Czechoslovakia. They intended to establish their matrimonial home in Johannesburg, where the husband had been promised employment, and arrived there about four months later. After the husband's death, it was to the wife's advantage to establish that the marriage was in community. Duties on her husband's estate would be lower. She contended that because the intended matrimonial home at the time of the marriage was in the Transvaal, the law of the Transvaal applied and the marriage was in community, there being no ante-nuptial contract. Under the law of the husband's then domicile, Germany, the marriage was not in community.

The court that first heard the case[86] undertook a lengthy review of Roman-Dutch and common law authorities touching upon the question before it. Some authorities supported the proposition that the law of the intended matrimonial domicile applied, but these were insufficient to persuade the court to depart from the conventional view in South Africa that the law of the husband's domicile applied in the absence of an ante-nuptial contract. The court was influenced

83 See Forsyth, 246-50; Kahn, *Husband and Wife*, 627-32. See also Cheshire & North, 573-81, which refers to South African law in discussion of English Conflict of Laws.

84 1950 (1) S.A. 220 (A.D.). See Kahn, *Notes on South African Private International Law*, (1950) 3 Int'l L.Q. 437, 439-43.

85 1975 (3) S.A. 707 (A.D.).

86 Frankel's Estate v. The Master, 1950 (1) S.A. 221A (N), aff'd, 1950 (1) S.A. 220 (A.D.).

primarily by pragmatic considerations. The "balance of convenience" favoured the conventional position.

South African law had always required certainty in regard to the property of married persons, so that third parties might know where they stood. Gifts between spouses were prohibited and ante-nuptial contracts had to be registered. This certainty had been easy to achieve with regard to originally-domiciled South Africans. The property rights of those who acquired a domicile in South Africa or were merely resident aliens were readily ascertainable if the rule as it had always been understood prevailed--that their property rights depended upon the law of their domicile at the time of their marriage. If the opposing contention prevailed, the property rights of spouses circumstanced as were the husband and wife in this case would be a secret locked in their own breasts. It would be simple for them to elect whether community of property was to apply and to be guided in the election by their financial situation at the moment. It was claimed that the spouses were married in community of property. If that claim was correct, the husband's estate would escape a substantial sum in taxation. It would have been a simple matter, had circumstances been different and had the claims of ordinary creditors been in question, to claim that the marriage was out of community. There was nothing just or convenient in a rule of law which made this possible.

On the widow's argument, the law of the intended matrimonial home would apply only if the intention were carried into effect. If so, the court asked, how soon must the intention be carried into effect? What was to happen if there was unforeseen delay? What was to happen if the intention was not carried into effect at all? What would be the spouses' property rights during the interval between marriage and the actual assumption of the new matrimonial home? All these considerations involved so much uncertainty that the balance of convenience was surely opposed to the widow's submission. The court added:

> the hitherto generally accepted rule . . . is based upon the fact that the husband's domicile is normally the matrimonial home. Many principles of our law have a similar basis in that they are founded upon the facts which exist in the majority of cases. There is no reason in logic why the minority of cases, where the facts do not exist, should be bound; that they are bound is part of the tribute which logic pays to certainty. The result is that the law is sometimes hard, but the alternative is that it should be

slippery.[87]

The Appellate Division came to the same conclusion as the lower court.[88] Four judgments were delivered, mostly devoted to analysis of Roman-Dutch and other writers. Insofar as the judgments went beyond what had been canvassed by the lower court, their most significant feature was to make clear that the spouses' agreement to establish their matrimonial home in a certain country was not an implied agreement to have their proprietary rights governed by the law of that country. An express agreement by the spouses that their matrimonial regime was to be governed by the law of South Africa might be given effect, but an agreement to live in South Africa could not put them on the same footing. The judgments dispute the notion that spouses' proprietary rights are based upon an implied agreement between them. It is unlikely that an intention concerning the law to govern, unexpressed in an actual agreement, would have been given effect. Absent an actual agreement on the subject, the law of the husband's domicile established the matrimonial regime.

This rule provided no answer to the question that arose in *Sperling v. Sperling*.[89] The Sperlings were domiciled in East Germany at the time of their marriage in 1954. They moved to West Germany in 1955 and emigrated to South Africa in 1957. Under the East German law then in force, the marriage was out of community. In 1965 East Germany adopted a new family law, which was said to emphasise the government's "socialistic, communistic" character. The 1965 law provided that property and savings acquired by either spouse through income from work belonged to both spouses in common. Upon termination of the marriage a court would divide the common property between the spouses. The division could be unequal. The law applied to spouses married before it came into effect and apparently applied to former domiciliaries of East Germany who had relocated elsewhere.[90] In 1974, after the Sperlings'

87 *Ibid.*, 221J.

88 Frankel's Estate v. The Master, 1950 (1) S.A. 220 (A.D.).

89 1975 (3) S.A. 707 (A.D.). See Brooks, *The Effect of Changes to the Law Regulating Matrimonial Property Regimes in South African Private International Law*, (1976) 9 C.I.L.S.A. 99; Forsyth, *What Happens When the Lex Causae Changes?*, (1975) 92 S.A.L.J. 368.

90 The court overlooked the fact that Mr. Sperling's counsel had contended that the East German law was not intended to apply to persons outside the

separation, a South African court was required to divide their matrimonial property. It became necessary to decide whether the Sperlings' property rights were governed by East German law as it stood at the time of their marriage or as amended in 1965.

The Appellate Division's judgment quoted the statement in Dicey and Morris that

> Changes in the *lex causae* present much the most important and difficult problems of time in the conflict of laws, especially when the change purports to have retrospective effect. The overwhelming weight of opinion among writers is that the forum should apply the *lex causae* in its entirety, including its transitional rules. This is certainly the prevailing practice of the courts on the continent of Europe. It is probably the prevailing practice of the English courts . . . .[91]

The court found authority supporting the statement, but its ultimate conclusion--that the 1965 law applied--was based primarily upon considerations of "justice and convenience" articulated by the court independently.

The Appellate Division quickly disposed of the notion that the governing law was "frozen" at the time of the marriage. A subsequent amendment to the law of the original matrimonial domicile (the husband's domicile at the time of the marriage) would be applied if it came into effect while the spouses retained that domicile. It would "hardly be consonant with either comity or common sense" for the marriage to revert to the pre-amendment regime when a new domicile was established. Mr. Sperling (who resisted application of the 1965 law) did not contest this. The real issue was whether a retrospective change in the law of the original matrimonial domicile applied to spouses who had already abandoned that domicile.

The court decided that the balance of justice and convenience in the case before it favoured adherence to the general principle that "a reference to a foreign *lex causae* includes the transitional law

country. If this was the case, there would seem to be no justification for applying the law to the Sperlings. Taking this factor into account would involve the application of *renvoi*. See Forsyth, *What Happens When the Lex Causae Changes?*, (1975) 92 S.A.L.J. 368, 371.

91 Dicey & Morris, Conflict of Laws 43 (9th ed. 1973).

thereof".[92] This conclusion was supported mainly by reference to the situation that might occur if the opposite conclusion were reached. It would be necessary to determine whether and when the spouses acquired a new domicile. This would add considerable uncertainty because of the difficult problems of law and fact attaching to the identification of domicile. The need for certainty, so that it would be known what matrimonial regime applied, would be better served by reference to the "transitional law": the retrospective element of the law of the original matrimonial domicile as amended. If the transitional law did not apply, what would be the position of spouses who later re-established a domicile in the original matrimonial domicile and then left again? Complications in this regard would have to be worked out.

The Appellate Division found no public policy objection to retrospective legislation or the application of foreign legislation on matrimonial property to South African domiciliaries. "As a matter of general principle, there appears to be nothing untoward in foreign legislation touching the rights of persons living in this country. Were this not permitted, the scope of Private International Law would be greatly reduced."[93] Even the "socialistic, communistic" character of the East German law was not contrary to South African public policy. The "community of acquests" was also found in the West. The 1965 law was held applicable to the Sperlings' property and the trial court was found to have divided the property in a manner consistent with that law.[94]

The judgment mentioned in passing the problem of characterisation (classification) inherent in certain matrimonial property cases.[95] Matrimonial property law can affect title to property, the effect of a transfer of property, succession to property, and (when there is a contract between the spouses or between a spouse and a third party) the validity and effect of a contract. When a choice of law question arises, might a court characterise it as one

92 Sperling v. Sperling, 1975 (3) S.A. 707, 724 (A.D.).

93 *Ibid.*, 723.

94 See Spiro, *Proprietary Consequences of Marriage and the Conflict of Laws*, (1976) 39 T.H.R.-H.R. 22, for criticism of the conclusions that a change in the law made after the spouses abandoned the original matrimonial domicile is applicable and that there is no public policy objection to its application.

95 On characterisation generally, see Laconian Maritime Enterprises Ltd. v. Agromar Lineas Ltd., 1986 (3) S.A. 509, 517-21 (D).

of title to property, succession or contract and apply the principles appropriate to those matters? Or must a court always apply the law of the original matrimonial domicile (the husband's domicile at the time of the marriage), in effect characterising the problem before it as an element of marital relations?

This problem was not taken up in *Sperling v. Sperling* but it was in *Powell v. Powell*.[96] The Powells' original matrimonial domicile was in England. Thus they were married outside of community of property. Some time later, after they had settled in South Africa, Mr. Powell purchased a motor car and gave it to his wife. After an estrangement between them, Mr. Powell purported to revoke the gift and claimed ownership of the car. Under South African law, donations between spouses were invalid and could be revoked; Mr. Powell's claim was valid. Under English law, the gift was valid and Mrs. Powell was now the owner of the car.

Mrs. Powell contended that the South African rule invalidating gifts was a direct consequence of the marriage and therefore did not apply to a marriage not contracted under South African law. Mr. Powell prevailed, convincing the court that the rule was part of the commercial law. It affected the spouses' capacity to conclude a "contract of donation". It was not a matter affecting "the proprietary rights of the spouses or the rights created at the time of the marriage in relation to property". In consequence, the proper law of the "contract" governed. This was clearly the law of South Africa, the spouses' domicile at the time and the place where the car would be used. One reason for the court's decision was its belief that while one of the original purposes of the rule prohibiting donations was concern about spousal "liberality", it had been retained in modern law for the protection of creditors.

It is submitted that the court reached the correct result for the wrong reasons. The court was correct in refusing to characterise the rule prohibiting donations as part of the matrimonial property regime, governed by the law of the original matrimonial domicile. The rule applied to any marriage whether in or out of community. In fact, its principal application was to marriages out of community.[97] That the spouses had once been domiciled in a country without the rule was not good reason to prevent the purpose of the rule from being achieved, whether it was the protection of a spouse's creditors or of

96 1953 (4) S.A. 380 (W).

97 See Hahlo, The South African Law of Husband and Wife 128-30 (4th ed. 1975).

an over-generous spouse. If the former, presumably it was South African creditors who were to be the principal beneficiaries of this rule of South African law. If the latter, there was no reason why South Africa should have been less concerned about spousal liberality on the part of persons who had acquired a South African domicile after their marriage than about the liberality of spouses whose first matrimonial domicile was in South Africa. The goal of certainty (or predictability) would not be well-served by requiring creditors to identify the spouses' original matrimonial domicile.

The court's "contractual" characterisation is unsound because it does not fit either of the stated purposes of the rule against donation and because there really was no contract at all, only a transfer of the property. The matter should have been characterised as one of title to property, involving the capacity to transfer property. This would justify application of either the law of the *situs* of the property or the law of the spouses' domicile at the time of the donation. South Africa was both the *situs* and the spouses' current domicile in *Powell v. Powell*, so application of its law was appropriate.

If the *situs* and the domicile should be different, perhaps the *lex domicilii* could be preferred to the *lex situs* on the basis that the difference between the local laws pertains to one spouse's capacity to donate property to the other--a matter with which the domicile has the greater concern.[98] The purpose of protecting creditors might point to application of the *lex situs*, but it is likely to be sufficiently served by application of the *lex domicilii*, as would the purpose of protecting spouses from their own generosity.[99]

A different characterisation issue arose in *Anderson v. The Master*.[100] The Andersons were domiciled in Scotland at the time of their marriage in 1923. Later they moved to South Africa. For the purposes of the proceedings before the court, it was assumed that

98 This is supported by another possible characterisation: that the rule on spousal donations relates to the personal consequences of marriage, which are governed by the *lex domicilii* at the time of the relevant act. See Forsyth, 243-46; Kahn, *Husband and Wife*, 626.

99 Southern African choice of law concerning rights to movable property is so unsettled that one cannot say whether the *lex situs* or the *lex domicilii* would apply on "general principle". See Forsyth, 291-94, which should be re-evaluated in light of Standard Bank of South Africa Ltd. v. Ocean Commodities Inc., 1983 (1) S.A. 276 (A.D.), discussed pp. 87-92, *supra*.

100 1949 (4) S.A. 660 (E). See Kahn, *Notes on South African Private International Law*, (1950) 3 Int'l L.Q. 437, 438-39.

they acquired a South African domicile. Mr. Anderson's will left nothing to his wife. After his death, Mrs. Anderson claimed one-third of the movables in Mr. Anderson's estate. The basis of the claim was that the *jus relictae* of Scottish law gave her a right to one-third of the movables.

Inasmuch as the right conferred upon the wife by the Scottish *jus relictae* (as described in the case) was a right of succession to a portion of her husband's estate and the beneficiaries of the will relied upon the freedom of testation afforded by South African law, the court should have characterised the choice of law issue before it as pertaining to succession to movables. Had it done so, South African law, as the law of the husband's domicile at death, would have applied.[101] Instead, the court adopted without discussion Mrs. Anderson's description of her claim--a claim to "'proprietary rights' . . . acquired . . . by virtue of her marriage in Scotland". It stated that since the matrimonial domicile was in Scotland, it could not be doubted that Scottish law governed "the question whether 'proprietary rights' were acquired by [Mrs. Anderson] in this estate by virtue of her marriage in Scotland".[102] A change of domicile after the marriage could not alter property rights acquired by the marriage. Accordingly, the court granted an order declaring that any "proprietary rights" obtained by the marriage must be determined according to Scottish law. Whether Scottish law actually gave Mrs. Anderson a right to one-third of the estate by virtue of the *jus relictae* was in dispute and not decided.

The court stated that the "proprietary rights" would be determined according to the law of Scotland as it was in 1923, "unless subsequent thereto in Scotland the rights have been extended or abridged by laws relating to a marriage in 1923". This implied what was held in *Sperling v. Sperling*--that application of the *lex domicilii* to matrimonial property rights included amendments subsequent to the marriage with retrospective provisions. The court also implied that any provision of Scottish law whereby proprietary rights were affected by the spouses' abandonment of their Scottish domicile would also be applied.

Pitluk v. Gavendo,[103] like *Anderson v. The Master*, involved a

101 See Graveson, 360.

102 Anderson v. The Master, 1949 (4) S.A. 660, 667 (E).

103 1955 (2) S.A. 573 (T). See Kahn, *A Lost Opportunity*, (1955) 72 S.A.L.J. 227.

will contested by the testator's surviving spouse, but the issues were quite different. A woman domiciled in the Transvaal made a will providing for various bequests. She then married a man domiciled in Southern Rhodesia. The couple established their matrimonial home in that country. Shortly thereafter, the wife died. A Southern Rhodesian statute provided that a will executed by a person prior to marriage becomes void upon marriage unless the testator endorses on the will his desire that it remain in effect. (The endorsement had to be duly signed and witnessed.) The husband contended that by virtue of this statute his wife's will was invalidated by their marriage. The case was heard in South Africa.

The principal issue addressed by the court was whether the statute was to be construed as applicable to wills of persons not domiciled in Southern Rhodesia at the time of the will's execution. The court decided that the statute did apply to foreign wills and governed the case before it. The marriage therefore operated to revoke the wife's will.

Pitluk v. Gavendo is another example of a correct result reached on the basis of an incorrect characterisation. The choice of law principle found in the judgment is that "upon marriage a woman acquires her husband's domicile and her property rights become regulated by the law of such domicile".[104] The court in effect characterised revocation of a will by marriage as a matter of matrimonial property rights and applied the conventional choice of law principle for questions of matrimonial property: the law of the husband's domicile at the time of the marriage governs. It is submitted that revocation of a will by marriage should be characterised as a matter of succession, as is revocation by other means.[105]

This would not necessarily result in application of the law of the testator's domicile at the date of death (which in *Pitluk v. Gavendo* was the same as the original matrimonial domicile). The law of the domicile at the time of the supposed revocation can be applied to a question of revocation of a will of movables. Thus, when marriage causes revocation under one local law the law of the original

104 Pitluk v. Gavendo, 1955 (2) S.A. 573, 575 (T).

105 See 2 Castel, 467-68. *Contra*, Cheshire & North, 613-14; Dicey & Morris, 638-41; Kahn, *Succession*, 619-20. In the Southern Rhodesian cases concerning the same statute and foreign polygamous marriages, discussed pp. 130, 134, *infra*, there is no suggestion that a question of matrimonial property rights was present.

matrimonial domicile would govern. (Application of a testatrix's last pre-marital domicile is unlikely, especially in view of the choice of law rule for matrimonial property.) This is preferable to applying the *lex domicilii* at the date of death, which would give changes of domicile the effect of revoking or reviving a will.[106]

In the foregoing cases, the spouses had not made an ante-nuptial or post-nuptial contract pertaining to matrimonial property. When the effect of such a contract is in issue, the argument naturally suggests itself that the applicable choice of law principles are those for contracts, not for identification of matrimonial property rights as such. *Ex parte Spinazze*[107] supports this.

A domiciliary of South Africa, Spinazze, went to Italy to marry his fiancée, who resided there. Prior to the marriage, they concluded an ante-nuptial contract which provided that there would be no community of property between them. The contract was signed and witnessed in Italy and attested by a British vice-consul there. After the marriage, both spouses were domiciled in South Africa. When the husband died, the question of whether the contract was effective to exclude community of property arose.

Because the original matrimonial domicile (the husband's domicile at the time of the marriage) was in South Africa, South African law determined the matrimonial property regime. South African law provided that the marriage was in community of property unless community of property was excluded by a valid contract. The court was required to decide the validity and effect of the contract the Spinazzes had made. To do this, the court applied contractual choice of law principles, which were distinct from the rule that chose South African law to govern the underlying matrimonial property regime.

Under Italian law, the ante-nuptial contract was completely void. Such a contract had to be executed by "public act" before a notary public or other authorised official. The British vice-consul was not an authorised official and did not have the status of a notary. Furthermore, there were only two witnesses instead of the required four. There is no indication in the case that the contract would have been invalid if executed before a notary public and four witnesses.

A South African statute provided:

106 See Anton, 536-37; Forsyth, 317-18.

107 1983 (4) S.A. 751 (T), aff'd, 1985 (3) S.A. 650 (A.D.). Some of the facts given in the text are found only in the judgment of the Appellate Division.

> An antenuptial contract executed outside the Republic shall be attested by a notary or otherwise be entered into in accordance with the law of the place of its execution, and shall be registered in a deeds registry within six months after the date of its execution . . . .[108]

The Spinazzes' contract met the second requirement (registration) but not the first. The contract was not attested by a notary because the vice-consul was not a notary, and it was not entered into in accordance with the law of the place of its execution (Italian law). The contract's failure to conform to the first requirement meant that it was not effective against third parties, *i.e.* persons other than the spouses. As far as third parties were concerned, the marriage was in community of property. However, the contract was binding on the spouses and their estates, irrespective of formalities. As far as they were concerned, the contract took the marriage out of community. South African law thus gave the contract the effect of creating a marriage which was out of community in respect of the property rights of the spouses and heirs *inter se*, while Italian law gave the contract no effect at all, in which case the marriage was entirely in community, as provided by the law that governed the matrimonial property regime (South African law). Which applied?

In the circumstances, another court might have regarded the choice of law problem before it as one pertaining to matrimonial property rights and applied the choice of law rule for matrimonial property regimes: the law of the husband's domicile at the time of the marriage governs. Instead, the court recognised that the relevant difference between Italian and South African law concerned the formalities required to make the contract effective. Under Italian law, the contract failed for want of formality (the British vice-consul not having the status required for the execution of a "public act" and the number of witnesses being insufficient). Under South African law, an informal ante-nuptial contract was effective except against third parties. From this, the court proceeded to decide that the appropriate choice of law principles were those applicable to contractual formalities. But what were these principles?

One possibility was that formalities were governed solely by the *lex loci contractus*. But the court was persuaded that an ante-nuptial contract which did not comply with the formalities required by the *lex loci contractus* ought to be held formally valid if it complied with

108 Deeds Registry Act, No. 47 of 1937, s. 87(2) (S. Afr.).

the formalities of the law of the husband's domicile at the time of the marriage. This was said to be the "proper law" of an ante-nuptial contract ("unless of course the parties have expressly or impliedly agreed that it should be governed by some other law").[109] Such a contract was valid if it complied with either the *lex loci contractus* or the contract's proper law. In this case, the contract met the requirements of the latter (South African law) for effectiveness of the contract among the spouses and their estates. Accordingly, Mr. and Mrs. Spinazze were married out of community *inter se*, but in community insofar as third persons were concerned.[110]

Ex parte Spinazze does not establish choice of law principles for cases in which an ante-nuptial contract is invalid (under one country's law) for reasons other than requirements of formality. It does, however, provide a basis for developing such principles. If the formal validity of a contract regulating matrimonial property is governed by the *lex loci contractus* or the contract's proper law, should not essential validity also be governed by the contract's proper law?[111] Whether a contract is effective to establish a matrimonial regime different from that which would otherwise apply is readily characterised as a question of contract.

If the contract's proper law is applied and the contract is valid under that law, the matrimonial regime will be determined by the contract and its proper law instead of the law of the husband's

109 It would have been more consistent with ordinary "proper law" principles to treat the husband's domicile as an important factor in determining the proper law. See Dicey & Morris, 661-63; McLeod, 374-75; Kahn, *Conflict of Laws*, 1983 Ann. Surv. S. Afr. L. 489, 503-04.

110 The Appellate Division confirmed this decision in a judgment that primarily considered Roman-Dutch authorities. Ex parte Spinazze, 1985 (3) S.A. 650 (A.D.). See Kahn, *Conflict of Laws*, 1985 Ann. Surv. S. Afr. L. 532, 535-40. Its conclusions were the same as the lower court's. The Appellate Division observed that to hold formally valid a contract which complied with the proper law (*lex causae*) but not the *lex loci contractus* was in conformity with modern private international law in western countries, including common law jurisdictions, and had the advantage of avoiding defeat of the reasonable expectations of parties who execute ante-nuptial contracts. To adopt the same approach to the formal execution of contracts generally seemed desirable. Ex parte Spinazze, 1985 (3) S.A. 650, 665 (A.D.).

111 See Dicey & Morris, 661-67; McLeod, 374-79; Sykes & Pryles, 502-04. The traditional view in Southern Africa is that it is governed by the law of the husband's domicile at the time of the marriage, with the exception that the *lex situs* governs the contract's effects upon immovable property. Forsyth, 250-52. See also Kahn, *Husband and Wife*, 632-37.

domicile at the time of the marriage. The court in *Ex parte Spinazze* believed that the proper law of an ante-nuptial contract was the law of the husband's domicile (in the absence of agreement to the contrary), but the proper law may well be the law of the state where the spouses intended to make their marital home.[112] As the place where the matrimonial property rights are to be enjoyed, it usually would have a closer connection with the subject-matter of the contract.

FOREIGN INSOLVENCY AND LIQUIDATION[113]

Several South African cases consider the effects of foreign insolvency and liquidation proceedings. In *Liquidator Rhodesian Plastics (Pvt.) Ltd. v. Elvinco Plastic Products (Pty.) Ltd.*,[114] the plaintiff had been appointed by a Southern Rhodesian court liquidator of a Southern Rhodesian company, pursuant to the provisions of the local Companies Act. In that capacity he brought suit in a South African court to recover a debt still due the company.

The defendant raised the defence that the plaintiff had not been recognised as liquidator by a South African court and consequently was not entitled to maintain an action to recover debts owed the company.[115] The plaintiff drew a distinction between a foreign

112 See Frankel's Estate v. The Master, 1950 (1) S.A. 221A, 221H (N), aff'd, 1950 (1) S.A. 220 (A.D.). The Appellate Division refrained from making general statements about the proper law of an ante-nuptial contract, but it held that the proper law of the Spinazzes' contract was the law of South Africa. Ex parte Spinazze, 1985 (3) S.A. 650, 665 (A.D.) This seems beyond dispute. South Africa was both the husband's ante-nuptial domicile and the parties' intended matrimonial home. Furthermore, the contract was in South African form (a printed form of a type sold by South African stationery shops), the husband brought it to Italy and instructed his then-fiancée to execute it, and it was made in order to avoid a matrimonial property regime (community of property) which prevailed in South Africa but not Italy.

113 This topic could have been included in the part of this work concerned with foreign judgments or, because insolvency and liquidation affect legal status, in the part concerned with personal status. Insolvency and liquidation are discussed at this point because they affect rights to property and therefore have some connection with the preceding topic and choice of law for property matters generally.

114 1959 (1) S.A. 868 (C).

115 Recognition is explained in Forsyth, 319-21.

liquidator's right to deal with or administer property in South Africa and the liquidator's right to institute legal proceedings for the recovery of property. While local recognition was necessary for the former right, it was not necessary for the latter. The plaintiff also submitted that it was really the company, not the liquidator, which was bringing suit, so no recognition was necessary.

The court held that the liquidator could not maintain the action in the absence of his recognition by a South African court. In general, a foreign administrator (such as a trustee under a will) could not maintain proceedings to recover money without prior judicial recognition. The court did not accept the plaintiff's distinction between dealing with property and instituting proceedings for the recovery of property. Instituting proceedings was dealing with property or an act of administration connected with it. The court believed it would be absurd if recognition were required before a foreign representative could take possession of property or collect debts, but not if he chose to sue for the property or debts.

The court was unpersuaded by the argument that it was really the company which was suing, not the liquidator, so no recognition was necessary. This was founded upon the fact that liquidation did not end the company's corporate existence or divest it of assets. It merely took control of the company from the directors and vested control in the liquidator. Arguably, the present suit was brought by the company as controlled by the liquidator. The court would not accept this because the named plaintiff was the liquidator and under the Southern Rhodesian Companies Act only the liquidator could bring an action on behalf of the company. Because only the liquidator was empowered to sue, the court would have held that it was the liquidator who was bringing the action and recognition was required even if the action had been brought in the company's name.

In *Hymore Agencies Durban (Pty.) Ltd. v. Gin Nih Weaving Factory*,[116] the plaintiff procured attachment of goods located in a Durban warehouse and alleged to be the property of a Hong Kong company. The attachment was for the purpose of founding jurisdiction in an action for breach of contract brought against the company in a Durban court. Shortly thereafter, the Supreme Court of Hong Kong issued a receiving order against the company and adjudged it bankrupt. The receiving and adjudicating orders purported to affect the company's property wherever located.

The Hong Kong company was notified of the South African

116 1959 (1) S.A. 180 (D).

proceedings. Its trustee in bankruptcy decided not to enter an appearance but requested that the proceedings taken by the plaintiff be stayed, restricting the plaintiff's claim to proof against the bankrupt's estate as an unsecured creditor. When the plaintiff moved for judgment by default, the court was required to consider what effect the Hong Kong orders had on the attachment used to found jurisdiction in the action.

The court held that the Hong Kong orders had no effect and granted the default judgment. It stated,

> It has been held that a Bankruptcy Statute is only of force in a State where it is enacted . . . . [T]he sequestration of a debtor by a foreign court does not preclude a creditor in this country instituting or proceeding with an action against the debtor in the ordinary way.[117]

The apparent *ratio decidendi*, however, is that the attachment preceded the bankruptcy orders. The fact that bankruptcy and receiving orders had been made against the defendant by the court of its domicile did not prevent the plaintiff from proceeding on the basis of a prior attachment of the defendant's goods.

The court said, "by comity of nations assignments in bankruptcy in one State are sometimes recognised as effective in another" and "A sequestration or bankruptcy order granted by the Court of the debtor's domicile *ipso facto*, does . . . normally divest the insolvent of all his movable property wherever situated."[118] The court was "not now concerned" with whether the goods attached still vested in the defendant and whether they could be attached in execution. The judgment thus leaves open the possibility that the Hong Kong orders would be recognised as divesting the defendant of his movable property in South Africa, with the effect of preventing subsequent attachment for the purpose of either founding jurisdiction or execution to satisfy a judgment against the defendant.

Viljoen v. Venter, N.O.[119] supports the view that a foreign insolvency order vests the insolvent person's movable property in his trustee. The court was in the jurisdiction where the trustee was appointed but not, at the time the matter came before the court, in

117 *Ibid.*, 182-83.

118 *Ibid.*, 183.

119 1981 (2) S.A. 152 (W).

the *situs* of the property involved. Mrs. Viljoen opened a butchery in Mafeking, South Africa, shortly before the estate of Mr. Viljoen was sequestrated. Sequestration was granted by a court in South Africa, where the Viljoens were domiciled. The trustee of the estate took possession of the butchery shop.

Mrs. Viljoen claimed that the butchery was owned by her, not her husband. She applied in South Africa for declaratory orders to the effect that the butchery did not vest in the trustee and he was not entitled to retain it. The court was not in a position to rule on this question but decided an additional question arising from the transfer of Mafeking from South Africa to Bophuthatswana soon after the trustee took over the butchery shop: did the South African sequestration order and appointment of a trustee vest in the trustee movable property that was now in a foreign country by virtue of a boundary change? This question was answered affirmatively. An insolvency order granted by a court of the insolvent's domicile vested foreign movables in his trustee. The trustee therefore acted lawfully in taking and retaining possession of the butchery if it belonged to Mr. Viljoen. Mrs. Viljoen's application for declaratory orders was dismissed.

Two related issues are dealt with in the judgment. One is whether the court had jurisdiction to make the declaratory orders sought by Mrs. Viljoen. The court decided not to consider this in view of its decision on the merits. (The question of whether the court had jurisdiction to order the trustee to release the butchery to Mrs. Viljoen was not considered because Mrs. Viljoen decided not to press for such an order.) The other issue arose from Section 21 of the South African Insolvency Act.[120] This provided that sequestration vested in the trustee the estate of the insolvent person's spouse, who then could obtain release of that estate in certain circumstances. If Section 21 applied to foreign movables, the trustee could retain the butchery even if it had belonged to Mrs. Viljoen. The court held that Section 21 did not so apply. There was a "general presumption against the extra-territorial operation of a statute" and "An insolvency or bankruptcy statute is only of force in the State where it is enacted, though by comity of nations assignments in bankruptcy in one State are sometimes recognised as effective in another."[121]

120 No. 24 of 1936.

121 Viljoen v. Venter, N.O., 1981 (2) S.A. 152, 155 (W), quoting from R. v. Etberg, 1932 A.D. 142, 145.

5

FAMILY LAW

JURISDICTION IN MATRIMONIAL CAUSES

Actions for divorce, judicial separation, restitution of conjugal rights and declarations of nullity present jurisdictional questions that have arisen in a number of Southern African cases. Nullity actions of course differ from the others in having the premiss that no marriage exists. There is a line of nullity cases in which the court assumed jurisdiction on the basis that one of the parties was domiciled in the court's area of jurisdiction when the action was instituted.[1] With one exception, the marriages had been celebrated in foreign states.

In *Ex parte Oxton*,[2] Oxton married his "wife" in England and resided with her there. He later discovered that she previously had married another man in Northern Ireland and this marriage had not been dissolved. Oxton and his "wife" separated and he emigrated to the Cape Province, where he sought an order declaring the marriage null and void. The court held that it had jurisdiction by virtue of the plaintiff's domicile, notwithstanding that the defendant (the "wife") had never been domiciled or resident in the Cape and the marriage had not been celebrated there.

The court reasoned that it was firmly established that in all matters affecting status, the exercise of jurisdiction was (in the

1 See generally Forsyth, 203-07, and Kahn, *Husband and Wife*, 559-65, which include the celebration of the marriage within the court's area of jurisdiction as a ground for the exercise of jurisdiction in nullity cases.

2 1948 (1) S.A. 1011 (C).

absence of express statutory power) confined to the court of the parties' domicile--their domicile at the time when the action commenced. The fact that a party submitted or failed to object to the court's jurisdiction did not confer jurisdiction in such matters or absolve the court from satisfying itself of the true domicile of the parties. In nullity proceedings respecting a voidable marriage, no difficulty of jurisdiction could arise. The wife had acquired the domicile of the husband. The decree of nullity, though retrospective in effect, clearly involved an alteration of the parties' status. The general rule of the domicile court's exclusive jurisdiction therefore applied.

In the case of a void marriage, the decree was merely declaratory of the parties' status. It did not alter it. The object of the decree, however, was to place on record by means of a judgment *in rem* the fact that the marriage was void *ab initio* and gave rise to no legal consequences. The direct issue in such proceedings was whether or not the parties were married. This would seem to be a question of status that should fall for decision in the *forum domicilii.*

Parties to a void marriage were not necessarily domiciled in the same country. The difficulty in the present case arose from the fact that the parties *prima facie* had different domiciles. Applying the "ordinary rule that the court of the domicile must decide on an issue of status", a South African court should have jurisdiction to decide the plaintiff's status and an English court should be the proper forum to determine the defendant's status. Under the law of England, the English court would have jurisdiction in any event by virtue of the fact that the marriage was celebrated there. However, a plaintiff should not be required to seek relief in the place of celebration, absent a common domicile there.

In the court's opinion, the fact that the determination of the status of each of the two parties was so inextricably woven together that a decision on the status of one necessarily decided the status of the other was no reason why the plaintiff should be deprived of the right to obtain a decree in the court of his domicile. It was in South Africa that he intended to live. It was for purposes of his life there that a decree of his status was of importance. If a South African court exercised jurisdiction, no conflict of laws could arise. Should it find that the marriage was bigamous, then by the laws recognised in both countries concerned the marriage was null and void *ab initio* and there never was a matrimonial status common to the parties. On the other hand, should the defendant oppose the suit and succeed in establishing that the marriage was valid, that decision itself would confirm the jurisdiction of the court as the court of the domicile of the husband and thus of the parties' common domicile. It appeared to the court to be in accordance with the principles underlying the decided cases and the "dictates of common sense and natural justice" for it to assume jurisdiction.

Later cases on annulment jurisdiction can be considered more briefly. In *Locke v. Locke*,[3] Locke's first wife, whom he married in England, disappeared and could not be traced. Believing that she could be presumed dead after seven years, Locke remarried in England. He then discovered that his first wife was living in Rhodesia. He came to South Africa to meet her but she divorced him. Having established a domicile in South Africa, Locke brought an action there to declare that his second marriage was a nullity. Following *Ex parte Oxton*, the court held that it had jurisdiction.[4]

In *Ex parte Cathrall*,[5] the court concluded that it had jurisdiction to grant a nullity decree if the defendant (the "husband") was domiciled in South Africa. The plaintiff was not domiciled or resident there. Because the basis of her action was that the marriage was void, the plaintiff could not be taken to acquire the domicile of her "husband" by marriage. The court saw no reason to distinguish for jurisdictional purposes nullity cases in which the defendant had a local domicile from nullity cases in which the plaintiff had a local domicile, believing it illogical that there would be jurisdiction in one category but not the other. That a court in the plaintiff's domicile might not recognise a nullity decree in this case was not reason for declining jurisdiction. The action was based upon South Africa's Prohibition of Mixed Marriages Act, which invalidated marriages outside South Africa by males domiciled in South Africa.[6] The court declined to consider whether the "husband's" being domiciled in South Africa at the time of the marriage would be sufficient to found jurisdiction.

The marriage in *C. v. C.*[7] was invalid because the decree dissolving the "husband's" prior marriage had not yet been granted.

3 1951 (1) S.A. 132 (N).

4 See also Locke v. Locke, 1950 (4) S.A. 240 (D), to the same effect.

5 1965 (2) S.A. 505 (N).

6 Prohibition of Mixed Marriages Act, No. 55 of 1949, repealed, Immorality and Prohibition of Mixed Marriages Amendment Act, No. 72 of 1985, s. 7 (S. Afr.). See pp. 127-29, *infra*.

7 1975 (1) R.L.R. 296 (G.D.), *sub nom.* S. v. S., 1975 (3) S.A. 440 (R).

The marriage was celebrated in Rhodesia, where the nullity action was brought, but that was not a factor in the court's decision. The court concluded that it had jurisdiction because, on the assumption that the marriage was void, the plaintiff "wife" established a separate domicile in Rhodesia before the proceedings were instituted. This was an *a fortiori* case because the "husband" had become domiciled in Rhodesia after commencement of the action.[8]

In *Kassim v. Ghumran,*[9] a fifteen-year-old girl from Zimbabwe had married a man domiciled in Malaŵi. Zimbabwe law required parental consent for the marriage of a minor. The couple obtained a false passport so that the girl could leave Zimbabwe and be married in Malaŵi. Her father, who had not given his consent, brought an action in Zimbabwe to declare the marriage void.

The court's judgment focused upon the merits of the action,[10] but the question before the court was whether it had jurisdiction to determine the validity of the marriage. The defendants had pleaded that the court was without jurisdiction. The plaintiff and his daughter were domiciled in Zimbabwe at the time of the marriage. He remained domiciled there and so did his daughter, if the marriage was void. (Otherwise, she was domiciled in Malaŵi.) The court's rejection of the plea must be taken as a decision that a court has jurisdiction in proceedings to nullify a local minor's marriage in a foreign country to a person domiciled there, at least when the marriage can be invalidated on grounds of *fraus legis* or the forum's public policy.

Ex parte Maclean[11] was not in form a nullity action, but if successful it might have had the effect of declaring that the plaintiff was not presently married. The plaintiff had married Maclean, who was domiciled in the Transvaal. They lived in various places in the Transvaal for a number of years, after which Maclean disappeared. The plaintiff then moved to the Cape, where she sought an order

8 Another *a fortiori* case is Narotam v. Narotam, 1970 (1) R.L.R. 84 (G.D.), in which the "wife" was a minor and her father attempted to have the marriage, entered without his consent, annulled. All parties were domiciled in Rhodesia. The court said that "logically, this court should have jurisdiction in a matter such as this" but made no decision on the question of jurisdiction, the parties having desired a decision on the merits.

9 1981 Z.L.R. 227 (G.D.), 1981 (4) S.A. 79 (Z).

10 See pp. 125-26, *infra.*

11 1968 (2) S.A. 644 (C).

presuming Maclean's death. The plaintiff submitted that the court had jurisdiction on the ground of domicile; she had established a domicile in the Cape and was the only party to the proceedings. The court disagreed and dismissed the action, saying, "In the first place it is doubtful whether applicant can *stante matrimonio* acquire a domicile of her own and secondly the order the Court is asked to make primarily affects the person whose death it is asked to presume and his property."[12]

Courts in nullity actions have assumed the invalidity of the marriage for purposes of identifying the domicile of the "wife". She could have a domicile separate from that of her "husband" and the courts of that domicile could entertain an action to declare the marriage void. There seems no reason why the court in *Ex parte Maclean* should not have adopted the same approach. *Ex hypothesi* the marriage did not exist when proceedings were commenced, so Mrs. Maclean could establish a domicile in the Cape. The situation was one of void rather than voidable marriage, terminated only by court order.

In South Africa at the time, however, it was likely that an order presuming death only permitted distribution of the estate of the "deceased" and did not affect the other spouse's marital status or freedom to remarry.[13] In these circumstances, only a court responsible for the administration of the "deceased's" estate--primarily the court of the "deceased's" domicile--should exercise jurisdiction.[14] The position probably should be that the court of the "surviving" spouse's domicile (identified on the assumption that the other spouse has died) has jurisdiction to presume or declare the death of the other spouse with the effect that the "surviving" spouse's status as a single person

12 *Ibid.*, 646.

13 See Kahn, *Conflict of Laws*, 1968 Ann. Surv. S. Afr. L. 429, 437. This has been changed by the Dissolution of Marriages on Presumption of Death Act, No. 23 of 1979 (S. Afr.).

14 In Ex parte Heinmann, 1952 (3) S.A. 149 (O), it was held that a declaration of death by the court of a person's last known domicile was not conclusive or sufficient evidence in an application for a South African order presuming death. The person concerned was a German beneficiary of a South African estate. In view of this decision it seems necessary that the court with jurisdiction over the administration of an estate exercise jurisdiction in an application to presume the death of the owner of the estate or of a person entitled to succeed to the estate, even if the person was not domiciled within the court's jurisdiction. The decision in Ex parte Heinmann is criticised in Pollak, *Conflict of Laws*, 1952 Ann. Surv. S. Afr. L. 311, 313.

is confirmed, but with no effect upon the distribution of the "deceased's" estate.

In actions for divorce and for restitution of conjugal rights,[15] the assumption is of course that the parties are validly married and have the same domicile (the husband's domicile being attributed to the wife). Only the court of the domicile has jurisdiction in such actions unless otherwise provided by statute.[16] *Winters v. Winters*[17] is an exceptional case in this respect. Mrs. Winters commenced proceedings in Swaziland for restitution of conjugal rights against Mr. Winters, who was domiciled in South Africa. The marriage was regarded as "valid in Swaziland" but a South African court would have regarded it as void by reason of the provisions of the Prohibition of Mixed Marriages Act.[18] A South African court would not entertain an action for restitution of conjugal rights or divorce for this reason.

The court discussed the rules that domicile was the basis of jurisdiction in a matrimonial action and that a wife acquired the domicile of her husband. If strictly applied, the court would not have jurisdiction and the plaintiff could not obtain restitution of conjugal rights anywhere. In order to avoid leaving Mrs. Winters with a right but no remedy, the court assumed jurisdiction. It believed that the "legal fiction" of attributing the husband's domicile to the wife "ought not to be taken to the length of requiring a court to deny a remedy which cannot be obtained in the courts of any other jurisdiction".

Ostensibly, the rule the court bent was the rule on attribution of domicile rather than the rule of jurisdiction as such. The "fiction" that the wife was domiciled with her husband in South Africa was disregarded because of the South African position that the marriage

15 Proceedings for restitution of conjugal rights usually were preliminary to proceedings for divorce on the ground of desertion. See Hahlo, The South African Law of Husband and Wife 407-18 (4th ed. 1975). Restitution proceedings were abolished in South Africa by the Divorce Act, No. 70 of 1979, s. 14 (S. Afr.).

16 See Forsyth, 195-98; Kahn, *Husband and Wife*, 539-46. It has been decided that the court of the spouses' domicile, which has jurisdiction to grant a divorce on the ground of adultery, does not thereby have jurisdiction to award damages or costs of action against the co-respondent. van Wyk v. van Wyk. 1952 (1) S.A. 760 (N) (damages); Carroll v. Menzies, 1961 (4) S.A. 672 (D) (costs).

17 1970-1976 S.L.R. 49 (H.C.).

18 See pp. 127-29, *infra*.

was void. But for this "fiction", the plaintiff was domiciled in Swaziland. The Swaziland court deemed itself the court of the plaintiff's domicile and accordingly assumed jurisdiction.

In *Winters v. Winters* it actually was not necessary for the court to entertain the action in order to avoid leaving the plaintiff with a right but no remedy. She brought the action in order to be able to divorce the defendant and marry another man. She could have obtained her freedom to remarry by bringing a nullity action in South Africa. This would have succeeded if *Ex parte Cathrall*[19] were followed. If the plaintiff had intended to claim rights to property or maintenance enjoyed only by a party to a valid marriage, then indeed she would have been left without a forum in which these rights could be enforced had the court in Swaziland refused to assume jurisdiction.

Winters v. Winters bears some comparison with *Granoth v. Granoth.*[20] The Granoths made a written agreement at a time when, it seems, they were domiciled and resident in Israel. The agreement provided that the husband would not institute divorce proceedings for at least one year (the wife could bring proceedings at any time) and that the Rabbinical Court of Israel would have sole jurisdiction in any divorce action. The husband specifically waived his right to seek a divorce in a South African court. He was planning to emigrate to South Africa at the time of the agreement and subsequently did so, establishing a domicile in the Cape Province.

When he entered this agreement, Mr. Granoth thought that if he obtained a divorce in Israel, it would be recognised in South Africa. However, an Israeli divorce obtained after he relinquished his Israeli domicile would not be recognised. Furthermore, as Mr. Granoth was no longer domiciled or resident in Israel, he no longer had access to the Israeli Rabbinical Court. (Mrs. Granoth, having retained Israeli residence, would have access to an Israeli court in divorce proceedings.) Mr. Granoth therefore brought an action for divorce in the Cape. Mrs. Granoth claimed that the spouses' agreement precluded the Cape court from entertaining the action.

The court held that the agreement was invalid. It was contrary to public policy because it left the plaintiff unable to sue for divorce at all. Notwithstanding the agreement, the court could exercise jurisdiction on the ground of the plaintiff's domicile in the Cape when the action was filed. The court distinguished a case in which

19 1965 (2) S.A. 505 (N). See pp. 113, *supra*, 128-29, *infra*.

20 1983 (4) S.A. 50 (C).

a forum-selection agreement left the plaintiff free to bring suit where the defendant was domiciled or resident. The case referred to[21] involved a money claim. It may be doubted whether a forum-selection agreement would be honoured in an action involving status, even if an alternative forum were available to the plaintiff.[22]

Restitution of conjugal rights is so linked to divorce that the jurisdictional requirements of divorce are applied to restitution actions, but separation proceedings are distinct. They do not affect marital status. Bases of jurisdiction other than domicile--especially the defendant's actual residence in the forum state--may be recognised.[23] This occurred in *Eilon v. Eilon.*[24] Mrs. Eilon commenced proceedings in the Cape Province for divorce and, alternatively, for restitution of conjugal rights or judicial separation. Mr. Eilon was resident in the Cape when the action was brought, but subsequently returned to Israel, from where he had come. Where the plaintiff resided was not stated. The plaintiff failed to establish that her husband had acquired a domicile of choice in South Africa.[25] This disposed of her prayers for divorce and restitution of conjugal rights.

The plaintiff's prayer for judicial separation was sustained against the contention that jurisdiction was absent. The court in the Cape had jurisdiction, the Appellate Division held, because the defendant was resident in the Cape at the commencement of the proceedings. Only the court of the domicile could pronounce a judgment affecting the parties' status, but a decree of judicial separation did not do so. In cases not affecting status, a court would assume jurisdiction when it could give an effective judgment. Because an effective judgment could be given if the defendant was

21 Commissioner for Inland Revenue v. Isaacs, N.O., 1960 (1) S.A. 126 (A.D.).

22 See Kahn, *Conflict of Laws*, 1983 Ann. Surv. S. Afr. L. 489, 491-93.

23 See Forsyth, 208-09; Kahn, *Husband and Wife*, 556-57.

24 1965 (1) S.A. 703 (A.D.). See also Lundy v. Lundy, 1962 (2) S.A. 481 (D). There the court concluded that a court in the Transvaal, where the husband had commenced divorce proceedings, would have jurisdiction over a counterclaim by the wife for separation because the defendant resided in the Transvaal and submitted to jurisdiction there. It was not necessary to jurisdiction in separation proceedings that both parties reside in the court's area of jurisdiction.

25 The Appellate Division was divided on this point but not on the jurisdictional questions.

physically present within the court's area of jurisdiction, the residence of the defendant there was a basis of jurisdiction. The defendant's residence in the Cape when the action was instituted therefore provided a ground on which the court could assume jurisdiction. The court left open the possibility of other grounds of jurisdiction in separation actions.[26]

South African legislation permits a wife to maintain divorce proceedings when she is ordinarily resident but not domiciled in the place where the proceedings are brought. Jurisdiction in a wife's divorce action exists if she is ordinarily resident in the court's area of jurisdiction on the date the action is instituted, ordinarily resident in the Republic for the preceding year, and alternatively (1) domiciled in the Republic when the action is instituted; (2) domiciled in the Republic immediately before marital cohabitation ceased; (3) a South African citizen immediately prior to the marriage; or (4) domiciled in the Republic immediately prior to marriage. If the court has jurisdiction on these grounds, it also has jurisdiction in respect of a counterclaim. The spouses' domicile in the court's area of jurisdiction remains a basis of jurisdiction in an action by either the wife or the husband, as does any other basis which might exist apart from this legislation.[27]

26 Kahn, *Jurisdiction to Grant a Separation Order*, (1965) 82 S.A.L.J. 142, agrees with the result but disputes the "effectiveness" rationale. The Appellate Division also decided that there was jurisdiction to grant certain ancillary relief claimed by the plaintiff: an order determining that assets acquired by the parties were joint property and dividing the assets between them; an order granting sole custody and guardianship of the parties' children to the plaintiff; and maintenance for the children. Jurisdiction in respect of the claims to property situated in South Africa and proceeds of the sale of property in Israel existed because the claims were ancillary to a decree of judicial separation and also presented a dispute within the jurisdiction to grant a declaratory order. However, there was no jurisdiction to determine rights to immovable property situated in Israel. Only the *situs* could entertain an action directly involving title to such property. (The court was not inclined to accept that the defendant's domicile would also have jurisdiction but did not entirely foreclose this possibility.) There was jurisdiction to determine custody and guardianship because the children were physically present in the Cape. There was jurisdiction over the claim to maintenance because it was a claim for the payment of money and therefore justiciable by the court where the defendant resided at the commencement of the action. Jurisdiction in child custody and guardianship proceedings is considered pp. 120-25, *infra*. On jurisdiction in actions for maintenance, see Forsyth, 209-11; Kahn, *Husband and Wife*, 565-69.

27 Divorce Act, No. 70 of 1979, s. 2 (S. Afr.). See Forsyth, 198-202.

Prior legislation extended, on somewhat different grounds, jurisdiction in a wife's action for judicial separation or restitution of conjugal rights. It also applied to divorce.[28] This legislation was repealed when South Africa abolished orders for separation and restitution. The corresponding statute of Zimbabwe provides that a wife's action for divorce, separation or nullity of marriage (and a counterclaim by the husband) can be entertained if the wife was (1) ordinarily resident in Zimbabwe for the preceding two years and a citizen of Zimbabwe; (2) merely resident in Zimbabwe for the preceding two years, if the marriage was celebrated in Zimbabwe; or (3) deserted by a husband who was domiciled in Zimbabwe immediately before the desertion.[29]

JURISDICTION TO ADJUDICATE STATUS AND CUSTODY OF CHILDREN

Numerous Southern African cases decide questions of jurisdiction in child custody proceedings.[30] It is unlikely that courts in common law countries would find it profitable to consider the judgments in these cases individually, but the principal features of these cases should be noted.

A distinction is made between a declaration that a parent (or other person) has the right of custody and an order that a child be delivered to the person entitled to custody. The distinction is occasionally overlooked, but usually it is sharply drawn. There is also a distinction between guardianship and the right of custody, but it usually has not been drawn in cases where jurisdiction was in question. The "touchstone" of jurisdiction to order that a child be "handed over" is the physical presence of the child within the court's area of jurisdiction. A court is considered the "upper guardian" of children present within its jurisdiction. On this basis, courts possess and usually have exercised jurisdiction in proceedings to obtain delivery of a child irrespective of the domicile of the child or the

28 Matrimonial Causes Jurisdiction Act, No. 22 of 1939, repealed, Divorce Act, No. 70 of 1979, s. 18 (S. Afr.). For comparison of the prior and present legislation, see Kahn, *Conflict of Laws*, 1979 Ann. Surv. S. Afr. L. 489, 490-96.

29 Matrimonial Causes Act, 1985, No. 33, s. 3 (Zimb.).

30 See generally Forsyth, 212-16; Kahn, *Husband and Wife*, 569-75.

domicile or residence of the parents.[31] Conversely, it has been decided that the court lacks the necessary jurisdiction when the child is not physically present.[32] Jurisdiction has, however, been assumed when the child was removed from the court's area of jurisdiction in violation of a prior custody order.[33] The court in *Mashaoane v. Mashaoane*[34] went further, holding that a court had jurisdiction to order the return of a child (who had been taken to another country about the time when the proceedings were commenced) because both parties were resident in the court's area of jurisdiction and the defendant was physically present there when the order was made. The order could be enforced against him by attachment and committal.

31 See Martine v. Large, 1952 (4) S.A. 31 (W) (court where mother and children resided had jurisdiction to order mother to allow children to spend holiday with father, in accordance with custody agreement); van Rensburg v. van Rensburg, 1957 (3) S.A. 283 (N) (court where parents and children resided but not domiciled ordered mother to return children to father); van Blerk v. van Blerk, 1960 (3) S.A. 494 (W) (court where mother and child resided ordered non-domiciliary father not to take child); Dickinson v. Dickinson, 1971 (1) R.L.R. 123 (G.D.), 1971 (2) S.A. 507 (R) (court where parents and children were physically present restrained father from removing child from country).

32 Handford v. Handford, 1958 R. & N. 352 (S.R.), 1958 (3) S.A. 378 (S.R.) (court of parties' domicile could not order mother, who lived elsewhere with child, to deliver child to father); Ceronio v. Snyman, 1961 (4) S.A. 294 (W) (court of mother's domicile could not order former husband, who had child in another province in violation of custody order, to deliver child to mother); Desai v. Engar, 1965 (4) S.A. 81 (W), rev'd, 1966 (1) S.A. 621 (T), rev'd, 1966 (4) S.A. 647 (A.D.) (court of father's domicile could not order delivery of child to father when child and defendants lived outside court's area of jurisdiction).

33 Allan v. Allan, 1959 (1) R. & N. 499 (S.R.), 1959 (3) S.A. 473 (S.R.) (court in Southern Rhodesia, where parents domiciled and resident, granted custody to mother and ordered father to deliver children, now in Scotland, to maternal grandmother living in England; by sending children from Southern Rhodesia to Scotland, father prevented mother from having children with her at least two nights per week, as provided by prior order); Matthews v. Matthews, 1983 (4) S.A. 136 (S.E.) (court ordered mother, who had taken children with her to another province, to return them to father, to whom court previously awarded custody; would not have ordered delivery of child removed outside country as order would be unenforceable). *Contra*, Ceronio v. Snyman, 1961 (4) S.A. 294 (W) (court that awarded custody to mother lacked jurisdiction to order father to hand over child held in another province).

34 1963 (3) S.A. 604 (N), aff'g 1962 (1) S.A. 628 (D).

The position with respect to jurisdiction in right-of-custody (and guardianship) cases has been more fluid. Clearly a court would have jurisdiction in custody proceedings between the child's parents if the child and its parents had a local domicile, even if the actual residence of the child or a parent was elsewhere.[35] The court of the child's domicile could exercise jurisdiction if one of the parents had become domiciled in another place.[36] It had been held that a court outside the domicile had no jurisdiction to award custody,[37] but since the Appellate Division's decision in *Eilon v. Eilon*[38] it has been clear that the court of the place where the child actually resides has jurisdiction to determine custody and guardianship even if the child's domicile is elsewhere.[39] It appears that the basis of jurisdiction is the child's

35 See Handford v. Handford, 1958 R. & N. 352 (S.R.), 1958 (3) S.A. 378 (S.R.) (parties had local domicile but defendant wife resided elsewhere with child; court had jurisdiction to declare that husband had right of custody); Allan v. Allan, 1959 (1) R. & N. 499 (S.R.), 1959 (3) S.A. 473 (S.R.) (parties had local domicile and residence but defendant husband sent child overseas; custody awarded to wife); Homan v. Bird, 1976 (2) S.A. 741 (T) (parties had local domicile but defendant ex-husband resided elsewhere and child overseas with grandmother; court had jurisdiction to vary prior order awarding custody to defendant). But see Vandermaelen v. Vandermaelen, 1973 (3) S.A. 584 (T) (court of domicile would not assume jurisdiction to declare father's right to custody of children residing with mother in foreign country), criticised in Kahn, *Conflict of Laws*, 1973 Ann. Surv. S. Afr. L. 428, 430-31.

36 Desai v. Engar, 1965 (4) S.A. 81 (W), rev'd, 1966 (1) S.A. 621 (T), rev'd, 1966 (4) S.A. 647 (A.D.) (court of father's domicile had jurisdiction to declare him entitled to custody; mother resident with child in another province).

37 Martine v. Large, 1952 (4) S.A. 31 (W) (children and defendant mother resided in court's area of jurisdiction, but father and therefore children domiciled elsewhere); van Blerk v. van Blerk, 1960 (3) S.A. 494 (W) (child and plaintiff mother resided in court's area of jurisdiction; father domiciled elsewhere). See also de Kock v. de Kock, 1960 (1) S.A. 582 (C) (child resided with grandparents in court's area of jurisdiction; plaintiff mother had left child at matrimonial home in another province).

38 1965 (1) S.A. 703 (A.D.).

39 See also Birkett v. Birkett, 1953 (4) S.A. 445 (T) (children resident with mother in court's area of jurisdiction at commencement of proceedings); Hubert v. Hubert, 1960 (3) S.A. 181 (W) (same); McConnell v. McConnell, 1981 Z.L.R. 12 (G.D.), 1981 (4) S.A. 300 (Z) (same); Ex parte Sakota, 1964 (3) S.A. 8 (W) (children resident with plaintiff uncle in court's area of jurisdiction); Dickinson v. Dickinson, 1971 (1) R.L.R. 123 (G.D.), 1971 (2)

physical presence rather than the child's residence as such. However, it was decided in *Littauer v. Littauer*[40] that a court should not ordinarily assume jurisdiction to determine the custody of a child who is merely present temporarily. The defendant's consent or submission to jurisdiction is a possible alternative basis of jurisdiction, recognised in a small number of cases.[41]

Jurisdiction in proceedings directly affecting a child's status is the subject of a few judicial decisions. In *Ex parte Egan*,[42] an application was brought in Southern Rhodesia, where the child and her mother resided, to declare that the child had been abandoned or neglected by her father, who resided in South Africa. South Africa was the domicile of the parents. The apparent purpose of the application was to make it possible for the child to be adopted without the father's consent.

The court held that although the parents and child were not domiciled in Southern Rhodesia, it had jurisdiction to make an "adoption order" (a term probably intended to include the declaration applied for) because the child was born and resident there. The court stated that it could visualise no reason why the courts of the parents' domicile would refuse to recognise an adoption order made in Rhodesia.[43]

In *Von Wintzingerode v. Von Wintzingerode*,[44] the plaintiff brought an application preliminary to an action to obtain orders declaring that he was not the father of the child born to his wife (the first defendant) and directing the Registrar of Births, Marriages and Deaths (the second defendant) to amend the birth register accordingly. The application was made in the Transvaal, where the child was born

S.A. 507 (R) (parents and child physically present in country but defendant father had removed child from residence there).

40 1973 (4) S.A. 290 (W).

41 Katzenellenbogen v. Katzenellenbogen, 1947 (2) S.A. 528 (W); Birkett v. Birkett, 1953 (4) S.A. 445 (T). *Contra*, Martine v. Large, 1952 (4) S.A. 31 (W).

42 1965 R.L.R. 518 (G.D.), 1966 (1) S.A. 379 (S.R.).

43 Whether an adoption order made outside the domicile would be recognised is questionable. See Cheshire & North, 466-69; Dicey & Morris, 498-501; Forsyth, 354-55.

44 1964 (2) S.A. 618 (T). See Kahn, *Illegitimacy: Jurisdiction and Choice of Law*, (1964) 81 S.A.L.J. 283.

and where she resided with her mother. The plaintiff and his wife were domiciled in Angola.

The court held that it had no jurisdiction; only the court of the domicile had jurisdiction to declare the status of the child as illegitimate. Custody proceedings were distinguished. A court could enquire into the legitimacy of a child with a foreign domicile "if the outcome of the enquiry is something incidental to the relief sought in the case", but this rationale did not support jurisdiction to order amendment of the birth register. No rights flowed from an entry in the register. Rectification of the register was ancillary to the issue of legitimacy. The court would correct the register if required after the court of the child's domicile had declared the status of the child.

This would be the court of Angola, where both of the principal parties (and therefore the child) were domiciled at all material times. No opinion was expressed concerning cases in which a party's domicile changed after the child's birth or cases in which the parents were perhaps not married to each other when the child was born. In the latter, the child's domicile would depend upon the question to be decided by the court: whether the child was legitimate.

This problem arose in *Ex parte Anastasio*.[45] A child had been born in the Congo to the plaintiff's wife. A Congolese court then divorced the plaintiff from his wife, who remarried. The plaintiff later established a domicile in South Africa, where he applied for an order declaring that the child was not his but that of his former wife and her new husband. They were on a temporary visit to South Africa and supported the application. After hearing argument on the jurisdictional question, the court granted the order. No reasons were stated, but the case represents a decision that the court of the putative father's present domicile has jurisdiction in his action to declare the child illegitimate.

One cannot be sure whether jurisdiction was exercised because the plaintiff now had a local domicile or because the child now had a local domicile if it was legitimate. Jurisdiction should not have been assumed on the ground that the child was presumed to be legitimate until declared otherwise and as a presumptively legitimate child his present domicile was the present domicile of the plaintiff. Jurisdiction should not be based upon a presumption opposed to the premiss of the plaintiff's action--that the child was illegitimate.

If jurisdiction was exercised because the plaintiff was now domiciled in the court's area of jurisdiction, no criticism is offered.

45 1969 (1) S.A. 36 (W).

The question of legitimacy can be described as a question of the plaintiff's status as parent and it involved a contingent obligation of maintenance. A putative father's domicile should have jurisdiction to decide such matters, at least concurrently with the domicile of the mother.[46]

VALIDITY OF MARRIAGE

It is generally accepted that in Southern Africa, the essential validity of a marriage is governed by the *lex loci celebrationis*, as in the United States, not a *lex domicilii*, as in England and other common law jurisdictions. Formal validity is also governed by the *lex loci celebrationis*.[47] This rule is subject to exceptions. The principal exceptions involve the doctrine of *fraus legis* and public policy.[48] Both were applied in *Kassim v. Ghumran*.[49]

Kassim v. Ghumran involved a marriage in Malaŵi between a man domiciled in Malaŵi and a fifteen-year-old girl domiciled in Zimbabwe. They could not have entered a valid marriage in Zimbabwe because the law of that country prohibited the solemnisation of the marriage of a minor without the consent of the minor's guardian or a High Court judge. Permission of the Minister administering the Marriage Act was also required because the girl was under the age of sixteen years. Neither parent of the girl consented to her marriage and no attempt to obtain judicial or ministerial consent is mentioned in the judgment. The girl and her intended husband managed to obtain a false passport for her so that she could travel to Malaŵi and be married there. At the time of the marriage they intended to remain in that country, but somehow the bride's father tricked the couple into returning to Zimbabwe. There, the groom was arrested on a charge of abduction and the bride's father sought a court order against the couple declaring that the marriage

46 See Forsyth, 219-20; Kahn, *Conflict of Laws*, 1969 Ann. Surv. S. Afr. L. 407, 423-24.

47 See Forsyth, 230-32; Kahn, *Husband and Wife*, 585-95.

48 See Forsyth, 237-43; Kahn, *Husband and Wife*, 596-622.

49 1981 Z.L.R. 227 (G.D.), 1981 (4) S.A. 79 (Z). See Christie, *Running Away to Marry*, 1982 Zimb. L.J. 8; Kahn, *Conflict of Laws*, 1981 Ann. Surv. S. Afr. L. 562, 574-75.

was void.

Both parties to the marriage defended the action. They asserted that the marriage was valid under Malaŵi law and therefore was to be regarded as valid in Zimbabwe. The plaintiff asserted that the marriage was invalid, irrespective of its validity under Malaŵi law, because it was *in fraudem legis* and to uphold the marriage would be contrary to the public policy of Zimbabwe (the forum state and pre-marital domicile of the bride).

The court agreed with the plaintiff. The *fraus legis* rule applied when one or both of the parties to the marriage were domiciled in the forum state and deliberately had their marriage solemnised elsewhere in order to escape some essential requirement of the *lex domicilii/lex fori*. A marriage valid by the *lex loci celebrationis* could be held invalid when the parties intended to evade a marriage requirement of the *lex domicilii*. This rule applied to the requirement of parental consent. The parties admitted that they travelled clandestinely to enter into a marriage that the bride could not have entered into in Zimbabwe. The marriage ceremony could have been an attempt to cheat or evade the laws of Zimbabwe. If so, the bride's father would be entitled to have that attempt annulled in the Zimbabwe court. The absence of evidence that the couple intended to return to Zimbabwe after the ceremony did not exclude application of the *fraus legis* rule. It could be applied even if the couple intended to remain in Malaŵi permanently. In any event, they had returned.

Alternatively, held the court, the marriage could be annulled on the ground of public policy. The marriage might be deemed repugnant to local moral principles because the bride, despite her youth, could have understood the immoral nature of her deceitful conduct and the groom, as an adult, could be presumed to have had this understanding. But the principle of public policy was not based solely upon the need to respect local moral values. Also involved was the need to prevent the laws and institutions of the country from being undermined or "stultified". The common law required the consent of a guardian to the marriage of a minor. This was endorsed by statute law, which added provisions for judicial and ministerial consent. The marriage in this case therefore could be "repugnant to the policy and institutions of Zimbabwe, as embodied in both its common and statute law". If facts had been put before the court revealing that there was reason to uphold the marriage in the interests of the bride, the court might find that public policy required that the marriage be upheld rather than annulled, but this could not be done on the facts presented so far.

The earlier case of *Pretorius v. Pretorius*[50] in effect adopted the *fraus legis* doctrine, although the term was not used. The parties to the marriage resided in the Orange Free State and were married in the Transvaal. The bride was a minor of eighteen years. Neither her father (who was deceased) nor her mother consented to the marriage. The couple had lived together as husband and wife for some time, during which they had children and the "wife" became an adult. She then sought a declaration of nullity in a court of the Orange Free State. "Clandestine" minors' marriages had been held to be void in the Free State. The Transvaal position apparently was that they were merely voidable.

The court's examination of Roman-Dutch authorities led it to the conclusion that the general *lex loci celebrationis* rule was subject to exceptions favouring application of the *lex domicilii*. If the parties left the state where they resided because local law prohibited the marriage they intended to enter or declared that they had no capacity to enter marriage without parental consent, and they then returned to that state, their action was regarded as avoidance of law and their marriage merited no recognition. If a minor went to live in another country with the consent of his parent and he was a "major" according to the *lex loci celebrationis*, his marriage would be valid. But if he left in order to marry and so avoid the parental power, the marriage was invalid.

The court rejected the "illogical" position taken in English decisions that parental consent was a matter of the formalities of marriage and thus governed by the *lex loci celebrationis*. Rather, it was a matter of essential validity. The objects of the *lex domicilii* would not be attained if people could enter legally valid marriages across the border and then return. Accordingly, it was the law of the Orange Free State which would give the answer to the question of the marriage's validity.

The court concluded that while the marriage could be void on the basis of fraud in the parties' action, the "wife" could be estopped by her conduct in going through the ceremony, in which she must have had a share in misleading the authorities, remaining in the marriage for five years after attaining the age of majority, and having children. Also, there might have been constructive consent to the marriage by the bride's mother. She took no steps to separate the parties until after her daughter's majority.

When a statute expressly regulates the validity of a foreign

50 1948 (4) S.A. 144 (O).

marriage, it must be applied by the courts of the state in which the statute is in force, despite a general *lex loci celebrationis* (or *lex domicilii*) rule. The principal example of such a statute in Southern Africa is South Africa's Prohibition of Mixed Marriages Act,[51] recently repealed. The act prohibited the solemnisation of marriages between "Europeans" and "non-Europeans". Marriages solemnised in violation of the act were void.[52] The act declared "void and of no effect in the Republic" certain marriages entered outside South Africa which could not be solemnised in South Africa because of the provisions of the act. These were marriages in which the male party was a citizen of or domiciled in South Africa.[53]

This feature of the statute was applied in *Ex Parte Cathrall.*[54] A white Englishwoman, temporarily employed in Australia, there married a black South African. After returning to England she sought an annulment in a South African court. The court was required to

51 No. 55 of 1949, repealed, Immorality and Prohibition of Mixed Marriages Amendment Act, No. 72 of 1985, s. 7 (S. Afr.). See Kahn, *Notes on South African Private International Law*, (1950) 3 Int'l L.Q. 91, 91-96. Another example is Marriage Act, No. 25 of 1961, s. 10 (S. Afr.). It applies where a person is authorised under the Marriage Act to solemnise marriages outside South Africa. The authority is limited to the marriage of South African citizens domiciled in South Africa. For all purposes the marriage is deemed to have been solemnised in the province in which the male party is domiciled. In effect this applies the law of that province (including the Marriage Act) to the validity of the marriage, given the general *lex loci celebrationis* rule. See Forsyth, 232-33.

52 S. 1(1). The repealing act provides for retrospective validation of marriages falling under the Prohibition of Mixed Marriages Act. Immorality and Prohibition of Mixed Marriages Amendment Act, No. 72 of 1985, s. 7 (S. Afr.). A party to such a marriage, with the consent of the other party if living, may apply to the Director-General: Home Affairs for a direction that the marriage shall be valid in the Republic with effect from the date on which it was contracted. The Director-General is to give this direction if he is satisfied that (1) the marriage would have been valid in the Republic but for the Prohibition of Mixed Marriages Act, (2) the marriage was not dissolved or declared invalid by a competent court on a ground other than the provisions of the act, and (3) neither party, after the contraction of the marriage and within the life of the other party, lawfully married a third person. Arguably, the Director-General's direction will override any legal impediment to marriage, not just that of the Prohibition of Mixed Marriages Act.

53 S. 1(2).

54 1965 (2) S.A. 505 (N).

hold the marriage void if the "husband" had a South African domicile at the time of the marriage, even if the marriage was valid in Australia.[55]

The effect of the Prohibition of Mixed Marriages Act upon litigation outside South Africa was in question in *Winters v. Winters.*[56] A marriage was celebrated in Swaziland between a white male domiciled in South Africa and a Coloured female resident in South Africa but domiciled in Swaziland. He was a citizen of Holland. She was a citizen of Swaziland. The couple never lived together. The wife returned to Swaziland and desired to marry another man. She brought an action in Swaziland for restitution of conjugal rights as a prelude to divorce proceedings. As far as the court was concerned, the marriage was "valid in Swaziland" despite its invalidity under the South African legislation.

The court with jurisdiction over an action for restitution of conjugal rights was the court of the spouses' domicile. As the wife of a man domiciled in South Africa, the plaintiff was domiciled in that country. But a South African court would not grant restitution of conjugal rights because it would not recognise the Winters' marriage. In order to avoid leaving the plaintiff with a right but no remedy, the court decided to treat her as a domiciliary of Swaziland for purposes of jurisdiction. It did this by putting aside the "legal fiction" that a wife's domicile was that of her husband.[57] In effect the marriage was treated as void for purposes of ascertaining domicile, and thus jurisdiction, because the marriage was void under South African law. The court believed it was not reasonable to apply the "fiction" when the law of the husband's domicile "proscribes" it by denying the existence of the marriage. The court apparently intended to treat the marriage as valid for the purpose of determining the plaintiff's entitlement to restitution of conjugal rights and divorce.

The validity of potentially polygamous marriages has been a recurrent problem in Southern African courts. At one time both actually and potentially polygamous marriages, valid according to the *lex loci celebrationis*, would not be recognised at all, limited statutory

55 At the time of the marriage, s. 1(2) of the Prohibition of Mixed Marriages Act applied only to the marriage of a male domiciled in South Africa. It was extended to all male citizens of South Africa by the Prohibition of Mixed Marriages Amendment Act, No. 21 of 1968 (S. Afr.).

56 1970-1976 S.L.R. 49 (H.C.).

57 See pp. 116-17, *supra*.

exceptions apart. Recognition was forbidden by the forum's public policy.[58]

This rule was applied in *Patel v. The Master of the High Court*.[59] In 1931 a man domiciled in Southern Rhodesia married a woman in India according to Hindu rites. They lived in Southern Rhodesia until the man's death in 1953. Under Indian law, they had entered a valid potentially polygamous marriage. The husband never took a second wife. Shortly before his death, the husband and wife went through a marriage ceremony in Southern Rhodesia. (The marriage register listed them as "married".) In 1950 the husband had made a will appointing his wife as sole heir. If they were validly married in 1931, the 1953 ceremony was a nullity. If the 1931 marriage was not valid, the parties were married by the 1953 ceremony and their marriage had the effect of revoking the 1950 will.

The court held that the 1931 marriage was not to be recognised because it was potentially polygamous. The only lawful marriage was that of 1953 and this revoked the husband's will. The court framed the question before it as whether the 1931 marriage was a marriage for the purpose of the statute providing for revocation of wills by marriage. It found no reason to give the term "marriage" in this statute anything other than its "ordinary meaning" of a monogamous union. This excluded potentially polygamous marriages even if the husband never took a second wife.

Acting Master, High Court v. Estate Mehta[60] involved a Hindu marriage in Bombay Province, India. As in the *Patel* case, the marriage was potentially polygamous and no second marriage was contracted. However, the husband was not then domiciled in Southern Rhodesia--both parties were domiciled in Bombay Province--and a Bombay statute enacted three decades later prohibited bigamous marriages by Hindus and declared them void. The will of the husband made his wife sole heiress. Southern Rhodesian law exempted from succession duty "any succession accruing from any predecessor to his surviving spouse". The question to be decided was

58 See Seedat's Executors v. The Master (Natal), 1917 A.D. 302; Forsyth, 239-43. This remains the position in South Africa, pending judicial acceptance there of the departure made in the Rhodesian cases described below.

59 1953 S.R. 160.

60 1957 (3) S.A. 727 (S.R.), rev'd, 1958 R. & N. 570 (F.S.C.), 1958 (4) S.A. 252 (F.S.C.).

whether the wife was such a "surviving spouse".

The lower court held that a party to a potentially polygamous marriage was not a "surviving spouse" and was not entitled to the exemption from succession duty. "Surviving spouse" meant the survivor of a marriage recognised in Southern Rhodesia as valid, which a polygamous marriage was not. However, the Bombay statute prohibiting bigamous Hindu marriages (*i.e.* terminating the capacity of a Hindu to take an additional spouse) could have made the marriage monogamous. If so, the marriage became valid and the wife was a "surviving spouse".

The statute prospectively invalidated bigamous marriages that were contracted in Bombay Province or contracted outside the province by a person domiciled in the province. In the court's opinion, the statute did not make the marriage before it monogamous if the spouses were domiciled outside the province at the time the statute came into force. Its only effect was to prohibit either party from entering a bigamous marriage within the province. If, however, the parties were domiciled within the province when the statute came into force, their marriage was converted into a monogamous one. They would be in the same position as persons married after the statute became effective. The wife would be a "surviving spouse". The court did not decide whether the parties were domiciled in Bombay Province or Southern Rhodesia at the critical time.

The executor of the estate appealed to the Federal Supreme Court, hoping to establish an entitlement to exemption from succession duty irrespective of the spouses' domicile. The appeal was successful.[61] The Supreme Court repudiated the view that a polygamous marriage would not be recognised in any circumstances. "Countervailing considerations" of "common sense and decency" warranted recognition of polygamous marriages for certain purposes, as had occurred in England.

The court agreed with the approach of a Canadian judge, expressed in a succession duty case involving a Chinese man who left two wives:

> It will be observed that this question has really no moral or religious aspect and no "consequent effects upon the position of the wife and legitimacy of the children," or prosecution for "polygamy which our law forbids" as a

61 Estate Mehta v. Acting Master of the High Court of Southern Rhodesia, 1958 R. & N. 570 (F.S.C.), 1958 (4) S.A. 252 (F.S.C.).

> felony . . . but is simply a business matter of the collection of a tax for revenue purposes . . . .
>
> May I not also ask what, in the comity of international jurisprudence "could be more absurd than" to refuse to recognize here the lawfully wedded and domiciled subjects of the admittedly civilized state of China when they merely seek to obtain that part of their domiciled Chinese husband's estate which happens to be in this, to them, foreign country, after paying the appropriate tax? . . . The difficulty in the case . . . is caused by the fact that this purely taxing statute . . . has . . . been erroneously approached as though it was the English Divorce Act, or some statute of a similar nature, under which conflicting litigants had invoked the jurisdiction of the Court to assert their domestic rights, hence the cases invoked by the Crown have no application to the fundamentally different question we have to deal with.[62]

The court took the absence of any special mention in the Death Duties Act of wives of polygamous marriages as an indication that the term "surviving spouse" was "used in a wide sense". When using the word "wife" the Southern Rhodesian legislature generally took care to exclude a wife of a polygamous marriage, if that was the intention, or to make special provision for such a wife.

> Although . . . "surviving spouse" must be used in the sense of a survivor of a marriage which the law recognises as valid, the Court should not . . . be astute to limit the phrase more by holding that recognition of a polygamous marriage would be contrary to the intention shown by use of the phrase.[63]

The marriage in the present case was to be recognised for the purpose of the exemption from succession duty. The wife was a

62 In re Lee Cheong, Deceased, (1923) 33 B.C.R. 109, 116, 127-28 (C.A.), *sub nom.* In re the Succession Duty Act; Lee Sheck Yew v. Attorney-General for British Columbia, [1924] 1 W.W.R. 753, 758, 767-68 (B.C.C.A.), *sub nom.* Yew v. Attorney-General for British Columbia, [1924] 1 D.L.R. 1166, 1171, 1183 (B.C.C.A.) (Martin, J.A.).

63 Estate Mehta v. Acting Master of the High Court of Southern Rhodesia, 1958 R. &. N. 570, 586 (F.S.C.), 1958 (4) S.A. 252, 261 (F.S.C.).

"surviving spouse". The court did not place any emphasis upon the fact that the marriage had in fact remained monogamous. It declined to express any opinion on whether the existence of a second wife would affect the judicial attitude toward a marriage.

The court declared that there was a need for a "flexible" rule. It denied that this would throw the law into a state of uncertainty. Laws pertaining to fulfillment of the obligations of marriage or dissolution of marriage for failure to observe them, which had been developed in regard to monogamous marriage, would be preserved. Courts administering a law which regarded polygamy with disfavour would only be persuaded to recognise polygamous marriages if strong reasons outweighing the general policy were present.

Tredgold, C.J., added the following apt comments in a concurring judgment:

> It is now clear that it is absolutely essential, if an intolerable situation is to be avoided, that foreign polygamous marriages, valid by the laws of the country in which they were contracted, should be recognised by our courts for certain purposes, however limited those purposes may be. Unless this is done the effectiveness of private international law, the system without which it would be impossible to maintain the legal relationships existing between the inhabitants of the various countries constituting the civilized world, would be most seriously impaired.
>
> . . . However much we may deprecate polygamous marriages, they are recognised by the law of a considerable number of countries which are accepted as civilized . . . . There are good and sufficient reasons for not recognising such marriages when the consequences of recognition would be to disturb the incidents of our own monogamous system. But where it is merely a question of recognising the marriage for the purpose of succession to property no such complication arises. On the contrary, there are the strongest reasons why recognition should be accorded, otherwise the consequences may be most serious for the successors of a great many blameless people who have lived and died on the not unreasonable assumption that their marriages were lawful in the eyes of the world. Under modern conditions, the movements of population and property will produce an increasing number of cases in which the succession to married persons falls, in whole or in part, to be determined by the law of a country other

> than their own. This must have an important bearing on the construction of a statute relating to succession, in which the legislature has used the expression "surviving spouse."
>
> I am strengthened in this conclusion by the fact that it is to my mind quite unrealistic to affirm that it is contrary to the policy of our law to recognise polygamous marriages for the purposes of succession when the majority of marriages in the Colony are under a polygamous system recognised for all civil purposes [by statutory enactment].[64]

It will be recalled that the court in *Patel v. The Master of the High Court*[65] would not recognise a potentially polygamous marriage for purposes of the statute providing for revocation of wills by marriage. It was decided that the spouses were married by a subsequent marriage ceremony and this caused revocation of a proven will. In *In re Estate Koshen,*[66] the question was whether a potentially polygamous marriage revoked a prior will. At his death, the testator was domiciled in British Somaliland, where Islamic law prevailed. The marriage in *Koshen* should not have had the effect of revoking the will if *Patel* was correctly decided, but the Federal Supreme Court's decision in *Mehta* had intervened.

The court in *In re Estate Koshen* held that the case fell within the principles of the *Mehta* case, especially in view of the remarks of Tredgold, C.J. The *Koshen* case related only to "succession of property". The marriage would be recognised for purposes of the relevant succession statute. Accordingly, it had the effect of revoking the will in question. The *Patel* case was not mentioned.

Kader v. Kader[67] presented the question of whether the wife of a potentially polygamous marriage was entitled to maintenance. The parties were married by Muslim rites in Malawi, where the husband was domiciled at the time. Thereafter they came to Rhodesia, where a magistrate ordered the payment of maintenance. The husband applied for rescission of the order on the ground that the beneficiary was not a wife for purposes of the legislation providing for

64 *Ibid.*, 588-89, 253-54.

65 1953 S.R. 160. See pp. 129-30, *supra.*

66 1960 R. & N. 157 (S.R.), 1960 (2) S.A. 174 (S.R.).

67 1972 (1) R.L.R. 302 (A.D.), 1972 (3) S.A. 203 (R.A.D.).

maintenance of spouses. There was no evidence of any additional marriage.

The Rhodesian Appellate Division held that the marriage was to be recognised for the purposes of the maintenance legislation. One consideration was that for some years after the maintenance legislation was enacted, magistrates courts entertained claims for maintenance by Africans, the vast majority of whom had polygamous marriages. In these circumstances it would be "extraordinary" if it was intended to exclude non-African wives of polygamous marriages from the legislation, absent an express provision to this effect. Another consideration was that Rhodesian law provided for reciprocal enforcement of maintenance orders of numerous countries whose laws permitted polygamy. Orders from these countries included orders in favour of wives of potentially polygamous marriages. The legislature would not have intended to permit a wife to enforce such an order while denying her the right to obtain a Rhodesian court order when deserted in Rhodesia. In addition, immigration legislation recognised polygamous marriages. One wife could be brought into the country. The legislature would not have intended that she could be abandoned with impunity, leaving the state to support her. The policy of the law being to frown upon polygamous marriages, this would be the worst way in which to discourage them.

The broader grounds of the court's decision were similar to those expressed in the *Mehta* case. It was not contrary to public policy to give recognition to polygamous marriages for certain purposes. In a country where the great majority of the population practised polygamy and whose polygamous marriages were recognised for all civil purposes except the High Court's matrimonial jurisdiction, it was illogical to withhold similar recognition to foreign polygamous marriages, particularly marriages monogamous in fact. Recognition of such a marriage or construction of the word "wife" depended upon the purpose for which the marriage was to be recognised and the objects of the statute. Foreign polygamous marriages would not be recognised when courts were exercising their "ordinary matrimonial jurisdiction".[68] Very different considerations applied when the question was whether a person was a wife entitled to support from her husband. In Rhodesia, unlike England,[69] a magistrate did not exercise matrimonial jurisdiction in making a maintenance order. The

68 For the reasons stated in Baindail v. Baindail, [1946] P. 122, 125-26 (C.A.).

69 Sowa v. Sowa, [1961] P. 70 (C.A.).

court could find no reason why the marriage should not be recognised for this purpose.

It is hard to deny the justice of the result reached in *Kader v. Kader*, but the court overlooked a critical question: could the right to maintenance be separated from the status of wife? One can readily accept that a provision of a succession statute or marital tax exemption extends to a person without this status, but it is much more difficult to accept that a person has an obligation to maintain a person who is not recognised as his wife. Rhodesian law treated as valid polygamous marriages contracted according to African customary law, but in all probability a foreign polygamous marriage would not be recognised as creating a marital relationship as such. This still would be contrary to public policy. The court did not cite any provision in the maintenance legislation that extended the obligation of maintenance to persons not enjoying a recognised marital status. Had the legislature thought of the problem that arose in *Kader v. Kader*, it might well have provided for maintenance, but it had not done so. It is no answer (as suggested in the judgment) that this was unnecessary in view of the *Mehta* case, as that dealt with an entirely different problem.

LEGITIMACY--CHOICE OF LAW

It is accepted in Southern Africa that the legitimacy of a child is determined by his domicile of origin. A child legitimate by the law of his domicile of origin is recognised as legitimate.[70] *Righetti v. Pinchen*[71] is an example of this rule's application. The child in question was born to Italian parents 197 days after their marriage. The parents were later separated by decree of an Italian court. The mother then acquired a "domicile" in Austria in order to give a court in that country jurisdiction in proceedings to nullify the marriage. The court granted a decree of nullity, the father having consented to the court's jurisdiction. Then, with the father's consent, the Austrian decree was declared valid and effective in Italy by the Italian Court of Appeal.

The mother took the child to South Africa, where the father sought an order declaring that he was entitled to custody and

70 Forsyth, 255. See also Spiro, Law of Parent and Child 491-96 (4th ed. 1985).

71 1955 (3) S.A. 338 (D).

requiring the mother to return the child to him. He relied upon the provision in the Italian separation decree giving him custody of the child and upon Italian law, which included the right of custody in the rights accorded to the father of a legitimate child.

This gave rise to the question of whether the child was legitimate. South African law treated the child of a nullified marriage as illegitimate, subject to the doctrine of "putative marriages". Under Italian law, a child born at least 180 days after the marriage of its parents or 300 days before the dissolution or annulment of the marriage was a legitimate child of the marriage. Except in cases where both parties to the marriage acted *mala fide*, a declaration of nullity did not affect a child's legitimacy. In this case it was not disputed that the father was *bona fide*. The child was therefore legitimate under Italian law.

The court decided that because the child was legitimate according to the law of his domicile of origin, Italy, his status as legitimate would be recognised in South Africa. Because the child was legitimate, the father was entitled to custody by virtue of Italian law as well as the Italian court's order. However, the court would not direct that the child be delivered to the father without satisfying itself that this would be in the child's best interests.[72]

The rule that a child's legitimacy is determined by its domicile of origin can readily be applied when the child's parents were domiciled in the same state at the time of the child's birth. The child's domicile of origin is in the state where its parents were domiciled at that time. But if the parents were domiciled in different states, the child's domicile of origin could be in either, depending upon whether the child is legitimate or illegitimate. If legitimate, the child's domicile of origin is derived from the father. If illegitimate, the child's domicile of origin is derived from the mother. When the issue before the court is whether the child is legitimate, which state's law is applicable?

Hamid v. Minister of the Interior,[73] an immigration case, decides that it is the law of the father's domicile that governs. In effect, the law of the state which would be the child's domicile of origin if it was legitimate determines whether it is legitimate. This is sound, at least in its result, because legitimacy concerns primarily a child's relationship to its father and it is the father's domicile which is most

72 See pp. 148-53, *infra*.

73 1954 (4) S.A. 241 (T).

concerned with this relationship.[74]

In the *Hamid* case, the father was domiciled in South Africa at all material times. He married the child's mother while on a visit to India. The child was born in India, where the mother continued to reside. The marriage would not be recognised as valid by a South African court because it was polygamous. By Indian law, the marriage was valid and the child legitimate.

The court treated the father's domicile at the time of the child's birth as the child's domicile of origin. By this law--the law of South Africa--the child was illegitimate because his parents were not validly married. As an illegitimate child, he did not derive South African citizenship from his father and had no right to reside in South Africa. If the father had been domiciled in India at the time of the child's birth, the child would have the status of legitimacy because he was legitimate by Indian law. He would have this status in South Africa even though his parents would not have the status of husband and wife.

CHOICE OF LAW IN MATRIMONIAL CAUSES

Undoubtedly a marriage may not be terminated except upon a ground established in the law of the forum.[75] This rule may be attributed to the forum state's position as the spouses' domicile--which originally it had to be in order for the forum to have jurisdiction--but it applies even when the forum state is not the domicile.[76]

74 See Nygh, 372-73.

75 See Kahn, *Husband and Wife*, 637-38.

76 By statute in South Africa, when a court has jurisdiction in a divorce action between parties not domiciled in the Republic, any issue is to be decided as if the parties were domiciled in the court's area of jurisdiction on the date the action was instituted. Divorce Act, No. 70 of 1979, s. 2(3) (S. Afr.). Therefore, the forum's law applies to the grounds on which a divorce can be granted and ancillary matters whether it is applicable *qua lex fori* or *qua lex domicilii*. See Kahn, *Conflict of Laws*, 1979 Ann. Surv. S. Afr. L. 489, 496. The parallel Zimbabwean statute applies to nullity and judicial separation proceedings as well as divorce actions. Matrimonial Causes Act, 1985, No. 33, s. 3(3) (Zimb.). Prior South African legislation applied to divorce, restitution of conjugal rights and (respecting mutual property rights) separation actions the law and practice of the provincial division in which the defendant (the husband) was domiciled or resident. In certain circumstances the

The courts in which *Holland v. Holland*[77] was litigated considered whether a divorce could be obtained on a ground afforded by the *lex fori* if the spouses were domiciled in another country when the ground arose and that country did not grant divorces on this ground. The plaintiff and her husband had been domiciled in England. There, the plaintiff's father discovered his son-in-law *in flagrante delicto*. Later that month, the husband emigrated to South Africa. He established a permanent home in Johannesburg. The wife had already established residence in Natal. She sued for divorce, on the ground of adultery, in the court for Johannesburg.

The trial court held that a divorce could not be granted on the ground of adultery committed beyond the court's jurisdiction at a time before the spouses established a domicile within its jurisdiction. One basis of its decision was that injustice to the wife might otherwise occur in many cases. The wife might commit an act which was no justification for a divorce in the matrimonial domicile. The husband could then move to a country where this act was a ground of divorce and, if he domiciled himself there, obtain a divorce "however anxious the wife might have been to atone for her misconduct".

On appeal it was held that adultery having been proved, the plaintiff was entitled to a divorce despite the fact that the adultery occurred in England and irrespective of whether adultery was a ground of divorce in English law (which was never ascertained). The judgment articulates a rationale for applying the law of the spouses' current domicile to divorce proceedings. In South Africa, as in all "Christian" nations, marriage, while resting upon the consent of the parties, was part of the "*jus publicum*". Married persons were absolutely subject to the *jus publicum* of the place where they were domiciled. The highest considerations of social order and morality rendered it desirable that any alteration in the relations between or status of husband and wife be determined by the domicile's courts and that, having been so determined, it be recognised in all countries. Marriage was of interest to the state. Its creation and destruction were matters determined by the state alone and not in any degree by

applicable law was to be determined as if the spouses were domiciled in the Republic at the time of the proceedings. Matrimonial Causes Jurisdiction Act, No. 22 of 1939, ss. 1(3), 6, repealed, Divorce Act, No. 70 of 1979, s. 18 (S. Afr.). See Kahn, *Husband and Wife*, 638-40.

77 1973 (1) S.A. 897 (T). See Kahn, *Choice of Law in Divorce Actions*, (1973) 90 S.A.L.J. 125.

the will of the spouses themselves.

The granting of a divorce, said the court, was not the punishment of an offence nor the setting aside by judicial process of a contract for a cause or condition in the contract. It was nothing but the regulation by the domiciliary state of the domestic affairs of its domiciliaries. The state of domicile was, therefore, alone concerned in the grant or denial of a divorce.

> In other words, where a divorce is granted as it can, subject of course to limited statutory exceptions, only be granted at the domicile of the parties, the cause for divorce and all the qualifications surrounding the granting of a divorce are to be determined in accordance with the law of the forum . . . .[78]

The court's conclusion that a divorce could not be refused in the circumstances of *Holland v. Holland* was based primarily on the fact that (statutory exceptions apart) jurisdiction to grant a divorce resided solely in the courts of the domicile at the commencement of the proceedings.

> Accepting thus, that . . . the jurisdiction to decree a divorce belongs exclusively to the Courts of the domicile, it follows that the domicile of the spouses at the date of the commencement of the proceedings for divorce, and not that at the date of the marriage, or of the event on account of which divorce is sought must rule . . . . It also follows that when such jurisdiction has been established, a divorce cannot be refused either by the *lex loci contractus* of the marriage, or by the personal law of the parties at the time of the marriage, or by the law of the place where any fact occurred upon which the action for divorce is granted, or indeed by the personal law of the parties at the time when any such fact occurred. No circumstance, thus, other than domicile is of importance in limiting the jurisdiction and this . . . is true of the residence of the parties, the nationality of the parties, the domicile of the parties at the time of the marriage, the place of the marriage, and the place where the offence in respect of which divorce is sought was committed, even if the offence did not give

78 Holland v. Holland, 1973 (1) S.A. 897, 900 (T).

> ground for a divorce in the place of its commission, or according to the then domiciliary law of the parties . . . .[79]

While not necessarily accepting this judicial leap from jurisdiction to choice of law, one may agree with the court that there is justification for the exclusive application of forum law in the fact that a divorce court undertakes to determine the desirability of the continuance of the marriage as a legal and social relationship within the society in which the court sits.

> Divorce is not a punishment for the act; it is the reaction of the State to the effect of an act upon the marital relation. The State where that effect is felt, that is, the State of domicile, judges that, as a result of the act, the longer continuance of the marital relationship is undesirable . . . .[80]

One should agree with the court's rejection of a *Phillips v. Eyre*[81] approach, in which the ground for divorce must be a wrongful act under the law of the place where it occurred (which may be deemed to be the then matrimonial domicile), as well as the law of the forum, in order to found a cause of action. As the court stated, there is no legal justification for regarding an act constituting a ground for divorce as similar to a delict for the purpose of determining whether the aggrieved party can seek redress in the court of his domicile. There is a fundamental difference between delictual liability and divorce. The former provides compensation for breaches of duty imposed by law. The latter provides relief from matrimonial obligations by extinction of an existing status.

The fear of injustice to the wife did not deter the court. This was met by "the domiciliary control over status". *Mala fides* could not be taken into consideration because domicile was an "objective factual relation between a person and a territorial jurisdictional area". Motive, as an integral factor of intention, would facilitate rather than hinder proof of a domicile's existence. If a change of domicile could be established, the motive with which the change was made was immaterial. A man might change his domicile to diminish his taxes,

79 *Ibid.*, 901.

80 *Ibid.*, 902.

81 (1870) L.R. 6 Q.B. 1 (Ex. Ch.)

to secure a divorce, or even to facilitate an illegal manner of life. One might change his domicile as a result of information of counsel that because of a difference of law the change was necessary to the accomplishment of a purpose. Only the intention to make a "real change of home" need be established.

FOREIGN JUDGMENTS IN MATRIMONIAL CAUSES

In Southern Africa, domicile has remained the only ground on which a foreign divorce can be recognised without statutory authorisation. Only divorces granted or regarded as valid by the spouses' (*i.e.* the husband's) domicile at the time proceedings were instituted have been recognised by Southern African courts.[82] In *Sauber v. Sauber*[83] and *Pink v. Pink*,[84] courts refused to recognise divorces granted to the wives by courts in Germany, where they resided. In *Sauber v. Sauber*, the wife seems to have resided in Germany since before the marriage. This may also have been the case in *Pink v. Pink*.

Ex parte Stern[85] is another case in which the divorce was granted in the country where the wife resided, but the wife had deserted the husband in another country and the divorce was obtained by the husband. The husband, domiciled in South Africa, met an Israeli woman while he was attending an English university. After celebrating their marriage in Israel, they resided in England. The wife then left the husband and returned to Israel. The husband instituted divorce proceedings there, which were successful. Uncertain whether the divorce would be recognised in South Africa, the husband applied in a South African court for a declaratory order recognising the Israeli decree.

The court refused the application, holding that the Israeli divorce was not entitled to recognition. The husband submitted that the court should follow English decisions which recognised foreign divorces when English courts would have exercised jurisdiction in analogous

82 See Forsyth, 339-46; Kahn, *Husband and Wife*, 646-54.

83 1949 (2) S.A. 769 (S.W.A.).

84 1957 (4) S.A. 41 (T).

85 1976 (2) S.A. 273 (C). See Kahn, *Conflict of Laws*, 1976 Ann. Surv. S. Afr. L. 522, 530-33.

circumstances[86] or when the petitioner had a "real and substantial connection", short of domicile, with the state in which the divorce was obtained.[87] The court doubted whether a foreign divorce was entitled to recognition in South Africa on a basis other than domicile. One reason was the enactment of legislation for reciprocal recognition of foreign divorces,[88] which had never been implemented and which in the court's opinion contemplated only a "minimal departure" from the principle that it is the domicile of the parties which determines a court's jurisdiction.

The court concluded that if a divorce could be recognised on the basis of "reciprocity" (parallel jurisdiction) or "real and substantial connection" neither basis was established in the present case. There was no evidence that the Israeli court exercised jurisdiction on a ground which "had the same ground been present in South Africa" would have entitled the petitioner (the husband) to claim a divorce from the South African courts or that the petitioner had a real and substantial connection with Israel. His wife was an Israeli citizen, but during the marriage she lived with her husband in England and was presently residing there.

The Rhodesian Appellate Division decided in *Moresby-White v. Moresby-White*[89] that the divorce court's finding that the husband was domiciled within its jurisdiction was not conclusive of the question when the husband never appeared to defend his wife's divorce action. Even though the divorce court, on the evidence before it, was justified in finding that the husband had a local domicile, the husband was entitled to establish that he was domiciled elsewhere at the time. If he proved this, the divorce would be denied recognition for want of jurisdiction. The matter was not *res judicata*. The husband did not lose his right to obtain a divorce in Rhodesia (which he claimed to be his domicile) by not defending the action his wife had brought in Zambia. He was free to adopt the attitude that the Zambian court lacked jurisdiction to try this action. Had he defended the action, the Zambian judgment might have been conclusive.

86 Travers v. Holley, [1953] P. 246 (C.A.).

87 Indyka v. Indyka, [1969] 1 A.C. 33 (H.L.).

88 See pp. 146-48, *infra*.

89 1972 (1) R.L.R. 199 (A.D.), 1972 (3) S.A. 222 (R.A.D.).

In *Sauber v. Sauber*[90] the wife, who had obtained a divorce in Germany, was permitted to maintain an action in South West Africa for restitution of conjugal rights and for divorce on the ground of desertion. The German divorce was not recognised because the divorce court was without jurisdiction, the spouses' domicile being in South West Africa at all times. It is submitted that if a person who defended a divorce action cannot set up want of jurisdiction against recognition of a divorce, as suggested in the *Moresby-White* case, *a fortiori* a person who initiated a divorce action cannot set up want of jurisdiction. But a case in which the divorce court exercised jurisdiction on the basis that the husband was domiciled in its area of jurisdiction, such as *Moresby-White v. Moresby-White*, can be distinguished from a case in which the divorce court exercised jurisdiction on another basis, as one may assume in *Sauber v. Sauber*. In the latter, the divorce court's judgment is not *res judicata* on the specific question on which recognition in principle depends--the location of the husband's domicile.[91]

Guggenheim v. Rosenbaum (2)[92] adopts the rule established in England by *Armitage v. Attorney-General*:[93] a divorce granted outside the matrimonial domicile is to be recognised when it would be recognised in the courts of the domicile. As in *Armitage v. Attorney-General*, the divorce had been granted to the wife in an American state. The husband was domiciled in another American state. This was the domicile of the wife as well under the law of the place (South Africa in *Guggenheim v. Rosenbaum*; England in *Armitage v. Attorney-General*) where recognition was in issue. The courts of the husband's domicile would recognise the divorce as valid.[94]

Armitage v. Attorney-General was followed in *Guggenheim v. Rosenbaum* because it was consistent with the general principle that questions of status, including marital status, were to be resolved by reference to the law of the person's domicile at the time of the

90 1949 (2) S.A. 769 (S.W.A.).

91 See Scoles & Hay, 495-96.

92 1961 (4) S.A. 21 (W).

93 [1906] P. 135.

94 The divorce would be recognised on the basis that the wife had the capacity to acquire a separate domicile and had done so in the state where the divorce was granted. This was also a basis for the divorce court's assumption of jurisdiction. See Leflar, 24-26, 615-17.

events allegedly affecting status. Because the divorce was recognised in the state which the South African court regarded as both spouses' domicile at the time of the divorce decree, the divorce gave the parties the status of unmarried persons in the law of that state.

There is not much Southern African case law on recognition of decrees in matrimonial causes other than divorce.[95] The court in *de Bono v. de Bono*[96] accepted that a court in Malta had jurisdiction in a nullity action by a man domiciled in Malta against a woman who, if the marriage was void, was domiciled in South Africa both before and after the marriage ceremony. The nullity decree was recognised even though the marriage was celebrated in South Africa and was valid by South African law. The marriage had been declared void for non-compliance with the requirement of Maltese law that the ceremony be a religious one. The parties were not married, held the South African court, because the marriage had been declared void in the domicile of the "husband".

An English separation order, granted when the spouses were domiciled in England, was recognised in *Ex parte Charlesworth.*[97] It was necessary for the plaintiff to have the separation order set aside in order to maintain an action for restitution of conjugal rights and divorce in Southern Rhodesia, where the spouses were now domiciled. The court held that a Southern Rhodesian court had no jurisdiction to set aside the separation. The plaintiff had to apply to the English court which granted the order.

This decision was followed in *Ex parte Pels.*[98] It was not alleged that the court which decreed the spouses' separation lacked jurisdiction, but the judgment indicates willingness to accept that a separation order granted in the spouses' then domicile is entitled to recognition.[99]

95 See Forsyth, 346-52; Kahn, *Husband and Wife*, 654-57; Silberberg, 24-26.

96 1948 (2) S.A. 802 (C).

97 1951 S.R. 146, *sub nom.* Ex parte Worth, 1951 (4) S.A. 230 (S.R.).

98 1957 R. & N. 27 (S.R.), 1957 (1) S.A. 632 (S.R.), rev'd, 1957 R. &. N. 853 (F.S.C.), 1958 (1) S.A. 196 (F.S.C.).

99 The Federal Supreme Court reversed on the ground that it was not necessary to have the order of judicial separation set aside in order for the plaintiff to proceed with an action to divorce his wife on the ground of cruelty. Ex parte Pels, 1957 R. &. N. 853 (F.S.C.), 1958 (1) S.A. 196 (F.S.C.).

In *De Sa Pessoa v. De Sa Pessoa*,[100] a South African court refused to recognise a foreign separation order on grounds of public policy. Recognition was contrary to public policy, held the court, because the order was immutable. Under the law of Moçambique, where the order was obtained, a separation order could never be set aside without the consent of both parties, even when the reason for which it was granted had ceased to exist. South African public policy did not countenance a separation that could not be set aside at the request of the guilty spouse on proof of reformation and desire for resumption of cohabitation. Ordinarily the separation order would entitle the defendant to live apart from the plaintiff. That would bar the plaintiff's present action--for restitution of conjugal rights. Because the order was not granted recognition, it did not operate as a bar.

The spouses were resident in Moçambique but domiciled in South Africa when the separation order was issued. One may surmise that the order was refused recognition on the ground of public policy, not want of jurisdiction, because the South African court believed that the court in Moçambique had jurisdiction, being the court of the spouses' residence. Inasmuch as South African courts had decided that they could exercise jurisdiction in separation proceedings when the defendant was resident but not domiciled locally,[101] it is likely that they would accept, for purposes of recognition of a foreign order, that a foreign court had jurisdiction in parallel circumstances.[102]

South Africa's Divorce Act makes provision for reciprocal recognition of foreign divorces.[103] The validity of a divorce granted in a country or territory in which the husband was not then domiciled is to be recognised by South African courts if the country or territory has been designated by proclamation. A country or territory may be

100 1967 (4) S.A. 629 (T).

101 See pp. 118-19, *supra*.

102 See Forsyth, 346-48; Kahn, *Husband and Wife*, 654-55. It might follow from the decision in De Sa Pessoa v. De Sa Pessoa that no foreign separation order should be recognised. Orders sufficiently variable to satisfy the forum's public policy would lack the finality generally required for recognition of foreign judgments. It seems, however, that the finality requirement is relaxed for separation orders, as it is for child custody awards. See Forsyth, 348-49.

103 Divorce Act, No. 70 of 1979, s. 13 (S. Afr.). See Forsyth, 344-46; Kahn, *Conflict of Laws*, 1979 Ann. Surv. S. Afr. L. 489, 499-503.

designated if the State President is satisfied that its law provides for the exercise of jurisdiction which substantially corresponds to the jurisdiction conferred upon South African courts in cases where the spouses are not domiciled in the Republic. A proclamation is not to be issued unless the law of the country or territory concerned makes "sufficient provision" for recognition by its courts of South African divorces of persons not domiciled in the Republic. No proclamation has ever been issued pursuant to the Divorce Act or its predecessor, which was enacted in 1953.[104] Although never implemented, the existence of legislation providing for recognition of divorces granted outside the husband's domicile makes the possibility that a South African court would itself decide to recognise such a divorce even more remote.[105]

Zimbabwe has legislation that can be applied without a governmental proclamation.[106] A court can "recognise the validity" of any decree or order of divorce, separation or nullity that was made in a country where the husband was not domiciled if a proclamation has been issued declaring that the laws of that country correspond substantially to Zimbabwe's statutory provisions concerning jurisdiction.[107] These provisions confer jurisdiction in certain actions by a wife for divorce, separation or nullity when the husband is not domiciled in Zimbabwe. A proclamation is not to be issued unless the President is satisfied that "adequate provision" has been made by the foreign country for recognition of Zimbabwean decrees and orders in cases involving husbands not domiciled in Zimbabwe. Alternatively, a court can recognise a decree or order, made in a country where the husband was not domiciled, if the court is satisfied that the laws of the foreign country contain provisions corresponding

104 Matrimonial Causes Jurisdiction Act, No. 22 of 1939, s. 6*bis*, inserted by Matrimonial Affairs Act, No. 37 of 1953, s. 9, repealed, Divorce Act, No. 70 of 1979, s. 18 (S. Afr.). The 1953 legislation applied to foreign orders for restitution of conjugal rights and judicial separation as well as divorce. No provision is made for the recognition of such orders in the Divorce Act, which provides that South African courts shall no longer issue orders for restitution of conjugal rights or separation. S. 14.

105 See Ex parte Stern, 1976 (2) S.A. 273 (C), discussed pp. 142-43, *supra*; Granoth v. Granoth, 1983 (4) S.A. 50 (C).

106 Matrimonial Causes Act, 1985, No. 33, s. 12 (Zimb.). See Kahn, *Husband and Wife*, 652.

107 Matrimonial Causes Act, 1985, No. 33, s. 3 (Zimb.), described p. 120, *supra*.

substantially to Zimbabwe's provisions on jurisdiction. This is not conditioned upon the foreign country's providing for recognition of Zimbabwean judgments.

FOREIGN CHILD CUSTODY ORDERS

Southern Africa has numerous reported cases concerning the effects of foreign child custody orders. All of the recent judgments assume that a foreign custody order has some effects and concentrate upon identifying these effects. None comes to grips with the question of why, as a non-final judgment, a foreign custody order should have any effect at all. Neither does any case decide questions of the foreign court's jurisdiction, beyond acknowledging (at least implicitly) that a court in the domicile of the parents and child had jurisdiction to make a custody order.

The present position in Southern Africa is adequately outlined in *Abrahams v. Abrahams.*[108] In this case, an order awarding custody to the husband had been made in an undefended divorce action in South Africa. The husband then brought an action in Bophuthatswana to enforce the order against his former wife. He submitted that enforcement of the order was not subject to a defence on the merits. It was a final judgment. The South African court would be unwilling to set it aside and the defendant had not expressed any intention to move for its rescission.

The court was of the opinion that the South African order lacked the finality required for its enforcement in another country. Under South African law, any custody order was subject to variation on good cause shown. Another consideration, which was "paramount", was the best interest of the child. South African courts had accepted and the Bophuthatswana court would accept the judgment of the Privy Council in *McKee v. McKee,*[109] where it was said:

108 (1981) 2 B.S.C. 97, 1981 (3) S.A. 593 (B). Significant prior cases include Ferrers v. Ferrers, 1953 S.R. 149, 1954 (1) S.A. 514 (S.R.); Righetti v. Pinchen, 1955 (3) S.A. 338 (D); Riddle v. Riddle, 1956 (2) S.A. 739 (C). See also Forsyth, 215-16, 354; Spiro, Law of Parent and Child 540-43 (4th ed. 1985); Kahn, *Husband and Wife*, 659-61.

109 [1951] A.C. 352 (P.C.).

> the welfare and happiness of the infant is the paramount consideration in questions of custody . . . . To this paramount consideration all others yield. The order of a foreign court of competent jurisdiction is no exception. Such an order has not the force of a foreign judgment; comity demands, not its enforcement, but its grave consideration. This distinction . . . rests on the peculiar character of the jurisdiction and on the fact that an order providing for the custody of an infant cannot in its nature be final.
>
> . . . Once it is conceded that the court of Ontario had jurisdiction to entertain the question of custody and that it need not blindly follow an order made by a foreign court, the consequence cannot be escaped that it must form an independent judgment on the question, though in doing so it will give proper weight to the foreign judgment. What is the proper weight will depend on the circumstances of each case. It may be that, if the matter comes before the court of Ontario within a very short time of the foreign judgment and there is no new circumstance to be considered, the weight may be so great that such an order as the Supreme Court made in this case could be justified. But if so, it would be not because the court of Ontario, having assumed jurisdiction, then abdicated it, but because in the exercise of its jurisdiction it determined what was for the benefit of the infant.[110]

The Bophuthatswana court was now the "upper guardian" of the child because the child was present within its jurisdiction. The court had to determine the child's position irrespective of the rights of the parents *inter se*.

As stated in the *McKee* case, the weight to be given to a foreign custody order depended upon the circumstances of each case. If the South African court had heard both parties in regard to the child's custody and had settled the question conclusively, and if the order was recent and no fresh circumstances had emerged, its persuasiveness might have been so great as to lead the Bophuthatswana court to recognise and enforce the order immediately. Common sense, "good neighbourship with South Africa and economic realities together with geographical complexity of the countries"

110 *Ibid.*, 365, 364.

demanded such an approach. Another consideration was that the South African and Bophuthatswana courts administered the same legal principles. The court observed later in its judgment that if it awarded custody to the defendant and the question of enforcing its order came before the South African court which issued the original order, that court would be bound (under the principles enunciated in *McKee v. McKee*) to consider whether the Bophuthatswana order should be recognised and enforced.

In the *Abrahams* case, the defendant had not been heard before the South African custody order was granted. The court concluded that all interested parties were entitled to place before it "such evidence and considerations . . . as may be relevant" to the determination of what was in the best interests of the child. The matter would be referred to trial. If the court then came to the conclusion that the plaintiff should be given custody, with or without qualifications, it would recognise and enforce the order of the South African court.

The weight to be given the foreign court's order was considered in *Jagoe v. Jagoe*:[111]

> The important aspects are whether a full inquiry was conducted by the foreign court, its reasons for awarding custody to a particular party, whether it recognizes the same principles of law as this court, whether its judgment on the issue was a reasonable one, and whether there has been a substantial change in the circumstances since its judgment.[112]

The foreign orders in *Jagoe v. Jagoe* had been made on the basis of an agreement giving custody to the plaintiff. The defendant had consented to this, the court found, because of a financial predicament from which he could not extricate himself without the plaintiff's signature, which was withheld until the custody agreement. There was no evidence that the foreign court had enquired into the "merits of the best interests of the child", who was then less than one year old. She was now three years and eight months.

The court concluded that in determining which party should now be awarded custody of the child, the weight to be attached to the

111 1969 (2) R.L.R. 266 (G.D.), 1969 (4) S.A. 59 (R).

112 *Ibid.*, 268, 61.

foreign orders was no greater than the weight to be attached to the parties' consent agreement. This was so slight as not to affect the view to which the court was required to come, independent of the orders, upon the evidence before it. Custody was awarded to the plaintiff, as in the foreign proceedings.

In *A. v. C.*,[113] the defendants had taken the children of their previous marriages from the United States to Rhodesia. Their former spouses, who had been awarded custody of the children in divorce proceedings, brought an action in Rhodesia to secure the return of the children to their custody. The defendants applied to have custody awarded to them. The court decided that only slight weight should be attached to one of the American custody orders because custody was not an issue disputed before the court that granted the order and there had been a substantial change in circumstances since the order was made, five years earlier. The Rhodesian court concluded that one of the children to which this order pertained should remain with the defendants. The others would be returned to the first plaintiff.

Much greater weight was given to the other custody order. The issue of custody had been contested. The American court had made a reasoned judgment, applying the same principles as would a Rhodesian court, arrived at after a full investigation of the matter. Also, within the previous three years there was a contested application for variation of the custody order, which was unsuccessful. The Rhodesian court decided that custody of the children to which the second order pertained should be awarded to the second plaintiff, who had prevailed in the American proceedings.

In *Riddle v. Riddle*[114] and *Kelly v. Kelly*,[115] it was held that a court could give effect to a foreign custody order by ordering delivery of the child to the parent awarded custody. The court could do this without first making its own order awarding custody to that parent or making the foreign order an order of the court. The court was required to exercise an independent judgment concerning the best interests of the child before enforcing the foreign order in this

113 1974 (2) R.L.R. 167 (G.D.). Additional details of the case are set forth in Rhodesian Printing and Publishing Company Ltd. v. X., 1974 (2) R.L.R. 207 (A.D.), *sub nom.* Rhodesian Printing & Publishing Co. Ltd. v. Duggan, 1975 (1) S.A. 590 (R.A.D.), aff'g 1975 (2) R.L.R. 281 (G.D.), 1974 (4) S.A. 508 (R), discussed pp. 342-45, *infra*.

114 1956 (2) S.A. 739 (C).

115 1957 H.C.T.L.R. 13 (Swazi. H.C.).

manner.

In marked contrast to the preceding cases, *Dube v. Dube*[116] reflects a virtually automatic enforcement of a foreign custody order. The parties had been divorced in South Africa. The divorce decree awarded custody to the mother. The father had not defended the proceedings. Two years later, he took the child from South Africa to Rhodesia. The mother consented on the understanding that the father would return the child at the end of the school holidays. The father failed to bring back the child, whereupon the mother applied in a Rhodesian court for an order requiring the child's return.

The order was granted. The court stated that it must assume that the court in Cape Town had jurisdiction to deal with the divorce and the "ancillary matter" of the custody of the child. Under these circumstances the defendant was not entitled to the custody of the child either in Rhodesia or in South Africa. If he desired a change of custody, the proper course for him was to take the appropriate proceedings in the Cape to have the order varied. The defendant had obtained temporary custody of the child by making an agreement with the plaintiff--an agreement which he broke by failing to return the child. "[A]s the Cape court had jurisdiction in this matter I must uphold the order of the Cape court, and as the respondent has not complied with his agreement to return the child I must now order him to do so."[117]

It is difficult if not impossible to reconcile the judgment in *Dube v. Dube* with the well-established "independent judgment" rule, which was not considered. However, the approach adopted in *Dube v. Dube* is to be welcomed. Courts should not exercise independent judgment in proceedings to enforce a foreign custody order. If the order was rendered by a court of competent jurisdiction and none of the common law defences to recognition of a foreign judgment[118] can be established, the order should be enforced without consideration of the merits of competing prayers for custody.

The best interests of the child would be well served by leaving that question to the court which granted the order, if it would entertain an application to modify the original order. (When

116 1969 (2) R.L.R. 410 (G.D.), 1970 (1) S.A. 331 (R).

117 *Ibid.*, 412, 332.

118 Such as fraud, failure of natural justice, repugnance to the forum's public policy. See Abrahams v. Abrahams, (1981) 2 B.S.C. 97, 1981 (3) S.A. 593 (B).

necessary for the protection of the child, enforcement of the custody order could be stayed pending an application to modify or annul the order.) The independent judgment rule affords a parent the opportunity of obtaining legally sanctioned or tolerated custody by taking the child across an international boundary. The approach of the court in *Dube v. Dube* denies this opportunity and substantially improves the enforcement of custody orders.[119]

119 See 2 Castel, 225-31.

II

SOUTHERN AFRICAN PRECEDENTS FOR THE LAW OF TORTS

6

NEGLIGENCE

DUTY TO TAKE POSITIVE ACTION

One of the fundamental and difficult questions of negligence law is that of when a person comes under a duty to take positive action. If such a duty exists, there can be liability for harm caused by "negligent omission". This has been addressed by Southern African courts in a number of important decisions.

In *Silva's Fishing Corporation (Pty.) Ltd. v. Maweza*,[1] the plaintiff sought damages for the death of her husband, drowned while a crew member of the *Antoinette*, a coastal fishing vessel. The *Antoinette* was part of a fishing fleet owned by the defendant. The defendant employed the skipper, who employed the remaining crew members and paid them a proportion of the value of the fish each caught. According to the plaintiff's declaration, the *Antoinette*'s engine failed and could not be restarted. When the vessel failed to return to its base, the defendant was notified that it was missing and "regarded as being in distress". The *Antoinette* drifted for nine days--the first six in calm weather and the last three in storms--during which the defendant was again informed several times that the vessel had not returned and was in distress. Ultimately the *Antoinette* was wrecked on coastal rocks and all crew members except the skipper were drowned. The plaintiff asserted that the defendant, knowing that the *Antoinette* was in distress, was under a duty to the crew members to undertake their rescue and failed to take reasonable steps to do so

1 1957 (2) S.A. 256 (A.D.). See 1 Boberg, 230-32; McKerron, *Liability for Omissions*, (1957) 74 S.A.L.J. 256.

when rescue could have been effected, causing the death of the plaintiff's husband.

The Appellate Division held that a duty of care was owed. A majority reached this conclusion on the basis of the defendant's prior conduct and the relationship between the defendant, the crew members and their vessel. While not employed by or otherwise in a contractual relationship with the defendant, the crew members were not merely persons permitted to take fish on the defendant's boat. They were engaged together with the defendant in the enterprise of catching fish, whose value was divided among the crew, the defendant and the skipper. In this enterprise, the crew went out to sea and risked its perils while the defendant stayed safely on shore and provided the boat. The defendant knew that a defective boat might endanger the lives of the crew. Under these circumstances of common enterprise, involving conduct by the defendant and known danger, the defendant owed the crew members a duty to provide a vessel which was reasonably safe--capable of taking the crew safely to and from the fishing grounds--and, even if that duty was discharged, a duty to rescue the crew should the vessel not be able to return on its own and rescue facilities be available. (Whether a fleet owner is under a duty in advance to have rescue facilities available was not decided.) The judgment also supports the existence of a duty to warn the crew of impending danger, such as from a dangerous storm or a newly-discovered defect in the vessel's gear, after the vessel has left its base.

Two judges concluded that a duty of care was owed on a narrower ground, albeit in a judgment rejecting the proposition that an omission unconnected with prior conduct is not actionable.[2] The defendant owed the crew a duty to maintain the *Antoinette* and its engine in a proper condition--a duty directed toward protecting the crew from the perils of the sea. This did not come to an end every time the boat left the shore, to revive only on the boat's return. The duty continued in full operation while the boat was at sea. The information that the *Antoinette* was in distress must have conveyed to the defendant that something was wrong with the boat or its engine. It then became the defendant's obligation to take reasonable steps to make the boat navigable or bring it and its crew back to shore. Leaving the crew adrift, to face the perils of the sea, was a breach of the defendant's duty to maintain the condition of the boat and engine.

2 *Ibid.*, 264-69 (Steyn, J.A., with whom Hall, A.J.A., concurred).

In *King v. Dykes*,[3] a veld fire burning on a farm during the dry season had spread to an adjoining farm and then to a third farm. The owner of the third farm claimed damages from the owner of the second farm. The plaintiff asserted that when the fire reached the defendant's farm and was observed by the defendant, he came under and breached a duty to take reasonable steps to extinguish the fire. The defendant did not commence action to extinguish the fire until some time after he first observed it. By then, the fire could not be contained.

Much of the judgment in the Rhodesian Appellate Division is devoted to attacking the process of developing specific rules on the existence of duties of care and of requiring that the facts of an "omission" case fit certain categories, such as "prior conduct" or "prior relationship", in order for a duty of care to arise. "'[T]he categories of negligence are never closed.' What is even more to the point, however, is that categories should never have been formulated."[4] One must apply the basic test of deciding whether or not a legal duty exists in the particular circumstances of the case--whether the reasonable man would foresee the possibility of harm to another and take steps to prevent its occurrence. Factors which had been given as justification for inflexible rules of duty, such as the drain on a defendant's financial resources, should instead determine the scope of the duty in each case, *i.e.* the steps which the defendant could reasonably be expected to take.[5] The court found support for its approach in the Privy Council's judgment in *Goldman v. Hargrave*.[6]

The court held that a duty of care was owed but not breached. Given his knowledge that veld fires in dry conditions often spread rapidly over a wide area, causing damage (particularly loss of forage

3 1971 (2) R.L.R. 151 (A.D.), 1971 (3) S.A. 540 (R.A.D.). See Dewhurst, *Culpable Omissions*, 1971 Rhod. L.J. 104.

4 King v. Dykes, 1971 (2) R.L.R. 151, 154 (A.D.), 1971 (3) S.A. 540, 543 (R.A.D.).

5 This approach is criticised in Boberg, *Law of Delict*, 1971 Ann. Surv. S. Afr. L. 141, 148-51, as insufficient to guide citizens in their conduct and lower courts in their decisions.

6 [1967] 1 A.C. 645 (P.C.). The facts of Goldman v. Hargrave are similar to the facts of King v. Dykes, but the defendant in *Goldman* commenced action to extinguish the fire when it was possible to do so and was not reasonably careful in his conduct.

for livestock) to farmers in the district, the defendant was under a duty of care to extinguish veld fires on his property. It mattered not whether he had any responsibility for starting the fire. It was difficult to ascertain the origin of such a fire and the need for prompt action to extinguish it precluded any prior detailed enquiry into its cause.[7] In this case the defendant had first observed smouldering debris, which he thought presented no danger, and then, after smoke was observed from the direction of the fire, completed loading his crop for transport before attempting to extinguish the fire. This was not unreasonable in the circumstances, so the defendant was not negligent. The judgment states that had the defendant been responsible for starting the fire, the steps he took would not have been sufficient. Thus the fact advanced by the defendant as establishing the non-existence of a duty of care--the defendant's not having started the fire--instead established a standard of care which the defendant did not fail to meet.

Minister of Forestry v. Quathlamba (Pty.) Ltd.[8] is another case in which a veld fire spread from the defendant's land to the plaintiff's. As in *King v. Dykes*, it was held that the defendant owed the plaintiff a duty of care but did not breach it by negligence. Adopting the type of categorical approach criticised in *King v. Dykes*, the Appellate Division held that when an owner or occupier of rural land becomes aware that fire has broken out on or spread to his property and foresees (or should foresee) damage to another's property if the fire is not controlled, he is under a duty to take reasonable steps to control or extinguish the fire. He falls outside the category of "mere omission", where no legal duty exists, by reason of his control of property which is a hazard to others because of the fire burning upon it.

7 An additional reason given in the judgment is that a fire started on one farm might well have been started by the negligence of an employee of another farm while on a social visit to the first farm, such social visits being frequent. King v. Dykes, 1971 (2) R.L.R. 151, 157-58 (A.D.), 1971 (3) S.A. 540, 546 (R.A.D.). Surely an employer's duty of care ought not to be premised upon employees' social visits. An employer has no responsibility for his employees while they are on social visits, outside the course of their employment. What the court may have had in mind is the undesirability of there being many fires which no farmer has a duty to extinguish--fires started by farm workers during their social activities and fires of natural origin. This would be the consequence if the duty to extinguish a fire depended upon responsibility for starting it.

8 1973 (3) S.A. 69 (A.D.).

The greater significance of *Minister of Forestry v. Quathlamba (Pty.) Ltd.* lies in its approval of the view expressed by two judges in *Silva's Fishing Corporation (Pty.) Ltd. v. Maweza*[9] that an omission unconnected with prior conduct could be actionable. In other words, there were circumstances in which a person who had not engaged in conduct causing danger could come under a duty to act for the protection of someone foreseeably threatened by that danger. In both cases, the existence of a duty of care was premised on the defendant's control of property--the fishing boat in one case and land in the other. But the implication was clear that there may be circumstances not involving prior conduct or control of property in which a duty to take protective action arises.

It was not long before this implication was tested in the Appellate Division. In *Minister van Polisie v. Ewels*,[10] it was alleged that an off-duty policeman had assaulted the plaintiff at a café. The plaintiff then went to the police station. At the entrance the same policeman, still off duty, assaulted him a second time. A sergeant and several constables, on duty at the station, became aware of the second assault but did nothing to protect or assist the plaintiff. The plaintiff claimed damages for both assaults from the assailant and for the second assault from the Minister of Police. The basis of the latter claim was that the sergeant and constables (for whose negligence the minister would be vicariously liable) owed the plaintiff a duty to protect him from the attack at the police station and were negligent in taking no action.

The Appellate Division held that a duty of care did exist. Cases of "unlawful omission", in which a person failed to discharge a duty to prevent harm to another, could exist when there was neither prior conduct nor damage caused by something connected with the person's land:

> an omission is regarded as unlawful conduct when the circumstances of the case are such that the omission not only occasions moral indignation but where the legal convictions of the community require that the omission be regarded as unlawful and that the loss suffered be

9 1957 (2) S.A. 256, 264-65 (A.D.) (Steyn, J.A., with whom Hall, A.J.A., concurred). See pp. 157-58, *supra*.

10 1975 (3) S.A. 590 (A.D.). See 1 Boberg, 213-14, 266-67.

compensated by the person who failed to act positively.[11]

Whether a legal duty to act existed, so that an omission was unlawful, depended upon all the facts of the case, it being impossible to determine in general when a legal duty arises.

The facts giving rise to a duty of care in the instant case were that the police had the function (conferred by statute) of preventing crime--a function which included protection of the citizen from crime as well as deterrence and detection of crime--the assault occurred in premises under control of the police, where a citizen had to go to lodge a complaint, and it took place within the sight of policemen for whom it was possible, even easy, to prevent or stop the attack on the plaintiff. It was an additional factor that the sergeant could have exercised authority over the assailant, *i.e.* ordered the assailant as a subordinate to cease his attack, but the result would have been the same had the assailant not been a policeman.

The judgment in *Minister van Polisie v. Ewels* accepts the principle that a person has no general duty to prevent harm to another. It gives no positive support to any argument that a private citizen is under a legal duty, as well as a moral duty, to rescue strangers from perils having no connection with the private citizen, such as a street-corner assault or drowning in public waters. But the judgment gives any plaintiff injured by an "omission" a basis for argument that a duty to act existed in the circumstances of his particular case. If the *Ewels* case is followed, one may not be able to determine in advance of a judicial decision whether an obligation to take positive action existed, and that decision may be based more upon *ad hoc* policy judgements or a judge's instinct to do justice in the particular case than upon any concrete legal principle.[12]

This is illustrated by the decision in *Mbhele v. Natal Parks, Game and Fish Preservation Board.*[13] The plaintiff had been attacked and seriously injured by a hippopotamus. He sought damages from a government board which managed a game reserve in the area. The plaintiff asserted that the hippo had come from the defendant's

11 Minister van Polisie v. Ewels, 1975 (3) S.A. 590, 597 (A.D.) (translation).

12 See the criticism of Minister van Polisie v. Ewels in Amicus Curiae, *The Actionable Omission--Another View of Ewels's Case*, (1976) 93 S.A.L.J. 85, responding to praise in Boberg, *The Wrongfulness of an Omission*, (1975) 92 S.A.L.J. 361.

13 1980 (4) S.A. 303 (D).

reserve and that the defendant was liable because of its failure to prevent the animal from leaving the reserve or recapture it prior to its attack upon the plaintiff. In order to recover damages, the plaintiff had to establish that the board owed him a duty of care to keep hippo from straying from the reserve, that the board failed to exercise reasonable care, and that the hippo which injured the plaintiff had come from the defendant's reserve.

The plaintiff's action failed on all three points. One might have thought that if a landowner owes his neighbours a duty to prevent the spread of a fire not originating on his land, a landowner owes his neighbours a duty to prevent the escape of animals living on his land. Moreover, the defendant board was charged with the conservation of hippo and the animals were protected from hunting and trapping (on or off the reserve), whereas persons threatened by fires were free to fight them. The court, however, assimilated the board to a private landowner and believed that the position of landowners would be "quite intolerable" if the law imposed upon them a duty to prevent wild animals naturally present on their property from causing damage to others. The court emphasised that the reserve had been a hippo habitat since "time immemorial" and the defendant's control of the reserve went no further than to "allow nature to take its course". The hippo population had increased because of protection, but the reserve was not overstocked. Fire was distinguised as a phenomenon introduced by human agency, overlooking fires of natural origin.

Any duty to the plaintiff would have been breached by the defendant's failure to take measures that could be reasonably expected of it. Hippo could be confined to the reserve only by construction of a fence at an enormous cost unwarranted by the danger to be averted, attacks by hippo upon humans being rare. If there was a duty, no breach occurred. But there being no duty, even reasonable steps to confine animals were not required.

It appears that the court would find no duty to keep animals within a reserve even when the animals are quite dangerous and can be confined without undue difficulty and expense. Arguably, the feasibility of confining an animal gives the reserve a degree of control over the animal which should place it under a duty of care,[14] but this argument finds no support in the *Mbhele* case. It seems that only such conduct as introducing wild animals onto land or breeding them in large numbers under artificial conditions would place a person under a duty to protect his neighbours from them.

14 See Burchell, *Law of Delict*, 1980 Ann. Surv. S. Afr. L. 173-76.

OTHER FAILURES TO PROTECT--HAZARDOUS PRODUCTS

Vast numbers of negligence actions are based upon the defendant's failure to take reasonable steps to protect the plaintiff from harm. Most are not "mere omission" cases because the defendant allegedly engaged in conduct that exposed the plaintiff to a risk of harm. The omission was the failure to reduce or eliminate the risk associated with the defendant's conduct. The negligence (if it existed) was to engage in the conduct unaccompanied by protective measures. Many such cases are resolved by addressing the question: did the defendant exercise reasonable care? More significant are cases which consider whether the defendant was under any obligation to act to protect the plaintiff, such as the following two hazardous products cases.

In *Hickey v. Donald*,[15] the plaintiff claimed damages sustained in a collision between his motor car and a lorry. The lorry had gone out of control when one of its front tyres burst. The defendants were the lorry's owner and its driver, a friend of the owner who borrowed it (at no charge) to haul some timber. The tyre was in a hazardous condition. This would have been discovered had either the owner or the driver inspected the tyre, but neither did. The plaintiff contended that the owner and driver were negligent in not inspecting the tyre before the lorry was taken on the road. The Federal Supreme Court held that the driver was not negligent but the owner was negligent and liable to the plaintiff.

The decision depended substantially upon the particular circumstances of the case. The tyre was on an aged vehicle, unlicensed until the driver borrowed it, which the owner had recently purchased at a minimal price--the type of vehicle a reasonable buyer would examine carefully before it was used. Also, the owner was the proprietor of a motor service station, leading the driver to assume reasonably that it was not necessary to inspect the tyres personally; the garage proprietor would have taken care of it. Notwithstanding its special facts, the case supports the broad proposition that it is negligence for a person to loan his vehicle, even gratuitously, without making a reasonable inspection for defects or warning the borrower that an inspection is necessary, unless he can expect that the borrower will make the inspection himself. The borrower's failure to inspect the vehicle and discover the defect does not relieve the lender of responsibility when inspection by the borrower is only a possibility,

15 1960 R. & N. 633 (F.S.C.), 1960 (4) S.A. 451 (F.S.C.).

not something to be anticipated. That the borrower in *Hickey v. Donald* could not reasonably be expected to discover the hazard served to support the conclusions that he was not negligent, the owner was negligent, and the borrower's ability to discover the hazard did not break the chain of causation from the owner's negligence to the collision with the plaintiff's vehicle.

A question of much greater economic consequence is whether a retail seller can be liable in negligence for failure to inspect his goods for defects. *A. Gibb & Son (Pty.) Ltd. v. Taylor & Mitchell Timber Supply Co. (Pty.) Ltd.*[16] gives it an affirmative answer--provided discovery of the defect by the buyer is not to be anticipated. The defendant was a retail building supplies merchant. It sold planks made of saligna--a wood widely used in the building industry--to the plaintiff, a building contractor. The plaintiff used the planks in the construction of scaffold platforms. The defendant allegedly knew that the plaintiff was a building contractor and that the planks would probably be used in scaffold platforms. A worker employed by a sub-contractor was seriously injured when one of the planks supplied by the defendant gave way under him. The plank was defective because it contained a large knot. The knot was clearly visible upon inspection of the plank, although not to the person working on the scaffold. The building contractor paid damages to the injured worker and then claimed contribution from the merchant. The basis of the contribution claim was that the merchant, as seller of the plank, owed the worker a duty to inspect the planks it sold for defects and prevent the delivery of defective planks, and would have been liable if sued by the worker.

The court rejected the position of the *Restatement (Second) of Torts*[17] that a seller is not liable in negligence for failure to inspect or test his product and thereby discover a dangerous condition. It embraced instead Prosser's conclusion that a retailer is under a duty to exercise reasonable care for the protection of buyers, including a duty to inspect goods or discover defects before the sale, and the problem is simply whether a reasonable man in the circumstances would make a certain examination.[18] The court then referred to various English authorities asserting that the possibility that the goods will be inspected after their sale does not exclude liability. Only a

16 1975 (2) S.A. 457 (W). See 1 Boberg, 205-06.

17 Restatement (Second) of Torts, s. 402 (1965).

18 Prosser, Law of Torts 632-34 (4th ed. 1971).

reasonable expectation that there will be an inspection which gives warning of the risk would do so.

In applying these principles it was necessary, the court said, to study the particular market-place in question, *i.e.* the kind of trade conducted, the methods employed and the expectations of those who customarily dealt in it. When the commodity is something not inherently dangerous and the potential of harm caused by defects depends upon how the commodity is used, the study of the market-place is refined to an enquiry into whether the diligent seller anticipates, as a probability, that the user will make the usual examination of the commodity before it is used and then use it for its customary purpose. If the seller anticipates an examination that will probably reveal a product's defects, danger is not foreseen and action to guard against it is not required. The court gave as an example of such a seller the proprietor of a timber yard. A timber merchant does not employ an army to inspect hundreds of thousands of pieces of timber. He merely supplies materials which will, after proper inspection, be fashioned into a whole very different from its individual components.

The defendant in the instant case was a more specialised merchant and the type of wood supplied (saligna) was reputed to be knot-free. A works foreman was charged with the duty of inspecting planks used for scaffold platforms. In the pressure of work and the belief that the planks supplied were reliable, the foreman failed to carry out the inspection. Arguably, the reasonable merchant would realise that builders regard saligna planks so highly that they are used without inspection, so there must be an inspection before sale. The court believed it more likely that the reasonable merchant would anticipate subsequent examination of the planks because builders must construct scaffolding with great care, in view of the risk of serious injury to workmen. The defendant in this case, therefore, was not negligent if it failed to inspect the plank which gave way.

INFORMED CONSENT

In common law jurisdictions, persons harmed by the unplanned effects of medical treatment have attempted to recover damages from the treating doctors or hospitals under the theories of "informed consent". One theory is that the defendant is liable to the patient for a battery (or "assault") for performing an operation or other procedure without consent. The consent that the patient in fact gave is regarded as legally ineffective because it was not an informed one, the risks of the treatment being unknown to the patient. The other theory is that it is negligence to perform an operation or other medical procedure without informing the patient of its risks. Those who should have informed the patient are responsible under the law of negligence when the patient suffers impairment of health from an undisclosed risk. The second theory appears to be supplanting the first.[19]

A 1957 case in South Africa, *Esterhuizen v. Administrator, Transvaal*,[20] supports the battery theory. The plaintiff was a minor suffering from a disease which caused tumours. Several years earlier, she had received low-dosage superficial X-ray treatment at the defendant's hospital. This was successful and caused no ill effects. She returned to the hospital when the disease manifested itself again. This time, she received "radical" high dosage deep therapy X-ray treatment of her hands and legs. The plaintiff's mother (her guardian) did not know and was not informed that this treatment differed from the earlier treatment. Nor was she or the plaintiff informed that it carried various risks, including that the radiation would cause necrosis (tissue death) requiring amputation of the affected limbs. This occurred. As a consequence of the X-ray treatment, the plaintiff suffered the amputation of both hands and both legs, for which she sought damages.

The court held that the treatment was an assault for which damages could be recovered because no lawful consent was given to it. An operation performed without consent was unlawful, and consent without knowledge of the risks was not an effective consent. The judgment asserts that to say a person consented to bodily harm or to run the risk of such harm presupposed knowledge of that harm or risk. This follows a brief consideration of the defence of *volenti non fit injuria*. One may question whether the court gave adequate weight to the distinction between the *volenti* defence in negligence cases, in which the plaintiff's appreciation of the risk is essential, and the *volenti* defence in intentional tort cases, in which the focus has been upon consent to the defendant's conduct.

The court did not undertake a comprehensive statement of the risks which must be disclosed and the circumstances in which disclosure must be made, in order to exclude liability. It was enough

19 See Linden, 64-66, 146-53; Prosser & Keeton, 120-21, 189-93; Winfield & Jolowicz, 706-07.

20 1957 (3) S.A. 710 (T). See Millner, *The Doctor's Dilemma*, (1957) 74 S.A.L.J. 384.

in the present case that the therapist administering the X-ray treatment knew it would cause disfigurement and a risk of amputation, knew that the treatment was different from the previous X-ray treatment received by the plaintiff, and did not explain the dangers of the treatment. It seems clear, though, that outside "life and death" situations, in which an operation should not be delayed in order to secure the informed consent of the patient or a guardian, disclosure of "serious risks" was required. Otherwise, a therapist acted at his peril. The judgment did not require the plaintiff to prove that she would not have undergone the X-ray treatment had its risks been disclosed. Perhaps that point was not taken up because the plaintiff succeeded on the alternative ground that it was negligent to use this treatment.

A second case, more recent than *Esterhuizen*, supports the negligence theory of liability in informed consent cases. In *Richter v. Estate Hammann*,[21] the patient suffered various disabilities as a result of a phenol block administered by her neuro-surgeon. The patient sued the neuro-surgeon's estate, alleging that he was negligent in administering the phenol block. The claim was then amended to assert liability in negligence on the ground that the neuro-surgeon failed to warn the patient of the dangers connected with a phenol block and she would not have undergone the operation if so warned. Liability for assault was not alleged.

After referring to the *Esterhuizen* case, the court stated:

> A doctor whose advice is sought about an operation to which certain dangers are attached--and there are dangers attached to most operations--is in a dilemma. If he fails to disclose the risks he may render himself liable to an action for assault, whereas if he discloses them he might well frighten the patient into not having the operation when the doctor knows full well that it would be in the patient's interests to have it. It may well be that in certain circumstances a doctor is negligent if he fails to warn a patient, and, if that is so, it seems to me in principle that his conduct should be tested by the standard of the reasonable doctor faced with the particular problem. In reaching a conclusion a Court should be guided by medical opinion as to what a reasonable doctor, having regard to

21 1976 (3) S.A. 226 (C).

> all the circumstances of the particular case, should or should not do.[22]

In this passage, the court appears to accept that a doctor is subject to negligence liability if he failed to inform the patient of a risk which the reasonable doctor would have disclosed. An additional element of liability, stated later in the judgment, is proof that the patient would have refused the operation if disclosure of the risk (including its incidence) had been made. The neuro-surgeons who testified in the *Richter* case stated that the complications suffered by the plaintiff were very unusual and there was no need to warn her of the risk that they would occur. The court concluded that non-disclosure of the risk was not negligent in these circumstances.

Richter v. Estate Hammann illustrates the disadvantages of the negligence theory of "informed consent" liability as compared with the battery theory. It would be no answer to a battery (or "assault") action that a reasonable doctor would not feel obliged to disclose to the patient the risk of the complications which ensued. The low incidence of risk, however, could be an answer to a claim of battery as well as a claim of negligence. If the complications, although serious, are as unusual as in the *Richter* case, the risk of their occurrence might be regarded as not serious and not one which would have material weight in an informed patient's decision whether to undergo treatment. The patient's consent to treatment may be regarded as effective despite the patient's ignorance of the risk.

THE REASONABLE MAN

Whether a person who caused loss or a person who suffered it acted with reasonable care in the circumstances so often determines the outcome of litigation that numerous cases on this subject can be found in the law reports of any common law jurisdiction. The same can be said of the South African Law Reports. They contain what must be the greatest concentration of traffic accident cases of any general series of law reports published in English. Numerous judgments give detailed consideration to whether a vehicle driver or owner or injured victim acted with the prudence of the *diligens* (or *bonus*) *paterfamilias*--the Roman-Dutch counterpart of the common

22 *Ibid.*, 232.

law's reasonable man.[23] Quantitatively, these constitute Southern Africa's greatest contribution to not only the law of negligence, but the law of Torts as a whole. Almost every variety of traffic mishap is represented. The conclusions reached depend to such an extent on the particular facts of the case and the evidence adduced in it that the judgments have very limited precedential value, even for cases with similar facts. For this reason, individual judgments on this subject will not be examined here.[24]

NERVOUS SHOCK

Bester v. Commercial Union Versekeringsmaatskappy van S.A. Bpk.[25] and *Masiba v. Constantia Insurance Co. Ltd.*[26] bear upon the scope of negligence liability for causing nervous shock. In *Bester*, a negligently driven car struck and fatally injured a six-year-old boy as he and his eleven-year-old brother were running across the road. As a result of this event, the surviving brother underwent a drastic change of personality, requiring medical treatment for several years. He had been a vivacious child, enjoying normal relations with other children and doing well at school. After the accident, he became aloof and aggressive. He suffered from nightmares and crying in his sleep, and his schoolwork deteriorated greatly. The child was diagnosed as having an anxiety neurosis resulting from shock sustained at the time of the accident. The shock was attributable in part to the child's fear that he himself would be struck by the car, but more to his witnessing the fatal injury of his younger brother and resulting feelings of guilt. Damages were claimed for his

23 Most of the cases are listed under "Negligence" in the indexes of the South African Law Reports.

24 A number of cases devoted to the question of reasonable care would be useful to Torts teachers to illustrate basic principles or provide interesting problems. *E.g.* Moore v. de Klerk, 1950 (4) S.A. 470 (T); Trimmel v. Williams, 1952 (3) S.A. 786 (C); Lomagundi Sheetmetal and Engineering (Pvt.) Ltd. v. Basson, 1973 (1) R.L.R. 356 (A.D.), 1973 (4) S.A. 523 (R.A.D.); Wessels v. Hall & Pickles (Coastal) (Pty.) Ltd., 1985 (4) S.A. 153 (C).

25 1973 (1) S.A. 769 (A.D.). See 1 Boberg, 182-84; Tager, *Nervous Shock and Mental Illness*, (1973) 90 S.A.L.J. 123.

26 1982 (4) S.A. 333 (C). See 1 Boberg, 192-93.

suffering and for medical treatment.

Damages could be recovered when nervous shock caused "physical" injury, *i.e.* physical disablement or impairment of health. The question in *Bester* was whether there was liability in negligence for psychological impairment unaccompanied by physical injury. The Appellate Division held that there was:

> there is no reason in our law why somebody who, as the result of the negligent act of another, has suffered shock or psychiatric injury with consequent indisposition, should not be entitled to compensation, provided the possible consequences of the negligent act should have been foreseen by the reasonable person who should find himself in the place of the wrongdoer.[27]

The principal bases of the decision were, first, application of the basic test of negligence liability: foreseeability. The injury for which damages were claimed was regarded as foreseeable by the driver. Foreseeability also met the argument that the child should not recover because the shock was caused more by witnessing the collision with his brother than by fearing for his own safety. It was sufficient that harm to the child was foreseeable. It was not necessary that the exact nature and extent of his injury should have been foreseen. Second, the court found it illogical to refuse damages for emotional shock on the ground that it did not coincide with physical injury. It was established that damages were recoverable when physical injury accompanied the nervous shock even if the shock was unrelated to the injury. Third, the court refused to accept a distinction between "physical" injury and "psychiatric" injury. The emotional or mental system was as much a part of the physical body as an arm or a leg and an injury to the emotional or mental system was as much an injury to a "physical organism" as an arm or leg injury. In the present case, the child's bodily fitness had been impaired. A person with his sufferings did not enjoy normal physical health.

It is not clear whether the court's concept of bodily health extended beyond certain manifestations of a person's psychological condition to the condition itself. Would there be impairment of health or fitness if a person were diagnosed as having psychiatric

27 Bester v. Commercial Union Versekeringsmaatskappy van S.A. Bpk., 1973 (1) S.A. 769, 779 (A.D.) (translation).

injury or illness but this did not cause any significant suffering or disability in employment, scholastic, social or other activities? The judgment does specify that the "shock or psychiatric injury with consequent indisposition" for which damages could be recovered, when foreseeable, does not extend to "insignificant emotional shock of short duration which has no substantial effect on the health of the person, and in respect of which compensation would not ordinarily be recoverable".[28] It is not entirely clear that liability extends to a person whose shock was not at all induced by fear for his own safety, but it appears that there is to be liability when the person was so situated that harm to him was foreseeable by the tortfeasor.

This is the interpretation of *Bester* adopted in *Masiba v. Constantia Insurance Co. Ltd.*[29] In that case, a vehicle whose driver failed to keep a proper look-out collided with the rear of a car stalled on a bridge. The stalled car's owner was outside the vehicle, but he had left his three-year-old daughter and a playmate inside. He saw his car propelled some distance along the bridge, almost toppling over onto the railway track below. The car owner exclaimed "Oh God, my children!" and went towards the car. Within two minutes he suffered a stroke that caused his death three days later.

The court held that shock was foreseeable and therefore the injuries caused by it (the stroke and subsequent death) were compensable. It was not necessary that shock follow upon a fear of personal injury, although this might well, depending on the circumstances of the case, be decisive in respect of foreseeability. So long as the fear of injury or harm was foreseeable, it was irrelevant that the injury or harm was threatening another person, such as the claimant's child--or for that matter the claimant's chattel, such as his motor car. While the reasonable man in the position of the negligent driver might not have foreseen that children would be inside the stalled car, he would have foreseen that among the bystanders, who were clearly visible on the road, was the car's owner and that the owner might suffer shock at seeing his car struck and propelled along the bridge. (One would have thought that the reasonable man would, first and foremost, foresee shock attributable to someone being injured inside the car, damaging a car being an event much less likely to cause shock.)[30] Harm being foreseeable,

28 *Ibid.*

29 1982 (4) S.A. 333 (C).

30 See Burchell, *Law of Delict*, 1982 Ann. Surv. S. Afr. L. 169, 176-80.

the defendant would have been liable for incapacity caused by the stroke, had the victim survived, and should be liable for the death the stroke caused. It was not necessary that the exact nature, extent or further consequences of the harm be foreseen.

The *Masiba* case differs from *Bester* not only in presenting an obviously "physical" injury but also in being regarded by the court as a "thin skull" case. The victim had a history of hypertension, which made him prone to a stroke. The court stated,

> It being a *sine qua non* of liability where non-physical injury is inflicted that this harm should have been foreseeable, the application of the "thin skull rule" to cases involving injury of this nature is that once a psychiatric injury of gravity sufficient to render it actionable is foreseeable, then the injured party can recover for more extensive psychiatric damage which is attributable to his pre-existing weakness . . . .[31]

Masiba was not a classic "thin skull" case because it was not established that the victim would have suffered injury of sufficient gravity to be actionable had he not been hypertensive. But the court applied the "thin skull" concept that the negligent defendant is bound to take his victim as he finds him. So long as harm was foreseeable and the defendant's negligent conduct materially contributed to the harm that ensued, the defendant is fully responsible even though the victim's pre-existing weakness or susceptibility is also a cause.

Masiba resembles a "thin skull" case in a second respect. The collision caused by the negligent driver was only the last of a series of events which led to the victim's stroke--his car stalling on the road; his pushing the car up an incline; an attack and robbery by a man who had been helping to push the car; his wife being struck down by a passing car; and then the collision and the car's being propelled along the bridge. No doubt the victim was under considerable stress, to which the stroke could be attributed, before the collision occurred. Nevertheless, the defendant was liable for the stroke so long as the collision made a material contribution to causing it, as the court found.

31 Masiba v. Constantia Insurance Co. Ltd., 1982 (4) S.A. 333, 342 (C).

LEGAL CAUSATION (REMOTENESS OF DAMAGE)

The emphasis given the foreseeability of nervous shock in *Bester v. Commercial Union Versekeringsmaatskappy van S.A. Bpk.*[32] implied that the Appellate Division considered the test of negligence liability for damage to be whether damage of that general nature was reasonably foreseeable by the tortfeasor. This was confirmed in *Minister van Polisie en Binnelandse Sake v. Van Aswegen.*[33] A man convicted of theft and housebreaking had escaped from prison and been recaptured. Two police constables were sent to pick up the prisoner. They drove an ordinary four-door car because the "Black Maria" (the vehicle designed for transporting prisoners) was out of order. On the way back, while the car was travelling at high speed, the prisoner grabbed the steering wheel and turned it to the right, causing the car to collide with a lorry travelling in the opposite direction. In the lorry were stud cattle belonging to the lorry's owner. The collision caused the lorry to overturn, injuring a number of the cattle so severely that they had to be destroyed. The owner claimed damages from the Minister of Police. It was alleged that the police constables were negligent in not controlling the prisoner in such a way as to prevent him from interfering with the driving of the car.

The Appellate Division sustained the trial court's award of damages to the plaintiff. It held that the trial judge had properly directed himself to the question of whether the damage was foreseeable and that damage was foreseeable in this case. (The damage involved is described in the most general terms--"damage to other road users". No consideration is given to whether damage to cattle was itself foreseeable.) The constables should have foreseen that this prisoner, if not adequately restrained, could attempt to escape (as he had in the past) and in the attempt affect the driving of the police car, endangering other users of the road. They were negligent in not taking such precautions as handcuffing the prisoner behind his back and having one of the constables sit beside the prisoner in the back seat. Liability was affirmed not only because the general nature of the loss was foreseeable but also because it was a loss which the reasonable person in the constables' position would have taken precautions to prevent. Thus, responsibility for the consequences of

32 1973 (1) S.A. 769 (A.D.). See pp. 170-72, *supra.*

33 1974 (2) S.A. 101 (A.D.).

negligence was linked to both of the principal tests of culpability: the foreseeability that one's conduct will cause harm to another and the failure to take reasonable steps to guard against its occurrence.

Contrary to the view of some commentators,[34] the approach adopted by the Appellate Division does not subsume the entire law of remoteness of damage. There is still a place for considering intervening causes and the relationship between the risks created by the defendant and the loss sustained by the plaintiff. In *Minister van Polisie en Binnelandse Sake v. Van Aswegen*, the act of the prisoner in attempting to escape was not an intervening cause breaking the chain of causation because the police constables' negligence was in failing to guard against this possibility. Similarly, in *Fischbach v. Pretoria City Council*,[35] an unknown person's removal of a cover protecting pedestrians from falling down a storm water catchpit did not break the chain of causation because the defendant was aware that covers were being removed and was negligent in failing to secure them against tampering. A defendant is liable for harm brought about by a third person's conduct if the defendant's negligence is in failing to guard against the consequences of that type of conduct.[36] In other situations, intervening conduct continues to present remoteness questions and it remains necessary to consider whether there was a sufficient relationship between the risks created by the defendant and the loss sustained by the plaintiff to support liability.

This is illustrated by *Portwood v. Svamvur*.[37] The defendant allowed his savage dog to run at large. At 4 a.m. one morning, the defendant's next-door neighbour, disturbed by the howling of this Doberman Pinscher, found it caught in his gate. The dog's back legs were in the wire mesh at the top of the gate and its forefeet were on the ground. At first the animal showed no signs of aggressiveness; but as the neighbour was in the midst of extricating it from the gate, the dog began to attack him. The neighbour sustained numerous bites, causing severe injuries for which he claimed damages.

The defendant was negligent in allowing the Doberman to run

34 See Boberg, *Law of Delict*, 1974 Ann. Surv. S. Afr. L. 156, 175-76.

35 1969 (2) S.A. 693 (T).

36 Restatement (Second) of Torts, s. 449 (1965). See Fleming, 197; Salmond & Heuston, 516-17.

37 1970 (1) R.L.R. 225 (A.D.), 1970 (4) S.A. 8 (R.A.D.).

at large unmuzzled. His conduct was a *sine qua non* of the plaintiff's injuries; the plaintiff would not have been bitten if the dog had been confined or muzzled. The foreseeable-consequences principle, to which the Rhodesian Appellate Division adhered, required that the general nature of the harm the plaintiff sustained be foreseeable. Clearly, it was. The very reason why the defendant was negligent was the danger that his dog would attack and bite a person. The defendant could not be expected to foresee that his dog would get caught in a fence and bite a person attempting to free it, but (following *Hughes v. Lord Advocate*)[38] unforeseeable events in the chain of causation did not render damage too remote when the damage itself was of a foreseeable type.

There remained an additional problem of causation: connecting the risk that made the defendant's conduct negligent with the injuries sustained by the plaintiff. The defendant was negligent in allowing his dog about unmuzzled only because the Doberman had a savage nature, *i.e.* a propensity to bite people much greater than the normal dog's. The risk stemmed from the dog's propensity to bite. The court found it necessary--correctly, it is submitted[39]--to determine whether the dog's savage nature was a material factor in causing the plaintiff's injuries, or whether the dog attacked the plaintiff only because it was caught in a gate, a situation in which a non-savage dog might well bite its rescuer. A "material" factor, it seems, was one that made more than a *de minimis* contribution to the result--perhaps too wide a definition. Only because the court found the dog's nature "played a material part" in the injuries (a finding well-grounded in the extent and severity of the injuries) was the plaintiff permitted to recover damages from the defendant.

A remoteness argument was seriously treated in *Sadomba v. Unity Insurance Co. Ltd.*[40] The plaintiff established that the defendant was liable for injuries sustained in a collision between his car and the defendant's negligently driven bus. The plaintiff lay unconscious by the side of the road for about half an hour, after which he was removed by an ambulance. When the plaintiff awoke in hospital, his watch and shoes were missing. Most likely, they were stolen by a member of the large crowd which gathered at the scene of the

38 [1963] A.C. 837 (H.L.).

39 But see the criticism in Boberg, *Uncommon Cause*, in Kahn, Fiat Iustitia--Essays in Memory of Oliver Deneys Schreiner 145, 161-63 (1983).

40 1978 R.L.R. 262 (G.D.), 1978 (3) S.A. 1094 (R).

accident. The plaintiff claimed damages for loss of the watch and shoes.

The court stated, "the question is whether the intervention of such acts by third persons made the collision so remote from the loss of the shoes and watch that the . . . defendant should not be held liable for those losses".[41] To answer it, the court first found that the unauthorised removal of the shoes and watch was foreseeable in light of various circumstances which themselves were foreseeable: the plaintiff was knocked unconscious in the collision and remained unconscious for at least an hour; about fifty spectators gathered and were able to approach the plaintiff; he was left unprotected; the spectators were not all affluent or for some other reason likely to resist any temptation to steal the watch and shoes; the darkness of the night and the confusion and excitement of the accident made it easy to accomplish the theft without interference.

The court then found it necessary to address an additional question drawn from the judgment in *Impress (Worcester) Ltd. v. Rees*:[42] whether the intervening cause (the removal of the watch and shoes) was "of so powerful a nature that [the] negligent driving was not a legal cause of the losses at all, but was merely part of the surrounding circumstances".

> If the plaintiff had not been unconscious, and had suffered the loss of his wallet through the act of pick-pockets whilst the spectators were milling around him as he stood at the scene, I would have said that only the pocket-picking was "the cause to which must be attributed decisive potency."[43] . . . But on the relevant facts of this case I think that the plaintiff's state of unconsciousness played so important a part in the removals that the negligent driving . . . was not merely a part of the circumstances surrounding the plaintiff's losses. It was sufficiently proximate to the losses to make the second defendant liable for them. To adopt the famous phrase in

41 *Ibid.*, 273, 1099.

42 [1971] 2 All E.R. 357, 358 (Q.B.D.).

43 Lord Wright, *Notes on Causation and Responsibility in English Law*, 1955 Camb. L.J. 163, 166.

> [*The Oropesa*],[44] because of his continuing unconsciousness, the heavy hand of the collision still lay upon the plaintiff when the thefts were committed.[45]

Consequently, the plaintiff was entitled to recover the value of the watch and shoes.

A different approach was taken to a somewhat similar problem in *Alston v. Marine & Trade Insurance Co. Ltd.*[46] A traffic accident for which the defendant was liable led to a stroke for which the plaintiff claimed damages. The plaintiff sustained a brain injury in the accident. This caused depression, for which the drug parstellin was prescribed. While on parstellin, the plaintiff ate some cheese. This caused the stroke--a recently-discovered effect of parstellin when combined with certain foods.

The court decided to apply the criteria of the first *Restatement of Torts*[47] to the question of whether the plaintiff could recover damages for his stroke. The *Restatement* directed, *inter alia*, consideration of whether an intervening cause brought about harm different from that which would otherwise have resulted from the actor's negligence; whether the results appeared after the event to be extraordinary rather than normal in the light of the circumstances at the time of its operation; whether the cause operated independently of any situation created by the actor's negligence and was not an act done as a normal response to such a situation; and whether it was due to the act of a third person or the victim.[48] The court concluded that the victim's eating of the cheese was a "superseding cause" and the defendant was not liable for the resulting stroke. The stroke was harm different in kind from the injury to be expected in a road accident; it was extraordinary and not predictable by medical science at the time the cheese was ingested; the cheese was consumed independently of the situation created by the tortfeasor's negligence

44 [1943] P. 32, 37 (C.A.).

45 Sadomba v. Unity Insurance Co. Ltd., 1978 R.L.R. 262, 274-75 (G.D.), 1978 (3) S.A. 1084, 1100 (R).

46 1964 (4) S.A. 112 (W).

47 Restatement of Torts, ss. 430 *et seq.* (1934).

48 *Ibid.*, s. 442. The *Restatement* included only the conduct of a third person, but there appears no reason why the court should not have added the conduct of the victim.

and not as a response to it; and the victim's act brought the stroke about.

Although described as "a classic on remoteness of damage in the jurisprudence of any country",[49] the judgment has been criticised by several commentators[50] and is unlikely to be followed outside the United States because of its rejection of the *Wagon Mound*[51] foreseeable-consequences doctrine. It is submitted, nevertheless, that the judgment reached the correct result, even if one accepts *Wagon Mound* and believes (contrary to the judge) that stroke is a foreseeable consequence of careless driving on the road.

The plaintiff's consumption of cheese had nothing to do with the accident or the negligence which caused the accident. The plaintiff did not eat cheese in response to his injuries or their treatment. The reasonably prudent driver could foresee that the victim of a traffic accident would eat cheese, a common food, but there is no reason why this should be in the driver's mind. The possibility that an accident victim will eat cheese and suffer an adverse reaction forms no part of the group of foreseeable risks which makes it negligent to drive carelessly. Only if eating cheese could be linked to these foreseeable risks would it be correct to hold the tortfeasor liable for the consequences. The plaintiff's consumption of parstellin, unlike his consumption of cheese, was definitely linked to the injuries sustained in the traffic accident, and it might be foreseeable that the victim of a traffic accident would suffer an adverse reaction to medicine prescribed for his injuries. However, it was not reasonably foreseeable that the plaintiff would be prescribed a drug that caused stroke when combined with common foods. Neither of the two elements which brought about the stroke (the cheese and the parstellin) involved foreseeable risks of careless driving, and the defendant should not have been held liable for the surprising consequences of the plaintiff's bring them together.

Mashaka v. Salisbury United Omnibus Co. Ltd.[52] is given as a

49 Boberg, *Law of Delict*, 1964 Ann. Surv. S. Afr. L. 148, 184.

50 *Ibid.*, 184-86; Honoré, *Remoteness of Damage*, (1964) 81 S.A.L.J. 410; Turpin, *Roman-Dutch Law--Remoteness of Damage--Wagon Mound Not Followed*, 1965 Camb. L.J. 34.

51 Overseas Tankship (U.K.) Ltd. v. Morts Dock & Engineering Co. Ltd., [1961] A.C. 388 (P.C.).

52 1964 R.L.R. 352 (G.D.).

final Southern African example of how other concepts of legal causation retain viability in a foreseeable-consequences regime. A train collided with a bus at a level crossing. An injured bus passenger sued the operators of both the train and the bus. The court found that the bus driver recklessly attempted to cross the tracks ahead of the train and the train's fireman failed to keep a proper look-out and give a timely warning of the bus to the engine driver. Both were at fault, but the court held the bus company solely liable by applying an inversion of the "last opportunity" rule. The last opportunity rule enables a negligent plaintiff to avoid the defence of contributory negligence when the defendant negligently failed to avail himself of a "last opportunity" to avoid injuring the plaintiff. The inversion in *Mashaka* is the court's applying the rule for the benefit of a defendant, absolving the railway of liability because the bus driver, knowing the train was approaching, failed to avail himself (by waiting for the train to pass) of a last opportunity to avoid the accident.

This is supported by older South African authorities,[53] but it is submitted that the court should have found no occasion for application of the last opportunity rule. The rule properly serves only to cast liability upon a defendant despite the plaintiff's negligence, not to relieve a defendant of liability because of another tortfeasor's conduct.[54] It would be ironic if defendants could avail themselves of the last opportunity rule in this fashion now that the rule has been abolished or repudiated in contributory negligence cases.[55] However, the result in *Mashaka* can be defended on the argument that a defendant whose negligence consists of failure to look out for danger to another should not be treated as causally responsible for harm when that other, knowing of the danger, recklessly or intentionally exposes himself to it. On this basis, the conduct of the bus driver can be regarded as the sole legal cause of the accident.[56]

53 See McKerron, 64.

54 See Fleming, 243; Prosser & Keeton, 462-64.

55 See Fleming, 250-52; Prosser & Keeton, 477.

56 See McAuley, *Last Opportunity Rule in Collision Cases*, 1965 Rhod. L.J. 12.

7

DEFENCES AND APPORTIONMENT OF DAMAGES

ASSUMPTION OF RISK

In *Lampert v. Hefer, N.O.*,[1] the Appellate Division recognised assumption of risk as a defence to a negligence action and applied it to reject the claim of a passenger who accepted a ride with an intoxicated driver. One of the grounds of negligence alleged in the plaintiff's declaration was that the driver was under the influence of liquor. The defendant pleaded and proved that the plaintiff chose to be a passenger knowing that the driver was too intoxicated to drive properly or exercise reasonable care and appreciating the risk to which she was exposing herself. The Appellate Division held that this constituted voluntary assumption of risk and was a good defence. It declined to follow the contrary decision in *Dann v. Hamilton*.[2]

The principle *volenti non fit injuria* was seen as applicable to the claimant in a negligence action who consented to be exposed to the risk of injury as well as to the plaintiff in an intentional tort case who consented to the intentional act. The court recognised that assumption of risk and contributory negligence overlap, in that both fit the facts of some cases. The defendant's plea in the *Lampert* case might be viewed as raising either.[3] The court did not find it

1 1955 (2) S.A. 507 (A.D.). See Millner, *Voluntary Assumption of Risk*, (1955) 72 S.A.L.J. 233.

2 [1939] 1 K.B. 509.

3 Schreiner, J.A., concurring, interpreted the plea as raising a defence of assumption of risk in relation to the plaintiff's acceptance of the ride and a

necessary to express a view on the question of whether *volenti non fit injuria* operated to exclude a duty of care or as a defence to liability for breach of duty. Nevertheless, *Lampert v. Hefer, N.O.* is authority for assumption of risk as a defence to negligence liability and for its application to a plaintiff who knew that the actor would not exercise reasonable care to protect her from the risk of the injury that occurred.

Assumption of risk was raised as a defence in the extraordinary case of *van der Vyver v. Netherlands Insurance Co. of S.A. Ltd.*[4] The plaintiff was a private detective. He had been employed by a Mrs. Ozen to watch her husband's movements. Late one afternoon, Mr. Ozen left his shop in Pretoria and drove away in an Austin Mini station wagon. He picked up a woman at a bus stop near the shop and drove with her to the northern part of town. After stopping at a roadhouse they left Pretoria. They turned off a dirt road and drove onto the veld, parking the car between some trees. The plaintiff, accompanied by his wife and a relative, van der Merwe, had been following Ozen's vehicle at all times. When Ozen turned off the dirt road, the plaintiff stopped his car in a place where Ozen could not see it. The plaintiff and van der Merwe crept toward Ozen's car. They could see that there were people in the rear of the vehicle. Ozen then climbed out, clad only in a shirt and socks, and began to put on his trousers. The woman went to the front seat. The plaintiff and van der Merwe then ran toward Ozen's car. Upon seeing them, Ozen jumped inside and began driving in the direction of the dirt road. Van der Merwe was standing ready with a flash camera and photographed Ozen and his companion. The plaintiff ran in front of the car. He asked Ozen to stop, holding up a card which identified him as a private detective. Ozen paid no attention and continued driving. The plaintiff tried to open the door on the driver's side, but it was locked. Van der Merwe went around to the passenger's side, opened the door and pulled the woman out of the front seat. He held onto her for some time. Ozen continued to drive toward the dirt road.

When the plaintiff realised that Ozen would not stop, he threw himself on the bonnet of the car. The plaintiff expected this would cause Ozen to stop. He hoped to obscure Ozen's view and prevent him from driving away. This tactic did not succeed. Ozen reached

defence of contributory negligence in relation to her conduct after the ride commenced. Lampert v. Hefer, N.O., 1955 (2) S.A. 507, 508-09 (A.D.).

4 1967 (2) S.A. 476 (T), rev'd, 1968 (1) S.A. 412 (A.D.).

the dirt road and increased his speed. The plaintiff rode on the bonnet, with one hand inside the driver's-side window and the other hand gripping the guttering on the roof. The plaintiff called out that he was a private detective and asked Ozen to stop so that he could have a talk with him, but Ozen continued to drive. The plaintiff claimed that he did not jump off the vehicle because its speed was too high and the road was too bumpy. He was afraid of injuring his back or neck.

Ozen then closed the side window. The plaintiff had to remove his fingers and change his position. He gripped the guttering of the roof and lay on top of it, with his left foot propped against the outside mirror and his right foot against the aerial. Shortly thereafter the vehicle reached a tarred road. Ozen drove toward Pretoria at a speed of fifty to sixty miles per hour. Several times, Ozen swerved from side to side across the road, apparently with the intent of throwing the plaintiff off the car. The plaintiff called to Ozen that he must stop so that the plaintiff could talk with him, but Ozen continued driving. Nor would he stop when the plaintiff fired two or three pistol shots into the ground.

After travelling for four miles on the tarred road, past a hotel, the car came to a fork in the road. Ozen turned toward the road on the left but suddenly swung toward the road on the right, which led to Pretoria. With the change in direction, the aerial on which the plaintiff propped his right foot broke. He slipped and fell off the vehicle, sustaining injuries. The trial court found that Ozen did not swing the vehicle to the right with the purpose of getting the plaintiff off the car. He had originally intended to drive on the road on the left side of the fork but suddenly decided to take the other road instead. Ozen continued to drive and eventually arrived at the Pretoria North police station.

The plaintiff sued the insurer of Ozen's vehicle for the injuries received when he fell off the car. He claimed that the injuries were intentionally inflicted or caused by negligent driving. The trial court found that Ozen was negligent because of the danger in driving at a high speed while the plaintiff was on the car. It rejected the defendant's claim that Ozen had acted in reasonable defence of his person or property. There was no evidence that his person or property was threatened and if Ozen was entitled to think that such a threat existed, the steps he used to avert danger were unreasonable. The plaintiff had identified himself as a private detective. It was only after Ozen sped along the tarred road and tried to get him off the vehicle that the plaintiff fired his pistol. If Ozen really had been afraid of the plaintiff, he would have turned in at the hotel.

The defendant contended that the plaintiff could not recover damages because by throwing himself onto Ozen's moving vehicle, he accepted the risk of the injuries that ensued. The plaintiff had acted voluntarily and knew that Ozen might not stop. He admitted that he was prepared to take the chance that Ozen would try to get away. He realised that persons caught in the circumstances in which Ozen found himself sometimes panicked and acted unreasonably. The trial court rejected this defence. If the plaintiff had fallen off at the beginning, while Ozen was trying to get away, the defendant might have a good defence, but the plaintiff did not accept the risk and agree to the consequences of what happened later. It was not his will and he had not consented to stay on the vehicle while it was being driven away at high speed. He tried to persuade Ozen to stop and had to hang on to the car so that he would not fall off and injure himself.

A divided Appellate Division upheld the trial court's ruling on this point.[5] The majority required clear proof of the plaintiff's knowledge and realisation of the nature and extent of the risk and of the plaintiff's consent in order for such a defence to be sustained. The evidence did not support the defendant's contention that the plaintiff was aware of the risk. This contention was based upon the plaintiff's realisation that a person who fell off a moving vehicle might be killed. But he thought that Ozen would be required to stop the vehicle by obstruction of his vision. The plaintiff was not aware of his dangerous position and what would happen to him until Ozen disregarded his attempts to persuade Ozen to stop. However, accepting that the plaintiff was aware of the risk of injury, he had not consented to it. His awareness did not mean that he had consented, and consent could not be implied from the fact that the plaintiff accepted the risk by intentionally getting on the bonnet of a moving vehicle. His uncontradicted evidence was that he would not have done this if he had known that Ozen would drive in the manner he did.[6]

5 Netherlands Insurance Co. of S.A. Ltd. v. van der Vyver, 1968 (1) S.A. 412, 421 (A.D.).

6 The court allowed the plaintiff's appeal from the trial court's decision that the plaintiff had been contributorily negligent. The trial court had held that the plaintiff and Ozen were equally at fault. The plaintiff had caused panic and, being aware of the risk that Ozen would try to get away, took up an exceedingly unsafe position on the car. This was the cause of everything that followed. The Appellate Division majority believed that Ozen's reckless actions were not reasonably foreseeable to the plaintiff and that there was no

Milne, A.J.A., dissenting, believed that the plaintiff's claim must fail on the ground of *volenti non fit injuria.*[7] He thought that the defence was at least as strong in this case as in *Lampert v. Hefer, N.O.* In his opinion the plaintiff, entirely of his own free will (and against Ozen's will), had assumed the risk of just the kind of harm as actually occurred. He appreciated the risk. The plaintiff's belief that Ozen would stop was of no consequence, for he took the risk tha Ozen would not stop. The plaintiff was determined to stay on the vehicle, despite the risk that he knew he was assuming, until it should stop and he could achieve his objective. Thus he elected to encounter the risk of the kind of damage that happened.

Volenti non fit injuria was again raised as a defence in *Vorster v. Santam Insurance Co. Ltd.*,[8] a case arising from a race on a country road. A Fiat and a Vauxhall raced each other for a R10 stake. Each carried a passenger sitting beside the driver. At a sharp bend, when the cars were travelling about seventy miles per hour, the Vauxhall swerved right. Its right-hand rear hit the left flank of the Fiat. The Fiat careered off the road through the veld, overturned, smashed through a farm gate and crashed into a transformer station. At the farm gate, the Fiat's passenger was hurled out of the vehicle and very severely injured. He claimed damages from the Fiat's driver and the Vauxhall's insurer.

The trial court found that both drivers were negligent--the Fiat's for attempting to overtake the Vauxhall at the bend at high speed and the Vauxhall's for driving around the bend at a dangerous speed with the Fiat in close proximity. The accident was caused by the negligence of both. By participating in the race as a passenger with knowledge that it was much more dangerous than non-competitive driving, the plaintiff was contributorily negligent. The reasonable person would not have taken part in the race. In the court's opinion, the plaintiff and the two drivers were equally blameworthy.

The plaintiff's knowledge of the dangers of racing and his consent to be a passenger in the Fiat, knowing that it was going to

causal connection between the plaintiff's actions and the consequences of Ozen's wrongful conduct. From the time he landed on the bonnet the plaintiff was powerless, practically a prisoner of Ozen. Ozen's conduct was the sole cause of injury.

7 *Ibid.*, 425-27.

8 1973 (2) S.A. 186 (W), aff'd, 1973 (4) S.A. 764 (A.D.). See Boberg, *Some Light on the Defence of Volenti*, (1974) 91 S.A.L.J. 19.

be raced on the road where the accident occurred, were the basis of the defence of *volenti non fit injuria* as well as of the plea of contributory negligence. As the trial court pointed out, it became more important to distinguish between the two defences when legislation introduced apportionment of damages for contributory negligence.[9] Contributory neglience now caused reduction of the award of damages, while *volenti* remained a complete defence to the plaintiff's claim.

The court rejected the *volenti* defence. It could only succeed if the plaintiff, before entering the Fiat, knew the nature and extent of the risk he would run, appreciated the risk, and freely consented to undergo the risk. Risk or danger was divisible into separate parts. A plaintiff might have consented to a particular type of risk but not another. It was necessary for the defendants to establish that the plaintiff was *volens* with respect to the particular "danger factor" which caused the damage. The court found that the plaintiff was *volens* with respect to mechanical hazards over which the drivers would have no reasonable control, such as the failure of a tyre or the steering mechanism when one of the cars was driven at maximum speed, but not with respect to negligent conduct on the part of the drivers during the race. The plaintiff had not agreed to negligent acts which endangered his safety. He did not know of or consent to the likelihood that the drivers would negotiate the bend in the road dangerously. Not being *volens* as to the cause of his injuries, the plaintiff was entitled to recover damages, reduced by one-third on account of his contributory negligence.

In the Appellate Division, to which the Vauxhall's insurer and the plaintiff appealed,[10] the plaintiff submitted that voluntary assumption of risk should be treated as "fault" for purposes of the contributory negligence apportionment legislation and thereby operate to reduce the plaintiff's damages rather than wholly defeat his claim. This submission was rejected because *volenti non fit injuria* had long been recognised as a defence and its criteria were radically different from the criteria of contributory negligence. Acknowledging that the two defences sometimes overlapped and that the subjective enquiry required by the *volenti* defence posed practical difficulties, the court found no justification for depriving the defendant in a "risk case" of a complete defence if the necessary facts were established.

9 Apportionment of Damages Act, No. 34 of 1956, s. 1 (S. Afr.). See pp. 192-93, *infra*.

10 Santam Insurance Co. Ltd. v. Vorster, 1973 (4) S.A. 764 (A.D.).

The essential elements of the defence were "knowledge, appreciation and consent". It was the consent element that caused considerable difficulty and upon which the court concentrated. When express consent existed, it was a matter of construction to determine what precisely was embraced by the consent. In cases such as the present one, in which the contention was that the risk of injury was accepted, the enquiry revolved around the ambit of the implied consent to be ascribed to the plaintiff and whether the injury was sustained in consequence of a risk falling within that ambit. The defence did not require an express or implied bargain or consensus between the parties whereby the plaintiff gave up his right of action for negligence.[11] Consent could be implied in other circumstances, although not whenever the plaintiff knowingly exposed himself to danger.

The court concluded that the required consent would ordinarily be established by showing, in addition to knowledge and appreciation of the danger, that the claimant foresaw the risk of injury to himself, provided the particular risk which culminated in his injuries fell within the ambit of the foreseen risk. Inasmuch as direct evidence was seldom, if ever, available and a plaintiff's negative *ipse dixit* usually carried little weight, a court was required to objectively assess the relevant facts in order to determine the inherent risks of the hazardous activity under consideration. Then it was to determine whether the plaintiff, despite his probable protestation to the contrary, must have foreseen the particular risk which eventuated and caused his injuries. If so, he would be held to have consented thereto.

Applying these principles, the Appellate Division came to essentially the same conclusion as the trial court: the plaintiff had been *volens* in relation to the risks ordinarily inherent in road racing, such as a burst tyre, but not the negligent driving that occurred and caused the accident. It believed that the driver's taking the bend in the manner proven and the subsequent events were not risks so inherent in this particular racing contest as must have been foreseen, and consequently consented to, by the plaintiff. The case was a borderline one, but there was no basis to disturb the trial court's decision that *volenti* had not been proved.[12]

11 The position advocated in Williams, Joint Torts and Contributory Negligence 306-15 (1951).

12 The Appellate Division also found no ground for disturbing the trial court's decision that the plaintiff and the two drivers were equally at fault. Neither court considered the argument, supported by *dicta* in Matthee v. Hatz, 1983

It is submitted that the disposition of this case was correct but that the Appellate Division should not have made the *volenti* defence dependent upon whether the plaintiff foresaw the specific risk that caused his injuries. Consent cannot be inferred from foresight alone. The enquiry in this type of case ought to be whether the plaintiff knew that another person would not exercise ordinary reasonable care for his safety in the respects relevant to causing his injuries. If he had this knowledge but nevertheless chose to expose himself to the risks resulting from the lack of reasonable care, he can be taken to have consented to these risks.[13] On this basis, the plaintiff consented to the risks flowing from high speed generally and from mechanical breakdown of the cars (assuming he knew that the cars were not specially equipped and maintained to withstand the rigours of racing). But the plaintiff did not know that the drivers would engage in highly dangerous manoeuvres carrying a substantial risk of serious accident. His expectation (and probably also the drivers' expectation) was that this would not occur. He therefore did not consent to the risk of this eventuality. This risk caused his injuries, so the defence of assumption of risk was properly rejected.

The finding that the plaintiff did not foresee the risk of what injured him is not inconsistent with the trial court's finding that he was contributorily negligent, which was not disputed on appeal. Clearly he was contributorily negligent if the reasonable man in his position would have foreseen the risk and been dissuaded by it from participating in the road race. However, the plaintiff was contributorily negligent even if this specific risk was not reasonably foreseeable. A contributory negligence defence, unlike a *volenti* defence, does not require that risks be drawn with particularity. It is sufficient that the risk which caused the injuries was of the same general nature as would have been foreseeable to the reasonable person in the plaintiff's position and caused him to act with greater care. The reasonable person in the plaintiff's position would not have been a passenger in a road race in the vicinity of the accident. He would have foreseen the risk of the cars colliding or at least the risk of the car in which he was riding going out of control. That was sufficient to sustain the defence of contributory negligence.

Within the scope of *volenti non fit injuria* are cases in which an

(2) S.A. 595, 600 (W), that parties engaged in a common illegal activity such as road racing owe no duty of care to one another.

13 See Prosser & Keeton, 480-82, 484-86. Different criticisms are collected in 1 Boberg, 768-71.

injured person had agreed in terms to accept the risk of injury or waive a right to be compensated. The effect of such an agreement upon liability for negligence was considered in *Bristow v. Lycett.*[14] The defendant was the owner of a wild animal farm open to visitors. At the entrance was a large notice, prominently displayed, reading "All persons entering these premises do so at their own risk." The notice also contained the prices of admission. The plaintiff saw and read this notice when she arrived at the entrance by car. Immediately upon entering the farm, the car was approached by a young elephant weighing 900 lbs. The elephant thrust its trunk through the car's window. The plaintiff and her companions, all elderly ladies, were alarmed by the elephant's action. The elephant's custodian, a teenage youth, told them not to be alarmed; the elephant only wanted a sweet. They gave a sweet to the elephant, who then withdrew his trunk. The youth was asked whether it was safe to get out of the car in the elephant's presence. He assured the ladies that it was perfectly safe to do so; the elephant was a "kind one" and would do no harm. Only because of this assurance did the ladies leave the car. They then paid the admission fee. More sweets were given to the elephant. It ran away, but a short time later it surprised and knocked down the plaintiff in an attempt to obtain more sweets. The plaintiff sustained a broken wrist, for which damages were claimed.

The Rhodesian Appellate Division held that the animal farm's owner was liable. It regarded the warning at the entrance to the farm, which the plaintiff had read, as the equivalent of an "exemption clause" in a contract to which the plaintiff had subscribed. The effect of this "exemption clause" depended upon the parties' intentions. It was necessary to ascertain what it was the parties proposed to exempt from liability. In order to do this, the court in substance identified the risks which could be encountered by a visitor to a wild animal farm and then considered which risks would have been within the visitor's contemplation when entering the farm, reading the notice and realising that animals were permitted to run free. It is implicit in the judgment that it is the visitor's and not the owner's contemplations which are controlling because, in case of doubt, an exemption is construed against the party stipulating for the exemption.

According to the court, a visitor would not expect to meet a man-eating lion. The risk that he would be injured because the animal farm's proprietor permitted such a dangerous animal to run free would be outside his contemplation and not covered by such an

14 1971 (2) R.L.R. 206 (A.D.), 1971 (4) S.A. 223 (R.A.D.).

exemption clause. On the other hand, a visitor would realise that the behaviour of all wild animals is unpredictable and that there is always a risk of injury from an animal that usually would not harm visitors. This is the risk a visitor would contemplate in connection with the exemption clause here. The plaintiff tacitly agreed to run the risk of this type of injury when she entered the park after seeing the posted notice. The injury which the elephant inflicted was within the scope of this risk. Therefore, absent other considerations, the notice would relieve the defendant of liability.

The custodian, however, had assured the plaintiff and her companions that the elephant was harmless. This was negligent of the custodian because he knew of the elephant's habit of persistently attempting to get sweets from visitors and did nothing to protect the ladies from the elephant's attentions. That an employee would mislead a visitor by a negligent assurance of an animal's safety was not within the contemplation of either the visitors or the owner, who was vicariously liable for harm caused by such negligence. Here, the plaintiff would not have left the car and entered the farm, but for the assurance. While agreeing to some risk in order to see the animals on the farm, the plaintiff did not agree to run the risk of being injured by this elephant when the assurance proved to be unjustified. The posted notice, therefore, did not protect the farm's owner from liability for the plaintiff's injuries.

The method adopted in *Bristow v. Lycett* is, in essence, to identify the potential risks faced by the party who agreed to exempt another from liability or accept the risk of loss, describing risks specifically in terms of their causes as well as the injuries involved, to ascertain which of these risks was in the contemplation of the parties, and to determine whether the injury was attributable to a contemplated risk, in which case there is no liability. Although the effect of any exemption clause will depend upon the particular type of contract involved and the circumstances in which it was made, this method may be applied to a wide variety of exemption clause and exemption notice cases.

ILLEGALITY

It is arguable that a plaintiff's claim to damages is not to be sustained if he was injured while engaged in illegal conduct or knowingly associated with illegal conduct by the defendant. This is considered in two South African cases, *Adam v. Latiff* [15] and *Matthee v. Hatz*.[16]

In *Adam v. Latiff*, the plaintiff was injured when the vehicle in which he was a passenger was involved in a collision. He claimed damages from the owner and driver of the vehicle. They raised as a defence the facts that they had committed a criminal offence in conveying the plaintiff as a passenger for compensation without being licensed to do so and that the plaintiff had committed a criminal offence (procuring or aiding and abetting the defendants' offence) by paying the defendants and having them convey him, knowing they were unlicensed.

The court held that the plaintiff could recover because it regarded his cause of action as arising solely from the driver's negligence and not, as the defendants contended, from the plaintiff's illegal acts. It distinguished an earlier case in which, on the same facts, passengers were denied recovery against a vehicle's liability insurer.[17] The insurance coverage applied only to passengers conveyed for reward, which it was illegal for the plaintiffs there to become, so there was a connection, not present in *Adam v. Latiff*, between the plaintiffs' unlawful conduct and the alleged liability of the defendant. If allowed to recover from the insurance company, the plaintiffs would have derived a beneit from their misdeeds. The court did not believe that the plaintiff in *Adam v. Latiff* would derive damages from his unlawful conduct if damages were awarded against the defendants.

In *Matthee v. Hatz*, the defendant was an unlicensed driver. The defendant's mother had lent her car to the plaintiff on condition that the defendant not be allowed to drive it. During the evening, the defendant took over the driving and caused a collision which injured the plaintiff. The defendant resisted liability on the ground that the plaintiff, knowing that the defendant had no licence, permitted the defendant to drive and rode with him as a passenger. It was a criminal offence to drive without a licence and an offence for the person in control of a car to permit an unlicensed person to drive it.

The court held that the plaintiff had not "permitted" the defendant to drive and the defendant's liability was not affected by the plaintiff's knowledge when he became a passenger that the defendant was unlicensed. It accepted, on the authority of such cases

15 1970 (3) S.A. 253 (N).

16 1983 (2) S.A. 595 (W).

17 Parity Insurance Co. Ltd. v. Marescia, 1965 (3) S.A. 430 (A.D.).

as *Smith v. Jenkins*[18] and *Ashton v. Turner*,[19] that a defendant may have owed a plaintiff no duty of care if they were engaged in a common illegal activity at the time of the alleged negligence. The court mentioned as examples parties engaged in housebreaking, escaping from crime, fleeing in a stolen car and road-racing. In the instant case, however, there was no common illegal activity because the plaintiff did not commit an offence, and the defendant's duty not to drive negligently was unaffected by the plaintiff's knowledge of the defendant's unlicensed driving.

Whether damages can be recovered for loss of illegally-derived income or damage to illegally-possessed property will be considered later.[20]

APPORTIONMENT OF DAMAGES

The Apportionment of Damages Act of 1956[21] introduced apportionment of damages and contribution among tortfeasors into South African law. Although its provisions have not been adopted in any common law country, this act constitutes one of South Africa's most significant contributions to the body of tort law and warrants the attention of any common law jurisdiction considering the reform of its contributory negligence or contribution legislation.

Section 1 provides for apportionment of liability in cases of contributory negligence. It is based upon the English contributory negligence act.[22] The South African act differs most significantly from the English act in explicitly abolishing the "last opportunity" rule[23] and in providing that the damages recoverable shall be reduced to such an extent as the court may deem just and equitable having

18 (1970) 119 C.L.R. 397.

19 [1981] Q.B. 137.

20 See pp. 240-44, 252, *infra*.

21 No. 34 of 1956. A detailed analysis of the act and its judicial interpretation is contained in McKerron, 289-319. See also 1 Boberg, 654-82; van der Walt, paras. 44, 61.

22 Law Reform (Contributory Negligence) Act, 1945, 8 & 9 Geo. 6, c. 28 (Eng. & Scot.).

23 S. 1(1)(*b*).

regard to "the degree in which the claimant was at fault in relation to the damage"[24] rather than to "the claimant's share in the responsibility for the damage".[25]

Section 2 regulates proceedings involving persons jointly or severally liable in delict for the same damage and provides for contribution between them. Although influenced by the 1935 English contribution statute,[26] Section 2 is an original and very complex piece of legislation. It attempts to meet a wide variety of problems which had arisen in other countries.

One problem was the uncertain legal position of tortfeasors who settled with the victim. For purposes of contribution, the South African act treats a full settlement as equivalent to a judgment for the sum agreed to be paid. (It is equivalent to the amount of damage actually suffered by the plaintiff, if this is less than the settlement amount.)[27] Another problem was multiplicity of litigation, with plaintiffs bringing successive actions against alleged tortfeasors and tortfeasors initiating contribution proceedings after the conclusion of plaintiffs' suits. The South African act meets this by providing that the plaintiff or defendant in an action may, before the close of pleadings, give notice of the action to any joint wrongdoer not sued in the action, who may thereupon intervene as a defendant. The court may, however, order separate trials. A joint wrongdoer who was not so notified cannot be sued thereafter for damages or contribution unless good cause for not giving notice is established.[28]

A third problem was to identify the limitation period applicable to contribution claims and, if necessary, to establish a more appropriate form of limitation. The South African act provides that the period of prescription (limitation) is calculated from the date of the judgment in respect of which a contribution is claimed or (when the judgment was appealed) the date of the final judgment on appeal. In cases of settlement, prescription is calculated from the date on

24 S. 1(1)(*a*).

25 Law Reform (Contributory Negligence) Act, 1945, 8 & 9 Geo. 6, c. 28, s. 1(1) (Eng. & Scot.).

26 Law Reform (Married Women and Tortfeasors) Act, 1935, 25 & 26 Geo. 5, c. 30, s. 6, repealed, Civil Liability (Contribution) Act, 1978, c. 47, s. 9(2) (Eng.).

27 S. 2(12).

28 S. 2(2)-(4).

which the wrongdoer agrees to pay the plaintiff in full settlement. The period is usually twelve months, but correspondingly less if the prescription period governing an action by the plaintiff against the joint wrongdoer was less than twelve months. Notice of claim requirements are treated analogously to limitation periods.[29]

The basic formula for apportionment of contribution is similar to the formula for apportionment in contributory negligence cases. A wrongdoer may recover from any other joint wrongdoer "such an amount as the court may deem just and equitable having regard to the degree in which that other joint wrongdoer was at fault in relation to the damage suffered by the plaintiff, and to the damages awarded".[30] This departs from the English formula of contribution "having regard to the extent of [the other tortfeasor's] responsibility for the damage".[31] When the plaintiff is given judgment against joint wrongdoers, the court may order, in lieu of contribution, an apportionment of the damages payable to the plaintiff.[32] When the full amount of contribution due cannot be recovered from a wrongdoer because of insolvency or other reason, the shortfall can be reapportioned among the remaining wrongdoers.[33]

Of the cases in which the Apportionment of Damages Act has been judicially interpreted, those concerned with the apportionment formula and with parties not liable in delict (tort) to the plaintiff would have the greatest interest for common law jurisdictions. With respect to the apportionment formula, the principal "bone of contention" has been whether the proportion of damages which each party must bear is to be assessed solely with regard to blameworthiness or whether the causal significance of each party's conduct is also to be considered. In the context of negligence liability, "blameworthiness" means not moral blame but failure to meet the standard of the reasonable man (*diligens* or *bonus paterfamilias*).

Causation could not be irrelevant because blameworthy (*i.e.*

29 S. 2(6)(*b*), (12).

30 S. 2(6)(*a*).

31 Law Reform (Married Women and Tortfeasors) Act, 1935, 25 & 26 Geo. 5, c. 30, s. 6, repealed, Civil Liability (Contribution) Act, 1978, c. 47, s. 9(2) (Eng.). The formula was re-enacted in the Civil Liability (Contribution) Act, 1978, c. 47, s. 2(1) (Eng. & N.I.).

32 S. 2(8).

33 S. 2(11).

negligent) conduct logically has no bearing upon negligence liability and apportionment unless it contributed to the injury. However, under one view a court should make an apportionment solely with reference to the degree to which conduct causally linked to damage was blameworthy--that is, the degree to which the conduct deviated from that of the reasonable person in the circumstances. The other view would consider in addition the relative importance and immediacy of each party's conduct in causing the damage. If, for example, the parties departed from the reasonable man standard to an equal degree, more of the loss could be apportioned to a party whose conduct created a substantial risk of harm or directly caused it than to a party who created a smaller risk of harm, which came about only because of some intervening circumstances. Furthermore, there would be a basis for apportioning damages to strictly liable parties.[34]

In *South British Insurance Co. Ltd. v. Smit*,[35] the Appellate Division appeared to adopt the first view. This was confirmed in *Jones, N.O. v. S.A.N.T.A.M. Bpk.*[36] This position rests primarily upon the decision of the South African Parliament to direct apportionment in accordance with the "degree" of "fault" rather than in accordance with "responsibility", as in the English legislation.[37] It was adopted by courts in Rhodesia[38] when that country enacted contributory negligence legislation similar to Section 1 of the South African act.[39] Accordingly, damages are apportioned according to a comparison of each party's degree of departure from the standard of reasonable

34 See South British Insurance Co. Ltd. v. Smit, 1962 (3) S.A. 826, 833-35 (A.D.); Boberg, *Contributory Negligence and the Apportionment Act*, (1959) 76 S.A.L.J. 253; McKerron, *Reduction of Damages under the Apportionment of Damages Act*, (1962) 79 S.A.L.J. 443.

35 1962 (3) S.A. 826 (A.D.).

36 1965 (2) S.A. 542 (A.D.).

37 See pp. 192-93, *supra*. Because of this variation in language, South African decisions would not carry much authority in determining the construction of the English statutes and the many replicas enacted in the Commonwealth. They are, however, quite relevant to the construction of the negligence legislation of the common law jurisdictions of Canada, which also provides for apportionment according to the "degree" of "fault".

38 Crow v. Royal Insurance Group, 1973 (1) S.A. 579 (R); James v. Fletcher, 1972 (2) R.L.R. 451 (A.D.), 1973 (1) S.A. 687 (R.A.D.).

39 Law Reform (Contributory Negligence) Act, c. 45 (1974) (Rhod.).

prudence.[40] Causation is not considered once it is ascertained that a party's negligence was one of the causes of injury.[41]

With respect to the Apportionment of Damages Act's application to parties not liable in delict to the plaintiff, two categories should be distinguished: parties liable to the plaintiff, but not in delict; and parties not liable to the plaintiff, although personally or vicariously at fault in causing the damage. The most important group of parties liable in damages, but not in delict or tort, consists of parties liable for breach of contract. It might be desirable to apportion damages between a plaintiff and a defendant liable in contract when the plaintiff could have avoided the loss through the exercise of reasonable care. It might also be desirable to extend contribution to parties liable in contract, so that there could be contribution when damage is caused by two persons' breaches of contract or the breach of contract of one person and the negligence of another person. In *O.K. Bazaars (1929) Ltd. v. Stern and Ekermans*,[42] however, it was held that neither the contributory negligence provisions (Section 1) nor the contribution provisions (Section 2) of the Apportionment of Damages Act applied when the plaintiff's action was for breach of contract.

The court summarily rejected the defendant's contribution claim, believing that because Section 2(1) of the act defined "joint wrongdoers" as two or more persons liable in delict to a third person for the same damage, Section 2 applied only to delictual liability. It did not apply to a person sued in contract, even though the parties from whom contribution was claimed were allegedly liable in delict. The defendant's attempt to obtain apportionment on the ground of the plaintiff's contributory negligence was considered at greater length. Section 1 did not specifically refer to liability in delict. It was addressed to contributory negligence. But contributory negligence was not a defence to liability in contract. The evident intent of the legislature in Section 1 was to provide that a claim for damages not be "defeated" by contributory negligence. Contributory negligence did not "defeat" a claim based upon breach of contract. Furthermore, it

40 The judgment in Jones, N.O. v. S.A.N.T.A.M. Bpk., 1965 (2) S.A. 542, 554-55 (A.D.), rejects a suggestion in South British Insurance Co. Ltd. v. Smit that apportionment in contributory negligence cases is determined solely by the degree of the plaintiff's negligence.

41 See McKerron, 301-04, 310-11; Boberg, *Law of Delict*, 1965 Ann. Surv. S. Afr. L. 174, 180-84.

42 1976 (2) S.A. 521 (C).

was difficult to construe the term "fault" in Section 1 as encompassing breaches of contract, for a contract could be breached without fault. Section 1, therefore, did not provide for apportionment of damages in contract cases generally, nor did it extend to cases in which the alleged breach of contract consisted of negligence, *i.e.* breach of a contractual duty of care.

Parties who caused damage to the plaintiff and were at fault in doing so may be insulated from liability by a contract, statute or rule of common law. The drafters of the Apportionment of Damages Act foresaw that a person who did incur liability might claim contribution from a person protected by a contract and provided that such a claim was not maintainable.[43] The result would probably be the same if a statute or common law immunity were involved. In *Kleinhans v. African Guarantee and Indemnity Co. Ltd.*,[44] the defendant established that the plaintiff husband was at fault in causing an accident in which his wife was injured. The wife could not hold her husband liable because they were married in community of property. The court held that because the husband was not liable, he was not a joint wrongdoer and the defendant could not obtain an apportionment of damages to the husband in respect of the defendant's liability for the wife's injuries.

In South African law, prior to the Apportionment of Damages Act, the "contributory" negligence of a decedent did not defeat a negligence action by his surviving dependants and the negligence of an injured wife or child did not defeat a husband's or parent's action to recover medical expenses or compensation for loss of services. Accordingly, when the Apportionment of Damages Act was enacted, no provision for apportionment in such cases was made in Section 1. Plaintiffs could recover full damages without reduction on account of the injured person's negligence.[45] This prompted defendants to claim contribution from the injured person or his estate under Section 2. The injured persons in these circumstances constituted another category of party at fault in causing the damage but not liable to the plaintiff. A wife or child incurred no liability for negligently causing the husband or parent to bear medical expenses and a decedent's estate incurred no liability for the decedent's negligently depriving dependants of support. For this reason, as held in *Saitowitz v.*

43 S. 2(6)(*c*), s. 4(1).

44 1959 (2) S.A. 619 (E).

45 McKerron, 66-67, 83, 87, 149, 157.

Provincial Insurance Co. Ltd.,[46] the injured person could not be required under Section 2 to bear any of the defendant's liability to the third party.

In 1971, the Apportionment of Damages Act was amended to provide for contribution in such cases and in the case of spouses married in community of property.[47] The injured person is now to be treated as a joint wrongdoer under Section 2 if his injury or death (in respect of which the plaintiff claims damages) was caused partly by his own fault. A person married in community of property is to be treated as a joint wrongdoer if he would have been a joint wrongdoer but for the marriage.[48] No provision is made for reduction of the plaintiff's recovery.

Zimbabwe's legislative provisions for apportionment of damages are much simpler than South Africa's. In its original form,[49] the Zimbabwe statute established apportionment only for contributory negligence. When the plaintiff claimed damages in consequence of the death or injury of some other person, fault on the part of that person would reduce the plaintiff's recovery.[50] In 1985, the statute was amended to add provisions for contribution.[51] Wrongdoers are to pay such proportions of the damages "as the court considers just and equitable, having regard to the respective degrees of fault of the wrongdoers".[52] A wrongdoer who makes a full settlement with the plaintiff or pays a greater amount than a court would apportion to the wrongdoer has a right of contribution.[53]

46 1962 (3) S.A. 443 (W).

47 Apportionment of Damages Amendment Act, No. 58 of 1971 (S. Afr.).

48 S. 2(1A)-(1B), (6)(*a*). See Boberg, *The Apportionment of Damages Amendment Act 58 of 1971*, (1971) 88 S.A.L.J. 423, reprinted, Boberg, The Apportionment of Damages Amendment Act 58 of 1971 (1971); Boberg, *Further and Better Reflections on the Apportionment of Damages Amendment Act 1971*, (1975) 92 S.A.L.J. 330.

49 Law Reform (Contributory Negligence) Act, c. 45 (1974) (Rhod.).

50 S. 4(4).

51 Law Reform (Contributory Negligence) Amendment Act, 1985, No. 28 (Zimb.), adding ss. 5-8 to the principal act.

52 S. 5.

53 S. 7.

The process is facilitated by requiring plaintiffs to join in one action all wrongdoers responsible for the damage. A subsequent action for damages against a wrongdoer who was not joined cannot be maintained without leave of court granted for good cause. Similarly, defendants are required to give notice to wrongdoers not already in the action, who may then intervene. Without leave of court, contribution may not later be claimed from a wrongdoer not given notice.[54] Fault on the part of the person whose death or injury gave rise to the plaintiff's claim no longer causes reduction of the plaintiff's recovery.[55] Instead, as under the 1971 amendment to the South African statute, the injured person is treated as a wrongdoer.[56] Consequently, contribution can be claimed by or against that person or his estate. The Zimbabwe statute appears to contemplate that only parties liable to the plaintiff will be liable for contribution, and its definition of "fault"[57] almost certainly excludes parties whose liability is not delictual.

AVOIDABLE CONSEQUENCES

When a plaintiff could have avoided the accident in which he was injured by exercising reasonable care, the defence of contributory negligence applies. At common law, the negligent plaintiff could not recover any damages to which his negligence contributed. Under statutes such as the Apportionment of Damages Act, Section 1, contributory negligence is not a complete defence but reduces the recovery in proportion to the plaintiff's relative fault. When, after the initial injury, the plaintiff could have reduced the resulting loss or expense by reasonable means, the "duty to mitigate damages" applies. The plaintiff who has failed to mitigate damages cannot recover compensation for the avoidable loss. This is not affected by

54 S. 6.

55 S. 3(b), repealing s. 4(4) of the original statute.

56 S. 8.

57 S. 3A: "'fault' means negligence, breach of statutory duty or any other act, omission or circumstance which gives rise to delictual liability, or which would, but for the provisions of this Act, give rise to the defence of contributory negligence".

contributory negligence apportionment statutes.[58]

Falling between classic contributory negligence cases and failure-to-mitigate cases are cases in which the plaintiff was not at fault in causing the accident but failed to take reasonable steps which would have reduced the extent or severity of the injuries sustained. These cases have long been the subject of considerable uncertainty. Under common law or statutory apportionment, are they to be treated as cases of contributory negligence, failure to mitigate, or neither--in which case the plaintiff recovers to the full extent of his loss?

The first South African case to consider this matter after the Apportionment of Damages Act came into force was *King, N.O. v. Pearl Insurance Co. Ltd.*[59] The plaintiff suffered serious head injuries in a collision between a car and the motor scooter she was riding. The defendant applied to add a plea that the plaintiff was at fault in relation to her injuries in failing to wear a crash helmet or similar device and, in consequence, her recoverable damages were subject to reduction under the Apportionment of Damages Act. The plaintiff denied that the act was applicable because failure to wear a crash helmet could not have been a cause of the collision.

The court held that the act was not applicable and refused the application. It acknowledged that the language of the act--"damage which is caused partly by his own fault"[60]--was wide enough to cover the present case if failure to wear a helmet was failure to take a reasonable precaution against damage. The court was of the view, nevertheless, that only conduct constituting contributory negligence at common law was "fault" for which the act provided reduction of damages. This view was supported by the court's perception that Section 1's purpose was to abolish contributory negligence as a complete defence and its definition of "fault"[61] did not go beyond an act or omission that would have given rise to the defence of contributory negligence.

The court believed that an act or omission which contributed

58 Fleming, 226-27; McGregor, Damages, para. 89 (14th ed. 1980); Street, 436-37.

59 1970 (1) S.A. 462 (W).

60 Apportionment of Damages Act, No. 34 of 1956, s. 1(1)(*a*) (S. Afr.).

61 S. 1(3): "For the purposes of this section 'fault' includes any act or omission which would, but for the provisions of this section, have given rise to the defence of contributory negligence."

only to the *quantum* of damage flowing from an event did not constitute contributory negligence, only an act or omission that was a cause of the event itself. Failure to wear a crash helmet was not a cause of the event (the collision). Therefore it was not contributory negligence. Because it was not contributory negligence, it could not be the basis for reducing the plaintiff's damages under the Apportionment of Damages Act. The judgment does not consider whether the plaintiff could be denied damages for the harm from which she would have been protected by a crash helmet on the basis of "failure to mitigate damages" or "avoidable consequences".[62]

This judgment has received criticism[63]--primarily for its premiss that an act or omission which contributed to the *quantum* of damage but was not a cause of the harmful event is not contributory negligence. It has been pointed out that negligence liability and the defence of contributory negligence depend upon the foreseeability and causation of damage, not an event or accident. This provides a basis for dividing the plaintiff's injuries between those which would have been avoided had the plaintiff taken a reasonable precaution, such as wearing a helmet, and those which would not have been avoided, and for treating the plaintiff as contributorily negligent with respect to the avoidable injuries. The judgment has also been criticised for its statement that

> If [the defendant's] contention is sound, it will presumably be open to a man who has negliently set fire to his neighbour's building to escape liability for part of the consequent loss by alleging and proving that his neighbour was not prudent enough to install fire extinguishers in the building; and perhaps the burglar who has stolen and sold

62 See Linden, 483-84; Prosser & Keeton, 458-59; Tager, *Safety Accessories--Should They Affect Apportionment?*, (1970) 87 S.A.L.J. 156. "Avoidable consequences" seems to be the best label for injuries which could have been avoided by such pre-accident precautions as wearing a helmet or seat belt. It can also be used to include losses avoidable by mitigation after the accident.

63 Boberg, *Law of Delict*, 1970 Ann. Surv. S. Afr. L. 155, 174-79; Lang, *Contributory Negligence and the Duty to Mitigate--the Decisions in King v. Pearl Assurance and Bowker's Park Komga Co-operative Ltd. v. S.A.R. & H. Re-examined*, 1981 Obiter 36. See also Vorster v. A.A. Mutual Insurance Association Ltd., 1982 (1) S.A. 145, 156-65 (T). But see Amicus Curiae, *Contributory Negligence and the Crash Helmet*, (1972) 89 S.A.L.J. 236, approving the result of not reducing the damages recoverable.

> scrip will be allowed to invoke the Apportionment of Damages Act to reduce his liability by showing that the plaintiff was at fault, within the meaning of the Act, by not keeping his scrip in a locked safe. The fraudulent company director may be heard to say, perhaps, in answer to part of a claim for damages against him, that a prudent board of directors would have kept a closer check upon his depredations and stopped them at an earlier stage.[64]

The examples of the burglar and company director are not in point, as their wrongs are intentional, not negligent. The example of the fire is in point, but why should the building owner not bear part of the avoidable loss if the reasonable man in his position would have installed extinguishers?

This hypothetical fire case foreshadowed *Bowkers Park Komga Co-operative Ltd. v. South African Railways and Harbours.*[65] In this case, the plaintiff claimed to have suffered damage from a fire which was started by one of the defendant's locomotive engines, ignited on the defendant's property, and then spread to the plaintiff's adjoining property. The defendant alleged that damage was due in part to the plaintiff's failure to keep the area near its boundary with the plaintiff free of grass and other vegetation--a fire hazard which resulted in the fire spreading from the defendant's land to the plaintiff's. The defendant alleged further that the plaintiff took "control" of the fire before it spread from the defendant's property and then failed to properly extinguish it or prevent its spreading to the plaintiff's property. How the plaintiff took control was not specified. The parties were at issue over whether the plaintiff's conduct, if proved, would constitute "fault" and be a ground for reduction of the plaintiff's damages under the Apportionment of Damages Act, Section 1.

The plaintiff relied upon the judgment in *King, N.O. v. Pearl Insurance Co. Ltd.* But for that judgment, with its emphasis on what caused the "event" in which damage was sustained, at least the last of the defendant's allegations (the plaintiff's failure to properly extinguish the fire after taking control of it while it was on the defendant's property) would appear to present contributory negligence in its traditional form. The court in *Bowkers Park* drew no

64 King, N.O. v. Pearl Assurance Co. Ltd., 1970 (1) S.A. 462, 464 (W).

65 1980 (1) S.A. 91 (E). See Boberg, *Multiple Causation, Contributory Negligence, Mitigation of Damages, and the Relevance of These to the Failure to Wear a Seat Belt*, (1980) 97 S.A.L.J. 204.

distinction between this and the plaintiff's alleged failure to keep its land free of inflammable grass and vegetation. It rejected the reasoning in *King* and held that the plaintiff's alleged conduct constituted "fault" for which recovery could be reduced if it was negligent, *i.e.* deficient under the reasonable man standard.

In essence the court rejected the proposition that conduct must be a cause of the "event" to constitute contributory negligence and accepted that it was causation of "damage" that mattered. It emphasised the references to "damage" in Section 1(1)(*a*) of the Apportionment of Damages Act:

> Where any person suffers damage which is caused partly by his own fault and partly by the fault of any other person, a claim in respect of that damage shall not be defeated by reason of the fault of the claimant but the damages recoverable in respect thereof shall be reduced . . . .

and the equation of "fault" with a negligent act or omission causally linked with damage in *South British Insurance Co. Ltd. v. Smit.*[66] In the court's opinion, contributory negligence might exist when the plaintiff's conduct was a cause of damage but not the event which caused it, and the Apportionment of Damages Act's definition of "fault"[67] did not exclude negligence causally connected with damage even if not strictly "contributory negligence". The judgment cites with apparent approval American authorities[68] to the effect that the court may make an apportionment between the damage which would have been suffered had the plaintiff not been negligent and the increased damage of which the plaintiff's negligence was a cause. The basis of such an apportionment is that the negligence is a cause of the increased damage but not of the damage which would have occurred in any event. The court did not specify how this apportionment would work in conjunction with the statutory apportionment of damages in proportion to fault.

If followed, the judgment in *Bowkers Park* was most likely to be applied not to fires but to traffic accidents in which injuries would

66 1962 (3) S.A. 826, 835-36 (A.D.).

67 S. 1(3), quoted in note 61, *supra*.

68 Restatement (Second) of Torts, s. 465, comment *c* (1965); Prosser, Law of Torts 433 (3d ed. 1964).

have been reduced by the use of a crash helmet or seat belt. This occurred in *Vorster v. A.A. Mutual Insurance Association Ltd.*[69] In *Vorster*, the plaintiff wife was injured while a passenger in a car driven by her husband. The car collided with a vehicle insured by the defendant. The driver of that vehicle was solely to blame for the collision. The wife's general damages amounted to R4000: R3000 for a foot injury and R1000 for other injuries that would have been avoided had she been wearing a seat belt. The husband paid R230,43 for the wife's medical expenses. The defendant sought reduction of the wife's damages on the ground that failure to wear a seat belt was "fault" under the Apportionment of Damages Act, Section 1.

The court first reached the conclusion that it always was negligent for a front-seat passenger in a car fitted with a seat belt not to use it. This conclusion was supported by the frequency of traffic accidents, the effects of seat belts in preventing and reducing injuries, the ease with which they are used, and recent legislation making it compulsory to wear them. The court then decided that failure to use a seat belt was "fault" and damages were to be reduced when not using a seat belt was a cause of injury--that is, when some of the injuries would have been avoided had the seat belt been worn. It endorsed the reasoning of the judgment in *Bowkers Park Komga Co-operative Ltd. v. South African Railways and Harbours* and amplified that judgment's criticism of *King, N.O. v. Pearl Insurance Co. Ltd.*

The court was of the opinion that only the R1000 of the wife's damages attributable to non-use of the seat belt was subject to reduction. The Apportionment of Damages Act did not expressly authorise reduction of only a part of a plaintiff's damages, but the court found no reason why this should not be done. It followed the English Court of Appeal[70] in regarding the unbuckled passenger as bearing a relatively small and somewhat standardised proportion of blame for the avoidable injuries in comparison with the negligent driver. Accordingly, the wife's R4000 damages were reduced by twenty per cent (R200) of the R1000 which use of a seat belt would have saved. Her husband recovered damages for payment of the wife's medical expenses without any reduction.[71]

69 1982 (1) S.A. 145 (T).

70 Froom v. Butcher, [1976] Q.B. 286 (C.A.).

71 The judgment indicates that the husband's claim would have been apportioned and reduced on the same basis as the wife's if the defendant had raised the

The "seat belt defence" eventually came before the Appellate Division in *Union National South British Insurance Co. Ltd. v. Vitoria.*[72] The plaintiff, a passenger in the front seat of a motor car, was injured when that car collided with another. The collision was caused wholly by the negligence of the driver of the second vehicle. The plaintiff's head struck the windscreen, causing extensive lacerations. She was not wearing the "lap belt" fitted to her seat. Had the belt been worn, the plaintiff probably would not have been propelled against the windscreen and suffered the lacerations. At most, her head would have struck the car's dashboard. There was no evidence of what injury this would have caused.

The trial court[73] had held that the plaintiff's failure to use the seat belt was not negligent:

> more often than not, [motor collisions] are caused by the careless and inconsiderate manner in which the motor cars involved are driven . . . . By applying his mind to his driving and by taking such precautions as the occasion demands, a reasonable man will expect little else than the enjoyment of a long and happy driving career. Should his passenger view his chances of reaching the end of their journey in safety more gloomily? When travelling with a competent and careful driver, the risk of becoming involved in a collision becomes so remote that . . . a reasonable man would not consider such a possibility as a real and likely one, unless the circumstances prove otherwise.[74]

It followed that the plaintiff had not acted without reasonable care and no question of applying Section 1 of the Apportionment of Damages Act arose.

The Appellate Division could not agree with this optimistic view. The reality was that large numbers of deaths and injuries were

matter. The *bonus paterfamilias* would, if the driver, advise his passengers to wear seat belts as well as wear one himself.

72 1982 (1) S.A. 444 (A.D.). See 1 Boberg, 436-39.

73 Vitoria v. Union National South British Insurance Co. Ltd., 1980 (4) S.A. 406 (T), aff'd, 1982 (1) S.A. 444 (A.D.).

74 *Ibid.*, 407. The "circumstances" referred to included the density of traffic, the behaviour of drivers on the road and other traffic conditions.

occurring in traffic accidents. Public policy demanded that passengers and pedestrians, as well as drivers, act carefully in order to avoid injury in such accidents. There would then be fewer injuries and a lower amount of damages payable, to the benefit of the community in general and insured motorists in particular. The use of seat belts was not compulsory at the time of the accident, but the plaintiff reasonably should have worn the seat belt, which could be used immediately and easily. She should have foreseen that the car in which she was riding could be involved in an accident and realised that the belt could protect her from certain injuries. Seat belts reduced the risk of injuries, according to findings of the trial court, and the advantages of the lap belt available to the plaintiff were greater than its disadvantages. The plaintiff would probably have hit her head on the dashboard, but lap belts prevented passengers from going through the windscreen or out of the door. Depending upon the construction of the dashboard, striking it might not have caused serious injury.

The Appellate Division's decision that the plaintiff was not reasonably careful for her safety required it also to decide whether she had been at "fault" for purposes of the Apportionment of Damages Act, Section 1. Its conclusion was "yes". "Fault" (and contributory negligence) was not limited to conduct which contributed to causing the accident or event in which damage was suffered. It could consist of failure to avoid consequential damage or loss by the exercise of reasonable care. The general principle of Section 1(1) (the principal apportionment provision) was that any blameworthy act or omission which contributed to the damage must be taken into account in determining the amount of damages recoverable. Contrary to what was said in *King, N.O. v. Pearl Insurance Co. Ltd.*,[75] the description of "fault" in Section 1(3)[76] did not limit the content of "fault" as meant in Section 1(1).

The plaintiff's damages, therefore, were subject to reduction in accordance with her degree of fault in relation to the damage she sustained. The court proceeded to consider apportionment of fault in "seat belt" cases. It was of the opinion that the fault of a driver whose negligence caused an accident was of a different type than the fault of a passenger who failed to use a seat belt and thereby avoid certain damage flowing from the accident. The fault of the

75 1970 (1) S.A. 462, 466-67 (W).

76 See note 61, *supra*, and accompanying text.

former was much greater than the fault of the latter. Also, the fault of a person who intentionally refused to use a seat belt was greater than the fault of a person who truly forgot to use one.

The judgment states that the fault of the average driver or passenger who forgets to wear a seat belt probably remains constant in most cases. But it refuses to follow the Court of Appeal's decision in *Froom v. Butcher*[77] that there should be a standard twenty-five per cent reduction of damages if use of the seat belt would have entirely prevented the injuries and fifteen per cent if the injuries would have been much less severe. However difficult it might be, it was necessary to determine the fault of the plaintiff and defendant in each case, whenever it was proved that the plaintiff suffered more damage on account of his omission. Only then could the plaintiff's claim be reduced in a just and equitable manner. The court seems to have contemplated that only the damages for injuries avoidable by use of the seat belt, not damages for all of the plaintiff's personal injuries, would be reduced in proportion to the plaintiff's fault. However, it was less than explicit on this point.

Ultimately, it was held that the plaintiff's damages in this case were not to be reduced at all. The court placed upon the defendant the burden of proving that the plaintiff's injuries were more severe than if the seat belt had been worn. The defendant had failed to discharge this burden, even though the plaintiff admitted that the seat belt probably would have prevented her facial injuries. Wearing a lap belt, the plaintiff probably would have hit her head against the dashboard. There was no evidence of what injuries this would have caused. The defendant failed to prove the facts necessary to reduction of the plaintiff's damages on account of her failure to use the belt.

It is submitted that the Appellate Division's treatment of the "seat belt defence" in this case is correct, assuming that apportionment of fault and consequential reduction of damages apply only to the injuries the passenger would have avoided had the seat belt been used. One expects that unreasonable failure to take other precautions against injury in an accident, such as use of a crash helmet while riding a motorcycle, would be treated in a similar manner. The element of the *Vitoria* case which may be most difficult to accept is the decision that there is no reduction of damages unless the defendant can prove that the passenger's injuries would have been less severe had the seat belt been used. This is especially difficult

77 [1976] Q.B. 286 (C.A.).

to accept when it has been established (as in the *Vitoria* case) that the plaintiff would not have suffered the same type of injuries.

Presumably, the defendant would have to prove not only that the injuries would have been less severe than those actually sustained, but also approximately how much less severe. Otherwise, the defendant could not establish that the plaintiff's damages ought to be reduced by a certain amount.[78] Generally, the plaintiff carries the burden of proof on the question of damages. The doctrine of mitigation of damages, in which the defendant carries the burden of proof, is not properly applicable to "seat belt" cases.[79] But the defendant carries the burden of proving contributory negligence ("fault" under the apportionment legislation). This requires not only proof that the plaintiff was negligent (acted without reasonable care) but also that this negligence was contributory--that is, a cause of the loss for which the plaintiff claims damages. If the defendant must prove that the plaintiff's negligence was contributory, it is for the defendant to prove that there is a loss to which the plaintiff's negligence contributed and to identify this loss. It is therefore appropriate to require the defendant to prove the avoidable loss in "seat belt" and analogous cases.

78 But see Boberg, *The Seat-Belt Saga*, (1982) 11 Businessman's Law 94, 96. His interpretation is that the defendant does not have the *onus* of establishing the extent of the preventable injuries. The plaintiff's injuries are regarded as indivisible unless the plaintiff proves them divisible. Therefore, once the defendant proves that some injuries were preventable by use of a seat belt, damages in respect of the entirety of the plaintiff's injuries are reduced in proportion to the plaintiff's fault unless the plaintiff can prove what portion of the injuries would have been suffered in any event.

79 See Charlesworth & Percy, Negligence, para. 5-44 (7th ed. 1983). Failure to use a seat belt, crash helmet, etc., is not failure to mitigate damages because the person concerned has not already been injured and has not made a decision to sustain loss rather than take reasonable preventive measures. When a plaintiff fails to mitigate, the loss suffered as a consequence should be attributed to the plaintiff's decision, not the defendant's wrongful act, and the plaintiff should recover no damages for it. When a plaintiff has unreasonably failed to take a safety precaution in advance of injury, the injury should be attributed to both the plaintiff's omission and the defendant's conduct and there should be apportionment under contributory negligence legislation. A contrary position is taken in Buchanan, *Apportionment of Damages and Fault*, (1982) 99 S.A.L.J. 209. See also Lang, *Contributory Negligence and the Duty to Mitigate--the Decisions in King v. Pearl Assurance and Bowker's Park Komga Co-operative Ltd. v. S.A.R. & H. Re-examined*, 1981 Obiter 36, 48-50 (contributory negligence and failure to mitigate should be governed by same rules).

8

VICARIOUS LIABILITY

Vicarious liability in Southern Africa closely resembles vicarious liability in common law jurisdictions. A decision on whether a person is vicariously liable for injury caused by another typically rests upon the facts of the particular case, but decisions in the following cases have precedential value.

EXISTENCE OF MASTER-SERVANT RELATIONSHIP

In *Goldberg v. Durban City Council,*[1] the plaintiff had been arrested after she failed to respond in court to summonses for traffic offences. She did not appear because she had never been served with the summonses. She was arrested and detained because the process server falsely stated that the summonses had been served. The process server (an off-duty traffic policeman) was liable for unlawful arrest. The plaintiff sought to hold the city council, which prosecuted the traffic offences, vicariously liable.

The council had entered into a written contract with the process server entitled "Contract for the Appointment of Persons to Serve Summonses in Criminal Cases on Behalf of the City Council". One clause provided that, "The contractor hereby acknowledges that he is an independent contractor and not the servant or agent of the Council which is in no way liable for any acts or omissions by the contractor." The court held, nevertheless, that the process server was the council's servant because of the degree of control the council

1 1970 (3) S.A. 325 (N).

exercised over the manner in which he was to perform his work.

The contract contained detailed instructions. The process server was obliged to receive all summonses delivered to him by the chief constable (they were not to be collected from the clerk of the court), he was to serve the summonses without delay between 6 a.m. and 9 p.m., and he could not delegate his duties. He was required to serve all summonses personally (rather than in another manner permitted by law), informing the recipient of the "nature and exigency of the summons", make a full and accurate account of all necessary particulars, and return all summonses and particulars to the chief constable (rather the clerk of the court) as soon as practicable. All that was left to the process server's discretion was the order in which summonses in a batch would be served and the time (when not on duty as a traffic officer) at which service would be effected--matters in which it would be difficult for the council to exercise direct control.

In *Rodrigues v. Alves*,[2] the defendants were members of a partnership which operated a vegetable farm. A fire spread from their farm to the plaintiffs' and caused loss for which the plaintiffs claimed damages. The man who started the fire was a former partner who, having nothing else to occupy himself, decided to perform work on the farm (primarily supervising the labourers) without compensation. This was of assistance to the partners and done with their knowledge and consent. The Appellate Division held that the partners had such a power or right of control over the work the former partner did that they were vicariously liable for his acts. It was not necessary to vicarious liability that the actor be controlled in the detailed manner in which the work was to be performed or deprived of all discretion. The partners had the right to control the manner in which the former partner worked on their farm and he was about their business when he started the fire. They were, therefore, liable for the damage the fire caused.

In *Bennetto v. Vryburg Municipality*,[3] the plaintiff's aircraft was damaged at an aerodrome owned by the defendant. The plaintiff was a student pilot being taught by a qualified instructor. After the plaintiff landed the aircraft at the aerodrome, the instructor took over the controls. While taxiing the aircraft's nose wheel fell into a hole that had been dug by meerkats. The defendant raised as a defence

2 1978 (4) S.A. 834 (A.D.).

3 1980 (2) S.A. 84 (N.C.). See Cheadle, *Industrial Law (Including Law of Master and Servant)*, 1980 Ann. Surv. S. Afr. L. 363, 378-79.

that the instructor was negligent and acting as the plaintiff's servant. The court held that the instructor was negligent in not obtaining information about conditions at the aerodrome before the flight, but he was not the servant of the plaintiff. The instructor, not the plaintiff, was in control of the training flight. The plaintiff's ability to decide the time and destination of training flights did not give him such control as to render the instructor his servant.

Orphanides v. Stratton (1)[4] arose from a collision between a car and another car being towed by a lorry. The court found that the collision and the death of a passenger in the first car (for which damages were claimed) were caused by negligence on the part of both the lorry driver, who was employed by the first defendant, and the towed car's driver, who was hired by the third defendant to drive the car before it broke down. The court applied the "borrowed servant" doctrine and held that neither the third defendant nor his employer (the second defendant) were liable for the negligence of the towed car's driver. When the tow was arranged, nothing was said to the third defendant about using his driver. It was the lorry driver who decided how the car would be towed, gave directions to the car driver, and to a substantial extent controlled the movement of the car while it was under tow. His control was such that the towed car's driver became the servant of the lorry driver or the lorry driver's employer. The car driver had left the service of the second and third defendants when the accident occurred.

NON-SERVANT PERFORMING TASK FOR ANOTHER

In *Boucher v. Du Toit*,[5] a car was stopped at an intersection. Its driver asked his passenger to remove a leaf or leaves from the windscreen. In response to this request, the passenger opened the door next to him. A motor scooter immediately collided with the door. The car driver sued the rider of the motor scooter for the damage to the car. The defendant contended that the passenger was negligent in opening the door, and the plaintiff was vicariously responsible for this negligence because the passenger had acted at the request and for the benefit of the plaintiff.

4 1952 S.R. 117.

5 1978 (3) S.A. 965 (O).

The court held that there was no vicarious responsibility in this situation. The car driver did not have a "right to control" over his passenger's conduct--applying the test often used to determine the existence of an employer-employee relationship. The driver and passenger did not contemplate that the former would have a right of control over the latter's opening the door, and opening the door was not an act which the passenger normally would be able to perform only with the driver's leave. The court found no policy considerations supporting the existence of vicarious responsibility, believing vicarious liability to be an undesirable consequence of a person's directing a "social request" to another. This is supported by various examples, involving persons who caused damage while driving a vehicle, closing a window or pouring a glass of wine, at the request and for the benefit of another person.

The example of driving a vehicle at another's request was drawn upon by the court in *Braamfontein Food Centre v. Blake*.[6] There, the defendant's proprietor wished to have a truck belonging to the defendant driven to the proprietor's home for a purpose of the defendant. Someone who was not the defendant's employee offered to do this. During the journey the truck driver was preceded by the proprietor in his car, so as to guide the truck driver to the proprietor's home. The plaintiff's vehicle was damaged in a collision caused by the truck driver's negligence.

The court held that the defendant was not liable. It quoted the assertions in *Boucher v. Du Toit*[7] that a right of control could not be found merely because a person drove a vehicle at the request and on behalf of another and that there was no justification for imputing negligence for this reason. The court then concluded that when there was no master-servant relationship, it was necessary that a person have had power to control the manner of driving in order to be held vicariously responsible for negligent driving. This was found not to exist in the present case. The proprietor's power to determine the route and the approximate speed of the journey did not amount to the control necessary to vicarious liability. It was doubted that such liability could exist when the person sought to be held responsible was not actually in the vehicle.

6 1982 (3) S.A. 248 (T).

7 1978 (3) S.A. 965, 973, 974-75 (O).

STATE SERVANT[8]

The leading cases on the delictual liability of the State for the wrongs of its servants involve members of the South African Police. They reflect a distinct trend toward the limitation and elimination of doctrines by which the State might avoid incurring vicarious liability for delicts committed by policemen while engaged in police work or even purportedly engaged in such work.

In *Sibiya v. Swart, N.O.*,[9] a constable assaulted a person whom he had arrested and was to take to the charge office. The victim sought damages from the Crown as well as from the constable. The Transvaal Provincial Division was of the opinion that if making the arrest was an act done in the course of the constable's employment as a Crown servant, the Crown was vicariously liable. The assaults would then be associated with the constable's performance of his duties *vis-à-vis* his employer. But in making the arrest the constable was carrying out a statutory duty, not acting as the agent or servant of his employer. Consequently, the Crown was not liable.

The Appellate Division disagreed.[10] The Crown was not liable if a police officer was performing a duty of a personal nature which made him independent of the Crown's control, but the mere fact that he was performing a statutory duty did not exclude vicarious liability. If it did there would be no vicarious liability, for example, when injury was caused by negligently driving a police van conveying an arrestee to the charge office. A policeman is engaged to perform duties of statutory law as well as duties entrusted to him by superior officers. In both he is under the control and subject to the commands of his employer, the Crown, and is a Crown servant. Here, the constable was acting as a Crown servant. He was not performing a duty of a personal nature and he was bound to take the plaintiff to a police station or charge office, so nothing depended upon any

8 The State Liability Act, No. 20 of 1957, s. 1 (S. Afr.), provides that "Any claim against the State which would, if that claim had arisen against a person, be the ground of an action in any competent court, shall be cognizable by such court, whether the claim arises out of any contract lawfully entered into on behalf of the State or out of any wrong committed by any servant of the State acting in his capacity and within the scope of his authority as such servant." Proceedings are to be taken against the minister of the State department concerned. S. 2.

9 1950 (2) S.A. 752 (T), rev'd, 1950 (4) S.A. 515 (A.D.).

10 Sibiya v. Swart, N.O., 1950 (4) S.A. 515 (A.D.).

discretion of his own. The Crown was, therefore, liable for the assaults the constable committed.

Neither court explained why an assault upon a person in custody should be regarded as within the scope of a policeman's employment. A rationale is included in the judgment in *Dladla v. Minister of Police.*[11] There, policemen assaulted the plaintiff in an attempt to elicit information about an armed robbery. Because the police were conducting a criminal investigation, seeking to elicit evidence which would facilitate prosecution of criminals, they were in the court's opinion "about their master's business" and within the scope of their employment. The assaults were a wrongful method of doing what the police were employed to do. That an act was unlawful, unauthorised or forbidden by the employer did not necessarily mean that it was outside the scope of employment. The doctrine that a policeman's employer is not liable when a policeman carries out a legal duty of a personal nature did not apply. When the assaults occurred, the police were not engaged in such a duty. They did not have such personal discretion in their conduct as to be independent of the control of their superiors. The State was liable for the assaults the plaintiff suffered.

In *Mhlongo v. Minister of Police,*[12] a policeman fired his pistol in an attempt to stop and arrest a man observed stealing something from a car. The bullet fatally injured the plaintiff's husband. It was accepted that the policeman acted negligently. The trial court held that the State was not vicariously liable. It regarded the policeman's acts in attempting to make the arrest as acts of a personal nature in which he had to exercise his discretion and did not perform as a servant of the State. The authority to make a warrantless arrest was conferred by statute. The statute regulated the manner in which an arrest could be made. A superior could not lawfully order the policeman to make an arrest that could not be brought within the statute's provisions.

The Appellate Division reversed.[13] In its view, the State is liable for a policeman's wrongful act unless the policeman was

11 1973 (2) S.A. 714 (W).

12 1977 (2) S.A. 800 (T), rev'd, 1978 (2) S.A. 551 (A.D.). See Aronstam, *State Liability*, (1978) 95 S.A.L.J. 26.

13 Mhlongo v. Minister of Police, 1978 (2) S.A. 551 (A.D.). See Forsyth, *The Liability of the State for the Delicts of the Police: A Step in the Right Direction*, (1979) 96 S.A.L.J. 12.

engaged in a duty or function personal to the policeman--personal in the sense that the State had no power to direct or control him in carrying out the duty or function. Only this takes a policeman "out of the category of servant *pro hac vice*". The State is liable when it has the power to direct or control a policeman in the execution of his duty or function, including the exercise of discretion. There was "much to be said" for the view that the decision of the policeman to arrest without warrant is "a function over which his employer, the State, has no power of direction or control". But the methods employed or action taken to effect an arrest were matters over which a policeman's superiors could and should exercise discretion and control. This was true in particular of the use of firearms. Policemen received training and instructions in their use. The policeman in this case apparently violated an instruction that a firearm may be discharged in a street to stop a fugitive offender only when this would not endanger the safety of other persons in the street. The statute which conferred the power of arrest did not regulate generally the conduct of a policeman in making an arrest or his duties to third persons in the vicinity and did not confer upon him a general discretion in this regard. The policeman fired his pistol in his capacity as a State servant and the State was liable for the resulting damages. The court left open the question of the State's liability when a policeman acts on the orders of his superior in making a warrantless arrest.

A policeman on duty generally makes an arrest because of his employment as a policeman, and it would seem that a policeman's superiors do have the power to direct or control a policeman's decision to undertake or not undertake a lawful arrest. It was, therefore, open to question whether the policeman's decision was "a function over which his employer, the State, has no power of direction or control" and whether a distinction between the decision to arrest and the method of arrest could be sustained.[14]

In *Minister van Polisie v. Gamble*,[15] the Appellate Division

14 See Naidoo v. Minister van Polisie, 1976 (4) S.A. 954 (T); Burchell, *Law of Delict*, 1978 Ann. Surv. S. Afr. L. 237, 269-71; Forsyth, *The Liability of the State for the Delicts of the Police: A Step in the Right Direction*, (1979) 96 S.A.L.J. 12.

15 1979 (4) S.A. 759 (A.D.). See Burchell, *Minister van Polisie v. Gamble*, (1980) 43 T.H.R.-H.R. 206; Forsyth, *State Liability for the Delicts of the Police: A Further and Better Step in the Right Direction*, (1980) 97 S.A.L.J. 207.

decided that "the State as employer is indeed vicariously liable for a wrongful arrest made by a police officer, acting in his capacity as such, within the scope of his employment, ie when he is about police business".[16] A police officer, when about police business, was always under the command, supervision and control of his seniors and thus under the control of the State. He remained an employee or servant of the State while exercising a statutory discretion within the scope of his employment. The court rejected the proposition that when making an arrest a policeman carried out a "personal duty". The State having accepted liability for a wrong "committed by any servant of the State acting in his capacity and within the scope of his authority as such servant"[17] (that is, within the scope of his employment), there was no reason why the State as employer could not be held vicariously liable for wrongful arrest. It followed from a finding that a constable made an unlawful arrest while acting as a police officer that the State incurred liability to the arrested person.[18]

CONDUCT WITH NON-EMPLOYMENT PURPOSE

Courts in Southern Africa have repeatedly held that an employer is not vicariously liable for damage when an employee, while engaged in the employer's work, does an act in pursuit of a personal purpose of the employee, not the master's business. This is illustrated by the following cases:

> *South British Insurance Company v. du Toit*,[19] in which a fire was caused by the defendant's servants bringing, for some purpose of their own, an open tin of petrol into a room occupied by the defendant and left in charge of his servants.
>
> *Carter & Co. (Pty.) Ltd. v. McDonald*,[20] in which the

16 Minister van Polisie v. Gamble, 1979 (4) S.A. 759, 768 (A.D.) (translation).

17 State Liability Act, No. 20 of 1957, s. 1 (S. Afr.).

18 Also important to State liability for the delicts of police officers is Minister of Police v. Rabie, 1986 (1) S.A. 117 (A.D.), discussed pp. 220-26, *infra*.

19 1952 S.R. 239, 1952 (4) S.A. 313 (S.R.).

20 1955 (1) S.A. 202 (A.D.).

defendant's employee was allowed to briefly leave work to do shopping, travelling to and from the market with the bicycle he used to make deliveries for the defendant; on the return journey the employee collided with the plaintiff. That the employee had been permitted to use the bicycle and was hurrying to return to work did not bring his use of the bicycle within the scope of his employment.

Dolf v. Heath,[21] in which the defendant's pay clerk, loading a revolver in connection with his duties, capriciously played with the revolver and pointed it at the plaintiff "to see if it would shoot"; it would and did.

Meyer v. Jackelson,[22] in which damage was caused by the defendant's farm labourers lighting a fire, contrary to the defendant's direct instructions, while they were engaged in their work; the fire was probably lit to cook meat, but in any event it was not shown to have been done in the employer's work.[23]

H.K. Manufacturing Co. (Pty.) Ltd. v. Sadowitz,[24] in which water seeped into the plaintiff's premises after one of the defendant's employees failed to completely turn off a wash basin tap; the tap had been used by the employee to obtain a drink of water or to wash her hands. This was regarded as a personal act not incidental to employment.

When an employee driving a vehicle on the employer's business conveys an unauthorised passenger, who is then injured in an accident caused by the employee's negligence, a court may decide that the employer is vicariously liable to the passenger because the employee's driving was within the course of his employment. Alternatively, a court may decide that the employer is not vicariously liable because the employee's conveyance of the passenger was not done in furtherance of the employer's business and therefore was

21 1959 (1) S.A. 714 (E).

22 1961 (3) S.A. 165 (T).

23 Boberg, *Law of Delict*, 1961 Ann. Surv. S. Afr. L. 187, 215-18, contends that there should have been liability on the basis that the labourers were negligent in failing to extinguish the fire and this negligence was in the course of their employment.

24 1965 (3) S.A. 328 (C).

outside the course of employment.[25] The latter position was adopted in *Rossouw v. Central News Agency, Ltd.*[26] and *Magage v. Murray & Stewart (Edms.) Bpk.*[27] For similar reasons, the Appellate Division held in *South African Railways and Harbours v. Marais*[28] that the railway administration was not liable for the death of a passenger in a train derailment caused by excessive speed. The passenger had been allowed by the train's driver to ride in the engine, contrary to instructions given the driver. The passenger would not have been killed had he remained in the coach where he belonged.

From the foregoing, one might have expected the court in *Barker v. Venter*[29] to hold that the employer was not vicariously liable, but the court decided the opposite. In this case, the defendant employed a man whose principal duty was to take care of sheep on the defendant's farm, but who also looked after cattle and generally kept an eye on the farm for the defendant, who lived elsewhere. Having completed one task on the farm and on the way to perform another, this labourer sat down to bask in the sun and smoke. He negligently set the grass alight, causing in dry conditions a veld fire which spread to the plaintiff's farm.

The court interpreted the case as one in which there was an improper execution of the work entrusted to the servant rather than an abandonment of his work. In support of its conclusion that the fire was started in the course of employment, the court quoted numerous judicial statements of the principles of vicarious liability. One cannot state with precision why the defendant was held liable, but it appears that the most important factors were that the servant had not completely abandoned his work for the defendant, the deviation from his duties was inconsiderable in time and space, the defendant should have foreseen that "inevitably" such a servant would smoke while about the master's business, and the risk of the harm sustained by the plaintiff was attributable to the defendant's employment of such a servant on his farm.

25 See Atiyah, Vicarious Liability in the Law of Torts 246-51 (1967); Dias & Markesinis, 309-11.

26 1948 (2) S.A. 267 (W).

27 1980 (4) S.A. 294 (O).

28 1950 (4) S.A. 610 (A.D.).

29 1953 (3) S.A. 771 (E).

In *African Guarantee & Indemnity Co. Ltd. v. Minister of Justice*,[30] the plaintiff sought damages for harm sustained in a collision between his car and a police van. The constables in the van were on patrol in the area in which the collision occurred, but the cause of the collision was the van's participation in a brief informal road race with a sports car. The Crown contended that in racing the sports car the constables were outside the scope of their employment, especially as they had not responded to radio messages to investigate complaints nearby, but the Appellate Division held that the Crown was liable.

The constables digressed from their employment but their digression, in the court's opinion, did not constitute an entire abandonment of their employment. Nor was it so great in respect of space and time that it could not be held that they were still exercising the functions for which they were appointed, which included control of the van in the patrol area. The constables were on duty during the race and subject to commands which presumably they would have obeyed, such as to act if they saw something which required immediate police action or received orders from their control station. That the constables did not immediately respond to the radio messages they had received did not constitute abandonment of their employment because the complaints apparently were not urgent and to race the sports car involved a delay of only a few minutes.

In *Ables Groceries (Pty.) Ltd. v. Di Ciccio*,[31] the plaintiff declared that the defendants were engaged to do the bookkeeping for the plaintiff's grocery business. The defendants delegated this task to an employee, de Klerk. The plaintiff's manager requested de Klerk to deposit the plaintiff's daily takings to the plaintiff's bank account. De Klerk withheld some of the takings from the deposits and kept them for himself. "As an integral part of his system of theft" de Klerk fraudulently manipulated the bookkeeping in the plaintiff's cash book so that the entries would tally with the bank deposits. The plaintiff sought to recover the amount stolen from it on the basis, *inter alia*, of vicarious liability.

The defendants naturally asserted that the fraudulent bookkeeping and theft were outside the scope of de Klerk's employment. The court was prepared to accept (although not definitely decide) that the theft was outside the scope of employment and that the plaintiff's

30 1959 (2) S.A. 437 (A.D.).

31 1966 (1) S.A. 834 (T).

claim would fail if it were based on the theft *per se*. But the wrongful act on which the plaintiff actually relied was the manipulation of the cash book. This could be the basis of vicarious liability, the court held, because making entries in the cash book was part of de Klerk's duties as an employee and a connection between this and the plaintiff's loss through theft had been alleged. The connection was not too remote. That de Klerk acted fraudulently, in his own interests, did not detract from the fact that he was doing his employer's work. An employer would be liable for his employee's doing fraudulently what he was authorised to do honestly. The plaintiff, therefore, stated a cause of action based upon vicarious liability.[32]

What if a policeman makes an unlawful arrest for reasons other than performance of the duties assigned to him or the duties of the police force generally? In *Minister of Police v. Rabie*,[33] the person who made the arrest was a member of the police force but his duties were those of a mechanic, repairing police vehicles during "office hours". On the evening of the arrest, this mechanic, Van der Westhuizen, attended a social function (apparently a New Year's Eve party) at the home of his ex-wife's family. He was asked to leave the function and did so after a complaint was made to the local police station. Shortly thereafter, the plaintiff walked down a nearby street. As he passed a newsagent's shop located opposite the house of Van der Westhuizen's former in-laws, Van der Westhuizen walked out from behind a tree, grabbed the plaintiff, and said "Why do you want to break in?" The plaintiff replied "I don't know what you are talking about." Van der Westhuizen's response was to say "Don't lie." and strike the plaintiff across the forehead with a wheel spanner. After identifying himself as a policeman and stating that he was taking the plaintiff to the police station, Van der Westhuizen banged the plaintiff's head against the window of the newsagent's shop and said "Did you try and break in here?" He then took the plaintiff across the street to the in-laws' house, spoke to his former wife, put

32 The court also held that the plaintiff stated an action against the defendants on the basis of personal liability for negligence. See p. 271, *infra*. The case illustrates the principle that even if the employee's wrongful act was outside the course of his employment, his employer can be held liable as personally negligent in the employment or supervision of the employee if reasonable care would have prevented harm to the plaintiff.

33 1986 (1) S.A. 117 (A.D.). See Stranex, *Liability for the Delicts of the Police: The Underwriter State*, (1986) 103 S.A.L.J. 190.

the plaintiff's hands through the window of Van der Westhuizen's car (a private vehicle), rolled up the window so as to jam the plaintiff's hands between the window and door frame, and (accompanied by his ex-wife) began to drive the car with the plaintiff dragging outside. His ex-wife persuaded Van der Westhuizen to stop. He then put the plaintiff inside the vehicle, drove to the local police station (not the station where he was employed as a mechanic), reported that the plaintiff had attempted to break the newsagent's window with a brick and wrote out a statement to this effect, which the plaintiff denied.

As a result, the plaintiff was charged with attempted housebreaking and attempted malicious damage to property. He was acquitted and claimed damages from both Van der Westhuizen and the State for assault, unlawful arrest, unlawful detention and malicious prosecution. It seemed clear that while Van der Westhuizen asserted his authority as a police officer and purported to act as a member of the police force in making the arrest and charge, he knew that the plaintiff had not attempted to break the shop window or otherwise attempt to commit a crime. Thus he had no ground for the exercise of police powers and no intention of furthering the police functions of investigation and prevention of crime or maintenance of law and order. (A warrantless arrest would have been lawful if there had been reasonable grounds for believing that the plaintiff had committed or was about to commit an offence.) It could be inferred that Van der Westhuizen acted out of frustration and anger at having been required to leave the home of his former in-laws. Having arrested and assaulted the plaintiff and taken him to the police station in the presence of witnesses, Van der Westhuizen laid a false charge in order to protect himself.[34]

Under *Minister van Polisie v. Gamble*,[35] the State was to be vicariously liable for a wrongful arrest made by a police officer, "acting in his capacity as such, within the scope of his employment, ie when he is about police business". The trial court in the *Rabie* case held that the State had incurred such liability.[36] The court appears to have concluded that the case came within the principle

34 See the analysis of the facts by Van Heerden, J.A. dissenting. Minister of Police v. Rabie, 1986 (1) S.A. 117, 124-32 (A.D.). The majority accepted this analysis for purposes of its decision.

35 1979 (4) S.A. 759 (A.D.). See pp. 215-16, *supra*.

36 Rabie v. Minister of Police, 1984 (1) S.A. 786 (W), aff'd, 1986 (1) S.A. 117 (A.D.).

expressed in *Gamble* because Van der Westhuizen ostensibly acted as a policeman exercising the police functions of investigating alleged offences and arresting, detaining and charging offenders. A police officer's duties and authority existed during the period he was off duty. That Van der Westhuizen was employed as a mechanic did not alter the result because there was no evidence that he had "police duties" any different from those of the other members of the force.

This decision was affirmed on appeal, but on a somewhat different basis. To the Appellate Division, the "cardinal question" was whether Van der Westhuizen was "acting 'in the course or scope of his employment' as a servant of the State, ie whether he was doing the State's work, viz police work, when he committed the wrongs in question".[37] His work as a mechanic was limited as to time and place, but his work as a police officer was not so circumscribed. In the absence of specific instructions to the contrary, he could embark upon the discharge of police functions. In some situations he might have a duty to do so. (Preventing the escape of a prisoner or offender was referred to.) Police functions included making an arrest, preliminary questioning of a suspect before arrest, taking the arrested person to the charge office and charging him with an alleged offence. Force could be employed in certain circumstances.

It was therefore necessary to enquire into the relationship between the acts done by Van der Westhuizen and his police functions. He identified himself as a policeman, asserted his authority as a policeman and professed to act as such. He later said that he considered himself to be on duty at the time he assaulted the plaintiff. Questioning a suspect, arresting him, taking him to the police station and charging him would normally be categorised as police work. However, it could be accepted that Van der Westhuizen knew the plaintiff was innocent and was actuated by malice and service of his own interests.

An act done by a servant solely for his own interests and purposes but occasioned by his employment might fall outside the course of the employment. In deciding whether a servant's act did so fall, some reference was to be made to the servant's intention. The test was, in this regard, subjective. But a master might be liable if there was a sufficiently close link between the servant's acts (for his own interests and purposes) and the master's business. This was an objective test. Also, according to Salmond, a master was liable

37 Minister of Police v. Rabie, 1986 (1) S.A. 117, 132 (A.D.).

for acts which had not been authorised, provided they were so connected with acts the master had authorised that they might rightly be regarded as modes, although improper modes, of doing them.[38]

The leading South African cases on the subject were mostly concerned with deviations by a servant from his duties at a time he was actually engaged in his master's work. To the Appellate Division, the tests applied in these cases did not seem wholly apposite to the instant case, in which the servant during the pursuit of his own private affairs ostensibly embarked on his master's business. It would be more apposite to proceed from the basis of vicarious liability mentioned by Watermeyer, C.J., in *Feldman (Pty.) Ltd. v. Mall*:[39]

> a master who does his work by the hand of a servant creates a risk of harm to others if the servant should prove to be negligent or inefficient or untrustworthy; that, because he has created this risk for his own ends he is under a duty to ensure that no one is injured by the servant's improper conduct or negligence in carrying on his work . . . .

Approaching the course of employment issue "from the angle of creation of risk", emphasis was shifted from the precise nature of Van der Westhuizen's intention and the precise nature of the link between his acts and police work to the question of whether those acts fell within the risk created by the State. By appointing Van der Westhuizen as a member of the force and thus clothing him with all of the powers involved, the State created a risk of harm to others. The risk was that he would be untrustworthy and abuse or misuse these powers, for his own purposes or otherwise, by unjustified arrest, excess of force constituting assault and unfounded prosecution. Van der Westhuizen's acts "f[e]ll within this purview" and "his appointment was conducive to the wrongs he committed". The Appellate Division did not find it necessary to define the limits of the State's liability in the context presented by *Minster of Police v. Rabie*. It sufficed to say that in the particular circumstances of the case and in view of the risk the State created, the State should be liable for Van der Westhuizen's wrongs.

38 Salmond & Heuston, 437.

39 1945 A.D. 733, 741.

Van Heerden, J.A., dissented. In his opinion, the trial court had erred in concluding that because Van der Westhuizen was a servant of the State, entrusted with the power of effecting arrests, he was acting as such when he arrested the plaintiff. It had lost sight of the principle that the State was liable for a policeman's act only if it was committed in the scope of his employment. Since only in exceptional cases would intentional wrongs have been authorised by the employer, the test of vicarious liability usually applied to intentional wrongs was whether the employee improperly carried out what he was employed to do or committed an act divorced from the employer's business. If harm was caused by "activities in his own affairs, unconnected with those of his master"[40] the master was not liable.

In determining whether the employee's activities were divorced from his employer's affairs, the employee's intention or motive was material. As a general rule, when the tortious act was not directed, at least partially, to furtherance of the employer's business but was done for some purpose of the employee's own having no relation to his employment, the employer was not liable. There was no vicarious liability if the employee's act was not performed for the accomplishment of an object for which he was employed but was motivated entirely by personal reasons such as malice or spite. If there was a sufficiently close connection between a capricious or wanton act and other conduct by the employee in furtherance of his employer's business, the latter might be liable. But if there was no connection, the intention with which the employee acted was generally decisive of the question of whether the wrong was committed within the scope of employment, even if the employee purported to act on behalf of his master.

There was no connection between the wrongs committed by Van der Westhuizen during his relatively brief encounter with the plaintiff and anything else he might have done in furtherance of his employer's business. He was not on duty and as a mechanic he would not normally perform ordinary police functions. The purpose for which he acted was therefore of critical importance. The arrest of and assault upon the plaintiff were activated by personal animosity engendered by anger and frustration. Van der Westhuizen then laid a trumped-up charge in order to protect himself. Although he professed to exercise police functions, he never intended to act on behalf of his employer or in furtherance of the employer's business.

40 Feldman (Pty.) Ltd. v. Mall, 1945 A.D. 733, 742 (Watermeyer, C.J.).

Van Heerden, J.A., was therefore of the opinion that the wrongs were independent acts for which the State could not be held liable.

Minister of Police v. Rabie has obvious importance to claims against the State for delicts committed by members of the police force. Applying the majority judgment of the Appellate Division, when a policeman purports to act as such and perform police functions, the State is subject to vicarious liability in all but the most exceptional cases. Cases in which a member of the police force acts ostensibly as a policeman but outside the risks associated with clothing a person with police status and powers will be few indeed. When a police officer abuses or misuses the powers conferred upon him, the State will not be able to avoid liability on the ground that the officer acted purely for personal motives without intending to serve the police functions of preventing and investigating crime, arresting and charging offenders, etc. But the decision has much wider significance. It appears to move strongly from a test of vicarious liability that emphasises the employee's purpose or motive to a test that emphasises the risks created by the employer in putting the employee in a certain position.[41] If conferring responsibilities or powers upon an employee may lead to injury to a third person, the employer can be held liable for such an injury even when the employee, in causing it, had a purpose other than service to the employer.

The Appellate Division distinguished cases in which a servant deviated from his duties during the time he was engaged in his master's work, but the "risk" approach may be applied to such cases. For example, a case like *Ables Groceries (Pty.) Ltd. v. Di Ciccio*, discussed above,[42] could be approached on the basis that to entrust a customer's bookkeeping and bank deposits to an employee carries with it the risk of embezzlement if the employee is dishonest; there should, therefore, be vicarious liability to the customer whose funds are embezzled. A case like *Dolf v. Heath*[43] could be decided on the basis that to have an employee carry a weapon presents a risk of

41 It also de-emphasises "control" as a basis of vicarious liability. See Stranex, *Liability for the Delicts of the Police: The Underwriter State*, (1986) 103 S.A.L.J. 190. But in *Rabie* and other cases in which the risk approach might be applied, the employer had at least theoretical control (power to direct the employee) in respects relevant to the risk.

42 See pp. 219-20, *supra*.

43 See p. 217, *supra*.

irresponsible or criminal use of the weapon. Permitting an employee to operate a vehicle without close supervision enables the employee to use the vehicle for personal errands or to carry unauthorised passengers (the road race in *African Guarantee & Indemnity Co. Ltd. v. Minister of Justice*[44] being a less obvious possibility). Isn't an injury sustained when a vehicle is so operated within the ambit of risk created by the employer? Whether *Minister of Police v. Rabie* will have the effect of applying the risk approach to such cases and expanding the scope of vicarious liability remains to be seen.

UNAUTHORISED CONDUCT WITH EMPLOYMENT PURPOSE

When a servant's conduct is not authorised by his employer but is intended to serve or does serve a purpose of the employer, the conduct is likely to be held to have occurred within the course of the servant's employment. But the conduct may be so far removed from the servant's authorised duties that it will be held outside the course of employment. This is considered in the following cases.

In *Sauer, N.O. v. Duursema*,[45] a postman drove a Post Office van to take mail bags from his post office to the local railway station. The van was involved in an accident with the plaintiff's car. The postman's authorised duties were to deliver mail. He did not have authority to drive a van and his superiors, who agreed to this, had no authority to appoint the postman to drive the van. The court held that driving the van was within the scope of the postman's employment. Because mail was being delivered in the van, the postman was not performing a function entirely different and independent from his authorised function. The court believed that driving the van was directly connected with the delivery of mail the postman was authorised to perform and was no more than a deviation from the authorised manner or method of performance. It distinguished the case of a servant who has no authorised delivery duties but drives a vehicle to deliver goods.[46]

44 See p. 219, *supra*.

45 1951 (2) S.A. 222 (O).

46 This distinction is not convincing. If the postman's duties were to carry mail on foot from the post office to the addressees (which was likely the case, but not specified in the judgment), they were entirely different from driving the mail van. See Schreiner, *Scope of Employment*, (1951) 68

In *Weir Investments (Pty.) Ltd. v. Paramount Motor Transport*,[47] a bus company was sued for damage caused when one of its buses crashed into a garage. The bus' conductor was driving the bus at the time. The most likely explanation of this was that the driver allowed the conductor to drive. The bus was on its normal route at the time. Another possibility was that the driver left the keys in the bus, which the conductor then started. The conductor had no authority to drive. The driver had a duty to keep control of the bus so that no one else would drive it.

The court held that the bus company was liable. The conductor, having no authority to drive the bus, was outside the course of employment. The defendant was not vicariously liable for his negligent driving. However, the driver was negligent in allowing the conductor (who was unskilled, unauthorised and unlicensed to drive the bus) to take possession of the keys. In the court's opinion, this negligence was in the course of the driver's employment whether he deliberately gave the keys to the conductor or simply left them in the bus. It was also a cause of the accident. The bus company, as the driver's employer, was therefore responsible to the plaintiffs.

The same conclusions were reached in a very similar case, *Francis Freres and Mason (Pty.) Ltd. v. Public Utility Transport Corporation Ltd.*[48] There, a bus driver allowed a mechanic's labourer to drive a bus to the company's workshop. The labourer had boarded the bus to travel to his work at the shop. During the journey, the bus ran into the entrance of the plaintiff's factory and hit two vehicles. The court held that the labourer's driving was outside the scope of his employment with the defendant because it had no relation to his functions as a mechanic's labourer. The scope of his employment was not enlarged to include driving when the driver, without authority, handed the bus over to him. However, the driver was negligent in handing over the bus to the labourer and this, held the court, was within the course of the driver's employment. It was an improper method of performing his authorised function of getting the bus to the workshop.

In *South African Railways and Harbours v. Albers*,[49] the

S.A.L.J. 244.

47 1962 (4) S.A. 589 (D).

48 1964 (3) S.A. 23 (D).

49 1977 (2) S.A. 341 (D).

defendant operated a garage business. The driver in this case was not employed by the defendant but was asked to look after the defendant's business for the morning. The defendant instructed him to receive money from customers having their vehicles serviced at the garage and to refer all requests for accident or breakdown service to a certain employee, who would go out in the defendant's truck. Despite this instruction and the fact that the defendant had previously forbidden him to use the defendant's trucks (because he lacked the necessary driver's licence and was too old), the man went out in a truck in response to a call for breakdown service. During this journey a collision occurred, for which the plaintiff claimed damages.

The court regarded the driver as a servant of the defendant but outside the course of his employment in driving the truck. Driving the truck was different in kind from anything the man was required or expected to do and had been put outside the range of his service by a "genuine prohibition". That he was about the master's business (responding to a call for service) did not necessarily mean that he was within the scope of employment. The court held, further, that the defendant was not liable on the basis that he was negligent in permitting the man left in charge of his business to take control of the truck's keys and the truck. The defendant was not negligent, for he could not be expected to foresee that the man would obtain possession of the keys (kept in an upstairs office) and, in violation of express instructions, drive the truck himself rather than telephone the employee who was supposed to drive it.

9

ASSESSMENT OF DAMAGES

PERSONAL INJURIES

The judgment in *Radebe v. Hough*[1] considers whether the plaintiff's economic, social or racial status affects the assessment of damages for pain and suffering. The plaintiff claimed damages for assault, having been shot by the defendant. The bullet wound caused severe pain for some days after the assault. The pain and discomfort had diminished over time but would never disappear completely. The trial judge awarded the plaintiff £16, stating:

> in awarding damages for pain and suffering one must take into consideration the standing of the person injured. For instance, in the case of a native, as is the plaintiff, who is earning the sum of £2 per week, I should most certainly not award the same amount for pain and suffering as I would for the same pain and suffering of a person who had more culture and, for instance, I would award a larger sum for damages in the case of an injury to a European woman than I would do for a native male, and so too in the present case, if it had been a European of some standing I would have awarded greater damages than I now propose to do . . . . I have come to the conclusion that if I award him for pain and suffering an amount equivalent

1 1949 (1) S.A. 380 (A.D.).

to two months' earnings, I would be doing justice.[2]

The plaintiff appealed against the adequacy of the award. The Appellate Division held that he should have been granted £200 for pain and suffering. The trial judge had applied an erroneous principle in assessing the damages. The "standing" of the person injured was not relevant in determining the extent of his pain and suffering.

> It may be that the learned Judge intended to convey that, even when the injury is the same, the extent of the pain and suffering varies with the standard of culture of the person injured. But even that proposition is of doubtful validity. A highly cultured man may be less sensitive to pain than his uneducated neighbour, and a robust society leader may be less sensitive to pain than a frail social nonentity. It is the physical and mental make-up of the person injured which must be considered in assessing his pain and suffering, and that make-up cannot be determined by reference to his social or cultural or financial status. Most decidedly it cannot be determined by reference to his race. If there had been evidence to support such a finding, the learned judge would have been entitled to find that the appellant was abnormally insensitive to pain. But . . . the fact the appellant is a native, earning only £2 a week, is not evidence that he is insensitive to pain.[3]

The Appellate Division believed the fact that the injured person was a "native" of small means, for whom money would have a high value, should have been excluded from consideration. It was true that compensation must sound in money and there was no relationship between pain and money which made it possible to express one in terms of the other with any certainty. But further uncertainty should not be introduced by taking into consideration the value of money to the person injured. A millionaire was not entitled to a higher award of damages for pain and suffering because money meant very little to him, and conversely a pauper was not to be prejudiced by the fact

2 *Ibid.*, 384-85.

3 *Ibid.*, 385.

that money meant a great deal to him.

In Blyth v. Van den Heever,[4] the Appellate Division approved the practice of awarding a "contingency allowance" as compensation for future losses whose occurrence is possible but not probable. The plaintiff had suffered severe damage to his arm as a result of the defendant's negligence. Doctors advised amputation of the arm but the plaintiff would not agree to it. There was a risk (assessed by one expert at ten to fifteen per cent) of future complications requiring amputation of the arm, and it was possible that the plaintiff might decide in the future that amputation was preferable to retaining the arm. There was thus a distinct possibility but not a probability that the arm would be amputated. It was uncertain not only whether this would occur but when. The time factor affected the number of prosthetic arms the plaintiff would have to purchase over his lifetime.

The judgment draws a distinction between "causation" and "quantification" of loss. The distinction is apparently that the "balance of probabilities" standard of proof is applied to causation of an injury but not assessment of losses flowing therefrom. Losses which may occur as a result of a proven injury need not be ignored in assessing damages when they are not, on balance, probable. The court did not find it necessary to express the possibility of amputation in terms of a percentage, which would then be applied to the damages incurred if the amputation took place. Instead, it awarded an amount (R3500) in respect of the costs of amputation (R9497) which would be fair in view of "the possibility and the various imponderables" involved. The same approach seems to have been applied to the plaintiff's claim for reduction of earning capacity. An amount was granted to compensate the plaintiff for his working disability and his disadvantage in the labour market should he, owing to unforeseen circumstances, be forced to give up his present occupation of farming.

The person for whom damages were claimed in *Gerke, N.O. v. Parity Insurance Co. Ltd.*[5] was injured so severely that he was unaware of his condition. The court was required to consider the basis of assessing damages for disability and reduction of life expectancy for a person never aware of the disability or loss of expectation of life. The court first stated that as the victim did not appreciate his condition, there was no mental suffering to be

4 1980 (1) S.A. 191, 224-26 (A.D.).

5 1966 (3) S.A. 484 (W).

considered. It then reviewed South African and English cases bearing upon the award of damages to a person unconscious of loss. The court identified an "objective" approach, which regarded the person unconscious of loss of amenities or shortened life expectancy as having suffered a loss for which compensation was due, and a "subjective" approach, which would award no compensation to a person unaware of the deprivation. The former had prevailed in *H. West & Son Ltd. v. Shephard.*[6]

The court adopted the "objective" approach. It decided, however, that compensation was "subjective" in that the *quantum* of damages depended upon the person's awareness. The suffering of a person aware of what he had lost would carry much heavier damages than the loss for which an unconscious person could recover. The court believed that awareness of the loss was the most important factor in assessing damages for loss of the amenities of life. Accordingly, the plaintiff was entitled to recover damages for loss of amenities and of expectation of life; but the amount[7] was small on account of the victim's unconsciousness of loss of amenities and the convention of awarding small sums for loss of life expectancy.[8]

In *de Harde v. Protea Assurance Co. Ltd.*,[9] the plaintiff sought compensation for loss incurred as a result of injuries sustained by her husband. She stated that she was "obliged" to resign her employment as a teacher in order to assist her seriously injured husband to conduct the affairs of his private company, which would "mitigate his damages". It was not alleged that the plaintiff had any legal obligation to assist her husband in this manner or that only she could provide such assistance. The plaintiff claimed as damages the difference between her salary with her husband's company and the higher salary she would have earned as a teacher.

The court upheld the defendant's exception to this claim. Not

6 [1964] A.C. 326 (H.L.).

7 R5000, of which one-fifth represented loss of expectation of life.

8 The judgment is criticised in Boberg, *Law of Delict*, 1966 Ann. Surv. S. Afr. L. 156, 172-79. The author asserts that it is illogical to allow compensation to an unconscious accident victim because awareness of loss is unnecessary, and then to award an additional sum on account of awareness. He espouses (rightly, it is submitted) the "subjective" approach, which recognises that the unconscious victim has suffered no non-pecuniary loss for which he can be compensated. See also 1 Boberg, 567-70.

9 1974 (2) S.A. 109 (E).

everyone "worse off" as the result of injury to another had an action against the person whose unlawful act caused the injury. It was the defendant and not the plaintiff who was liable to compensate the husband for his injuries. If she was worse off because of his injuries, her loss did not "lie in law at the door of the defendant" because it was not a direct consequence of his injuries. The position might have been different (although further difficulties would face the plaintiff) if it had been alleged that the husband had a legal right to demand the plaintiff's assistance and she a legal duty to provide that assistance for the upkeep of the joint household.[10]

The court noted that the husband could recover in his action the cost of paying an assistant he required because of his disability (putting aside the complicating feature that the husband's business was conducted through a company). It distinguished the plaintiff's claim for loss of earnings as too remote. The court might have added that the plaintiff's mitigation argument was misplaced. Assuming her salary as a teacher exceeded the salary of an assistant, to mitigate damages would be for the husband to hire an assistant and for the wife to remain a teacher. This would be true even if the wife would accept a lower salary as an assistant than another person.

Mitigation of damages was the basis of the court's assessment of damages for future medical expenses in *Williams v. Oosthuizen.*[11] The plaintiff claimed an amount which would cover the cost of an operation at a private clinic. The court held that only the "nominal" cost of treatment at a public hospital would be awarded because there was a public hospital which would be obliged to admit the plaintiff and would provide comparable treatment. The plaintiff's duty to mitigate damages required that he choose treatment at a public institution rather than indulge in costly private treatment at the defendant's expense.

FATAL INJURIES

In *Ongevallekommissaris v. Santam Versekeringsmaatskappy*

10 Boberg, *Law of Delict*, 1974 Ann. Surv. S. Afr. L. 156, 157-59, suggests that the plaintiff's claim would be allowable if supported by such allegations, on analogy to a husband's or father's action for medical expenses incurred as a result of injuries to his wife or child.

11 1981 (4) S.A. 182 (C).

Bpk.,[12] the defendant claimed it was not liable to the widow of a fatal accident victim because she would be in employment after her husband's death and her earnings would exceed the amount of support her husband would have provided her, had he survived. A number of South African cases had taken into account a widow's earnings or capacity to earn in assessing damages for loss of a husband's support, but the court regarded the propriety of this practice as an open question.

The court began with the premiss that a dependant's remedy in a fatal accident case was compensation for pecuniary loss sustained as a result of the death. Material losses, benefits and prospects were to be taken into account. In this regard, one started with the value of the support which the widow would have enjoyed had her husband survived, and then considered any pecuniary advantage which came to the widow from any source by reason of the death. The question, therefore, was whether the widow's earnings or earning capacity was a pecuniary advantage resulting from death.

The court, following *Carroll v. Purcell*,[13] held that it was not. A widow might choose to take employment because of her husband's death but her employment or earning capacity did not result from death. It existed during the marriage, even if the then wife chose not to exercise it. Capacity to earn was distinguishable from capacity to remarry, which was acquired only upon the husband's death and therefore was considered in assessing damages. A widow's damages were for loss of support, which was derived from the marital relationship. Loss of support was not diminished because she could create other sources of revenue, which did not constitute support. A widow's earnings were not to be considered on the basis of the duty to mitigate damages. A duty to mitigate by seeking employment could arise only if the prospective earnings were relevant to the loss, which in the court's opinion they were not.

It followed that the widow's present and potential earnings were not to be subtracted from damages for loss of support. They could, however, be taken into account in estimating the amount of support which the husband would have provided had he survived. As an alternative, the court held that if a widow's earning capacity was to be taken into account in assessing damages no deduction could be made in this case, for there was no evidence that the claimant's

12 1965 (2) S.A. 193 (T).

13 (1961) 107 C.L.R. 73.

earnings or earning capacity arose from or were increased by her husband's death.[14]

The court's reasoning and its conclusion that there was to be no deduction from damages for loss of support on account of the widow's earning capacity were endorsed by the Appellate Division in *Peri-Urban Areas Health Board v. Munarin*.[15]

In *Constantia Versekeringsmaatskappy Bpk. v. Victor, N.O.*,[16] an action was brought on behalf of a child who lost both parents in a traffic accident. Damages for loss of support by his parents were claimed. The child was adopted a few months after the accident. His adoptive parents would provide him with as much support as he could have expected from his natural parents. The defendant submitted that the child had lost support only during the period between the death of his parents and his adoption and could recover compensation for loss of support only in respect of this period. If the child received an award for loss of support over the full period he would have been supported by his natural parents, with support from his adoptive parents he would be put in a better position than if his parents had not died. The defendant drew an analogy between a child's adoption and a widow's remarriage. The practice of considering a widow's remarriage or prospects of remarriage in

14 Such evidence could be presented when the wife, prior to the fatal accident, had refrained from taking employment in order to look after an invalid husband. Boberg, *Damages for Wrongful Death--Relevance of Widow's Earning Capacity--a New Direction*, (1965) 82 S.A.L.J. 277, 278. Considering the care which the husband had required as a maintenance expense saved by the husband's estate upon his death might be preferable to considering it an element of the wife's earning capacity.

15 1965 (3) S.A. 367, 375-76 (A.D.). See Boberg, *Law of Delict*, 1965 Ann. Surv. S. Afr. L. 174, 201-04. South Africa and Rhodesia followed England and numerous other common law jurisdictions in enacting legislation that excludes from the calculation of damages insurance money, pensions and benefits (from trade unions and friendly societies) paid as a result of the death. Assessment of Damages Act, No. 9 of 1969 (S. Afr.); Assessment of Damages Act, c. 40 (1974) (Rhod.). See Boberg, *Good News for Dependants in Actions for Wrongful Death*, (1969) 86 S.A.L.J. 339. On the treatment of insurance premiums "saved" on account of the death, see Groenewald v. Snyders, 1966 (3) S.A. 237 (A.D.); Boberg, *Dependants' Damages and the 'Saving' of Insurance Premiums*, (1966) 83 S.A.L.J. 411.

16 1986 (1) S.A. 601 (A.D.).

calculating damages for loss of support by her husband had become well-established in South Africa.

The Appellate Division held that the claim for loss of support which the child otherwise would have was not to be reduced on account of his adoption and support by his adoptive parents.[17] It said that in determining compensation for loss of support, a court tries to place the child in the position in which he would be if his father had not died. It was probably logical and reasonable to take into consideration the benefits which the death of the father brought to the child. But the adoption of a child was not a consequence that flowed from the father's death. Also, a child's right to be supported by his parents was not unqualified. When a child had his own income, it could be applied to his support before his parents would be obliged to use their own resources. The damages claimed in the present case would provide such income. They could therefore be applied by the child's adoptive father for his support. The child would not then be doubly compensated. If, instead, the adoptive father decided to use his own means to support the child, this was not to diminish the defendant's obligation to pay damages.

This factor was used to distinguish a child's claim for loss of support from the claim of a widow. But it appears that the Appellate Division refused to apply to an adopted child a rule analogous to that applied to a remarried widow primarily because of its doubts about the soundness of the widow's remarriage rule. The remarriage of a widow, like the adoption of a child, was not seen as a consequence flowing from the death of the husband. Thus it was not necessarily a factor which had to be taken into account in calculating damages. Remarriage did not reinstate a widow's right to support. It gave her a new right to support from her new husband. If a right to support from someone other than the deceased existed, it did not necessarily follow that it was properly taken into consideration in calculating compensation. The Appellate Division accepted the defendant's assumption that a widow's remarriage or chance of remarrying was to be brought into the calculation of damages in fatal accident cases, but it was not convinced that legal principles or considerations of logic or reasonableness required an analogous approach to a child's adoption after the death of its parents.

17 The trial court had reached the same conclusion. Victor, N.O. v. Constantia Insurance Co. Ltd., 1985 (1) S.A. 118 (C), aff'd, 1986 (1) S.A. 601 (A.D.).

It is submitted that in fatal accident cases adoption of a child after its parents' death should not be distinguished from remarriage of a widow after her husband's death.[18] In both cases, a family relationship carrying with it a right of support is terminated by the death, and in both cases a like relationship also carrying with it a right of support is created. The second relationship never would have been created but for the severance of the first. Therefore, the second relationship and the support derived from it are consequences (although not necessary consequences) of the death. In both situations the amount of support to be derived from the second marital or parental relationship should be taken into the calculation of damages for loss of support, at least when remarriage or adoption has already occurred (thus avoiding speculative and distasteful assessments of a dependant's prospects of remarriage or adoption). The real loss to the survivor is the difference between the support that would have been provided by the deceased husband or parent, but for his death, and the support that will be provided by the new husband or parent.

Awarding a greater amount of damages puts the dependant in a better position than if the death had not occurred and is not justified by the argument that the defendant should not benefit from the remarriage or adoption.[19] It is true that over-compensation would be avoided if damages were calculated without regard to remarriage or adoption and then applied to support the wife or child, but this would relieve the new husband or father of the obligation of support. If a man wishes to have the benefit of a marital or parental relationship, he ought to bear the normal obligation of support and not avoid it because his wife or child can receive an award of damages on account of a prior relationship.

18 See Boberg, *The Relevance of Other Sources of Support for Dependants*, (1966) 83 S.A.L.J. 402. In Burchell & Dendy, *Law of Delict*, 1985 Ann. Surv. S. Afr. L. 179, 210-12, adoption is distinguished from a widow's remarriage on the grounds that remarriage waives a claim for loss of support subsequent to the new marriage (the widow takes her new husband "for better or worse, for richer or poorer") and the adoptive parent acts primarily out of charity, to which is attached the rule that the benevolence of third persons toward a plaintiff must be disregarded in assessing damages.

19 See Parmanand, *An Exercise in Altruism?*, 1985 De Rebus 617, criticising the judgment of the trial court, and the more general analysis in Koch, *Damages for Personal Injury and Death*, (1986) 49 T.H.R.-H.R. 215.

LOSS OF EARNING CAPACITY

In *Swart v. Provincial Insurance Co. Ltd.*,[20] the injured plaintiff had been employed as a postman, within the uniformed division of the Department of Posts. He received leg injuries in an accident for which the defendant was liable. These injuries permanently prevented him from doing work which required walking or standing. He therefore could no longer work as a postman. Neither could he do sorting, which carried a higher salary and led to possible promotion to inspector. He could not be transferred to clerical work because that was in another division of the postal department, which required a Standard VIII education. The plaintiff had attained only Standard VI. The Post Office continued to employ the plaintiff in the uniformed division and assigned him to drive the mobile post office.

The plaintiff sought compensation for the income he would be denied because of his inability to advance from postman to other positions in the uniformed division. The defendant objected to this on the ground that the plaintiff could earn a comparable income if he entered the clerical division, which he could do by obtaining further education and passing the Standard VIII examination. This could be attained in two years of evening study. Evidence was given that the plaintiff had been a good worker of above average intelligence and had better prospects of advancement in the clerical division than in his current position.

The trial court held that in assessing damages for loss of earning capacity, the applicable test was whether refusal by the plaintiff to return to school to improve his chances of financial promotion was reasonable or not. In its opinion, the question was in principle the same as the question of whether it was reasonable for a plaintiff to refuse to undergo an operation. It concluded that the plaintiff should undertake the education required to attain Standard VIII. He would be reasonably compensated for loss of earnings by an amount (R1000) which covered the costs of this education and postponement of a promotion until after he entered the clerical division.

The Appellate Division held that the trial court had erred because its decision was unsupported by the evidence. The problem of further study had never been properly put before the court. The plaintiff had not been questioned about his desire, capacity or aptitude for further study and the possibilities pertaining thereto. Among the factors affecting the matter but not in evidence and not taken into

20 1963 (2) S.A. 630 (A.D.).

account by the trial court were the plaintiff's performance in Standard VI and the examination; his psychological capacity to successfully reach Standard VIII in evening classes, especially in light of his age (twenty-seven) and twelve-year absence from school; his ability to attend school regularly; his aptitude for working in the clerical division of the Post Office; and conditions of employment (appointment age requirements, duties, salary scales and promotion prospects) in that division. The evidence did not support a decision that the plaintiff ought to obtain further education to qualify for a clerical position. The plaintiff was entitled to a much higher award based upon the difference between what the plaintiff was likely to earn with his present education and physical condition and what he would have earned had he not been injured. However, this amount was adjusted to reflect numerous contingencies affecting his employment and income, one of which was the possibility that the plaintiff would obtain further educational qualifications.

It was said in the Appellate Division's judgment that while the plaintiff had a duty to take all reasonable steps to minimise damage, the burden rested on the defendant to prove that the plaintiff failed to do what the reasonable person would do in the circumstances.[21] This passage was applied in the plaintiff's favour in *Van Almelo v. Shield Insurance Co. Ltd.*[22] The defendant was held not to have discharged the *onus* upon it when the plaintiff, a municipal employee, chose to accept a lower-paying job with the city rather than take private employment with no loss of salary but less security and perhaps lower medical benefits. The court stated that the plaintiff carried the *onus* of proving only his disability and the defendant carried the *onus* of proving the plaintiff's residual ability, *i.e.* the ability remaining after he sustained injuries.

The accuracy of this proposition was at issue in *Krugell v. Shield Versekeringsmaatskappy Bpk.*[23] On the basis of the judgment in *Van Almelo*, the plaintiff submitted that once it had been shown that the plaintiff would not be able to resume his former work, the defendant had the *onus* of showing that the plaintiff could do "lesser work"; if the defendant did not discharge this *onus*, the plaintiff was to be considered to have lost all earning capacity. The court distinguished *Van Almelo* as involving the question of whether it

21 *Ibid.*, 633.

22 1980 (2) S.A. 411 (C).

23 1982 (4) S.A. 95 (T).

would be reasonable for the plaintiff to take a certain lesser job, but went on to express disagreement with *Van Almelo*'s view of the parties' burdens of proof. In general it was for the plaintiff to show not only that his earning capacity had been reduced, but also what the amount of the loss was. He was required to quantify his damages for loss of earning capacity. Only when the plaintiff had discharged this *onus* would the principle of mitigation come into play. Loss of employment could be used as evidence that the plaintiff's earning capacity had been affected, but the mere fact that a particular job had been lost or that a particular direction had been closed to the plaintiff did not necessarily mean that earning capacity had been completely or partially lost.

The court found that the evidence did not exclude the plaintiff's being able to work. He would be able to perform a lesser job, although perhaps not on a continual basis. However, his future earnings could not be estimated. The court decided for this reason to adopt an admittedly unscientific approach to assessment of damages. Had the plaintiff lost all earning capacity, the court would have awarded the plaintiff the value of all that he would have earned in his former occupation, reduced by a contingency allowance of ten per cent. In order to take account of the plaintiff's residual earning capacity, the court increased the contingency allowance to thirty-five per cent.

LOSS OF ILLEGALLY-DERIVED INCOME

In *Dhlamini v. Protea Assurance Co. Ltd.*,[24] the plaintiff's injuries prevented her from continuing in her occupation as a seller of fruit. She had been selling fruit in public places for twenty years and intended to continue in this trade until she had brought up her eleven children. Because she did not have a hawker's licence, the plaintiff's trade was illegal--as she well knew, for she had unsuccessfully applied for a licence on several occasions. The trial court held that the plaintiff could not recover damages for loss of earning capacity because the earnings were derived from knowingly conducting an illegal trade.

The Appellate Division affirmed. It stated that damage calculated on the basis of income from an immoral or criminal activity would not be compensated because it was against public

24 1974 (4) S.A. 906 (A.D.).

policy to do so. This rule would also apply to income from a "colourless" activity forbidden by statute ("colourless" in the sense that it could not be regarded as immoral or criminal) when the income from the activity was not enforceable due to invalidity. In order to decide whether or not the plaintiff's income from selling fruit was "legally valid", the Appellate Division enquired whether the sale of fruit (a lawful activity *per se*) had been made subject to possession of a licence because of concern for public health or other considerations of public policy. If considerations of "public interest" played a role in the granting of a licence, the unlicensed plaintiff's income was illegal and to be regarded in the same light as, for example, a thief's.

Such considerations were present here, in the court's opinion, particularly because of the public interest, served by control of hawkers, in preventing the sale of unhealthful or adulterated food or the trading in foodstuffs by persons suffering from infectious disease. (The Appellate Division did not find it necessary to consider whether the municipality's long toleration of the plaintiff's activities affected the question of public policy because this toleration was not investigated in the trial court.) Accordingly, the plaintiff's income was illegal and she could not recover damages for loss of income or earning capacity. The court did not specify whether "validity" would always be the test in cases of a "colourless" illegal activity or what the result of the plaintiff's claim would have been if her income was valid or enforceable, despite the absence of a license.

In *Booysen v. Shield Insurance Co. Ltd.*,[25] the victim derived income from illegal sales of liquor and from weekly dances and cinema, also illegal because not licensed. Had he sought damages for loss of this income, his claim would have been denied because of the decision in *Dhlamini v. Protea Assurance Co. Ltd.* But here the victim's injuries were fatal and his dependants claimed damages for loss of support. The question was whether the dependants could recover for loss of support derived from the decedent's illegal income.

Although the dependants' action for loss of support was considered to belong to the dependants in their own right and not through the decedent's estate, the court refused to distinguish the plaintiffs' claim on this basis. It regarded the considerations of public policy expressed in *Dhlamini* as fully applicable to the dependants' action. There might be room for distinguishing cases in

25 1980 (3) S.A. 1211 (S.E.), aff'd, 1979 (3) S.A. 953 (A.D.).

which the illegality was merely "technical" and would not have prevented the deceased from continuing with the activity or from enforcing payment for goods or services. But where, by reason of public policy, the proceeds of the activity were not recoverable, the dependants, like the victim himself, could not rely on the income as a basis of compensation. Courts would not, for example, grant the survivors of a deceased prostitute damages for the loss of maintenance derived from the proceeds of prostitution. Consequently, the dependants could recover only for loss of support attributable to lawful income.[26]

The question of whether a dependant's claim for loss of support should be denied on the ground that the source of support was illegal activity reached the Appellate Division in *Santam Insurance Ltd. v. Ferguson.*[27] The decedent for many years had earned his income from his panel-beating business. He did not obtain the licence for such businesses required by a provincial ordinance. He was committing an offence by conducting the business without a license. The decedent probably could not have obtained a licence because the premises he used had defects "from a health point of view" and were not sufficiently fire-resistant. Also, the area was zoned for residential purposes.

The trial court[28] believed it unjust and on principle unsound to non-suit a widow or child because the deceased husband or father was making a living out of illegal or criminal conduct that was not *turpis*. The widow or child may have known nothing about the decedent's activities, and if the illegality were discovered and stopped, the husband would have resorted to some other form of livelihood. The court was of the opinion that *Dhlamini v. Protea*

26 This decision was soon followed in a case where the decedent operated an unlicensed taxi, Mba v. Southern Insurance Association Ltd., 1981 (1) S.A. 122 (Tk. S.C.). Compare Fortuin v. Commercial Union Assurance Co. of S.A. Ltd., 1983 (2) S.A. 444 (C), in which a widow was allowed to recover for loss of support on a finding that her husband would have applied for and received a hawker's licence had he not been killed. The judgment in *Booysen* is criticised in Blommaert, *Booysen v. Shield Insurance Co. Ltd.*, 1981 T.S.A.R. 176, for failing to distinguish the dependants' action from a personal injury claim by the earner of illegal income and recognise the legislative policy of favourable treatment of dependants. See also 1 Boberg, 591-94.

27 1985 (4) S.A. 843 (A.D.). See Burchell & Dendy, *Law of Delict*, 1985 Ann. Surv. S. Afr. L. 179, 209-10.

28 Ferguson v. Santam Insurance Ltd., 1985 (1) S.A. 207 (C), rev'd, 1985 (4) S.A. 843 (A.D.).

Assurance Co. Ltd. was not binding authority for dependants' actions and should apply only to cases in which the injured person's income was not legally recoverable--for example, where the income was derived from robbery; it should not apply to cases in which he could recover the price of goods sold or services rendered. The present case fell into the second category. The court therefore awarded the panel-beater's widow the amount of support she would have received if her husband had not been killed.

The Appellate Division held that this award was erroneous. Under *Dhlamini*, the income received by the deceased from his business was unlawful, and because the widow's claim of loss of support was based upon unlawful income it could not be maintained. The Appellate Division emphasised, as it had in *Dhlamini*, the important considerations of public policy pertinent to issuance of a licence for the victim's business. Here, health, safety, fire danger and the residential comfort of the neighbourhood played important roles. The conduct of business without a licence was therefore not a "colourless" statutorily forbidden activity and its consequences, including the income derived therefrom, were not lawful. Loss of unlawful income could not be a basis of compensation for a dependant, just as it could not be a basis of compensation for the injured person. As the court had not been properly presented with a basis on which it could be found that some of the decedent's income was lawful, the widow's entire claim for loss of support failed.

Despite the outcome of *Santam Insurance Ltd. v. Ferguson*, the court in *Mankebe, N.O. v. A.A. Mutual Insurance Association Ltd.*[29] concluded that damages might be recovered when maintenance had been derived from an illegal source. The right of a dependant to recover damages resulting from the death of a person who derived income from carrying on an illegal trade or business depended upon the nature of the trade or business carried on, the nature of the prohibition, and the reason for the prohibition. A court would not readily deprive a dependant of the right to recover damages on account of death unless the prohibition of the deceased's activities of necessity indicated that it was the intention of the applicable legislation to regard such activities as both illegal and invalid.

Where the illegality constituted a danger to the public or, perhaps, was of such a nature as to cause "general public opprobrium", public policy would demand that the plaintiff be deprived of the right to recover damages for loss of maintenance

29 1986 (2) S.A. 196 (D).

derived from the illegal source. This presented a question of fact. It was necessary to receive evidence concerning the nature and degree of the illegality and the effect of this illegality on the transactions entered into by the deceased. In South Africa, many otherwise lawful activities were rendered unlawful by failure to obtain a permit or similar authorisation. Where this failure did not constitute a danger or potential danger to the public, as it had in *Dhlamini* and *Ferguson*, public policy did not demand that the activities carried on be declared invalid.

Accordingly, the court ordered a hearing on the nature of the trade conducted by the deceased in the instant case, a self-employed hawker who had not obtained the licence required to carry on his trade. The judgment contains a useful review of overseas as well as South African decisions concerning recovery for loss of illegally-derived income or maintenance.

COLLATERAL BENEFITS

In Southern Africa, as in common law jurisdictions, a plaintiff's recoverable damages are usually not reduced when the plaintiff has received payment on account of his loss from a "collateral source".[30] The receipt of compensation from the plaintiff's insurance company or a third party (other than a concurrent tortfeasor) does not terminate or diminish the plaintiff's claim against the defendant. It is merely *res inter alios acta*.[31] This may not be true, however, of certain

30 See 1 Boberg, 489-92; McKerron, 123-34. Subject to the substantial statutory changes referred to in note 15, *supra*, benefits received from a collateral source on account of death do reduce damages in a fatal accident claim. See *e.g.* Legal Insurance Company Ltd. v. Botes, 1963 (1) S.A. 608, 620-21 (A.D.) (accident insurance proceeds and benefit of accelerated receipt of life insurance proceeds deductible); Indrani v. African Guarantee and Indemnity Co. Ltd., 1968 (4) S.A. 606 (D) (state "pension" or allowance granted widow and children on account of death deductible; not considered to be paid on account of death if continued after payment of damages because of need at that time).

31 See Du Randt v. Eriksen Motors (Welkom) Ltd., 1953 (3) S.A. 570 (O) (truck owner had paid plaintiff damages when wheel came off truck and struck plaintiff's car; plaintiff could maintain action against garage whose employee placed wheel on truck negligently); Botha v. Rondalia Versekeringskorporasie van Suid-Afrika Bpk., 1978 (1) S.A. 996 (T) (hire-purchase agreement required purchaser to insure motor vehicle; seller, who retained ownership, could maintain action for damage to vehicle after

payments received from an employer. If a plaintiff was given a salary or a substitute for salary while he was disabled from working, it is arguable that the amounts received are not to be ignored as payments from a collateral source, but are to be considered in computing the loss of earnings sustained as a result of the plaintiff's injuries.

In *van Heerden v. African Guarantee and Indemnity Co. Ltd.*,[32] the court refused to award damages for loss of earnings when the plaintiff's employer had continued to pay the plaintiff wages while he was out of work. It distinguished benefits received under an insurance policy or out of charity. Such benefits resulted not from the wrongful act but from a "new cause supervening"--the obligation arising from the insurance contract or the charity or affection of the person providing the benefit. They were to be ignored on the same principle that shielded the defendant from liability for damage flowing from a new supervening cause. It could not be said that the plaintiff in such circumstances did not suffer damage. In contrast, the plaintiff whose wages were continued did not suffer loss of earnings and the payment of wages was not due to the supervening of a new cause. Nor was it charity. Payment of wages was a circumstance undisturbed by the plaintiff's injury. The plaintiff was, therefore, not entitled to recover damages in this respect.

This decision was criticised on the ground that payment of wages when an employer is not obligated to pay an employee absent from work is indistinguishable from payment made out of charity, and the wrongdoer should not derive a benefit therefrom.[33] The judgment in *van Heerden* was not followed in later cases. In *Henning v. South British Insurance Co. Ltd.*,[34] it was held that the plaintiff could recover damages for loss of earnings when his employer had paid the plaintiff the amount he would have earned if not injured less the amount of workman's compensation he received. The court regarded the employer's payments as a collateral matter, or *res inter alios acta*, because the employer was not under a contractual

purchaser's insurer paid for repair of damage), discussed in Burchell, *Law of Delict*, 1978 Ann. Surv. S. Afr. L. 237, 276-79.

32 1951 (3) S.A. 730 (C).

33 McKerron, *Damages: Collateral Source Rule*, (1951) 68 S.A.L.J. 372; McKerron, *Law of Delict*, 1951 Ann. Surv. S. Afr. L. 129.

34 1963 (1) S.A. 272 (O).

obligation to pay the plaintiff, although the payments constituted sick leave provided for by Public Service regulations. Its distinction of obligatory and non-obligatory payments was questionable,[35] and in *Bosch v. Parity Insurance Co. Ltd.*[36] it was held that a plaintiff entitled to full-salary sick leave pay under his employment contract could recover the same damages as if no sick leave had been paid. The court drew an analogy between wage continuance or sick leave under an employment contract and payment under an insurance contract the plaintiff had purchased. The alternative of granting the plaintiff the value of the sick leave he consumed was rejected.

The court in *May v. Parity Insurance Co. Ltd.*[37] reached the same result, and in *Morris v. African Guarantee and Indemnity Co. Ltd.*[38] not only the employer's continuation of wages but also its meeting the plaintiff's medical expenses was disregarded in assessing damages. (The employer was not under a contractual obligation to do either.) In *Oberholzer v. Santam Insurance Co. Ltd.*,[39] a plaintiff whose injuries permanently disabled him from employment was permitted to recover damages without setting off his disability pension against his loss of earnings. The Appellate Division held in *Santam Versekeringsmaatskappy Bpk. v. Byleveldt*[40] that when the victim's employer took him back into employment but his brain injuries rendered him incapable of performing work of value to the employer, the amounts he received as wages were to be disregarded in assessing damages for loss of earning capacity, for they were paid out of compassion.[41]

35 See Boberg, *Law of Delict*, 1963 Ann. Surv. S. Afr. L. 210, 237-39.

36 1964 (2) S.A. 449 (W). See Luntz, *Damages for Loss of Wages*, (1964) 81 S.A.L.J. 288; Luntz, *Damages for Loss of Wages*, (1964) 81 S.A.L.J. 516.

37 1967 (1) S.A. 644 (D).

38 1964 (4) S.A. 747 (W).

39 1970 (1) S.A. 337 (N).

40 1973 (2) S.A. 146 (A.D.). See Boberg, *Law of Delict*, 1973 Ann. Surv. S. Afr. L. 135, 185-91.

41 Trollip, J.A., dissented, believing that the wages had to be deducted because the victim was employed and receiving a salary for his services, irrespective of the employer's benevolent motive and the poor quality of the services. Santam Versekeringsmaatskappy Bpk. v. Byleveldt, 1973 (2) S.A. 146, 168-76 (A.D.).

These decisions seemed to establish that no injury-related benefit received by an employee from his employer reduced the damages payable by a defendant. But then the Appellate Division held in *Dippenaar v. Shield Insurance Co. Ltd.*[42] that the value of the plaintiff's retirement pension was deductible when the plaintiff was required to retire early because of his injuries. After canvassing the divergent views expressed in the House of Lords in *Parry v. Cleaver*,[43] the Appellate Division stated:

> the notion of "capacity to earn" excludes receipts and benefits arising from benevolence or ordinary contracts of insurance, and . . . that is the real reason why such receipts and benefits are generally excluded, though not without criticism. When the capacity to earn is sought to be proved by the plaintiff by means of a contract of employment, the monetary value of the contract can only be assessed when one looks at the contract as a whole. In this regard it seems clear that, if in terms of such contract there is a compulsory deduction from salary plus a contribution by the employer in order to pay the employee money as sick leave or as a pension, it is the intention of the parties that that money shall be paid when it is due, in terms of the contract. In fact, the "income" of the employee is in terms of the contract not confined to his salary (in its ordinary connotation) but includes also sick pay or pension when such pay or pension is due. If a monetary value is sought to be put on the earning capacity based on this contract, every benefit received under the contract, such as a pension, must therefore be considered . . . . To suggest that wages and pensions are of a different kind or that pensions are some form of insurance may be partly true if one looks only at the meaning of the words "wages", "pensions" and "insurance" without looking at the context of the contract as a whole and without considering the purpose for which such contract as a whole is used in determining a plaintiff's loss of earning capacity. . . . [I]f the plaintiff claimed that he lost his salary and part of a pension receivable under the terms of his

42 1979 (2) S.A. 904 (A.D.). See Burchell, *Law of Delict*, 1979 Ann. Surv. S. Afr. L. 179, 209-12.

43 [1970] A.C. 1 (H.L.).

> employment with the Government, he must acknowledge that under the same contract he is receiving payment of pension benefits.[44]

This statement suggested that not only retirement pensions, but other benefits forming part of an employee's contractual "compensation package" and received after the injury, would be deductible from damages for loss of earning capacity. The damages would, though, include the value of benefits (such as retirement pension and sick leave) lost or consumed on account of the injury. Lower courts have interpreted *Dippenaar* as requiring that salary continuance (sick leave) and medical expenses to which the plaintiff was entitled under his contract of service be deducted from damages recoverable for loss of earnings and medical expenses respectively. The plaintiff could recover only for his actual loss of income and expenses, taking into account his employment benefits.[45] No consideration was given to adding to the damages the value of the leave the plaintiff consumed.[46]

Gehring v. Unie Nasionaal Suid-Britse Versekeringsmaatskappy Bpk.[47] maintains a distinction between benefits received by the

44 Dippenaar v. Shield Insurance Co. Ltd., 1979 (2) S.A. 904, 920 (A.D.).

45 Serumela v. S.A. Eagle Insurance Co. Ltd., 1981 (1) S.A. 391 (T) (sick pay); Krugell v. Shield Versekeringsmaatskappy Bpk., 1982 (4) S.A. 95 (T) (sick pay); Gehring v. Unie Nasionaal Suid-Britse Versekeringsmaatskappy Bpk., 1983 (2) S.A. 266 (C) (medical expenses). The court in *Gehring* was uncertain whether such benefits were to affect the assessment of damages only when the plaintiff sought to prove damages for loss of earnings by reference to his employment contract or whenever the benefits affected the plaintiff's actual economic loss under the heads of damages claimed. Ultimately, it refused to permit a plaintiff who made no claim for loss of earnings to recover damages for medical expenses actually borne by his employer.

46 In Serumela v. S.A. Eagle Insurance Co. Ltd., 1981 (1) S.A. 391 (T), the plaintiff lost nothing by using up his sick leave because he subsequently left his employment. Accumulated sick leave had no monetary value upon termination of this employment. In Krugell v. Shield Versekeringsmaatskappy Bpk., 1982 (4) S.A. 95 (T), the plaintiff was dismissed from work as medically unfit. He used both sick leave and normal leave. It was not argued that the salary the plaintiff received on normal leave reduced damages for loss of earnings. Both the pension he received after his dismissal and the pension he lost on account of his dismissal were taken into account in the calculation of damages.

47 1983 (2) S.A. 266 (C).

employee as an entitlement under his contract of service and benefits received in the employer's discretion. Sick pay which was a "privilege" rather than a "right" was held not to offset damages for loss of earnings. Thus, the question of whether a payment or other benefit is a contractual entitlement or discretionary has become critical in the assessment of damages for personal injury.[48]

48 See Gough, *Ghering* [sic] *v. Union* [sic] *Nasionaal Suid-Britse Versekeringsmaatskappy Bpk.*, (1983) 46 T.H.R.-H.R. 474. The author argues that the distinction ought not to be between obligatory and non-obligatory payments, but between benefits which an employer can be expected to pay and payments which are completely gratuitous or voluntary.

10

NUISANCE AND TRESPASS TO LAND

Only a few Southern African cases of nuisance and trespass to land have precedential value for common law jurisdictions.

RIGHT TO ACTION

In *Kanniappen v. Govender*,[1] the plaintiff had entered a written agreement for the purchase of a farm of 158 acres. The agreement provided that possession and occupation of the farm would be delivered to the plaintiff on the 30th June 1959, after which the plaintiff would receive the rents and income of the farm and be responsible for rates, insurance and other outgoings. Ownership of the farm was not to pass to the plaintiff and the property was not to be registered in his name until the purchase price (payable in annual installments) had been fully paid or guaranteed. This had not occurred at the time of the litigation. The plaintiff brought an action of trespass in order to obtain ejectment of a tenant who occupied fifteen acres of the farm and refused to vacate it on the 30th June 1959.

The court held that the plaintiff could not maintain an action of trespass because he had not obtained possession of the fifteen acres occupied by the defendant. Trespass was described as a wrong against actual possession, a disturbance of possession from which arose a right to restoration of possession and damages. It afforded no remedy to one entitled to obtain possession but not disturbed in

1 1962 (1) S.A. 101 (N).

possession. The plaintiff was not disturbed in possession, never having acquired it. The court rejected the plaintiff's submission that the seller of the farm, intending to divest himself of all interest in the property including possession, had placed the plaintiff in "constructive possession". It appears that the plaintiff's remedy was against the seller: enforcement of the seller's contractual obligation to deliver possession of the entire farm. The seller, having retained ownership, would in turn have a "vindicatory action" (not an action of trespass) to recover possession from the tenant.[2]

In *Amod v. Andrews Bakery (Pty.) Ltd.*,[3] the plaintiff, a sub-tenant of residential premises, sought to interdict the defendant from carrying on its business in such a way as to constitute a nuisance. The defendant raised the point that the plaintiff's occupation of the dwelling was illegal. The dwelling was in an area reserved for white persons. The plaintiff was not white and he was liable to be criminally prosecuted for failing to vacate the premises. The court held that the plaintiff, being in illegal occupation, could not maintain an action for nuisance. In relation to the property he occupied, he had no right to be free of interference with his comfort, convenience, peace and quiet and enjoyment of the land--the right on which the action was based. The court was unconvinced by the argument that there was a duty not to disturb the peace of a neighbouring "trespasser" on analogy to the duty of care (in certain circumstances) not to injure a trespasser. The court did not distinguish the case before it from a case in which the plaintiff's occupation of land is unlawful because it is without the consent of the true owner, but it may not have intended to preclude an action in the latter.[4]

2 The trial court in Hefer v. Van Greuning, 1978 (3) S.A. 942 (T), rev'd, 1979 (4) S.A. 952 (A.D.), reached a similar conclusion: an owner of land who never took possession of it could not maintain a trespass action for damages; actual possession was required except in the case of an owner who had prior possession and claimed for injury to his reversionary right to possession. The Appellate Division reversed on the ground that under South African law an owner of land had an Aquilian action for damages against a person who unlawfully occupied or damaged it.

3 1965 (2) S.A. 433 (T).

4 See Mathews, *Law of Property (Including Mortgage and Pledge)*, 1965 Ann. Surv. S. Afr. L. 222, 233.

NUISANCE--RESTRICTING USE OF PLAINTIFF'S PROPERTY

Assagay Quarries (Pty.) Ltd. v. Hobbs[5] raised the question of whether there is a right under the law of nuisance to be free of an activity that has no physical or aesthetic effect upon the plaintiff's land but results in the plaintiff's being prohibited by law from conducting a profitable activity there. The plaintiff was the tenant of land on which it operated a quarry. This required blasting operations. A regulation provided that blasting could be conducted within five hundred yards of a power line only with the written permission of the Inspector of Mines. The plaintiff required and obtained this permission. The defendant Electricity Supply Commission then commenced construction of an additional power line within five hundred yards of the blasting point. The Inspector of Mines notified the plaintiff that permission to blast would be withdrawn. Allegedly, the defendant knew that this would be the effect of erecting the new power line. The plaintiff sought damages for loss of profits from its quarrying and an order that the defendant remove the power line to a place more than five hundred yards from the plaintiff's land. The word "nuisance" was not used in the declaration but it was interpreted to raise an action of nuisance in substance. The declaration asserted that erection of the power line interfered with the plaintiff's use and enjoyment of the land and the beneficial enjoyment thereof.

The defendant contended that apart from disturbances of a servitude, there is no private nuisance unless something deleterious has come onto the plaintiff's land. The court regarded the escape of something deleterious as a typical example of a nuisance, not part of its definition. It cited English and American cases in which conduct not causing such an escape was regarded as a nuisance--operating a smallpox hospital (from which no infection spread), "watching and besetting" premises, conducting prostitution, and establishing a funeral parlour in a residential district.[6] In the court's opinion, if it was a nuisance to interfere with a neighbour's enjoyment of his property by interfering with his comfort, it could also be a nuisance to interfere with his ability to enjoy his property by putting it to profitable use. The power line was capable of being a nuisance in the circumstances of the case. Whether it was actionable depended upon whether the power line was a reasonable user of land by the defendant and

5 1960 (4) S.A. 237 (N). See McKerron, *The Nuisance that Never Was, or The Cause of Action that Blushed Unseen*, (1962) 79 S.A.L.J. 28.

6 See Fleming, 385; Prosser & Keeton, 619-20.

whether the plaintiff's user was so exceptional that the law of nuisance did not afford protection. This was not decided.

While one must agree with the court that there is no logical distinction between conduct which has the effect of depreciating the value of property by allowing something to escape onto it and conduct which brings about the same result without any escape, the cases cited by the court--"watching and besetting", the house of prostitution, etc.--involved conduct which caused discomfort in the use of the plaintiff's property. This did not occur in the *Assagay Quarries* case. That the defendant's use of land is a nuisance because the plaintiff will then be prevented by law from making a beneficial use of his property is an original proposition. It rests primarily upon the interference caused to the plaintiff in its use of land. *Assagay Quarries* is not a case in which the defendant simply made it less profitable for the plaintiff to use his land without interfering with that use. But one wonders whether the defendant should have been deemed responsible for loss flowing from a regulation and a decision (the Inspector of Mines') the defendant did not make.

11

MISREPRESENTATION

ACTIONABLE STATEMENTS

The law in Southern Africa recognises liability for misrepresentations made fraudulently. It also appears, despite the broad language used when the Appellate Division held there was no liability in *Herschel v. Mrupe*,[1] that there can be liability for misrepresentations made negligently.[2] But until recent times, plaintiffs prevailed in few of the reported cases.

In *Murray v. McLean, N.O.*,[3] the plaintiff attempted to recover from the Minister of Health costs incurred in the expectation of selling prefabricated houses to the Ministry of Health. The plaintiff claimed that he was induced to make purchases of materials and make other preparations for sales of houses by the representations of the ministry's officials, including the Secretary for Health, that the

1 1954 (3) S.A. 464 (A.D.), with Centlivres, C.J., dissenting. See 1 Boberg, 81-83; McKerron, *Liability for Negligent Statements: Hershcel v. Mrupe*, (1954) 71 S.A.L.J. 316; Price, *Negligent Misrepresentation Again*, 1955 Butt. S. Afr. L. Rev. 154. The plaintiff wanted to recover legal costs wasted in pursuing a claim against a company which the defendant erroneously identified as her liability insurer. (The actual insurer could have been sued directly by the plaintiff.)

2 See Administrateur, Natal v. Trust Bank van Afrika Bpk., 1979 (3) S.A. 824 (A.D.), and cases discussed in this chapter.

3 1969 (2) R.L.R. 541 (G.D.), 1970 (1) S.A. 133 (R). See Dean, *Put Not Your Trust in Princes, Nor in the Son of Man, in Whom There is no Help--Psalm 146, Verse 3*, (1970) 87 S.A.L.J. 149.

ministry would purchase numerous houses from the plaintiff. The sales were never made because funds were not made available to the ministry. The plaintiff sought damages on the ground of negligent or reckless misrepresentation, including misrepresentation that funds to buy the houses would be available.

The court had no doubt that an action might lie for damages resulting from negligent statements. The applicable principles were those stated by the New York Court of Appeals in *International Products Company v. Erie Railroad Company*,[4] from which Schreiner, J.A., had quoted in *Herschel v. Mrupe*:[5]

> Liability in such cases arises only where there is a duty, if one speaks at all, to give the correct information. And that involves many considerations. There must be knowledge or its equivalent that the information is desired for a serious purpose; that he to whom it is given intends to rely and act upon it; that if false or erroneous he will because of it be injured in person or property. Finally the relationship of the parties, arising out of contract or otherwise, must be such that in morals and good conscience the one has the right to rely upon the other for information, and the other giving the information owes a duty to give it with care . . . .
>
> When such a relationship as we have referred to exists may not be precisely defined. All that may be stated is the general rule. In view of the complexity of modern business each case must be decided on the peculiar facts presented.[6]

Another element, drawn from the judgment of van den Heever, J.A., in *Herschel v. Mrupe*,[7] was that the person making the statement could expect the recipient to use ordinary prudence in avoiding injury

4 244 N.Y. 331, 155 N.E. 662 (1927).

5 1954 (3) S.A. 464, 480 (A.D.).

6 International Products Company v. Erie Railroad Company, 244 N.Y. 331, 338, 155 N.E. 662, 664 (1927).

7 1954 (3) S.A. 464, 481-91 (A.D.).

to himself.[8]

Applying these principles, the court held that the plaintiff had no cause of action. In its opinion, this was not a case in which the recipient of the information had a right to rely on it and hold the supplier of the information responsible. The ordinary prudent seller engaged in negotiations with a prospective purchaser knows that a sale may not eventuate for a number of reasons. The plaintiff here could have protected himself from loss by either waiting until the contract was finalised before incurring expenses on it or by seeking an agreement by the government to reimburse his expenses if a sales contract was not concluded. Moreover, it did not appear that the plaintiff ever specifically enquired of the ministry's officials about the availability of funds for the purchases. Such an enquiry would have put the officials on notice that the plaintiff attached importance to this point and would rely on their responses. No action would have lain in the circumstances had the defendant been an ordinary commercial company. *A fortiori* no action should lie against the government for representations made by a civil servant. Otherwise, the government's ability to allocate funds in the public interest would be fettered.

In *Scottish Rhodesian Finance v. Taylor*,[9] the purchaser of a car unsuccessfully attempted to prevent a finance company's repossession of the car on the ground that the company had breached a duty of care to him. The purchaser had enquired of the Rhodesian "Hire-purchase Institute" (H.P.I.) whether anyone claimed a hire-purchase interest in the car. He received a negative reply and then bought the car. The finance company had taken an interest in the car and reported it to H.P.I., but with an incorrect registration number. H.P.I. had no record of a hire-purchase under the correct number, which the purchaser used. The court, following the principles set forth in *Murray v. McLean, N.O.*, held that the finance company owed a subsequent purchaser no duty to transmit correct information to H.P.I. Also, the company had made no misrepresentation relied upon by the purchaser because the company did not represent that it had no interest in the car.

Damages for fraudulent misrepresentation were claimed in *Jones*

8 The court also referred to Hedley Byrne & Co. Ltd. v. Heller & Partners Ltd., [1964] A.C. 465 (H.L.), and the dissent of Denning, L.J., in Candler v. Crane, Christmas & Co., [1951] 2 K.B. 164, 174-85 (C.A.).

9 1972 (2) R.L.R. 165 (G.D.).

v. Mazza.[10] The plaintiff, the landlord of business premises, alleged that he was induced to reduce the second defendant's rent by representations that this defendant could not afford to pay more than a reduced rent, when in fact the defendant's profits were such that it could afford the original rent at all material times. (There were also representations that the premises were badly situated for a motorcycle business, that the second defendant would have moved its business to other premises had it been able to do so, and that it had a "hand to mouth business getting merely the crumbs of motor cycle business in Salisbury". It was conceded that they were statements of opinion or mere "puffing" and did not give rise to liability if false.) The trial court awarded damages to the plaintiff. It regarded the misrepresentations of inability to afford certain rents as statements of opinion which included statements of fact and therefore were actionable. The misrepresentations involved a statement of material fact to the extent they asserted that the defendants held the stated opinion concerning the amount of rent they were in a position to pay--a matter about which the defendants knew more than the plaintiff.

The Rhodesian Appellate Division[11] held that the defendants were not liable. When two businessmen were "haggling about a price" a statement that "I cannot afford to pay what you are asking." was mere "puffing in reverse". It was not to be taken to mean that the declarant could not raise the amount of money to pay the amount demanded. Rather it would be understood as a meaning either that the declarant did not in the circumstances regard it as prudent to spend as much as the other demanded or simply that he was trying to make a good bargain. A statement that "I cannot afford it." unaccompanied by particulars of the declarant's financial condition was too imprecise to found an action for false representation. In any event, if the statement was actionable by a plaintiff who understood it to mean "I have just not got the money to pay the rent you ask." the plaintiff here had failed to prove that he so understood it.

In *Lourens v. Genis*,[12] the plaintiff alleged that the defendants had fraudulently represented to him that water would be found if the plaintiff sunk a bore hole at a certain place on his farm. Acting

10 1972 (2) R.L.R. 377 (G.D.), 1973 (1) S.A. 570 (R), rev'd, 1973 (1) R.L.R. 88 (A.D.), 1973 (2) S.A. 740 (R.A.D.).

11 Mazza v. Jones, 1973 (1) R.L.R. 88 (A.D.), 1973 (2) S.A. 740 (R.A.D.).

12 1962 (1) S.A. 431 (T).

upon this the plaintiff sunk the bore hole, at substantial cost, but did not find the water expected. The plaintiff sought to recover from the defendants the cost of drilling the hole. One would expect the plaintiff's action to succeed upon proof of these allegations. This was the result in the magistrate's court, but on appeal judgment was granted in the defendants' favour because of the underlying facts.

The defendants, father and son, had been introduced to the plaintiff as persons who could divine water for him. During discussions between the parties, the son had been represented as a person with "X-ray eyes" who could see water or its radiation under the ground and point out its location. It was agreed that for payment to the defendants of £15, the son would point out for the plaintiff a place where water could be found by drilling. The son walked around the farm, standing still at various places and saying "Here I see 1500 gallons [an hour].", "Here I see 2000 gallons.", and so on. But the plaintiff wanted more. The parties came to a place where the son said there would be at least 3000 gallons at about 250 feet. "I see water running." The father confirmed this and added that if the son said there were at least 3000 gallons, the plaintiff could be sure that the amount was closer to 4000 gallons. The plaintiff had a hole drilled at a cost of £207,10s. Only 120 gallons per hour were found after drilling 415 feet. After the plaintiff complained about the failure of the bore hole the defendants returned the £15 they had received, but the plaintiff sought to recover the £207,10s drilling cost.

The court held that the plaintiff could not recover damages because no reasonable person in his position would have believed the defendants' representations and acted upon them. No fraud was committed if the plaintiff was not misled or should not have been misled. When the circumstances were such that a representation could not mislead the normal reasonable careful person, there could be no question of fraud. The plaintiff, a normal practical farmer, should have realised that he could not rely on the defendants' divination of water. He had believed the defendants but now admitted that the results of sinking a bore hole could not be predicted and that water was not always found where it was divined. In addition, he admitted that one Viljoen, who also claimed to have X-ray eyes, had previously divined a dry bore hole for him. In the circumstances, the plaintiff had acted at his own risk and had caused himself loss by his own unreasonable foolishness.[13]

13 The judgment is criticised in Hunt, *The Man with X-Ray Eyes*, (1962) 79 S.A.L.J. 120. The author asserts that liability for fraudulent misrepresentation does not require that the representee's belief in the misrepresentation's truth

A defendant was held liable for damages caused by a negligent statement in *Wood v. Northwood Service Station (Pvt.) Ltd.*[14] The engine of the plaintiff's Mercedes had seized. The plaintiff sought advice from a director of the defendant garage. He was told that it was uneconomic to repair or replace the engine and that the car was worth between $600 and $800 in its present condition. Acting on this advice, the plaintiff sold the Mercedes for $800. He soon learned that the buyer repaired the car for $200 and sold it for $2400 (without disclosing to the purchaser that the engine had seized).

The court applied the principles laid down in *International Products Company v. Erie Railroad Company.*[15] The defendant's director knew that the plaintiff desired the information for a serious purpose and would act upon the advice. He also must have realised that damage would result if the advice was wrong. In the court's opinion, when a regular customer of a garage asks for this sort of advice about his car, in morals and good conscience the garage has a duty to advise him with care and the customer has a right to rely on the garage for the information given. The court awarded the plaintiff the difference between the amount for which he sold the Mercedes and the true value of the car, taking into account its history and the probability of putting it in good condition with relatively minor repairs.

In *E.G. Electric Co. (Pty.) Ltd. v. Franklin,*[16] the plaintiff declared that when she purchased her house, the defendant electrician had given the seller a certificate that the house's electrical wiring complied with municipal regulations. The deed of sale required that the seller furnish the plaintiff with such a certificate, as the electrician knew or should have known. When the plaintiff sold the house, she similarly undertook to furnish such a certificate to the purchaser. When she attempted to obtain the certificate, she found that the wiring (which had not been altered) did not comply with municipal regulations. It cost her a substantial amount to remedy the defects and thus meet her obligation to the purchaser. She alleged that the defendant was liable for this cost because he had negligently issued a certificate without ensuring that it was correct.

or his action in reliance upon it be reasonable. Accord, McKerron, 213.

14 1974 (1) R.L.R. 49 (G.D.).

15 244 N.Y. 331, 155 N.E. 662 (1927). See p. 256, *supra*.

16 1979 (2) S.A. 702 (E).

The electrician, conceding that there could be liability for negligent misstatement in certain circumstances, contended that there was no liability when the plaintiff's pecuniary loss resulted from a certificate provided to another person under a contract with that person. The court held that the plaintiff stated a cause of action. Its judgment is devoted primarily to asserting that this was not the type of case in which recognition of liability would open the door to a limitless number of claims against the person who made the misstatement--a fear which had led courts to deny that a duty of care was owed to persons who relied on misstatements. Here there was only a single loss, suffered by the person who the defendant knew would be handed the certificate. The court did not consider whether the plaintiff actually established that reliance upon the defendant's certificate was the cause of the damages claimed.[17]

The judicial concern with a potentially unlimited number of actions arising from negligent misstatement is particularly apposite to suits against accountants and auditors.[18] Since 1982, their delictual liability has been regulated in South Africa by statute. The Public Accountants' and Auditors' Act[19] provides that when in the ordinary course of his duties an accountant or auditor expresses an opinion, gives a certificate, makes a report or statement, or certifies a statement, account or document, he will incur no liability to a client or third party unless he acted negligently or maliciously. Apart from liability arising from contract or statute, there can be no liability to a third party for financial loss suffered as a result of reliance on an accountant's or auditor's work unless he knew or reasonably could be expected to know, at the time the negligent performance of duties occurred, that his work would be relied upon in certain ways by the third party or used by the client for inducement of the third party to act or refrain from acting. If an accountant or auditor represents to a third party that a previous opinion, certificate, report, statement, account or document is correct, he can be liable if he then knows or reasonably could be expected to know that the third party will rely upon this representation in ways outlined by the statute.

17 See Ranger v. Wykerd, 1977 (2) S.A. 976 (A.D.), discussed pp. 265-66, *infra*.

18 See Ultramares Corporation v. Touche, 255 N.Y. 170, 174 N.E. 441 (1931), quoted by the court in E.G. Electric Co. (Pty.) Ltd. v. Franklin.

19 No. 51 of 1951, s. 26(5)-(8), as amended by Public Accountants' and Auditors' Amendment Act, No. 42 of 1982 (S. Afr.). See Larkin, *Company Law*, 1982 Ann. Surv. S. Afr. L. 262, 268-70.

The principal issue in *Kern Trust (Edms.) Bpk. v. Hurter*[20] was whether a person induced to enter a contract as a result of the other contracting party's negligent misstatement (made during negotiations leading to the conclusion of the contract) could recover damages from the latter. The court held that an action could be maintained. A person induced to enter a contract by misrepresentation was not limited to the established remedies of cancellation of the contract or reduction of the purchase price. Liability in non-contractual cases had been established, and the court did not believe the availability of the other remedies justified rejection of delictual liability in cases involving a contract. These remedies might be totally inadequate to compensate the plaintiff for the loss he suffered. Neither was the party's option of requiring the other contracting party to guarantee the truth of his representations a valid reason for refusing a remedy in damages. The other party might not be prepared to guarantee a statement, and the recipient of the statement might be satisfied without a guarantee when it appeared (wrongly) that the person making the statement had taken all reasonable steps to satisfy himself as to its correctness. An action would not exist in all cases of negligent misstatement made in a contractual context, but the court found it unnecessary on this occasion to establish the limits of liability or set forth guidelines.[21]

A secondary issue in *Kern Trust* was whether an action could lie for negligently making "assurances" about future events during the negotiations leading to the conclusion of the agreement. The defendant allegedly assured the plaintiff that the building society of which the defendant was chairman would increase the amount of a loan and that a company would pay sufficient dividends to enable loans to be made to the plaintiff. The defendant submitted that these assurances were no more than opinions or forecasts and no action for

20 1981 (3) S.A. 607 (C). See Hutchison, *Damages for Negligent Misstatements Made in a Contractual Context*, (1981) 98 S.A.L.J. 486.

21 See also Pilkington Brothers (S.A.) (Pty.) Ltd. v. Lillicrap, Wassenaar and Partners, 1983 (2) S.A. 157 (W), rev'd, 1985 (1) S.A. 475 (A.D.), discussed pp. 275-82, *infra*, and Autorama (Pvt.) Ltd. v. Farm Equipment Auctions (Pvt.) Ltd., 1984 (3) S.A. 483 (Z.H.C.), discussed in Boberg, *Inducing a Contract*, (1984) 14 Businessman's Law 35. In the latter case, the court held that the plaintiff stated a cause of action in alleging that he bought a motor vehicle at an auction conducted by the defendant, who negligently misrepresented that it was selling the vehicle on behalf of its owner. The auctioneer's client was in fact a hire-purchaser, and the plaintiff was required to pay the owner the balance outstanding under the hire-purchase agreement.

damages could be based upon the negligent (as distinct from fraudulent) expression of an opinion or forecast. The court rejected this submission. In its view, once it was recognised that liability could arise from a negligent statement that induced a contract, there was no reason why a negligently expressed opinion could not give rise to an action. A person who expressed an opinion or made a forecast without reasonable justification could--depending upon all the circumstances, including the position he occupied and the extent to which others might attach weight to the opinion or forecast--be guilty of negligence.

CAUSATION AND DAMAGES

In *Siman & Co. (Pty.) Ltd. v. Barclays National Bank Ltd.*,[22] the Appellate Division divided on the question of whether an allegedly negligent statement caused the loss for which the plaintiff sought damages. One Friday afternoon, officials of the plaintiff heard that the South African currency would probably be devalued over the weekend. They telephoned the branch manager of the defendant bank, of which the plaintiff had long been a customer, to arrange forward cover for foreign currency commitments. The manager told them it was too late for cover to be obtained that afternoon. The plaintiff did not obtain cover and the South African currency was devalued during the weekend. It cost the plaintiff at least R90,000 more to meet its foreign commitments than if cover had been procured. The plaintiff claimed this amount as damages from the bank, alleging that the branch manager's statement was false--it was not too late for him to arrange forward cover when this was requested--and made negligently.

A three-two majority of the court held that the plaintiff could not recover. Two of the majority interpreted the branch manager's conduct as consisting of two acts: his communication to the plaintiff of his decision not to arrange forward cover that afternoon and his statement of the reason for refusing to act--that it was too late to do anything. The plaintiff's case was based on this erroneous statement, but the two judges attributed the plaintiff's loss to the branch manager's refusal to act. The plaintiff's loss was caused by the misstatement only if it induced the plaintiff not to seek and obtain forward cover from another source, and it was probable that the

22 1984 (2) S.A. 888 (A.D.).

plaintiff could not obtain cover from another branch or bank on the Friday afternoon. Thus, the plaintiff was in the same position as if the misstatement had not been made. It followed that the plaintiff had no action. It also followed that the plaintiff had failed to show that the branch manager was negligent. This required proof that he knew or ought to have known that forward cover was still procurable elsewhere that afternoon.[23]

The third judge of the majority did not identify two separate acts (refusal to arrange forward cover and intimation of the reason) in what the branch manager said. He interpreted the branch manager's attitude as one of refusal to act. He agreed that the misstatement did not cause the loss because there was no proof that the plaintiff could have obtained forward cover elsewhere if it had realised that it still had time to do so.[24]

The two dissenting judges were of the opinion that causation as well as the other elements of negligence liability had been made out. The question of causation was here to be answered by ascertaining what would have happened had the branch manager not been negligent. This required the substitution of non-negligent conduct for the negligent conduct and identification of the probable consequences of the hypothetical non-negligent conduct. It was not necessary to determine whether the plaintiff could have obtained forward cover at another branch or bank. Had the branch manager acted with reasonable care, he would have informed the plaintiff's representatives that there was still time for his bank to process an application for forward cover, one of the representatives would have hurried to the bank branch with the required records, the bank would have duly processed the application, and cover would have been obtained. Therefore, the manager's negligence caused the loss. He made no decision to refuse to arrange cover. His attitude was one of willingness to procure cover for the plaintiff if this were possible.[25]

The majority judges had come to the same conclusion about the

23 *Ibid.*, 898-909 (Trollip, A.J.A., with whom Wessels, J.A., concurred).

24 *Ibid.*, 909-10 (Nicholas, A.J.A.).

25 *Ibid.*, 910-26 (Corbett, J.A., with whom Miller, J.A., concurred, dissenting), 926-28 (Miller, J.A., dissenting). The dissenting judges are supported in Dendy, *Law of Delict*, 1984 Ann. Surv. S. Afr. L. 208, 223-27. See also Boberg, *A Financial Disaster and a Legal Débâcle*, (1984) 101 S.A.L.J. 603, where it is contended that the manager's statement was to the effect that cover could not be obtained from his own bank and the plaintiff's loss was caused by reliance upon this misstatement.

bank manager's attitude. Had he realised that there was still time for forward cover to be arranged, he would have acted to do so for the plaintiff, a valued customer obviously in urgent need of protection in its foreign currency commitments. It is therefore submitted that the branch manager never "refused" to act and that the dissenting judges correctly identified the probable result had the branch manager not been negligent. However, one can agree with the majority that it was not the negligent statement which caused the plaintiff's loss. Rather, it was the branch manager's failure to arrange forward cover when requested by the plaintiff. The statement was merely the expression of his reason for inaction. The reasonably prudent manager would have realised that cover could be obtained and would have acted so as to avoid loss to his customer. For this reason, the plaintiff's loss was caused by the manager's negligence, provided it was possible for him to arrange forward cover for the plaintiff on Friday. But the plaintiff did not contend that the bank was under a non-contractual duty to take such action. It was therefore appropriate not to hold the bank liable.[26]

In *Ranger v. Wykerd*,[27] the Appellate Division addressed the measure of damages in an action for fraudulent misrepresentation. The plaintiff had purchased a house from one of the defendants. He was particularly interested in the house's swimming pool. The defendants misrepresented the pool as structurally sound and in good condition, whereas they knew it was defective in material respects. After purchasing the house, the plaintiff discovered the defects and had them repaired. He claimed the cost of the repairs as damages.

The trial court absolved the defendants on the ground that the plaintiff had failed to prove that the market value of the property (in its actual condition) was less than what he paid for it and therefore failed to prove that he suffered any loss as a result of the defendant's fraud. The Appellate Division, in a majority judgment which extensively but rather inconclusively considers the principles of assessing damages in such cases, held that the plaintiff had sustained damages equivalent to the cost of repairing the pool and was entitled to recover this amount.

The dissenting judge believed that this was a "contractual" measure of damages, "making good" the misrepresentations of the defendant. (The majority denied this, referring to the damages which

26 See van Warmelo, *Unlawful Act in Delict*, (1985) 102 S.A.L.J. 414.

27 1977 (2) S.A. 976 (A.D.). See McLennan, *General Principles of Contract*, 1977 Ann. Surv. S. Afr. L. 85, 89-92.

would be assessed in a delictual action against a person who damaged the pool.) The "delictual" measure of damages was the loss the plaintiff had actually sustained, comparing the price paid for the property with the value of the property he received. The plaintiff had not shown that the property was worth less than what he paid for it. He therefore had no claim against the defendant who was not the seller of the house. However, there was precedent for awarding the "contractual" measure of damages in a delictual action against a party to a contract who made a fraudulent misrepresentation bearing upon the contract. The other defendant, the seller of the house, could therefore be held liable for the cost of repairing the pool.[28]

28 Ranger v. Wykerd, 1977 (2) S.A. 976, 980-90 (A.D.) (Jansen, J.A., dissenting). See Coomers Motor Spares (Pvt.) Ltd. v. Albanis, 1979 R.L.R. 96 (G.D.), 1979 (2) S.A. 623 (R), for a simpler case in which the court awarded the difference between what the plaintiff paid and the actual value of the property the defendant sold (the amount the plaintiff presumably would have paid had there been no misrepresentation and had the plaintiff still been willing to make the purchase).

12

ECONOMIC LOSS

LOSS CONSEQUENT UPON INJURY TO ANOTHER

South African courts usually have refused to sustain actions for economic losses flowing from negligently-inflicted injuries to another person or his property. However, it can no longer be said there is a general rule of non-liability in such circumstances.

In *Union Government v. Ocean Accident and Guarantee Corporation Ltd.*,[1] a magistrate employed by the South African government was injured while a passenger in a taxi, which he was using for the purposes of his official duties. He was absent from duty for two and a half months during which, under the regulations governing his service, the government continued to pay his salary. The government sought to recover the salary it paid during this period from the insurer of the taxi. It alleged that it had suffered damages in this amount for loss of the magistrate's services as a result of the taxi driver's negligence.[2]

The Appellate Division held that, with the possible exception of the employer of a domestic servant, an employer had no cause of

1 1956 (1) S.A. 577 (A.D.).

2 It is unlikely that this allegation could have been substantiated without proof that none of the magistrate's work during the two and a half months could have been covered without employing an additional magistrate or other staff. The government would not have suffered loss to the full extent of the magistrate's salary if other persons or the magistrate himself (overtaking the arrears when he returned to duty) could discharge some of his functions. See *ibid.*, 582-83.

action for injury to his employee. The court could not accept as a general proposition that persons contractually linked to the injured person could sue the careless injurer for the loss they suffered. This would create an "unmanageable situation" and lead to absurdities. Establishment of liability in the particular case of an injured employee was not justified by considerations of justice or convenience. Liability would be unsatisfactory because, among other reasons, it would exist only if the employee's terms of service provided for payment of salary during his absence from duty, and the injured employee's contributory negligence would not be a defence. An employer could protect itself from loss by providing that salary was not payable during any period of absence for which another person was liable to compensate the employee.

In *Franschhoekse Wynkelder (Ko-operatief) Bpk. v. South African Railways and Harbours*,[3] a wine-making co-operative claimed damages for economic loss caused by the spraying of weed killer along the defendant's railway line. The weed killer contaminated soil and damaged grape vines on adjacent farms, with the result that the co-operative no longer received wine grapes from those farms. The court held that no duty of care was owed the co-operative. It found no consideration of policy which could justify the extension of liability to this case. No "special relationship" between the parties was alleged. Even if harm was reasonably foreseeable, its risk was so remote that the reasonable man would not have taken steps to guard against it.

In *Osborne Panama S.A. v. Shell & B.P. South African Petroleum Refineries (Pty.) Ltd.*,[4] a negligently navigated tanker collided with and damaged a mooring buoy. Another ship, intending to discharge its cargo of oil at the buoy, was delayed because of the damage, thereby incurring liability for demurrage. The charterer of the ship sued the owner of the tanker to recover the demurrage. The Appellate Division summarily held that no duty of care was owed the plaintiff. It agreed with the reasoning of the trial judge,[5] who believed that a decision that the defendant owed a duty of care would

3 1981 (3) S.A. 36 (C).

4 1982 (4) S.A. 890 (A.D.).

5 Shell & B.P. South African Petroleum Refineries (Pty.) Ltd. v. Osborne Panama S.A., 1980 (3) S.A. 653 (D), aff'd, 1982 (4) S.A. 890 (A.D.). See Burchell, *The Policy Limits for Recovery of Pure Economic Loss*, (1981) 98 S.A.L.J. 1.

be a radical departure from the conservative approach to liability found in *Union Government v. Ocean Accident and Guarantee Corporation Ltd.* The judge had noted that it had not been shown that loss to the plaintiff specifically was foreseeable. Loss was foreseeable only on the basis that the plaintiff belonged to an unascertained class of potential victims, namely the owners or charterers of vessels intending to discharge oil at the mooring buoy.

This aspect of the *Shell & B.P.* case was used to distinguish it from *Coronation Brick (Pty.) Ltd. v. Strachan Construction Co. (Pty.) Ltd.*[6] There the defendant's bulldozer, building a road opposite the entrance to the plaintiff's works, allegedly severed the cables that supplied electricity to the works. The power was cut, resulting in loss of production of bricks. The plaintiff claimed damages for this loss. The court held that a duty of care existed. The plaintiff had alleged specifically that the defendant knew the cables were present and knew the plaintiff would suffer a loss of production and hence income if the power were cut. In the *Shell & B.P.* case the plaintiff was only a member of an unascertained class of potential victims, not specifically contemplated. The result of *Shell & B.P.* would probably have been different, the court thought, had the plaintiff's ship been discharging oil at the time the defendant's ship collided with the buoy.

After an extensive review of the general principles of duty of care, the court stated:

> in determining in a given case whether the defendant's conduct which resulted in foreseen or foreseeable economic loss was unlawful or wrongful the question is whether it would in all the circumstances be reasonable to recognise that defendant owed the plaintiff a legal duty or duty of care or, to put it differently, whether the reasonable man in defendant's position would in all the circumstances have recognised that he owed the plaintiff a duty of care. Although it is not possible to lay down hard and fast rules, certain guidelines have been laid down by our Courts. A defendant's conduct, including an omission, is regarded as unlawful when the circumstances of the case are of such a nature that it not only incites moral indignation but also that the legal convictions of the community demand that it

6 1982 (4) S.A. 371 (D). See 1 Boberg, 144-49; Hartford, *Some Problems on Unlawfulness in Aquilian Actions for Damages for Pure Ecomomic Loss*, (1984) 101 S.A.L.J. 42.

> ought to be regarded as unlawful and that the damage suffered by the plaintiff ought to be made good by the defendant.[7]

A special relationship between the plaintiff and defendant was not a prerequisite to liability for pure economic loss.

In determining whether conduct was unlawful, the court was required to carefully balance and evaluate the interests of the concerned parties, the relationship of the parties, and the social consequences of imposing liability in the particular situation. In coming to its conclusion the court was to have regard to the probable or possible extent of the foreseeable or foreseen loss, the degree of risk that the loss would be suffered as a result of the conduct complained of, the value to the defendant and/or society of the object which the defendant was seeking to achieve when he conducted himself in the manner complained of, whether there were reasonably practicable measures available to the defendant to avert the loss, what the chances had been that those measures would be successful, and whether the costs of such measures would have been reasonably proportionate to the loss which the plaintiff could have suffered.

These principles persuaded the court that a duty of care existed. The defendant's alleged conduct (failing to take care to avoid damaging the cables, knowing this would cause the plaintiff substantial loss of income) did incite moral indignation and offend against the legal convictions of the community. The community attitude would be that the defendant was under a duty of care to avoid the loss and that there should be liability for the loss. The loss appeared to be one which could have been avoided by practicable, simple measures, and the value to society of the defendant's activities was no higher than the value of the plaintiff's activities. As for the danger of multiplicity of actions and overwhelming potential liability, which had led courts to be cautious in finding duties of care, the court asserted that it did not follow from the decision that a duty of care was owed in this case, in which the defendant allegedly knew that a particular user of electricity would suffer loss, that a duty of care was owed to all users of electricity when the defendant did not know their identity or whether they would suffer damage.

7 Coronation Brick (Pty.) Ltd. v. Strachan Construction Co. (Pty.) Ltd., 1982 (4) S.A. 371, 384 (D).

OTHER CIRCUMSTANCES

In *Ables Groceries (Pty.) Ltd. v. Di Ciccio,*[8] the plaintiff declared that the defendants were engaged to do the bookkeeping for the plaintiff's grocery business. The defendants delegated the task to an employee, de Klerk. The plaintiff's manager requested de Klerk to deposit the plaintiff's daily takings to the plaintiff's bank account. De Klerk withheld some of the takings from the deposits and kept them for himself. "As an integral part of his system of theft" de Klerk fraudulently manipulated the bookkeeping in the plaintiff's cash book so that the entries would tally with the bank deposits. The plaintiff brought suit to recover the amount stolen from it. It asserted that the defendants were under a duty of care to employ an honest person to execute the bookkeeping or do it personally and breached the duty by employing a dishonest person, de Klerk, thereby causing the plaintiff to suffer loss.

The court held that this claim stated a cause of action. It had been accepted that the negligent choice of an employee could be a wrongful act and that there could be liability for consequential damage to a third party. If an employer directed an employee to perform a task for someone else, the employer was under a duty to take care in the choice of the employee, particularly when the employee would be in a position of trust. The employer ought to consider the honesty of the employee and the risk of damage to others in case of dishonesty. Here, the contract provided that the defendants would do bookkeeping and the theft was actually in depositing funds. However, the reasonable person would realise that dishonesty in bookkeeping would offer a chance of theft and fraud, and the plaintiff had made out a causal connection between the bookkeeping and the loss suffered. The duty resting upon the employer was in addition to his contractual duty. There could be delictual liability even though the plaintiff and defendant had a contract and the employee was instructed to do the work provided for in the contract.[9]

The plaintiffs in *Bedford v. Suid-Kaapse Voogdy Bpk.*[10] declared that they were three of the four sisters who were residuary heirs of

8 1966 (1) S.A. 834 (T).

9 The court also held that the plaintiff stated an action against the defendants on the basis of vicarious liability. See pp. 219-20, *supra.*

10 1968 (1) S.A. 226 (C).

an estate. They were entitled to inherit in equal shares. The defendant, a company in the business of acting as administrator of estates, was administrator of this estate. The residuary estate included 37,900 shares of Volkskas Bpk. The estate was given the opportunity to purchase 6510 additional shares at R0,85 each, less than their market price. With the approval of the heirs, the executors instructed the defendant to acquire the additional shares. The defendant, knowing that the heirs had consented, accepted this mandate and applied on the necessary forms for allotment of the 6510 shares to the estate. Although funds were available, the defendant failed to make payment with the application, as required. Volkskas therefore rejected the application and the estate did not receive the shares. Ten months later, when the plaintiffs discovered these facts, the shares were worth R1,20.

The plaintiffs sought damages on the basis that they would have received 4881 of the 6510 shares and had lost the difference between the R1,20 market value and the R0,85 purchase price of each of the 4881 shares. They claimed that the defendant owed them as heirs a duty to carry out with care the mandate to purchase the shares, breached it by negligently failing to make payment at the same time as the application, and thereby caused loss by diminishing the estate coming to the plaintiffs.

The plaintiffs failed to persuade the court that they had any contractual relationship with the defendant, so their ability to recover damages depended upon whether the defendant was subject to delictual liability. The court held that on the facts alleged the defendant owed the plaintiffs a duty of care. The defendant knew that it was acting on behalf of an estate with residuary heirs who approved of the transaction and would receive an advantage therefrom. Reasonably it must have foreseen that if it performed its mandate negligently and the estate did not receive the shares, the plaintiffs would be among those who would suffer prejudice as a result. The court emphasised that it was not deciding that each heir of every estate would have an action against a person who acted for the estate negligently. This would depend on the facts of each case. But where it was alleged that the defendant knew that a particular transaction specifically touched one or another of the heirs, it would follow that the defendant must have foreseen that his negligent act could cause disadvantage to the person affected. The "neighbour principle" of *Donoghue v. Stevenson*[11] was quoted in this connection.

11 [1932] A.C. 562, 580 (H.L.) (Lord Atkin).

The plaintiffs' action succeeded to this extent, but ultimately it failed because the pleadings did not establish that the plaintiffs had suffered any damage. It did not follow from the fact that shares which could have been purchased at R0,85 were worth R1,20 when the plaintiffs discovered the facts of the matter that they had been damaged. Shares were not to be assigned to the plaintiffs until the estate was wound-up. There was no allegation that the estate had been wound-up. The plaintiffs sustained damage only if the shares were worth more than R0,85 on the date that they would have been distributed to the plaintiffs.

The judgment in *Tobacco Finance (Pvt.) Ltd. v. Zimnat Insurance Co. Ltd.*,[12] unlike the judgments in the preceding two cases, expressly considers the general question of negligence liability for pure economic loss. The court concluded that there could be liability in negligence for economic loss provided that the loss was not "indeterminate and unmanageable". In any given case, the problem was pragmatic rather than jurisprudential. If the loss was finite, there was no need to speculate on the identity of possible claimants, and if it was a single loss with no multiplicity of actions likely to follow in its train, there was no "pragmatical" objection to allowing recovery provided that other requirements of liability, such as foreseeability of harm, were present.

The court was satisfied that the case before it met these conditions. Rhodesian legislation[13] provided for the registry of "stop-orders" with the Registrar of Farmers' Stop-Orders. A "stop-order" was a written agreement or undertaking by which a farmer gave to another person (the "holder") an interest in or right to a crop produced in Rhodesia and authorised payment to the holder of all or part of the proceeds of the crop. Insurers of a crop in respect of which a stop-order had been registered were required to pay money due under the insurance policy to the Registrar, who would then pay the holder of the stop-order the amount due him. The farmer would receive the residue, if any.

A farmer, Marshall, had registered a stop-order in favour of Tobacco Sales Warehouse (Pvt.) Ltd. (T.S.W.) as security for loans advanced to him. The stop-order was in respect of one year's wheat crop. T.S.W. ceded to the plaintiff, an affiliated company, its right to payment. The stop-order remained registered in the name of

12 1982 (1) Z.L.R. 47 (H.C.), 1982 (3) S.A. 55 (Z.H.C.).

13 Farmers Stop-order Act, c. 110 (1974) (Rhod.).

T.S.W. The crop was insured with the defendant. The defendant was required to pay a substantial sum under the policy for hail damage to the crop. Contrary to the provisions of the legislation, the defendant paid this amount directly to Marshall instead of to the Registrar of Farmers' Stop-Orders. Marshall disappeared and the plaintiff never received the amount due it. The plaintiff sought to recover from the defendant the amount the defendant should have paid to the Registrar. The Registrar would have paid it to T.S.W., which in turn would have transmitted it to the plaintiff.

It was admitted that the defendant had not exercised reasonable care. It should have made enquiry of the Registrar in order to ascertain whether a stop-order existed. The principal issue was the existence of a duty of care to the plaintiff. (Liability for breach of statutory duty was discussed briefly, but no decision was required.) One element was that the plaintiff was not the registered holder of the stop-order. The defendant, which issued much agricultural insurance, knew that insurance proceeds were supposed to be sent to the Registrar if a stop-order had been issued and that it was supposed to ascertain the existence of stop-orders. It therefore knew that creditors who relied on a stop-order as security would not receive the insurance payment if the proceeds of the insurance were not sent to the Registrar. In the court's opinion, it made no difference that the plaintiff was not the registered holder of the stop-order. Loss to creditors other than registered holders was foreseeable to the defendant.

A second element was the nature of the damage: pure economic loss. The court believed that permitting recovery in this case would not open the door to an "indeterminate and unmanageable flood of actions". No calamitous results would ensue. The loss was finite and singular. It could occur only once. The plaintiff's precise identity was not known to the defendant, but this did not matter. Any creditor of an insured farmer could legitimately count on the insurer paying the proceeds of crop insurance to the Registrar. Liability would be limited to this class of creditors, when they were directly affected by failure to pay insurance proceeds to the Registrar. The loss ought to be borne by the insurer in these circumstances. If creditors who advanced money to farmers on security of stop-orders did not have this remedy, they would be less inclined to extend credit, to the detriment of agriculture and the country's economy. Also, liability would deter carelessness in complying with the statutory requirements. Public policy therefore favoured recognition of a duty of care. The defendant owed a duty of care and became liable to the plaintiff for the amount it should have transmitted to the

Registrar.

In *Combrinck Chiropraktiese Kliniek (Edms.) Bpk. v. Datsun Motor Vehicle Distributors (Pty.) Ltd.*,[14] the plaintiff had leased a new car manufactured by the defendant. The leasing company had purchased the car from a garage for the purpose of letting it to the plaintiff. The lease contract provided that the lessor would not be liable for any loss arising from any fault in the vehicle, and the lessee could not cancel the lease or pay a reduced rental on account of any fault. Allegedly there were numerous defects in the car, which the plaintiff soon discovered. It claimed damages from the manufacturer for loss of the use of the vehicle and expenses incurred in its attempts to have the car repaired.

The court held that the plaintiff had no cause of action. Its principal reason was unwillingness to extend delictual liability for economic loss. The court believed that delictual liability would constitute an unjustifiable invasion of the field of contract. Here, if the manufacturer contracted out of liability for defects when it sold the car, the contract would be frustrated if the plaintiff could bring suit. If the manufacturer did not contract out of liability, it could be sued by the party to whom it sold the car as well as by the plaintiff. Furthermore, it could not be said that the manufacturer ought to have foreseen that a later successor to the vehicle would waive his common law remedies to claim from his predecessor for the defects.[15]

Pilkington Brothers (S.A.) (Pty.) Ltd. v. Lillicrap, Wassenaar and Partners[16] involved a contract between the plaintiff, a manufacturer of glass, and the defendant, a firm of consulting and structural engineers. The defendant was to carry out a subsoil investigation of

14 1972 (4) S.A. 185 (T).

15 The decision is criticised in Boberg, *Law of Delict*, 1972 Ann. Surv. S. Afr. L. 130, 133-34. The court in Tobacco Finance (Pvt.) Ltd. v. Zimnat Insurance Co. Ltd., 1982 (1) Z.L.R. 47, 58-59 (H.C.), 1982 (3) S.A. 55, 64-65 (Z.H.C.), discussed pp. 273-75, *supra*, expressed agreement with this criticism, not finding a reason why, if the manufacturer of a defective car may be liable to anyone who suffers physical injury as a result of its negligent manufacture, it is not also liable for the "far more limited and distinctly foreseeable economic loss" of the hirer of a defective vehicle.

16 1983 (2) S.A. 157 (W), rev'd, 1985 (1) S.A. 475 (A.D.). See Boberg, *Back to Winterbottom v. Wright?--Not Quite!*, (1985) 102 S.A.L.J. 213; Burchell & Dendy, *Law of Delict*, 1985 Ann. Surv. S. Afr. L. 179, 181-87; Davis, *Professional Negligence and the Lillicrap Case*, (1985) 9 S. Afr. Ins. L.J. 32 & 54; Pearmain, *A Delictual Remedy for Breach of Contract--To Be or Not To Be?*, (1985) 7 De Jure ac Legibus 22.

the suitability of a site for a glass plant, design works for the plant, and supervise construction. The defendant advised the plaintiff that the site was suitable and designed the works. After construction had begun, the plaintiff assigned its agreement with the defendant to the main construction contractor. The defendant continued to act as engineer for the project, its contractual obligations now running to the contractor. The plaintiff alleged that the defendant was negligent in carrying out the soil investigation, designing the works and supervising construction. The plaintiff was required to employ other experts to carry out a proper soil investigation. Much reconstruction and additional work was necessary to put the plant in a proper condition for the manufacture of glass, and additional manufacturing costs would be incurred.

The plaintiff framed its action in delict because its cause of action in contract had become prescribed. The trial court, in deciding whether the plaintiff had a delictual action to recover its expenses, first rejected the defendant's submission that the plaintiff's claim was entirely for pure economic loss. It regarded claims of damages to remedy defects in construction as claims for physical damage, not pure economic loss, when the defects threatened to cause personal injury or property damage.[17] The court also attributed the damages to alleged negligent conduct in the design and supervision of the plant, not statements made in reports, designs and advice given the plaintiff. The negligence in preparing the soil investigation report, however, involved negligent misstatement, and the resulting loss--the cost of employing additional experts to carry out a proper soil investigation--was purely economic.

By this time it had been established that there could be liability for economic loss caused by misstatement or conduct. Analysing numerous authorities from South Africa and common law jurisdictions, the court concluded that whether a duty of care exists in a particular case depends upon the relationship between the parties and various policy factors, including the need to avoid "indeterminate liability". The factors on which the defendant principally relied were that the parties were in a contractual relationship, with the alleged negligence constituting a breach of the defendant's contractual

17 It follows from this conclusion and the court's approval of the judgment of Lord Denning, M.R., in Dutton v. Bognor Regis Urban District Council, [1972] 1 Q.B. 373, 396 (C.A.), that the plaintiff's claim in Combrinck Chiropraktiese Kliniek (Edms.) Bpk. v. Datsun Motor Vehicles Distributors (Pty.) Ltd., p. 275, *supra*, should have been sustained if any of the car's alleged defects could have caused an accident.

obligations to the plaintiff, and that the plaintiff then assigned the contract to the main construction contractor, to whom the defendant's obligations ran thereafter.

That the negligent conduct also constituted breach of an express or implied contractual obligation to the plaintiff was no obstacle to delictual liability, in the court's opinion. A duty of care could co-exist with a contractual obligation even though it was accepted by the defendant in a contract. In the present case, there was no question of "frustration" of the contract. The contract did not exclude liability in delict, nor did the assignment. If the defendant had an answer to the claim within the terms of a contractual limitation or disclaimer of liability, or because all of the plaintiff's rights were assigned to the main contractor, it could be pleaded. There was no reason to suppose that the defendant could be held liable for the same loss twice--once to the plaintiff and once to the main contractor. The court concluded that the plaintiff's claim could be maintained insofar as it was based on a cause of action in delict. However, the claim to recover the cost of proper soil investigation appeared to be one for contractual damages only. It sought to enforce the defendant's contractual undertaking to do this work. The delictual claim for this cost was therefore struck out.

The defendant successfully appealed to the Appellate Division. That court, one judge dissenting, held that the plaintiff had no delictual claim on the facts alleged.[18] It rejected the trial court's conclusion that the plaintiff had presented a case of damage to property. There was nothing in the pleadings which alleged or implied that the defects in the construction of the plant created a danger of damage to the plaintiff's property. The plaintiff's case was that the defects in the construction of the plant rendered it unsuitable or less suitable for its purpose–a "non-material" loss. The court thought that it would serve no useful purpose to decide whether the plaintiff's claim should be categorised as one based upon negligent misstatement. This would not affect the court's assessment of the relevant policy considerations, on which liability would depend.

The Appellate Division stated that the fact that the plaintiff

18 Lillicrap, Wassenaar and Partners v. Pilkington Brothers (S.A.) (Pty.) Ltd., 1985 (1) S.A. 475 (A.D.). Smuts, A.J.A., dissenting, was in substantial agreement with the trial court concerning liability for economic loss. He would not, however, have struck out the claim for the cost of proper soil investigation. In his opinion, the cost was recoverable as part of the plaintiff's delictual damages if it was incurred in order to take necessary steps to mitigate the loss.

might have framed its action in contract (insofar as the damages arose before the assignment) did not *per se* debar it from claiming in delict. All that it need show was that the facts pleaded established a cause of action in delict. That the relevant facts might have been pleaded so as to raise a claim for contractual damages was, in principle, irrelevant. However, the court's assessment of whether delictual liability should exist was heavily influenced by the existence of contractual liability.

In its opinion, there was no need for delictual liability. Each party had adequate contractual remedies for breach occurring while there was a contractual *nexus* between them. The relief now claimed by the plaintiff could have been claimed in an action based upon breach of contract. Moreover, the delictual action "[did] not fit comfortably in a contractual setting like the present". When parties enter into such a contract, they normally regulate those features which they consider important for the relationship they are creating and contemplate that the contract should lay down the ambit of their reciprocal rights and obligations.

If a delictual action were generally available for defective performance of contractual obligations, a party's performance would presumably have to be tested by the standard of the *bonus paterfamilias* (reasonable man) as well as by the definition of his duties in the contract. If the former standard differed from the contractual one it was excluded by the contract, for the parties had agreed to be bound by the contractual standard. If it were argued that the *bonus paterfamilias* would always comply with the standards laid down in his contract, this would in effect say that the law of delict could be invoked to reinforce the law of contract. No policy considerations justified such a conclusion, and it would be anomalous that the delictual standard of fault should be governed by what was contractually agreed upon by the parties.

Weighing against extension of delictual liability was the fact that a contract may regulate aspects of the parties' relationship other than the parties' respective duties. The contract might limit or extend liability, impose penalties, grant indemnities, or provide special methods of settling disputes, such as arbitration. The law of delict should not operate to eliminate such provisions. That the contracting parties could have expressly excluded delictual liability and failed to do so was no answer. The law of delict should not set a trap for the unwary.

The considerations that led the court to the conclusion that there should be no delictual liability remained applicable upon assignment of the contract. The relationship between the three parties had its origin in contract. It had to be assumed that their respective rights and obligations were regulated to accord to their wishes and that the contractual remedies which would be available were those the parties desired to have at their disposal. A delictual remedy was unnecessary and the parties should not be denied their reasonable expectation that their rights and obligations would be regulated by their contractual arrangements, not circumvented by application of the law of delict.

The court drew a distinction between South African law and English law, reflected in such cases as *Anns v. Merton London Borough Council*[19] and *Junior Books Ltd. v. Veitchi Co. Ltd.*[20] In English law, a *prima facie* duty of care exists if there is a sufficient relationship of proximity or neighbourhood between the parties such that, in the reasonable contemplation of the alleged wrongdoer, carelessness on his part may be likely to cause damage to the victim. One then examines any considerations which ought to negative, reduce or limit the scope of the duty. South African law approaches the matter in a more cautious way. It does not extend the scope of the delictual action to new situations unless there are positive policy considerations which favour such an extension. Also, one of the factors affecting English tort liability for professional negligence--the unenforceability of an agreement made without consideration--was inapplicable to South African law.

The judgment concludes with a reference to the damages that might be awarded. The delictual measure of damages was the loss sustained because of another's wrongful conduct. It had not been alleged that the value of the glass plant was less than what the plaintiff paid for it. The plaintiff's "patrimony" might have been enhanced by erection of the plant, despite its alleged defects. The plaintiff claimed the amount which would have to be spent to bring the plant up to the standard laid down by the contract. In the court's view, this amount did not represent a "loss in the ordinary sense of the word". The plaintiff was in effect suing for the monetary equivalent of its bargain--the contractual measure of damages. This was another reason for refusing to entertain a delictual claim. The plaintiff's complaint was that its plant did not comply with its requirements. To remedy this wrong, damages had to be computed according to the contractual measure because the wrong itself was

19 [1978] A.C. 728 (H.L.).

20 [1983] 1 A.C. 520 (H.L.).

essentially a breach of contract, not a delict.

The Appellate Division's judgment may be read broadly to the effect that there is no delictual liability for "negligent breach" of a contract of professional employment, or negligent performance of professional services rendered pursuant to a contract, unless there would be liability independently of the parties' contractual relationship. An even broader reading is possible, excluding delict when there would be liability absent a contract. One now expects negligence liability for foreseeable economic loss when the loss results from reliance upon professional advice seriously given to the plaintiff, although there was no contract between the parties. The *Pilkington* case may mean that this otherwise-existing liability is excluded when there is a contractual relationship.[21]

On the other hand, the judgment does not deny that performance of a professional contract may create circumstances in which a delictual duty of care is owed. It is aimed at the proposition that a delictual duty arose because the defendant was performing for the plaintiff a contract that included an obligation of reasonable care. Any duty would have to have a broader foundation. That a duty could not arise but for a contract did not necessarily exclude a delictual duty.

The most likely effect of the Appellate Division's decision is to emphasise the distinction between physical damage and economic loss and to increase the burden of justification borne by the plaintiff who makes a delictual claim for economic loss.[22] For personal injury and property damage, delictual liability will be the norm. It will not be excluded by the existence of a contractual relationship. The patient injured by unskillful medical treatment or the lessor whose property is damaged by the lessee's carelessness will be considered to be owed a duty independently of the contract.[23] For economic loss, delictual liability will be extended only when policy considerations warrant.

Rarely will this be the case when a direct or indirect contractual

21 See Hurchison & Visser, *Lillicrap Revisited: Further Thoughts on Pure Economic Loss and Concurrence of Actions*, (1985) 102 S.A.L.J. 587, 590-95.

22 See *ibid.*, 587-90; Davis, *Professional Negligence and the Lillicrap Case*, (1985) 9 S. Afr. Ins. L.J. 32, 58-59.

23 This interpretation is supported by Correira v. Berwind, 1986 (4) S.A. 60 (Z.H.C.) (patient had delictual action against surgeon for harm caused by negligent performance of operation).

relationship existed. The parties had an opportunity to address themselves to economic loss and compensation for it when the contract was formed. An action for breach of contract would usually provide an adequate remedy for economic loss unless the plaintiff had agreed to exclusion of the remedy. The parties could be expected to provide in the contract for losses and expenses of serious concern to them, if not satisfied with the usual contractual obligations and remedies. Where economic loss is concerned, a court would seldom be justified in effectively varying contractual arrangements. A plaintiff's desire to avoid prescription of a contractual claim would not justify application of the law of delict.

In the absence of a contractual relationship, there will remain a wide field in which delictual liability can usefully be extended. Policy considerations will warrant application of the law of delict because it cannot be expected that certain economic losses, whose compensation is desirable, be provided for by contract. The same can be said of most personal injury and property damage caused by negligence: compensation is desirable and cannot be expected to be provided for by contract. When there is a contract, the parties may not have addressed themselves to property damage and, especially, personal injury. Alternatively, they may have had an expectation, which application of the law of delict only confirms, that there would be liability for such harm if negligently caused.[24]

If this interpretation of the *Pilkington* case is accepted, the

24 This point is best illustrated by cases in which the defendant's negligence caused economic loss by cutting off the supply of a product to the plaintiff. In a large proportion of such cases, no contractual relationship between the two parties existed. There was no reason for them to form a contractual relationship. The only remedy is delictual. Delictual liability will be found justified in some cases, but not others. See *e.g.* Franschhoekse Wynkelder (Ko-operatief) Bpk. v. South African Railways and Harbours, 1981 (3) S.A. 36 (C), which distinguishes (not very convincingly) Caltex Oil (Australia) Pty. Ltd. v. The Dredge "Willemstad", (1976) 136 C.L.R. 529. See also Coronation Brick (Pty.) Ltd. v. Strachan Construction Co. (Pty.) Ltd., 1982 (4) S.A. 371 (D), discussed pp. 269-70, *supra*. If the interruption of supply was caused by property damage, the property owner usually will have a delictual remedy against the defendant. The existence of a contract between the owner and the defendant should not exclude delictual liability--at least when the contracting parties did not address events of this nature when they formulated the contract. In contrast, if supply of the product has been cut off by the supplier's negligence, there is no justification for delictual liability for economic loss. The plaintiff has a contractual relationship with its supplier and should be confined to the contractual remedies for interruption or termination of supply.

Appellate Division's judgment warrants favourable consideration in common law jurisdictions, notwithstanding the differences between South African law and English law noted by the court.[25]

25 The judgment is criticised in Beck, *Delictual Liability for Breach of Contract*, (1985) 102 S.A.L.J. 222; Boberg, *Back to Winterbottom v. Wright?--Not Quite!*, (1985) 102 S.A.L.J. 213; Burchell & Dendy, *Law of Delict*, 1985 Ann. Surv. S. Afr. L. 179, 181-87; Pearmain, *A Delictual Remedy for Breach of Contract--To Be or Not To Be?*, (1985) 7 De Jure ac Legibus 22. Its distinction of delictual and contractual liability is supported in van Warmelo, *Liability in Contract and in Delict*, (1985) 102 S.A.L.J. 227. Notwithstanding the criticisms, it is submitted that the Appellate Division was correct in distinguishing between physical damage and economic loss, finding that the plaintiff claimed only economic loss, insisting that justification for subjecting the defendant to delictual liability for economic loss be established, and concluding that in the contractual context found in the *Pilkington* case a delictual remedy was not warranted.

13

PASSING OFF

The principles of liability for "passing off" in Southern Africa are essentially the same as in common law jurisdictions. The result of passing off litigation usually depends upon the facts of the particular case and the relief the court is asked to grant.[1] The following cases are significant because of their consideration of general issues of passing off liability.

GEOGRAPHIC EXTENT OF PROTECTION

Pockets (Holdings) Ltd. v. Oak Holdings Ltd.[2] would have been a very typical passing off case but for the fact that the plaintiffs did little business where the defendant traded. The plaintiffs, a holding company and two subsidiaries, owned businesses in Salisbury, Southern Rhodesia, which had long traded under the name "Pockets". The defendant established similar businesses under the name "Pockets" in Bulawayo, apparently for the deliberate purpose of taking advantage of the goodwill attached to the name. Only one of the plaintiffs actually did business in Bulawayo, and the amount of business it did was small. However, the plaintiffs were well-known to the public there.

The court restrained the defendant from doing business under the

1 See *e.g.* William Bartfield & Co. (Pty.) Ltd. v. Job Hypermarket, 1976 (3) S.A. 157 (T).

2 1953 S.R. 21, 1953 (2) S.A. 659 (S.R.).

name "Pockets". It believed the case fell within the principle that the law will not permit one person to represent that his business is that of another; one could not use a name so as to lead the public to believe that his business was that of another concern. The area in which the goodwill of a business was effective would ordinarily correspond with the area in which the business was carried on. But a reputation might well be established beyond the limits of its immediate operations. In such a case the business must be entitled to protection from the use by others of its good name, provided there is a reasonable prospect that such use may interfere with its trade, present or future.

As an example, if it were possible to find a village in Southern Rhodesia in which there existed no branch or agency of Barclays Bank or the Standard Bank of South Africa, it would be "absurd to suggest" that the courts would not interdict the use of either of these names by a banking house in the village. It was not necessary to prove that anyone actually had been deceived or that confusion actually had arisen. Loss of trade or other actual damage need not be proved in order for the plaintiffs to obtain a restraining order. All that was necessary was that the plaintiffs have a business reputation in the area where the defendant commenced to trade and that there be a "clear probability that deception or confusion may arise".

Under the judgment in *Slenderella Systems Incorporated of America v. Hawkins*,[3] it is not enough that the plaintiff have a business reputation in the sense of being known in the country where the defendant operates. The plaintiff must actually have trade within the country. The plaintiff in this case carried on an extensive weight-reduction business in North America and Europe under the name "Slenderella", marketing both goods and services. For years it had advertised in foreign magazines having a wide circulation in South Africa. It wanted to have the defendant restrained from conducting a "slenderising" business in South Africa under the name "Slenderella", claiming that the defendant misrepresented to the public that it was a branch or subsidiary of the plaintiff. The plaintiff alleged that it intended to open weight-reduction "salons" in South Africa and that it suffered a loss of goodwill because of the defendant's use of the same name.

The court refused the relief sought. The "right of property existing . . . in regard to the name or goodwill enjoyed . . . in

3 1959 (1) S.A. 519 (W).

respect of a trade or goods" would be protected only in relation to a name or goods within the jurisdiction of the court. It was not necessary that the plaintiff actually carry on business in the jurisdiction. It was sufficient if his goods were sold there and gave him a "right of property therein in a reputation, name or goodwill attaching to the goods or business". The plaintiff had no "right of property" in South Africa because it had not marketed anything there. It acquired no right of property through its business in other countries and advertisements read in South Africa. Nor did it suffice that the plaintiff contemplated opening business in South Africa and had registered a patent and trade-mark in preparation for this.

A similar result is found in *Pick-'n-Pay Stores Ltd. v. Pick-'n-Pay Superette (Pvt.) Ltd.*[4] The plaintiff had developed a chain of "Pick-'n-Pay" supermarkets in South Africa. The name "Pick-'n-Pay" was now well-known there. It also had become well-known in neighbouring Rhodesia because of travel between the two countries and advertisements in newspapers circulated in Rhodesia. The Pick-'n-Pay chain did not carry on business in Rhodesia but averred that it was planning to open stores there within the next two to four years if it could use its established name and protect the name from use by others. A supermarket in Salisbury traded under an identical name and copied the logo used by the chain in its South African newspaper advertisements. The chain's proprietor sought to restrain this supermarket's use of the name and logo.

The court held that the chain had no right to the relief sought. It quoted at length from the judgment in the *Slenderella* case but devoted more attention to English cases, especially the "*Crazy Horse*" case, *Alain Bernadin et Compagnie v. Pavilion Properties Ltd.*[5] There it had been decided that for purposes of a passing off action a trader could not acquire goodwill in a country without some sort of user in that country. Advertisement of a foreign establishment did not constitute user. The acquisition of a reputation within the country through advertisements or travel was insufficient to establish the goodwill required in passing off litigation. Reputation without user did not suffice. That the plaintiff intended to expand into the area where the alleged passing off occurred did not persuade the

4 1973 (1) R.L.R. 244 (G.D.), 1973 (3) S.A. 564 (R), aff'd, 1974 (1) S.A. 597 (R.A.D.).

5 [1967] R.P.C. 581 (Ch.).

Rhodesian court that the plaintiff should be protected from the defendant's use of the same name.[6]

PARTIES NOT IN COMPETITION

A related problem arises when the party seeking relief has done business in the area where the opposing party trades but is no longer engaged in business there. This was considered in *Polakow Brothers (Pty.) Ltd. v. Gershlowitz.*[7] The plaintiff had long run a toy shop called "Treasure Island". Because a satisfactory lease could not be obtained and the proprietor's health had declined, the plaintiff closed the shop and sold the stock and fixtures. The plaintiff unsuccessfully attempted to sell the business' goodwill. Another person commenced a similar business, under a different name, at the same location. Two weeks later, the defendant opened a business called "Treasure Island", allegedly with the intent of leading the public to believe that this was the business the plaintiff had conducted. The plaintiff asked that the defendant be restrained from using the name.

The defendant submitted that he became free to use "Treasure Island" when the plaintiff closed its shop; the plaintiff had abandoned the name and no goodwill now attached to the name or the advertisement of it. Moreover, it was generally known that the plaintiff had closed its business and having done so, the plaintiff could suffer no injury as a result of deception or confusion. The court held that a person who had closed his business could be protected if his business name (and advertising) continued to have a reputation and its use by others might cause deception or confusion. It was for the plaintiff to prove the existence of a residual reputation. This had been proved in the present case. Then, however, the defendant had an opportunity to prove abandonment of the right to the name and the goodwill attaching to it. If abandonment was proved, the defendant was free to use the name. This would be determined at a trial, pending which the court granted a temporary interdict against the defendant.

The court did not specify the purpose served by restraining a person from trading on the reputation of a closed business or the

6 The court's judgment and reasons were confirmed by the Rhodesian Appellate Division. Pick-'n-Pay Stores Ltd. v. Pick-'n-Pay Superette (Pvt.) Ltd., 1974 (1) S.A. 597 (R.A.D.).

7 1976 (1) S.A. 863 (S.E.).

harm the proprietor of the closed business would suffer if this conduct were not restrained. The court apparently had in mind that the proprietor might (as the plaintiff in this case did) wish to sell the business' goodwill after its closure, and the goodwill would be saleable only if other traders were prevented from appropriating it free of charge.

Competition between the parties may also be absent because they conduct different types of businesses. This was considered by the Appellate Division in *Capital Estate and General Agencies (Pty.) Ltd. v. Holiday Inns Inc.*[8] The parent and members of the Holiday Inn group of companies, which operated hotels and motels around the world, brought an action against companies which were using the name "Holiday Inn" in a shopping centre and a complex of forty-four "duplex chalets". The defendants contended that the name "Holiday Inn" was distinctive of the plaintiffs' hotel and motel business only; its right to the exclusive use of the name was limited to those businesses.

The court disagreed, holding that a "common field of activity" was not required. If, despite the absence of a common field, there was a reasonable likelihood of the public being confused into believing that the defendants' business was connected with the plaintiffs', relief could be granted. That the parties' activities were different went only to the factual issues of the likelihood of confusion and damages. It could not be accepted as axiomatic that damage could not arise when there was no common field of activity. The trial judge had found that confusion was likely. People who saw the name "Holiday Inn" on the shopping centre or the duplex chalet project would assume a connection with the hotel chain. This finding was upheld by the appellate court.

Regarding damage, there could be no diversion of custom but the Appellate Division found "sufficient potential prejudice" to warrant restraining the defendants' use of the name. The plaintiffs' reputation could be damaged if the shopping centre or chalet project were run in an unsatisfactory way or had financial difficulties. Even in the absence of evidence of unsatisfactory conduct in the past, it could be assumed that it might occur in the future. The plaintiffs would be granted protection so that their reputation would not be at the mercy of parties who wrongly conducted themselves so as to cause confusion.

The judgment in *Lorimar Productions Inc. v. Sterling Clothing*

8 1977 (2) S.A. 916 (A.D.).

Manufacturers (Pty.) Ltd.[9] contains the most comprehensive review of the common law's application to "character merchandising" to be found in any law report. As described in the judgment, character merchandising involves the commercial use of names and likenesses of the personages, characters, locations, titles, logos and derivatives therefrom of a television series, feature film or other entertainment programme. Programme producers and their agents offer and sell (for substantial sums) licences and endorsements to business interests. Those interests contemplate increasing consumer demand for their products or services by associating them with a popular film, television programme, celebrity, fictitious character, etc.

In this case the plaintiffs were Lorimar Productions, the producers of the popular American television series *Dallas*; an American company engaged in character merchandising and distribution of films and television series, which Lorimar had appointed to do character merchandising for *Dallas*; and a company which had received an exclusive appointment to do *Dallas* character merchandising in South Africa, one of the countries in which *Dallas* was televised. There were three defendants, all of which used features of *Dallas* without a licence from Lorimar or its agents. One was a company which marketed "Southfork" jeans and used the letters "JR" in its advertising.[10] A second was the proprietor of a major chain of retail stores, which procured and sold numerous items of "Dallas" clothing and accessories in its "Western Departments". It also used "JR" in its advertising. The third was the owner of the "Dallas Restaurant" in Pretoria, which named menu items after *Dallas* characters and allegedly had a caricature of J.R. Ewing on the front door. The plaintiffs sought an interim order restraining the defendants from use of any characters, locations, persons, titles, logos and concepts depicted in the *Dallas* television series.

The court held that there was no passing off in this case. In order for a plaintiff to have an action, it must have a reputation or goodwill in the respect in which the alleged passing off occurs. Otherwise, there can be no deception of the public. Lorimar had a reputation and goodwill in South Africa pertaining to the entertainment field, but it had none in relation to clothing or

9 1981 (3) S.A. 1129 (T).

10 The fame of *Dallas* is such that it is probably unnecessary to mention that "JR" represents the initials of "J.R. Ewing", the most prominent character of *Dallas*, and "Southfork" is the ranch on which live J.R. Ewing and the other principal characters, the members of the Ewing family.

restaurants. Neither Lorimar nor its agents (the other plaintiffs) had taken any steps to create an association between *Dallas* and clothing or restaurants. That the *Dallas* names, characters, locations and logos could be used to attract custom did not give Lorimar goodwill in whatever field it intended to use these features. Where a goodwill or reputation exists, a name, mark, logo, etc., will "conjure up" in the public mind the particular class of article or service for which the holder is known.

The court considered separately the likelihood of deception or confusion. It found no such likelihood. The defendants attempted to take advantage of the publicity and public interest generated by the *Dallas* series, but their conduct did not represent that Lorimar had a proprietary interest in them or approved their merchandise or cuisine. The plaintiffs claimed that deception was likely; character licensing was a well-known fact of contemporary life and the public would assume the existence of a licence from or association with the production company when elements of a television or film production were used to market products. However, character merchandising was not well-known in South Africa and no evidence of actual deception was adduced. The court believed that the public would perceive the true situation: "blatant copying without permission". It was not moved by the plaintiffs' fears that *Dallas*' popularity as well as the marketing of licences could be adversely affected if the defendants' products were poor or unsuitable. Neither was it deterred by the fact that it would be difficult, if not impossible, for the plaintiffs to licence the use of *Dallas* features in South Africa if the defendants' unlicensed user was not restrained.[11]

NON-COMMERCIAL PARTIES

Old Apostolic Church of Africa v. Non-White Old Apostolic Church of Africa[12] is one of the few reported passing off actions between two charitable organisations. The Old Apostolic Church sought to prevent a breakaway group from using the name "Non-White Old Apostolic Church". Apparently the principal grievance was the defendant's use of "Old". Among the issues presented was whether the law of passing off was applicable to parties not carrying

11 The plaintiffs also sought relief on the ground of the South African delict of "unlawful competition". See pp. 298-300, *infra*.

12 1975 (2) S.A. 684 (C).

on a trade.

The court held that it was. In the case of a church, it did not trade but was "something akin to a business". It required money from donations and might be joined or left at will. If its "business" was likely to be adversely affected by unlawful activities, the activities could be restrained. The defendant's name was likely to cause confusion and constituted passing off because it would lead uninformed persons to believe that the defendant was a branch of the plaintiff. Potential church members and benefactors would be misled into joining or donating to the defendant, to the detriment of the plaintiff.

DEFENDANT TRADING UNDER PERSONAL NAME

The plaintiff in *Boswell-Wilkie Circus (Pty.) Ltd. v. Brian Boswell Circus (Pty.) Ltd.*[13] owned and operated the Boswell-Wilkie Circus. The defendants established a new circus called the "Brian Boswell Circus". The plaintiff claimed that in using the Boswell name, the defendants were passing off their business as that of the plaintiff. The defendants were Brian Boswell and a company solely owned by him, Brian Boswell Circus (Pty.) Ltd. He was a member of the Boswell family, which had founded Boswell's Circus, a predecessor of the Boswell-Wilkie Circus. The family controlled Boswell's Circus for almost fifty years but had been out of the circus business for two decades.

The trial court's first step was to determine whether the name Boswell, when attached to a circus, had gained a "secondary meaning" which denoted the plaintiff's circus. The court found it did; the name was distinctive of the plaintiff's circus in the minds of the public. The name had been tied exclusively to the plaintiff's circus, a highly popular one, for seventy years. There was evidence that the Boswell-Wilkie Circus was still known as "Boswell's Circus". The reputation of the Boswell name was such that it continued to be included in the name of the circus after the Boswell family lost control and after the circus' merger with Wilkie's Circus. The next step was to determine whether the defendants' use of the Boswell name would lead the ordinary person to believe that the defendants' circus was the same as the plaintiff's circus or connected with it.

13 1984 (1) S.A. 734 (N), aff'd, 1985 (4) S.A. 466 (A.D.). See Boberg, *Of Bread and Circuses*, (1985) 14 Businessman's Law 233.

The court believed this was highly likely. Thus the plaintiff made out a *prima facie* case of passing off.

The court then began to consider the circumstance that the defendants were using the personal name of their circus' proprietor, Brian Boswell. Could a person be restrained from trading under his own name? In this regard, the court saw no reason to distinguish between Brian Boswell and the company of which he was sole proprietor. If he was free to run Brian Boswell's Circus himself, he was equally free to run it through a wholly-owned company. The court undertook a lengthy and incisive examination of the English cases bearing on the question. They reflected a diversity of judicial opinion, but it had been recognised repeatedly that a name which truthfully identified a business' proprietor, product or service could falsely represent that the business or product was that of another. This would occur when the name had come to signify particularly the business or product of the latter person and thus have a secondary meaning.

The court concluded that an interdict could be granted in these circumstances. A person's use of his own name was no exception to the law's prohibition of passing off of businesses and products. While Brian Boswell understandably believed that as a member of the Boswell family he was entitled to capitalise on its reputation in presenting circuses, that reputation now belonged to the plaintiff. The defendants could not trade on it without "poaching on the [plaintiff's] property". They were enjoined from operating a circus or presenting or promoting a circus performance under the name Boswell or any name of which Boswell was a part.

The Appellate Division dismissed an appeal by the defendants.[14] It substantially agreed with the trial court's conclusions but believed that the defendants should not have been prohibited in absolute terms from using the name Boswell. Use of the name would be permissible if it were made clear to the circus-going public that the defendants' circus was not the plaintiff's or connected with the plaintiff's. The Appellate Division altered the trial court's order by adding the proviso "without clearly distinguishing their circus or performance from the circus of the [plaintiff]". This would permit the defendants to use the name Boswell, without first obtaining modification of the order, if they devised an effective means of preventing confusion of their circus with the plaintiff's.

14 Brian Boswell Circus (Pty.) Ltd. v. Boswell-Wilkie Circus (Pty.) Ltd., 1985 (4) S.A. 466 (A.D.).

PRODUCT SIMULATION

The judgments in *John Waddington Ltd. v. Arthur E. Harris (Pty.) Ltd.*[15] make it clear that a defendant will not be prevented from selling a product that deliberately copies almost all features of the plaintiff's product, so long as the defendant distinguishes his product in such a way that potential buyers are unlikely to be deceived into thinking that the defendant's product is the plaintiff's. The plaintiff was the British manufacturer and distributor of the board game "Monopoly". After years of exporting Monopoly sets to South Africa, the plaintiff had appointed an agent to manufacture and distribute Monopoly there. The agent was the only source of Monopoly in South Africa. The defendant (which had been the plaintiff's agent) commenced manufacture and distribution of its own board game, "Big Deal". Big Deal copied Monopoly in all significant respects except for the game's name and the use of South African names rather than English names in the properties on the board.

The plaintiff alleged that the defendant was passing off Big Deal as Monopoly. Its attempt to have the manufacture and sale of Big Deal restrained on an interim basis failed. The plaintiff's patent on Monopoly had expired, so the defendant was entitled to copy the plaintiff's product, provided it was not passed off as the plaintiff's own. The plaintiff's game was well-known by the name "Monopoly". The defendant's game was clearly labelled "Big Deal" and there was no evidence that anyone was led to believe that Big Deal was Monopoly. A person might think there was a trade connection between Monopoly and Big Deal because of their similarity, but it was more likely that purchasers would realise that Monopoly's manufacturer would never allow its product to be sold under a different name. A likelihood of deception, therefore, was not established.

In *Agriplas (Pty.) Ltd. v. Andrag & Sons (Pty.) Ltd.*,[16] the principal plaintiff manufactured plastic irrigation devices called "drippers". They carried no mark or trade name except the letters "DII". The plaintiff sued to have the defendant restrained from selling drippers of the same size, shape and colour (black) as the plaintiff's. The defendant contended that these features were purely functional and that the plaintiff was not entitled to stop the defendant

15 1968 (3) S.A. 405 (T), aff'g 1968 (1) S.A. 38 (T).

16 1981 (4) S.A. 873 (C).

from marketing a product with the same features.

The court held that the reputation and goodwill which could be protected must relate only to the non-functional elements of an article. A newcomer was not required to distinguish the functional features of his article from an established trader's. Purely functional features and features common to the trade were not part of a trader's "get-up" and could be freely copied. If this were not so, reasoned the court, no rival could use the most effective or efficient design. His product would not serve its function in the best manner. Also, a trader who marketed a purely functional article under a patent would be able to claim a perpetual monopoly after the patent lapsed because, as the sole trader, he might well claim a reputation and goodwill in respect of the functional shape and size.

The court in effect defined a "purely functional element" of an article as one which could not be altered without in some way limiting or otherwise affecting the article's function. It also appears to have regarded as functional elements those which made the manufacture or distribution of the article less expensive or difficult. The court's judgment contains an additional formulation of the distinction between purely functional features and non-functional features: the former are required for effective use of the article at an economic price and the latter are added with the object of successfully marketing the article. The court found that apart from the letters "DII" the plaintiff's dripper had functional features only. Thus it had no distinctive get-up. Also, no features of the defendant's dripper (including its colour) could be changed without sacrificing functionality. Accordingly, the court refused the plaintiff's application for an interdict. The court also held that the plaintiff was not entitled to relief because it failed to establish that it had acquired a reputation based on its dripper's size, shape and colour and that the defendant's dripper would be confused with the plaintiff's.

In *Rusmarc (S.A.) (Pty.) Ltd. v. Hemdon Enterprises (Pty.) Ltd.*,[17] the plaintiff imported and distributed cigarette holders and refill cartridges manufactured by a Japanese company, Terasaki. Terasaki usually sold these goods under the "Friend" trade-mark, but the goods Terasaki provided the plaintiff were trade-marked "Win" by agreement with the proprietor of that mark. The defendant subsequently imported identical cigarette holders and refill cartridges manufactured by Terasaki and trade-marked "Friend". Win and Friend products had the same distinctive packaging. Nothing was added by the importers

17 1975 (4) S.A. 626 (W).

or distributors in South Africa.

The court did not decide the issue of whether the defendant was passing off Friend cigarette holders and cartridges as Win products. It held that the plaintiff, as an importer who contributed nothing to the get-up of the Win products, had acquired no reputation or goodwill through the get-up and therefore was not entitled to have the defendant restrained from using it. The Win name was associated with the product, not the plaintiff. If anyone acquired a reputation through the get-up and could prevent the defendant from using it, it was the manufacturer.

This decision was relied upon by the defendant in *Salusa (Pty.) Ltd. v. Eagle International Traders*.[18] The plaintiff imported from Europe a product entitled the "MD4 Stop Smoking Method". This was a set of four cigarette holders designed to progressively reduce a smoker's intake of "tar" and nicotine and enable him to give up the habit. It came in a distinctive packaging--essentially the same as the packaging used in Europe except for language variations. The European manufacturer gave the plaintiff the exclusive right to market MD4 holders in Southern Africa. The plaintiff undertook an expensive campaign to develop the market. The holders were sold by retail pharmacies at a substantial mark-up.

The defendant then began to import MD4 holders from Europe, manufactured by the same firm as the plaintiff's. The defendant had them packaged in a "bubble pack" which used the same lettering and colours as the plaintiff's product and incorporated the name "MD4 Stop Smoking Method". The defendant sold them to a chain of stores. The stores sold the MD4 holders for about half of the price charged by the retail pharmacies. It was clear from the packaging and the stores' advertising that the holders sold by these stores were the same as the plaintiff's. The plaintiff claimed that the defendant was passing off its goods as the plaintiff's.

The court sustained the plaintiff's claim and granted an interdict. It found that the plaintiff had established a reputation and created a demand for the MD4 holders, which the defendant was exploiting. In South Africa, the name and get-up had become distinctive of the plaintiff rather than the manufacturer. Although the court did not say so explicitly, this is what distinguished the case before it from the *Rusmarc* case. One of the relevant factors was that the European manufacturer generally stayed in the background and allowed the holders to become identified with the concerns in various countries

18 1979 (4) S.A. 697 (C).

with whom the manufacturer had exclusive sales agreements. Also, it was the plaintiff's decision to use the MD4 name and the same get-up as used in Europe.

The restraint imposed upon the defendant was limited. The defendant was prohibited from making up a pack for the holders which used the name "MD4 Stop Smoking Method" and so resembled the plaintiff's pack that it could reasonably be taken for it. The defendant was not prohibited from importing holders already packaged by a foreign trader in the same pack as the plaintiff's, for the defendant and the foreign trader had a right to lawfully sell the holders as the foreign firm's goods.

The law of passing off does protect a person who places his own trade-mark on products manufactured by another. Passing off would literally occur if his trade-mark were attached by someone else to identical products of the same manufacture. Legal relief for this probably could be obtained. One might therefore accept that the plaintiff in the *Salusa* case, having decided that "MD4 Stop Smoking Method" should be the name of the product it sold, was entitled to have the defendant restrained from attaching the same name to the product the defendant sold. But the MD4 name was actually attached to the product in Europe, from which both the plaintiff and defendant imported it. The plaintiff's complaint really was not that the defendant was misrepresenting to consumers that the defendant's product was the plaintiff's. It was that the defendant was effectively informing consumers of the fact that the product sold by the defendant was the same as the product sold by the plaintiff. The required element of deception was not present.

The court's decision created a substantial barrier to competition by requiring the defendant to bear the cost of importing the product fully packaged or creating a market for a "new" product--that is, one distinct from the plaintiff's product. The defendant might find it necessary to give a new brand name to the holders it sold. Generally, the law of passing off should not be used to restrain a person from selling a product under a certain brand name and packaging if it is the "genuine article", even if the plaintiff has a reputation for selling the same product under the same name or packaging.[19] The plaintiff's reputation as distributor of the MD4

19 In Hampo Systems (Pty.) Ltd. v. Audiolens (Cape) (Pty.) Ltd., 1985 (4) S.A. 257 (C), the court concluded that in selling genuine Pentax cameras, the defendant did not pass off its business as being that of or connected with the authorised Pentax distributor in South Africa, and it was not necessary for the defendant to expressly disavow any connection with that distributor. See

holders could have been appropriately protected by requiring that the defendant be identified as the distributor or importer on the packages the defendant sold. This would have enabled the persons concerned with the identity of the distributor to discover it, while making clear to retail consumers (who ordinarily would not care who distributed the product) that the product distributed by the defendant was the same as the product distributed by the plaintiff.

Visser, *Law of Patents, Designs, Trade Marks and Copyright*, 1985 Ann. Surv. S. Afr. L. 371, 377-80.

14

UNLAWFUL COMPETITION

A business interest which fears loss of trade caused by means other than passing off may obtain a judicial remedy in South Africa under the doctrine of "unlawful competition". This encompasses some more specific causes of action found in common law jurisdictions, such as injurious falsehood[1] and breach of confidence.[2] The scope of "unlawful competition" is unsettled, but it could cover as wide a field as its American counterpart, "unfair competition".[3]

FALSE REPRESENTATIONS

The conduct alleged in *Gove v. Geary & Son (Pty.) Ltd.*[4] was the reverse of passing off. The defendant was a firm of springsmiths. It competed with the plaintiff, a firm which manufactured and dealt in motor vehicle springs. Allegedly, the defendant falsely advertised that it manufactured suspension coil springs and sold as being of its own manufacture suspension coil springs manufactured by the plain-

1 See Post Newspapers (Pty.) Ltd. v. World Printing & Publishing Co. Ltd., 1970 (1) S.A. 454 (W).

2 See pp. 304-06, *infra*.

3 See Callmann, The Law of Unfair Competition, Trademarks and Monopolies, ch. 2 (4th ed. 1981); McCarthy, Trademarks and Unfair Competition 12-31 (2d ed. 1984).

4 1963 (4) S.A. 95 (D), rev'd, 1964 (1) S.A. 434 (A.D.).

tiff, thereby gaining an improper advantage in its competition with the plaintiff. As a result, the plaintiff lost customers to the defendant.

The trial court identified as the governing principle that interference with the trade of another was not unlawful and not actionable unless the defendant used unlawful means.[5] The court held that the means alleged were unlawful and the plaintiff stated an action.

> [Allegedly, undue and improper] advantage was obtained as a result of the attribution by the defendant to itself of the skill and experience of the manufacturer of the suspension coil springs which it utilised and sold, that is to say, of the skill and experience of the plaintiff. Just as in the case of passing off the law does not permit a trader to pass off his goods as those of his rival and thus reap the benefit of the latter's reputation by deceiving the public, so also in my view is it wrongful conduct to hold out in trade competition that the product of the skill and experience of a rival is of one's own manufacture.[6]

The Appellate Division, interpreting the plaintiff to have alleged wilful falsehood, agreed that conduct of this type was actionable but held that the necessary allegations had not been made with sufficient clarity.[7]

MISAPPROPRIATION

In the "*Dallas*" case, *Lorimar Productions Inc. v. Sterling Clothing Manufacturers (Pty.) Ltd.*,[8] which was discussed in connection with passing off,[9] the plaintiffs argued "unlawful

5 The court declined to express an opinion on whether otherwise lawful conduct could be unlawful when the defendant was actuated by malice. Malice was not alleged.

6 *Ibid.*, 102.

7 Geary & Son (Pty.) Ltd. v. Gove, 1964 (1) S.A. 434 (A.D.). See Gemini, *Trade Competition and False Representations*, 1964 Comm. & Muni. L. Rptr. 62.

8 1981 (3) S.A. 1129 (T).

9 See pp. 287-89, *supra*.

competition" as an alternative ground of action. They contended that it was unlawful for the defendants to use for their own business advantage the creations of the producers of *Dallas*--characters and names from the television series and the publicity and goodwill which the producers had generated--and deprive the plaintiffs of opportunities to profit from the publicity and goodwill by character merchandising, *i.e.* the sale of licences permitting the use of *Dallas* characters and names in products and advertising.

The court declared: "the norm to be applied is the objective one of public policy. This is the general sense of justice of the community, the *boni mores*, manifested in public opinion."[10] In determining and applying this norm in a particular case, the interests of the competing parties were to be weighed, bearing in mind also the interests of society. The business ethics of that section of the community where the norm was to be applied were of major importance. Relevant factors were the protection already afforded by statutes and established common law remedies, such as passing off; the morals of the market-place, *i.e.* the ethics of the business community concerned; "an inherent sense of fairplay and honesty"; the importance of a free market and strong competition in the economic system; whether the parties concerned were competitors; and international conventions such as the Convention of Paris for the Protection of Industrial Property.

The court's consideration of these factors led it to decide that the plaintiffs could not succeed on the basis of unlawful competition. Common law principles, statutes and international conventions in related fields provided no basis for concluding that the plaintiffs should be protected or that the defendants' conduct was *contra bonos mores*. The American law of "unfair competition" did not protect characters or prevent the copying of products and designs--even when a defendant thereby appropriated the skill and labour of the plaintiff and avoided the expense involved in designing and preparing an article, putting himself in a position to undercut the plaintiff. There was no clear proof of business ethics in the relevant sections of the community: traders, manufacturers, television producers and their agents. Licensing was a common practice and it was arguably unfair to deprive the plaintiffs of royalties from it. On the other hand, infringements of their so-called rights were "legion", commercial enterprises engaged in competition were forever seeking new and

10 Lorimar Productions Inc. v. Sterling Clothing Manufacturers (Pty.) Ltd., 1981 (3) S.A. 1129, 1152 (T).

more attractive methods of presenting their goods to the public, and undue restriction upon imitation might inhibit a free market and the advertising necessary to full competition. That mere copying was not necessarily contrary to the community's sense of justice was indicated by the fact that articles made under an expired patent could be reproduced with impunity.

The court considered the fact that the plaintiffs and defendants were not competitors "in the normal sense of the word" to be a factor of major importance. The defendants did not affect Lorimar (the producer of *Dallas*) in its "normal business", the entertainment field. Also, Lorimar could not acquire sole rights in geographic names such as "Dallas" even if it had made the names famous. Overall, the court concluded that neither the morals of the market-place nor the interests of society required that the defendants' conduct be adjudged against public policy and unlawful.

Sea Harvest Corporation (Pty.) Ltd. v. Irvin & Johnson Ltd.[11] posed the question whether it was unlawful competition for a trader to adopt descriptive words prominently featured in a rival's advertising campaign. The parties were the two leading distributors of frozen fish products in South Africa. The plaintiff commenced an advertising campaign which described its products as "prime cuts" of fish. Until that time, the term "prime cuts" had not been used in South Africa in relation to fish, although it was well-known in relation to meat. (It had been applied to fish in North America.) The campaign was claimed to be extremely successful. Despite the extensive use of the words "prime cuts" in the plaintiff's advertising, they appeared on the plaintiff's packages only in small print in descriptions of fish products, such as "boneless prime cuts of natural hake". About a year after the plaintiff's advertising was launched, the defendant introduced a new product called "Kingklip prime cuts". The plaintiff applied for an order restraining the defendant from passing off its "Kingklip prime cuts" as the product of the plaintiff and from otherwise selling fish products bearing the appellation "prime cuts".

The court decided that there was no passing off. Each party packaged its products under its well-known trade name--Sea Harvest and I & J respectively--and there was no confusion between them. The defendant therefore could not be restrained from using the term "prime cuts" on the basis of passing off. There remained the plaintiff's argument that it was entitled to relief on the ground of unlawful competition. The basis of this argument was that the

11 1985 (2) S.A. 355 (C).

plaintiff's successful advertising campaign, featuring the words "prime cuts", was a valuable asset acquired at considerable expense, which formed part of the plaintiff's right to attract custom. It would be damaged by the defendant's adoption of "prime cuts". This was unlawful competition because the defendant was deliberately misappropriating or "filching" the plaintiff's asset in order to share in the plaintiff's success without payment, and also to dilute the effect of the plaintiff's marketing campaign.

The court rejected the claim of unlawful competition--primarily because it regarded "prime cuts" as descriptive words, appropriate to the product, in which no trader could have a monopoly. It was prepared to accept for the sake of argument that when a trader, for the purpose of a structured and cohesive advertising campaign, develops and uses a slogan or catchword which forms a prominent component of the campaign, there may be circumstances in which a competitor's use of the same slogan or catchword is unlawful, even though there is no passing off. But in assessing whether this conduct offended against the general sense of justice of the community--the criterion of unlawful competition--it was relevant to have regard to principles which had already been laid down in relation to established remedies such as passing off and injurious falsehood.

A long line of passing off and trade-mark cases had established that where descriptive words (as opposed to invented or fancy words) were used in a trade name or mark, courts would not easily find that the words had become distinctive of the business or products of the person using them and would not grant what amounted to a monopoly in such words. The court viewed this principle as applicable to cases of alleged unfair dealing other than passing off. If a trader could not claim a monopoly in descriptive words as part of the name of his business or product, equally he could not claim a monopoly for those words if used as part of an advertising campaign. Another person was free to adopt the same words. That the defendant deliberately made use of the words for its own benefit, at the plaintiff's expense, did not render its conduct unlawful.

In *Butt v. Schultz*,[12] the plaintiff and defendant built and sold boats. Over a period of twenty-four years, the plaintiff had developed and produced "Butt-Cat" hulls for a catamaran-type boat. The hulls were made from moulds. The plaintiff sold someone a Butt-Cat hull that had been rejected because of its unsatisfactory

12 1984 (3) S.A. 568 (E), aff'd, 1986 (3) S.A. 677 (A.D.). See Boberg, *All's* Not *Fair in Business Competition*, (1986) 16 Businessman's Law 62.

finish. The defendant acquired this hull and used it to construct a mould, substantially identical to the plaintiff's mould, from which hulls nearly identical to the Butt-Cat could be produced. The defendant then made such hulls for boats that he sold in competition with the plaintiff. The plaintiff contended that the defendant had engaged in unlawful competition. A lower court and the Appellate Division agreed. The defendant was restrained from using in the manufacture of his catamaran hulls any Butt-Cat hull manufactured by the plaintiff or mould made therefrom, with or without modifications.

The lower court's decision rested principally upon two lines of authority. One line consisted of breach of confidence cases. These indicated that design information which gave the producer an advantage over a competitor was judicially protectible when the materials used and the finished product were freely available to the public. The other line of authority originated in the American "*I.N.S.*" case, *International News Service v. Associated Press*.[13] There, the Supreme Court of the United States sustained an action by a news agency against a competing agency for copying news published by the plaintiff's member newspapers and selling the copied news to its own customers. This indicated that the sale of a product to the public did not necessarily permit a competitor to copy or use the product freely. The Supreme Court had said:

> The right of the purchaser of a single newspaper to spread knowledge of its contents gratuitously, for any legitimate purpose not unreasonably interfering with complainant's right to make merchandise of it, may be admitted; but to transmit that news for commercial use, in competition with complainant . . . is a very different matter. In doing this defendant, by its very act, admits that it is taking material that has been acquired by complainant as the result of organization and the expenditure of labor, skill, and money, and which is salable by complainant for money, and that defendant in appropriating it and selling it as its own is endeavoring to reap where it has not sown, and by disposing of it to newspapers that are competitors of complainant's members is appropriating to itself the harvest of those who have sown. Stripped of all disguises, the process amounts to an unauthorized interference with the normal operation of complainant's legitimate business

13 248 U.S. 215 (1918).

> precisely at the point where the profit is to be reaped, in order to divert a material portion of the profit from those who have earned it to those who have not; with special advantage to defendant in the competition because of the fact that it is not burdened with any part of the expense of gathering the news. The transaction speaks for itself, and a court of equity ought not to hesitate long in characterizing it as unfair competition in business.[14]

This provided the basis for judicial action to prevent the defendant from taking advantage of the plaintiff's industry, inventiveness, expertise and expenditures, unburdened by the labour and expense to which the plaintiff was put, and depriving the plaintiff of the expected profit. Breach of confidence cases also supported this.

In the court's opinion, it followed that it was unlawful for a person to construct hulls not to his own design, but according to a competitor's drawing and plans or ("even more reprehensible") by use of a mould made by the competitor. Copying might be lawful if features of another person's design were incorporated into one's own design, but slavish adaptation of another's design, even as the starting point prior to modification, would usually be unlawful. Competitors were entitled to design a hull with similar features to the plaintiff's, but they had to "start from the beginning, not on the second or third rung of the ladder".

The Appellate Division[15] disapproved the lower court's judgment insofar as it was based on principles of breach of confidence. The design of the Butt-Cat hull was in the public domain; there was nothing confidential about it. But the appellate court accepted the application of *I.N.S.* The principles enunciated in *I.N.S.* were said to be generally in accordance with the approach adopted by South African courts in unfair competition cases, as were the principles of other Western legal systems as summarised in a recent text:

> foreign jurisdictions *selectively* control slavish imitation through their unfair competition laws. In the absence of specific industrial property rights, by no means all copying is prohibited; but where it is felt to be "unfair", the law will provide a remedy. As well as the fact of copying, the

14 *Ibid.*, 239-40.

15 Schultz v. Butt, 1986 (3) S.A. 667 (A.D.).

> judge can consider the scale of the plaintiff's initial investment, the originality and commercial success of his product, the ease with which it was copied, the technical and commercial feasibility of product differentiation, and the economic sense or nonsense of requiring investment in redesigning a satisfactory product from scratch. He can also scrutinise the behaviour of the parties, taking account, for example, of any unfairness in the way information was obtained, impropriety of motive, and dubious marketing practices, including public deception. His aim is to reach a decision which is fair as between the parties while paying due regard to the public's interest in free, as well as fair, competition.[16]

Applying these principles, the defendant's conduct constituted unfair competition. The community would condemn as unfair and unjust the use of the plaintiff's hull, evolved with considerable expenditure of time, labour and money, to form a mould with which to make boats in competition with the plaintiff. There was no sufficient countervailing public interest that shielded the defendant from liability.

The Appellate Division deflected the defendant's submission that the copying of something not protected by the Copyright Act, the Patents Act or the Design Act was not unlawful. The question to be decided was not whether one could lawfully copy the product of another but whether "A, in making a substantially identical copy, with the use of B's mould, of an article made by B, and selling it in competition with B, is engaging in unfair competition". The court believed that the United States Supreme Court, in deciding decades after *I.N.S.* that the copying of an article not protected by a federal patent or copyright could not be prohibited under state unfair competition law,[17] had ruled on a constitutional question that had no bearing on the present problem.

BREACH OF CONFIDENCE

In *Dun and Bradstreet (Pty.) Ltd. v. S.A. Merchants Combined*

16 Fellner, The Future of Legal Protection for Industrial Design 200 (1985).

17 Sears, Roebuck & Co. v. Stiffel Co., 376 U.S. 225 (1964); Compco Corp. v. Day-Brite Lighting, Inc., 376 U.S. 234 (1964).

Credit Bureau (Cape) (Pty.) Ltd.,[18] the plaintiff and the defendant carried on the business of supplying credit information. The plaintiff supplied information to subscribers in a publication entitled *Credit Records*. Subscription carried the condition that the information contained in *Credit Records* be held in confidence and not revealed to other persons. Allegedly the defendant, which was not a subscriber, obtained and recorded information from *Credit Records* and used it to furnish credit reports to the defendant's subscribers. The plaintiff sought damages for loss of trade, an accounting of income derived from the defendant's use of the information, and an order requiring the defendant to deliver up all records containing information reproduced from *Credit Records*.

The defendant had supplied its subscribers with both oral and written reports. The court did not address the written reports, for which the plaintiff's action was based on its statutory copyright. The plaintiff presented a common law claim with respect to the oral reports as these did not breach the statutory copyright. Believing that there was no common law copyright in South African law, counsel for the plaintiff relied upon "breach of confidence". He submitted that the defendant's obtaining and using confidential information from *Credit Records* was actionable in delict either as the unlawful misappropriation of the plaintiff's property or as unlawful interference with the plaintiff's business.

The court would not accept that the information was property under the common law or that the plaintiff had any action based upon rights to information as such. The plaintiff's rights under its contracts with subscribers could be treated as property, but the plaintiff did not allege that the defendant caused or induced any breach of contract by subscribers. The court did, however, accept that in certain circumstances breach of confidence was actionable as unlawful interference with trade or business. It did not find helpful the proposition that interference with trade was unlawful when the defendant used unlawful means, believing that this begged the question of what constituted unlawful means. Instead, the primary criteria were fairness and honesty. Dishonest and fraudulent means of competition were unlawful.

The court characterised conduct of the type alleged in this case as "dishonest and a fraud upon the compiler of the information". It decided that

18 1968 (1) S.A. 209 (C). See Copeling, *Dun and Bradstreet (Pty.) Ltd. (Plaintiff/Respondent) v. S.A. Merchants Combined Credit Bureau (Cape) (Pty.) Ltd. (Defendant/Excipient)*, (1968) 31 T.H.R.-H.R. 180.

> where, as in this case, a trader has by the exercise of his skill and labour compiled information which he distributes to his clients upon a confidential basis (*i.e.* upon the basis that the information should not be disclosed to others), a rival trader who is not a client but in some manner obtains this information and, well knowing its nature and the basis upon which it was distributed, uses it in his competing business and thereby injures the first mentioned trader in his business, commits a wrongful act *vis-à-vis* the latter and will be liable to him in damages.[19]

In reaching this conclusion, the court appears to have been influenced less by the English authority recognising breach of confidence as actionable than by the *I.N.S.* case and its condemnation of the defendant who is "endeavoring to reap where it has not sown".[20]

A person who was not a rival trader could be liable for certain types of interference with trade, but the court decided that in this case it was necessary for the plaintiff to establish that the defendant acted as one of its competitors. Otherwise, the plaintiff could not meet the essential condition of proving that the defendant's conduct caused damage to the plaintiff, damage here being the loss of actual or potential customers. The court held that the plaintiff's pleadings failed to allege the competition element (that the defendant was in competition with the plaintiff or used the information from *Credit Records* in a competing business) and otherwise failed to state a cause of action for unlawful competition with sufficient clarity. The defendant's exceptions were therefore upheld.[21]

19 Dun and Bradstreet (Pty.) Ltd. v. S.A. Merchants Combined Credit Bureau (Cape) (Pty.) Ltd., 1968 (1) S.A. 209, 221 (C).

20 See pp. 302-03, *supra*. Compare Multi Tube Systems (Pty.) Ltd. v. Ponting, 1984 (3) S.A. 182 (D), in which the court's approach to misuse of confidential information by one of the plaintiff's employees resembled the approach of the English courts.

21 Compare Harchris Heat Treatment (Pty.) Ltd. v. Iscor, 1983 (1) S.A. 548 (T) (customer of plaintiff interdicted from using furnace it had substantially copied from plaintiff's furnace; defendant's furnace used for treating defendant's own steel plate). See also Prok Africa (Pty.) Ltd. v. N.T.H. (Pty.) Ltd., 1980 (3) S.A. 687 (W), in which it was held that a plaintiff who was not the owner of confidential information but was licensed by the foreign owner to use it had standing to sue for wrongful use of the information. The defendant was a manufacturer who began sales of the same product as the plaintiff.

15

DEFAMATION

While an independent course has been set in recent years, defamation law in Southern Africa retains much in common with defamation law in common law jurisdictions.[1] This is especially true of the traditional elements of the *prima facie* case: publication by the defendant of a defamatory statement about the plaintiff. (No distinction is drawn between libel and slander.) In a majority of the cases discussed below, the presence of one of these elements was at issue. Also received into Southern African law have been the defence of truth (justification) and the various privileges, including fair comment.[2]

WHAT IS DEFAMATORY

Whether the defendant's statement was defamatory or capable of conveying a defamatory meaning is the subject of numerous reported judgments.

In *Schoeman v. Potter*,[3] a magazine article written by the defendant described his encounter with the plaintiff some years earlier. In conjunction with references to the plaintiff's wealth and eccentricity, the article said, "He was that queer combination of

1 See generally Burchell, *The Law of Defamation in South Africa* (1985).

2 See *ibid.*, 13-17.

3 1949 (2) S.A. 573 (T).

garrulousness and courtesy, squalor and dignity, that one often finds in country districts." The court held that the word "squalor" conveyed that the plaintiff lived "under conditions and amid surroundings characterised by personal filth or dirt" and was defamatory. It "tends to degrade him in the eyes of his fellow-men and is thus clearly actionable".

In *Jonker v. Davis*,[4] the defendant said to the plaintiff in Afrikaans, "You must remember that I am the son of a rich man and that I have been well brought up (educated). I will not stand for a boy like you, who grew up in a *krot* and obtained a little education from your father, sending me such an insulting letter." The meanings of "*krot*" included "hovel" and "hut". The court held that this comparison of the wealth and upbringing of the plaintiff and defendant was not defamatory. In contrast to the statement in *Schoeman v. Potter*, there was no imputation of personal squalor. Early disadvantages in life and the defendant's boasting would not cause feelings of hatred, ridicule or contempt in the right-thinking or fair-minded person or cause the plaintiff to be shunned.

Botha v. Shaw[5] arose from an interview the defendant gave to newspaper reporters upon the dissolution of her marriage to the plaintiff. The gist of the story, printed in two newspapers, was the plaintiff's refusal to have sexual intercourse with the defendant during their marriage and the defendant's despair about not being able to attract the plaintiff physically. She reportedly said that the plaintiff "appeared to have a psychological block about wanting me".

The plaintiff submitted that "when it is said of a newly married husband that his wife did everything within her power to have sexual relations with him, but did not succeed, something must be wrong with the man, and . . . the reasonable reader would conclude that he was impotent or suffered from an abnormality as regards sexual intercourse". The court disagreed, finding no defamation. The reasonable reader would see the "lament of a woman deserted in her love and who eventually flounders in the darkness of doubt". It was not defamatory to say of a man that he refuses to have intercourse with his wife. The normal reader would not see impotence or abnormal lack of sexual interest in this. The reader would instead understand that the plaintiff lacked interest in his wife for various possible reasons. Nor would the term "psychological block" be

4 1953 (2) S.A. 726 (G.W.).

5 1972 (1) S.A. 257 (O).

understood to mean that the plaintiff was impotent. A "mental obstruction" could have many causes.

In *H.R.H. King Zwelithini of Kwa Zulu v. Mervis*,[6] the plaintiff's complaint was the opposite: he had been portrayed as having too much interest in persons of the opposite sex. The plaintiff was hereditary king of the Zulu nation. An article on him in the defendants' newspaper was headlined, "Yes, I'm a Ladies' Man . . . Says Zwelithini as Wife No 3 bears his fifth child". The article quoted him as saying "I am a ladies' man." and mentioned a "conquest". The plaintiff asserted that this would be understood to mean that the plaintiff, although king of a large nation, was promiscuous and a man of loose sexual morals.

The court found no such defamatory meaning. It was not defamatory to describe a married person as a "ladies' man". The dictionary definitions of "ladies' man" did not suggest that the interest which such a man shows in women is an immoral one. The ordinary readers of the defendants' newspaper would not read the article in the defamatory senses claimed by the plaintiff. The word "conquest" appeared to refer to one of the plaintiff's wives and in any event did not impart a derogatory meaning to "ladies' man".

According to the court, the plaintiff's royal status could affect only the *quantum* of damages, if liability were established. If the words "ladies' man" were not defamatory of a commoner, they were not defamatory of a king. The fact that a statement might lower a person in the estimation of a particular population group (here, the Zulu nation, which did not comprise the whole of the defendants' readership) did not make the statement defamatory. That depended upon the estimation of right-thinking people generally. That Zulus would regard it as disrespectful to call their king a "ladies' man" could not convert words having an innocent meaning in English into words bearing the defamatory meanings pleaded by the plaintiff.

Kritzinger v. Perskorporasie van Suid-Afrika (Edms.) Bpk.[7] arose from an ambiguous newspaper article introduced by a misleading headline. The writer of the article likely intended to report that in judicial proceedings involving two well-known former rugby players, Nelie Smith and Klippies Kritzinger, the personal estate of the former had been sequestered and the company of which the latter was a director had been liquidated. However, the article referred to the

6 1978 (2) S.A. 521 (W).

7 1981 (2) S.A. 373 (O).

company as if it belonged to Kritzinger and could be read as reporting that the personal estates of both Smith and Kritzinger had been sequestered. This impression was reinforced by the article's headline: "Nelie and Klippies declared bankrupt". Kritzinger claimed damages for defamation from the publisher and distributor of the newspaper.

The court was of the opinion that a reasonable reader would not infer from a report that the plaintiff's company was in liquidation or sequestration that the plaintiff was guilty of maladministration; this was not defamatory. The court therefore focused upon the description of the plaintiff as bankrupt and a person whose estate had been sequestered. The defendants contended that this was not defamatory of the plaintiff because he was not a "businessman". The court agreed that, insofar as the law of defamation had treated specially reflections on the credit of a businessman, the plaintiff was not such a person. A businessman for this purpose was someone who operated a business himself, out of which he made his living or profits; someone whose own credit was an important aspect of the operation of the business activities. While described in his pleadings as a businessman and company director, the plaintiff was at most a director with a shareholding and probably also an employee of the company concerned. His personal credit was not at stake in it.

The court held, nevertheless, that the plaintiff had been defamed and awarded damages. This conclusion was based primarily upon Roman-Dutch law, but much of the reasoning is applicable to the common law of defamation--for example, the dependence of non-business individuals in modern society upon the availability of credit, which could become unavailable if there was no redress for the spread of false reports, and the protection which would be given a person who intended to go into business at a future date if statements going to the credit of a person not then a businessman were actionable. The court regarded reflections on credit as affecting the reputation of a person even though he was not a businessman.

It was a question of fact whether a statement about a person's finances diminished the regard in which he was held and was actionable in a given case. It was necessary to distinguish between a statement which caused injury to reputation and a statement which only caused hesitation or unwillingness to extend credit, in self-protection. In this case, there was evidence that the newspaper article did cause and could in the future cause the plaintiff difficulty in obtaining credit and employment. The court found that the esteem in which the plaintiff was held by others was sufficiently connected to his financial standing that the newspaper article was injurious to his reputation and defamatory.

In *Fortune v. African International Publishing Co. (Pty.) Ltd.*,[8] a magazine reported that the Department of African Languages at the University of Rhodesia was having trouble continuing its Ndebele courses. The head of the department was reported to have said that "Ndebele is becoming a dead language." The head was aggrieved by this erroneous report. He went to "considerable pains" to let it be known that the magazine's assertions were incorrect and wrote a letter to the magazine's editor challenging its correspondent "to show when and where I made the extraordinary remark that 'Ndebele is becoming a dead language.'" The magazine published this letter. Beneath it, an editorial note said that according to the magazine's correspondent, the head of the department made the disputed statements at a given time and place.

The head sued the magazine's publisher, claiming that publication of the correspondent's confirmation of the original report together with his own emphatic denial made him out to be a hypocritical liar, denying in public what he said in private. The court held that this would not be how readers of the magazine would understand what was published. They would simply take it as a dispute between the plaintiff and the correspondent, for which there were many possible reasons. Nothing said by the magazine indicated that the correspondent's version was to be accepted in preference to the plaintiff's denial.

The plaintiff in *Coulson v. Rapport Uitgewers (Edms.) Bpk.*[9] alleged defamation by a newspaper's statement that he had been "summarily dismissed" as editor of another newspaper. This appeared in an article reporting the appointment of the plaintiff's successor. The plaintiff drew a distinction between being "summarily dismissed" and being "requested to resign". The former implied that the plaintiff had committed misconduct, for serious misconduct was grounds for lawful summary dismissal. It also implied that his employer could not tolerate him for a moment longer.

The Appellate Division did not agree. It thought that when an employer offers an employee a choice between resignation and summary dismissal, the employer's motive is usually to save the employee embarrassment. One might infer in the case of summary dismissal that the breach between employer and employee is more serious than in the case of an employee requested to resign, but so

8 1976 (2) R.L.R. 223 (G.D.).

9 1979 (3) S.A. 286 (A.D.).

far as defamation was concerned there was little difference between the two.

The court did not accept that a report of summary dismissal implied misconduct. There could be grounds for dismissal to which no such unfavourable connotation attached, and summary dismissal without lawful grounds frequently took place. A newspaper editor might have differences of opinion with the owner in regard to numerous matters. Serious disputes might arise, leading to summary dismissal. The main topic of the article complained of was the new editor's appointment and previous career. The "overwhelming impression" given to a reasonable reader was that the plaintiff had to give way to the new appointee, who on account of his qualifications, his experience and possibly his political convictions was more acceptable to the publisher than the plaintiff. Such a reader would not find in the report an allegation of dishonesty, incompetence, breach of duty, moral untrustworthiness, or unfitness to serve as editor. For the foregoing reasons, the Appellate Division concluded that the plaintiff had not been defamed.

In *Good v. Smith*,[10] the plaintiff claimed that the defendant represented the plaintiff as having failed to join the armed forces during World War II although eligible to do so. The plaintiff asserted that the defendant's words, gestures and "sneering and aggressive manner" conveyed that he was a coward for not having enlisted. He relied upon the alleged attitude of English-speaking South Africans that members of this group, such as the plaintiff, should join one of the armed forces. Other South Africans were said to consider that persons who supported the war effort had a duty to join if eligible.

The court held that the defendant's conduct could not reasonably be understood to impute that the plaintiff was a coward. In view of the large numbers of English-speaking South Africans who were eligible to join the forces but did not do so for wholly creditable reasons, no reasonable person could regard another as a coward solely because he had not joined. Thus the defendant had not defamed the plaintiff.

The plaintiffs in *Prinsloo v. S.A. Associated Newspapers Ltd.*[11] wished to prevent a newspaper from publishing an article and photograph identifying a university student as a suspected police informer. The plaintiffs were the father of a person identified in the

10 1964 (4) S.A. 374 (N).

11 1959 (2) S.A. 693 (W).

judgment as "Miss X" and the colonel in charge of the security branch of the South African Police. There had been articles in the press alleging that a young woman at the University of the Witwatersrand had been doing "espionage" work for the South African Police at the university, reporting to the police on activities at the university. The article the plaintiffs sought to suppress reported that the president of the university's Students' Representative Council and another person took Miss X from her home at midnight to a flat where she was interrogated by fellow students about reporting to the police; the two appeared in a magistrate's court to answer questions in connection with this incident; Miss X categorically denied knowledge of allegations they had made.

The plaintiffs contended that the article and photograph defamed Miss X in portraying her as a person who made reports to the police. The court, following *Byrne v. Deane*,[12] held that this was not defamatory. It might well be that a section of the community thought such behaviour was not correct, but in the court's opinion no right-thinking person would think less of a student for reporting criminal activities. Whether the court's conclusions were correct is open to question. It must be doubted that the South African Police were receiving reports only of criminal activities and that the right-thinking person would not think ill of a student who engaged in "espionage" concerning fellow students.[13]

The defendant in *Karim v. Wetterings*[14] was alleged to have made several statements to the effect that the plaintiff had been declared a prohibited immigrant by the Botswana government and had to leave the country within six months. The plaintiff, an attorney, claimed that the statements carried the innuendo that he was an undesirable person or had been guilty of some unlawful conduct. The court held that to say of a person that he is a prohibited immigrant is not defamatory. It was not capable of causing the plaintiff to be shunned or avoided, exposing him to hatred, contempt or ridicule, lowering him in the estimation of right-thinking people, etc. The court had in view the various categories of persons who could be declared prohibited immigrants in Botswana. The president could declare all of the nationals of a particular country to be prohibited immigrants. The plaintiff failed to establish that the defendant's

12 [1937] 1 K.B. 818 (C.A.).

13 See Boberg, *Law of Delict*, 1959 Ann. Surv. S. Afr. L. 113, 120-22.

14 1974 (2) B.L.R. 34 (H.C.).

statements were understood to mean that he had been guilty of unlawful conduct. The judgment leaves open the possibility that had this innuendo been proved, the statements would have been found defamatory.

de Klerk v. Union Government[15] arose from the South African government's publication of its version of action taken under the Suppression of Communism Act[16] to remove Communists and Communist influence from trade unions. This included the statement that a secretary of the leatherworkers' union had been revealed as a Communist and forced to resign his post but control of the union "remained in the hands of men sympathetic to the former secretary"; an anti-Communist group was set up in the union and then registered as a second union in order "to overcome the difficulties of overthrowing the present executive". A member of the executive council of the leatherworkers' union claimed damages for defamation.

The court sustained the claim and awarded damages. It held that the article was defamatory in imputing to members of the executive council, who controlled the leatherworkers' union, at least an inclination toward Communism. This implied unfitness for membership of a union executive and was defamatory in view of the provisions of the Suppression of Communism Act and contemporary public opinion. The court did not mention that the act itself recognised that it could be defamatory to describe a person as a Communist. In order to make it easier to inform the public about supposed Communists, the act provided that in certain circumstances there would be no liability in damages for describing a person as a Communist.[17]

In *Gayre v. S.A. Associated Newspapers Ltd.*,[18] the defendant had published in its newspaper an article entitled "Pro-apartheid Scot's Visit Causes Stir". It concerned the South African Genetic Society's invitation to the plaintiff to be its guest of honour at the society's congress and adverse reaction to this invitation. According to the plaintiff's declaration, the article stated that Johannesburg scientists

15 1958 (4) S.A. 496 (T).

16 No. 44 of 1950, repealed, Internal Security Act, No. 74 of 1982, s. 73 (S. Afr.).

17 Suppression of Communism Act (now Internal Security Act), No. 44 of 1950, s. 17*bis* (S. Afr.).

18 1963 (3) S.A. 376 (T).

were shocked by the invitation, a number said they would boycott the congress, one professor had declined to deliver a paper as a result, and at least one member had resigned from the society in protest. It was reported that the plaintiff had been called a "Fascist geneticist". The article allegedly conveyed that the plaintiff's scientific views were racialistic and he was misusing scientific evidence to "bolster up ideological concepts". The plaintiff claimed to have been defamed in his avocation as an anthropologist and ethnologist by imputations that he had committed disreputable conduct in and was unfit for his avocation and unworthy of the honour bestowed upon him by the South African Genetic Society.

The court held that the plaintiff had a cause of action with respect to the averments that the defendant had represented him as possessing racialistic views, being a "Fascist geneticist", and having misused scientific evidence to bolster up ideological concepts. To say of an anthropologist that his views were racialistic imputed to him an unscientific approach to his subject, warped by antagonism to certain races. To call him a "Fascist geneticist" was to impute to him an approach to genetics which was unscientific and influenced by unwarranted political considerations. The overtone now attached to the word "Fascist" was well-known to be one of extreme and intolerant nationalism which ill combined with science, especially in a field so closely related to race as genetics.

The reference to the plaintiff as a "Fascist geneticist" was capable of defaming him as an anthropologist and ethnologist. The sciences were related. A person with "Fascist" views on genetics was likely to have them on anthropology and ethnology as well, and such a person would not be worthy of an invitation to be a guest of honour at a conference of scientists in the "broad field of the study of mankind". To convey that the plaintiff misused scientific evidence for ideological reasons was also defamatory as guilt of "disreputable conduct".

The report that scientists were shocked by the society's invitation to the plaintiff and some would boycott the conference was held not to be defamatory. To found a defamation action, it was necessary to establish that the views ascribed to the plaintiff were so abhorrent that they repelled decent and right-thinking people. "Copernicus was shunned and despised by some people because of his views on a heliocentric universe, but one would have to suggest that they were right in doing so before it would be defamatory of him."[19]

19 *Ibid.*, 380.

The paragraphs complained of mentioned only a few individual people who were going to shun the plaintiff, not that "a body of scientists" were determined to shun him.

In *Chesterton v. Gill*,[20] the issue was whether it was defamatory to label the plaintiff as a "Nazi". This word appeared in a headline to a newspaper article on a bequest made to the plaintiff, the leader of a British right-wing group that subsequently joined the National Front. Although "Nazi" had more sinister overtones than "Fascist", *Chesterton v. Gill* was not an *a fortiori* case in relation to *Gayre v. S.A. Associated Newspapers Ltd.* because the offending newspaper article did not concern the plaintiff in his profession. Neither was there a government operation (including criminal sanctions) to destroy the influence of Nazis and Nazism in South Africa, as there was with respect to Communism in *de Klerk v. Union Government.* As the defendant contended, it was not defamatory *per se* to ascribe extreme political views to a person.

Nonetheless, the court had no hesitation in concluding that the word "Nazi" could be defamatory.

> I think I am entitled to have regard to the fact that the word "Nazi" is an abbreviation for the words National Socialist German Workers Party which had its origin in pre-war Germany and which party is now defunct. To describe a person as a Nazi to-day does not necessarily ascribe to him allegiance either to a defunct or even an existing political party. In its generally accepted sense to-day the description "Nazi" might very well have sinister and ugly connotations associated with the Nazis of pre-war Germany and the atrocities perpetrated by them which are still fresh in the memories of millions of people living to-day. To say of a person that he is a Nazi is in my opinion something much stronger than to say of him that he belongs to an extreme right-wing political movement or party, and conceivably members of such a right-wing political party might strongly resent being called Nazis. To label a person a Nazi might very well lower that person in the estimation of right-thinking members of society.[21]

20 1970 (2) S.A. 242 (T).

21 *Ibid.*, 247.

According to other criteria, a statement was defamatory if it was calculated to expose the defamed person to hatred, contempt or ridicule. In the court's opinion it required very little imagination to foresee a distinct possibility of exposing a person to hatred and contempt by labelling him a Nazi.

In *Golding v. Torch Printing & Publishing Co. (Pty.), Ltd.*,[22] the court considered whether it was defamatory to call the plaintiff a "quisling". The court held that it was not; while "quisling" had become synonymous with "traitor" that was not how it would be understood in this case. The context of the article was the division and dispute within South Africa's Coloured community concerning participation in the government-appointed Coloured Advisory Council (C.A.C.). The plaintiff was chairman of the C.A.C. and an advocate of participation. The defendants' paper adopted an attitude of uncompromising opposition to the C.A.C. The term "quisling" had been widely used by opponents of the C.A.C. to describe those persons who had joined it. The court believed that a reasonable person with knowledge of these facts would not read the defendants' article as a personal attack on the plaintiff. The article would be read only as an attack upon the plaintiff's membership in the C.A.C. and cooperation with the government. He was portrayed as guilty of treachery to his people in the sense that he was letting them down by the policy he was following. As such the article was not defamatory.

What seems to have been a milder criticism of a political opponent was found to be defamatory in *Greeff v. Raubenheimer*.[23] The eight-member council of a country town had divided into two factions of four members each. One faction was led by the defendant. The other faction consisted of the two plaintiffs and two other councillors. All councillors stood for re-election in 1972. The defendant's faction triumphed. The plaintiffs and a third member of their faction were defeated. Subsequently, the defendant was unanimously elected as mayor. His ceremonial induction took place at a large public function. Addressing the gathering, the defendant said:

> I have certain ideals for Oudtshoorn and I ask my council to follow me in working in the interest of the town. I am aware of the fact that the office embraces

22 1949 (4) S.A. 150 (C).

23 1976 (3) S.A. 37 (A.D.), aff'g 1975 (3) S.A. 236 (C).

> many responsibilities, but I also know that I shall receive strength for this great task. This is my third term as mayor, but whereas previously I could not move forward as I had to defend my back, tonight I have trusted guards around me and I can move forward.
>
> Should Councillors differ from me, I ask them to do so in the interest of the town.

The plaintiffs contended that the statement "whereas previously I could not move forward as I had to defend my back" defamed them. They interpreted this as imputing to them treachery and/or disloyalty toward the defendant in carrying out his duties as mayor and advancing the interests of the town. The Appellate Division accepted this interpretation and upheld the trial court's award of damages. It rejected the defendant's contention that his statement would be understood to mean that the plaintiffs had engaged in nothing more serious than tactical conduct behind the defendant's back, such as holding a caucus. The political background and the knowledge of it by those who heard or read of the defendant's statement would not mean that the defendant's words were not defamatory. It could be inferred from the statement as a whole that the plaintiffs had differed from the defendant in order to advance their own interests, not those of the town, and it could not be doubted that the plaintiffs' reputation had suffered a "serious setback".[24]

The plaintiff in *Demmers v. Wyllie*[25] claimed that he was defamed in a newspaper article published by the defendants. The article concerned sales of expropriated land by the Department of Community Development. The majority of the article concerned the department's handling of the land transactions, which were strongly criticised. Also featured was the purchase of the "plum parcel" and other "bargains" by the plaintiff. The plaintiff was protrayed as a prominent supporter of and substantial contributor to the National Party, which had governed South Africa for almost three decades. The article's headline was "Nat Scoops Huge Land Deal".

24 See Pienaar v. Argus Printing and Publishing Co. Ltd., 1956 (4) S.A. 310 (W), for another case in which political criticism was found to be defamatory as imputing discreditable conduct and improper motive to the persons criticised. The context was a major issue of national politics. The case is discussed pp. 325-26, *infra*.

25 1978 (4) S.A. 619 (D), aff'd, 1980 (1) S.A. 835 (A.D.).

The trial court, whose judgment was affirmed by a majority in the Appellate Division,[26] carefully considered the various defamatory meanings which were allegedly conveyed by the article and headline. The court found that the article did not suggest to the ordinary reader that the plaintiff had actively used his connections with the National Party to gain favourable treatment from the Department of Community Development or that the plaintiff made a large gift to the party in consequence of favours to him by the department. The size of the gift would be taken as an indication of the plaintiff's dedication to the party's cause. The article would probably suggest to the ordinary reader that the department had done him undue favours (land sales at low prices) because of his political allegiance, but this was not defamatory of the plaintiff. Portrayal as the passive recipient of such favours would not disparage a businessman in the estimation of right-thinking persons generally.[27]

The judgments delivered in the trial court and Appellate Division are of interest because of the judges' comments on the general principles employed in determining whether a statement is defamatory, particularly with reference to the hypothetical characters of the "ordinary reader", "reasonable reader" and "right-thinking person". Two judges in the Appellate Division dissented, believing that the plaintiff had been defamed.[28] One reasoned:

> It may well be that a lawyer would hesitate to infer that the plaintiff had "used" his link with the Party to gain favour in the absence of some allegation that he had actively taken steps to solicit or encourage the bestowing of such favour, but in the case of the layman, the ordinary reader untrained in the law and the demands of logic, we must accept . . . a certain amount of loose thinking and not only loose thinking, but implication read more freely, "especially--when it is derogatory". As was pointed out by Lord Devlin "the layman's capacity for implication is much greater than the lawyer's".[29] In this case we are

26 Demmers v. Wyllie, 1980 (1) S.A. 835 (A.D.).

27 The majority in the Appellate Division did not rule on whether this was defamatory, believing the point not to have been raised by the pleadings.

28 *Ibid.*, 839-40 (Jansen, J.A., dissenting), 846-52 (Diemont, J.A., dissenting).

29 Lewis v. Daily Telegraph Ltd., [1964] A.C. 234, 277 (H.L.) (Lord Devlin).

> concerned only with the layman.
>
> I must picture the Sunday afternoon reader of this newspaper who relaxes with his feet up and a glass by his side. He is in no mood to subject the article to close scrutiny and analysis. He is reading for his pleasure; sensational matter is provided for his entertainment. He will browse through the article, probably once only and, having done so, is likely to come to the conclusion that plaintiff's politics have brought him financial favours. It is improbable that he will caution himself and say that there has been no impropriety because it is nowhere stated in the article that plaintiff has actively used his political influence to canvass for favours. Indeed, if he does pause to think about the matter, he may well say to himself--this man has used his political connections to enrich himself because he has accepted undue favours knowing that such favours were extended to him because of his party political affiliation. In short he has "used" his politics by availing himself of the opportunities offered.
>
> Having come to this conclusion the ordinary reader will, in my view, regard the plaintiff with diminished respect. The article, will, in the well worn phraseology of the law, "tend to lower the plaintiff in the estimation of right-thinking members of society generally".[30]

The other dissenter suggested that in interpreting a newspaper article, the standard to be applied was that of the "average ordinary reader of that newspaper"--how, on the probabilities, he would have understood the article. Abstract and ideal qualities of being balanced, right-thinking and reasonable--if "reasonable" be understood in the sense of "sound of judgment"--should only be ascribed to the reader and should only come into play (if at all) when addressing the subsequent question of "whether the meaning attached to the article by the average ordinary reader (including the implications seen by him) is to be considered to be defamatory and therefore actionable".[31]

The principal points made in the majority judgment were that an article was defamatory if, on the balance of probabilities, it bore a defamatory meaning to ordinary readers, even if there was room for

30 Demmers v. Wyllie, 1980 (1) S.A. 835, 851-52 (A.D.) (Diemont, J.A., dissenting).

31 *Ibid.*, 840 (Jensen, J.A., dissenting).

a non-defamatory interpretation, and the ordinary reader was a person who gives a reasonable meaning to the words used within the context of the document as a whole and not a person who is prepared to give a meaning to those words which cannot reasonably be attributed thereto.

REFERENCE TO PLAINTIFF

In *Potgieter v. Ellis*,[32] the defendants' newspaper published an article concerning government meat control:

> CONTROLLERS STEAL THE UNDERCUT
>
> Meat control has been accused of causing many strange and unpleasant things, but its latest manifestation is in the nature of a phenomenon. For it has led to some Durban butchers finding an animal that defies all the laws of nature. This is a slaughter animal that has been quite unable, possibly owing to the drought, to grow an undercut.
>
> Many a sirloin that graces a Durban dinner table to-day lacks that succulent, much sought after titbit, so that the housewife, trying as ever to prepare a meal fit for the breadwinner to eat, buys a chunk of beef that has a big proportion of bone. The pre-meat scheme sirloin, bony though it might have been, at least had an undercut.
>
> But times have apparently changed since then and so have the oxen that we eat.
>
> One butcher, asked where the undercut had got to, confessed that he did not know.

The defendants regarded the article as an impersonal criticism of the meat control scheme and contended that the word "controllers" in the headline referred to "the whole army of controllers . . . , everybody engaged in the administration of the meat scheme from the highest to the lowest". The plaintiff was the chief official in the Durban area of two meat control authorities. He claimed that the article was defamatory of him individually.

The court held that the article was published "of and concerning

32 1948 (3) S.A. 1183 (D).

the plaintiff" to the readers of the defendants' newspaper who were in the meat trade in the Durban area. They called him the "Meat Controller" or "Controller" and would undoubtedly and reasonably understand the article as referring to him. Accordingly, the plaintiff had a cause of action if the article was defamatory. The court then held that it was not. The word "steal" in the headline would not be understood by those who connected the article with the plaintiff--persons in the meat trade--as meaning that the plaintiff had stolen sirloins. Rather, the article would be understood as a serious but non-defamatory criticism of the plaintiff as responsible for consumers being supplied sirloins without undercuts, criticism which did not attack his honesty, integrity, fitness for office or even his efficiency in the performance of his duties.[33]

The principal issue in *Vermaas v. Pelser*[34] was whether a handbill attacking an opposition party during a by-election campaign could be interpreted as defamation of that party's candidate in the by-election. The handbill denounced the United Party's policy on Communism and urged electors to vote for the candidate of the Herenigde Nasionale Party (H.N.P.). The United Party candidate claimed damages from the H.N.P. candidate, his election agent and the party's provincial organising secretary, all of whom "virtually accept[ed] responsibility" for the handbill's publication.

The court assumed for the purpose of its decision that the handbill was defamatory because readers could draw the inference that the United Party favoured Communism and the establishment of a black Communist republic in South Africa. The judgments in *Knuppfer v. London Express Newspapers, Ltd.*[35] provided the authority upon which the court principally relied in deciding whether the

33 Compare A. Neumann C.C. v. Beauty Without Cruelty International, 1986 (4) S.A. 675 (C). The defendant, an organisation opposed to the fur trade, placed at railway stations in suburban Cape Town posters depicting a woman dragging a fur coat from which blood was dripping, with the captions "It takes up to 40 dumb animals to make a fur coat. But only one to wear it." and "If you don't want millions of animals tortured and killed in leg-hold traps, don't buy a fur coat." The plaintiff was one of the six furriers in Cape Town which sold furs. The court held that the posters were not reasonably capable of being understood to refer to fur dealers or sellers as a group, let alone to the plaintiff specifically. If defamatory of anyone, the posters defamed the wearers or buyers of fur coats as stupid or brutish. If others were referred to, they encompassed everyone in the fur industry.

34 1951 (1) S.A. 752 (T).

35 [1943] K.B. 80 (C.A.), aff'd, [1944] A.C. 116 (H.L.).

handbill could be regarded as defaming the plaintiff individually. When defamatory words were written or spoken of a class of persons, a member of the class had no action for defamation unless there was something to show that the words about the class referred to him as an individual. The court held that the plaintiff could not meet this requirement. The handbill attacked the United Party as a whole and its policies and activities. The plaintiff had not been singled out for attack under the guise of an attack on his party. The handbill would probably have been issued whoever was the United Party candidate. It could not be regarded as referring to the plaintiff individually. The plaintiff's action therefore failed.[36]

In *South Africa Associated Newspapers Ltd. v. Estate Pelser*,[37] a newspaper reported strong criticism of the South African government's failure to stop the execution of a black man convicted of murder after reprieving the white man convicted of the same murder. The criticism was made by a law professor who was director of the Society for the Abolition of Capital Punishment. His reported remarks included the following:

> "The execution of Makinitha must fill all South Africans with shame.
>
> "Two persons of different races commit the same crime and are sentenced to the same punishment by a court of law; yet they are treated differently by the Executive on the plea of mercy.
>
> "One would have expected the Government to save the life of Makinitha, to avoid the obvious inference of discrimination; that they did not do so speaks volumes for their lack of concern for justice and the reputation of our law."
>
> . . . [I]f extenuating circumstances meriting reprieve were present in Wilson's case they were also present in Makinitha's case.

The plaintiff was Minister of Justice at the time the Executive Council (cabinet) made the decisions to reprieve the white man and

36 See McKerron, *Law of Delict*, 1950 Ann. Surv. S. Afr. L. 132, 133-34, which suggests that the court looked at the handbill's language but not the circumstances in which it was published and therefore applied too narrow a test.

37 1975 (4) S.A. 797 (A.D.).

not to reprieve the black man. He claimed damages for defamation from the newspaper and the professor who made the published statement. The plaintiff asserted that the statement imputed to him having acted shamefully and dishonestly, with racial bias and a gross lack of concern for justice. The defendants portrayed the statement as non-defamatory criticism of governmental action, referring to no particular individual.

The published statement might have been taken to refer to the plaintiff individually because, as newspaper readers might know, the Minister of Justice's portfolio was the one most concerned with the administration of justice and this minister was likely to have taken a leading, or at least active, part in the Executive Council's deliberations on reprieves of persons sentenced to death.[38] Instead, the Appellate Division proceeded to decide whether the statement reasonably could be understood as referring to any individual in the Executive Council.

Its conclusion was "yes". Criticism of the Executive Council's decision, such as "The execution . . . must fill all South Africans with shame.", was not defamatory of cabinet members. But the court drew a distinction between a statement that an Executive Council policy or decision resulted in shameful discrimination or gross injustice and a statement that a policy or decision resulted from an intention to discriminate (racially) or disregard of the requirements of justice. In the context of this case--a life-or-death decision--the latter was defamatory and could be understood as referring to the members of the Executive Council, such as the plaintiff, who made the policy or decision at issue. The court, following Lord Atkin in *Knupffer v. London Express Newspaper, Ltd.*,[39] recognised no special rules of law applicable to class or group libel. It was necessary only that the matter published concern the plaintiff personally. The matter here could be so interpreted. The plaintiff therefore stated a cause of action against the defendants.

The proposition that "group defamation" was actionable in the *Pelser* case was moderate in comparison with the proposition that there could be liability for defaming members of the group involved

38 This is implied in the trial court's judgment, Pelser v. South African Associated Newspapers Ltd., 1975 (1) S.A. 34, 43 (N), which the Appellate Division affirmed. See also the brief reference to this in the Appellate Division, South Africa Associated Newspapers Ltd. v. Estate Pelser, 1975 (4) S.A. 797, 813 (A.D.).

39 [1944] A.C. 116, 121-22 (H.L.).

in the earlier case of *Pienaar v. Argus Printing and Publishing Co. Ltd.*[40] It had long been the goal of the National Party, which came into government in 1948, to remove Coloured persons from the common roll of voters in the Cape Province. Other tactics having failed, the government decided to obtain an amendment to the South African constitution permitting this. This required a two-thirds vote of both houses of Parliament in a joint sitting. Unable to secure a two-thirds majority, the government obtained (by a simple majority in each house) legislation which would enlarge the Senate and change the electoral system for the Senate in such a way as to give the National Party seventy-seven of the eighty-nine Senate seats. The party would then have a two-thirds majority in Parliament as a whole, which would be used to remove Coloured voters from the common roll. All this met much criticism and opposition.

One newspaper found an opportunity for renewed criticism when it learned that the National Party in the Transvaal, which would fill twenty-seven Senate seats, was taking applications for the seats from party members, who were required to pay £20 for the privilege of being considered. In a leading article, the newspaper described this procedure as a "party lottery in which the prize is a senatorship at £1400 a year". There were said to be 150 applicants, swelling the party's coffers by some £3000. The article, entitled "The Senate Disgrace", contained biting criticism of this method of selecting senators, as well as of the whole Senate plan.

> [The aspirants for places in the Senate] are volunteering--for a handsome fee--to do the dirty work of the Nationalist Government by providing the two-thirds majority . . . . That this majority is now being created by a disreputable subterfuge apparently leaves them quite unmoved. The Government, at the taxpayers' expense, have invented a number of attractive new jobs, and they will vote for anything if they can get them.

A few days later, the newspaper published a list identifying the 156 applicants for Transvaal Senate seats. Two of them were the plaintiffs in the *Pienaar* case. They alleged that the article was understood to mean that they and the other applicants were persons of a base moral standard, who were prepared to act dishonestly provided they were paid for such acts, and consequently were not fit

40 1956 (4) S.A. 310 (W).

to associate with respectable people. The defendant newspaper contended that the leader was understood as criticism of National Party policy and the Senate legislation and not as imputing some improper motive to each individual aspirant.

The court sustained the plaintiffs' action. In its opinion, the article undoubtedly referred to each member of the group of Senate aspirants while also denouncing the procedure being followed. The article strongly criticised the applicants' participation and linked it to the "prize" of a senatorship and senator's salary. The court was also of the opinion that the article imputed an improper, discreditable or corrupt motive to the applicants; they were prepared to do dishonourable things in order to get seats in the Senate and the emoluments that went with them. This was such as to lower the reputation of the persons to whom it referred. Members of the class defamed, including the plaintiffs, therefore had a cause of action for defamation. The court awarded £100 to each plaintiff. The court had in mind that "when a large number of people are defamed the sting becomes diffused among them". It warned that damages awarded subsequently to other members of the class would be different (presumably lower) because their honour, as well as that of the two plaintiffs, had been vindicated by the outcome of this case.[41]

PUBLICATION

A defendant must have published defamatory matter about the plaintiff to a third person in order to be liable for defamation. If there has been no publication, the plaintiff has suffered no loss of reputation. If the defendant has not caused defamatory matter to be published, he is not responsible for any loss of reputation which the plaintiff may have suffered. *Pretorius v. Niehaus*[42] presented the question of the defendant's responsibility for publication when a letter sent by the defendant was opened by someone other than the person to whom it was addressed.

The plaintiff and his wife lived in a house in Sasolburg rented from the National Housing Commission. The commission's housing in Sasolburg was under the administration of the Housing Officer of

41 This is criticised in McKerron, *Defamation of Large Group of Persons*, (1957) 74 S.A.L.J. 14, on the ground that the injury to their reputations was the same as the injury to the plaintiffs' reputations.

42 1960 (3) S.A. 109 (O).

S.A.S.O.L. Dorpsgebiede Bpk., Muller. Muller received a written complaint from one Venter that the plaintiff was undressing at a open window and exposing himself in front of Venter's wife. In the course of his duties, Muller sent a copy of this complaint to Niehaus, the district representative of the National Housing Commission, and asked him if he could do something about the matter. Niehaus responded by sending a letter to the plaintiff at his residence. The letter said that a complaint had been received that the plaintiff was exposing himself at an open window before his neighbour's wife and he would be removed from the housing if this did not cease immediately. Niehaus sent a copy of this letter to the Housing Officer, S.A.S.O.L. Dorpsgebiede Bpk. The letter addressed to the plaintiff was opened and read by his wife before it was handed over to him. The copy was opened by staff members of S.A.S.O.L. Dorpsgebiede, who opened letters addressed to the Housing Officer, before it was handed over to Muller.

The plaintiff claimed damages from Niehaus and the National Housing Commission for publication of the defamatory letter to the plaintiff's wife and of the copy to personnel of S.A.S.O.L. Dorpsgebiede. (Publication to Muller was admittedly privileged as within the duties of Niehaus as district representative of the National Housing Commission and Muller as Housing Officer in Sasolburg.) The plaintiff contended that the defendants were liable for defamation because Niehaus caused publication of the letter and copy. The defendants contended that there was no liability because Niehaus addressed the letter and copy to the plaintiff and the Housing Officer respectively and did not expect that other persons would open and read them.

The court held that the test of responsibility for publication was whether the defendant knew or reasonably could have expected that publication would result from his conduct. A person who posted a defamatory letter was not responsible for all the consequences whether foreseeable or not. Accordingly, the court proceeded to consider whether Niehaus reasonably could have expected that the letter and copy would be opened and read by persons to whom they were not addressed. It concluded that the plaintiff had failed to establish this in the case of either the letter or the copy, and further that it had not been proved that the copy had been read by personnel of S.A.S.O.L. Dorpsgebiede. The action therefore failed for the plaintiff's failure to prove publication by the defendants.

The court thought it could generally be expected that a letter addressed to a firm or company would be opened and read by clerks when not marked "Private" or "Confidential", but here Niehaus did not have knowledge of a section of S.A.S.O.L. Dorpsgebiede that opened letters addressed to the Housing Officer and it had not been proved that he reasonably could expect that persons other than the Housing Officer would read what Niehaus had sent him. In the case of the original letter, the court's opinion was that it would reasonably be expected that a letter sent to a private person in his personal capacity would be opened and read only by that person. This was the expectation testified to by Niehaus, who had never found it necessary in his long experience in the Public Service to label correspondence to private persons as "Private" or "Confidential". The court did not accept that Niehaus should have expected that the letter would be opened by the plaintiff's wife in view of his knowledge that the plaintiff was married (houses were rented only to married persons), the stamp of the National Housing Office on the envelope (which would lead the plaintiff's wife to believe that it contained a communication about the house which she and the plaintiff rented), and the absence of "Private" or "Confidential".

In *Grindlays Bank Ltd. v. Louw*,[43] it was claimed that Grindlays had defamed Louw in a letter sent to him in his capacity as chairman of a public company, Impala. The letter allegedly implied that Louw had improperly caused Impala to assume responsibility for private debts owed by him, his wife and his private company. The letter was opened by Louw, who then discussed its contents with other directors of Impala.

The defamation claim was based upon the theory that the defamatory contents of the letter were published to Impala because it was addressed to Louw in his capacity as chairman of Impala and because it was necessary for him to bring a communication affecting the company's interests to the attention of members of the board of directors. The court held that the letter was never published. That Louw received the letter as chairman of Impala did not mean that its defamatory contents were published to Impala. Only he saw the letter. Consequently, his reputation could not have been damaged. That Louw felt obliged to disclose the letter to his fellow directors did not establish publication to Impala because such disclosure was unnecessary. Louw knew that the letter's suggestion that Impala had guaranteed the private loans was patently incorrect. He could have telephoned Grindlays' attorneys, pointed out the error in the letter, and requested a corrected letter which he could then safely have discussed with the other directors. Grindlays in fact quickly sent a

43 1979 R.L.R. 189 (G.D.).

corrected letter of its own volition.

Does a speaker publish a defamatory expression if his hearer does not then understand its defamatory meaning but discovers it a few minutes later? This was the issue in *Vermaak v. Van der Merwe.*[44] One Mrs. Claassens had telephoned the defendant and asked to speak with his wife. The defendant responded, "Haven't you heard that she is staying with that damned lesbian?" The person referred to as a lesbian was the plaintiff. At the time, Mrs. Claassens did not know what the word "lesbian" meant, so it had no defamatory significance for her. At the end of the telephone conversation, she asked her husband what a lesbian was. He told her.

The defendant submitted that there was no publication because the defendant's statement was not understood in any defamatory way at the time it was communicated. The plaintiff conceded there was no publication at that time but submitted that there was publication when Mrs. Claassens learned the meaning of "lesbian". The court held that publication had occurred.

> In our view the law would be deficient in a most material respect if a person who did everything he thought necessary to defame another could escape liability simply because the person to whom he addressed his defamatory statement did not immediately grasp the true significance of what he had been told. If the person addressed discovered the defamatory significance of the statement at a later stage, the defamer should be held liable, regardless of the length of the time lapse between communication and understanding.[45]

The court was influenced by the consideration that South Africa was a multilingual country, where persons could be addressed in a language other than their mother tongue and not immediately grasp a statement's defamatory meaning. Also, it regarded as applicable a South African decision[46] that a person has a cause of action when the reader of a defamatory statement did not know immediately that it

44 1981 (3) S.A. 78 (N).

45 *Ibid.*, 83.

46 Ferreira v. Sardinha, 1917 T.P.D. 477.

referred to the plaintiff but was so informed soon afterwards.[47]

One may well agree with the court that the law would be deficient if the plaintiff in *Vermaak v. Van der Merwe* had no remedy, given that only a few minutes elapsed between the defendant's statement and the plaintiff's understanding of it and that the plaintiff's reputation was damaged as much as if Mrs. Claassens understood the statement instantly. But it is difficult to accept that "the defamer should be held liable, regardless of the length of the time lapse between communication and understanding". Can it really be the law that there is liability when a statement is not understood as defaming the plaintiff until years after its communication?[48]

CONSENT

In *Fortune v. African International Publishing Co. (Pty.) Ltd.*,[49] the plaintiff claimed defamation by a magazine's confirmation of an earlier report of remarks allegedly made by the plaintiff. The plaintiff, the head of a university department of African languages, had asked the magazine's editor to publish a letter in which he denied making the remarks. The letter asserted that the number of Ndebele students in the department was a healthy one and challenged the magazine's correspondent "to show when and where I made the extraordinary remark that 'Ndebele is becoming a dead language'". The magazine published this letter together with an editorial note. The note stated, "Our Rhodesian correspondent reports that at a University Internal Review Sub-Committee meeting on June 5, Professor Fortune said, 'We are struggling for Ndebele students from an ever-decreasing pool. It is in imminent danger of becoming a dead or extinct language.'"

The court rejected the plaintiff's contention that the magazine

47 This principle was applicable to Pienaar v. Argus Printing and Publishing Co. Ltd., 1956 (4) S.A. 310 (W), discussed pp. 325-26, *supra*.

48 See Morgan, *Lesbians, Lies and Liability*, 1981 Camb. L.J. 245, which refers to statements published to a person who subsequently learns the meaning of the defamatory words, statements published to a person who subsequently obtains a translation of defamatory words spoken in a foreign language, statements published to a person who subsequently learns of facts that give defamatory meaning to the statements, and statements published to a person who subsequently learns the identity of the person defamed.

49 1976 (2) R.L.R. 223 (G.D.).

had defamed him by publishing the note.[50] In addition, it upheld the defence of *volenti non fit injuria* raised by the defendant. By sending a letter to the editor for publication and challenging the correspondent to state when and where the disputed remarks were made, the plaintiff assumed the risk that the magazine would publish with his denial the particulars of the occasion on which the plaintiff supposedly made the remarks. The plaintiff expected a response to his challenge and had been informed by the editor that the substance of his letter would be referred to the correspondent for comment prior to publication of the letter. The plaintiff, confident in the knowledge that he did not express the opinions attributed to him, may have anticipated that the correspondent's response would confirm his refutation of the original report, but he knowingly invited and assumed the risk of the publication that took place. The court distinguished the plaintiff's "challenge" here from the case of a plaintiff who "dared" the defendant to repeat in public or unprotected by privilege defamatory remarks made in private or under privilege. The plaintiff there would not be held to have consented to the defamation.

JUSTIFICATION (TRUTH)

South African Associated Newspapers Ltd. v. Yutar[51] presented the issue of whether evidence of the plaintiff's conduct after publication of a defamatory statement is admissible to support a plea of justification. The defamatory statement was a newspaper poster declaring "How Dr. Yutar Misled the Court". This concerned the plaintiff's conduct as prosecutor in a certain trial. The defendants sought to justify their statement by evidence of incidents occurring at previous and subsequent trials as well as incidents occurring at the trial to which the poster referred.

The plaintiff had pleaded that the poster would be understood to mean, first, that he had been guilty of disgraceful and unprofessional conduct; second, that he was a dishonest person; and, third, that he was unfit for the office of prosecutor in a court of law. The Appellate Division held that the evidence the defendants wanted to use was admissible because it was relevant to prove the truth of the

50 See p. 311, *supra*.

51 1967 (3) S.A. 454 (A.D.).

third meaning alleged by the plaintiff. The plaintiff's alleged conduct at previous trials was of unquestionable relevance to the question of his fitness for office at the time of the defamatory publication. Conduct at subsequent trials, not long after publication, was also relevant.

> Unfitness for office, as manifested by conduct, arises from disabling qualities or a lack of enabling qualities. Such qualities or the lack of them in the holder of an office are inherent in his mental equipment, make-up, disposition or turn of mind. Their presence or absence is not a fugitive feature which is there the one moment and gone the next, and cannot be confined to a particular date. To say of a man that he is unfit for his office is not merely an invitation to survey his past performance up to the date of the statement. It inevitably also raises the prospect of significant behaviour in the near future. If the unfitness is a fact it may be expected to be exposed not by a single isolated incident or by past occurrences only, but from time to time, and conduct subsequent to a particular date upon which it is alleged to exist would be as relevant to demonstrate its presence at that date as anterior conduct would be, provided, of course, that in both cases the conduct is not too remote to be of any probative value. [There is] no ground on which such a case is to be distinguished from one in which the defamatory statement expressly relates to possible or probable future conduct.[52]

One must accept the court's decision as correct, given the plaintiff's pleadings. If the plaintiff had relied only upon the literal meaning of the words on the newspaper poster, the evidence proferred by the defendants should have been inadmissible. A specific allegation of misconduct upon one occasion is not justified by misconduct at other times.[53] It seems that the plaintiff could have pleaded the literal meaning of the words complained of, treating them as defamatory because they imputed to him conduct discreditable in an advocate (at least if misleading the court was intentional). If so, the plaintiff was the victim of his own pleadings.

52 *Ibid.*, 458.

53 See Clerk & Lindsell, para. 20-61.

PRIVILEGES

In *Pogrund v. Yutar*,[54] the Appellate Division formulated and applied principles governing an advocate's liability for defamatory remarks made in a judicial proceeding. The case stemmed from newspaper accounts of torture and beating of prisoners at a South African prison. A prison warder had made a statement concerning this to a reporter. The reporter took the warder to an attorney, before whom the warder swore to the truth of the statement. Subsequently, the warder was prosecuted for knowingly making a false statement under oath. He pleaded guilty at a trial in which evidence of the falsity of his statement was adduced. Addressing the court on the question of sentence, the prosecutor made defamatory remarks about the reporter. The reporter sued the prosecutor for defamation.

The Appellate Division held that the limits of an advocate's privilege to make a defamatory statement in a trial were that the statement must be pertinent or germane to the issue in the case and have some foundation in the evidence or circumstances surrounding the trial. The court then concluded that the majority of the defendant's defamatory remarks were germane to the question of sentencing the prison warder, given the reporter's involvement in the case, and had a foundation in the evidence. There was, however, one remark which implied that the reporter deliberately falsified the warder's statement because this better suited the story the reporter wanted to bring out. This was thought not relevant to the question of sentence, because it did not add to the "depravity" of the warder's conduct, and to have no foundation in the evidence. The remark was, consequently, not privileged and damages were awarded in respect of it.

The Appellate Division was concerned in *Joubert v. Venter*[55] with the privileges of attorneys (solicitors) and witnesses as well as of advocates. With respect to advocates and attorneys, the court reiterated that a statement was privileged if it was pertinent or germane to the issue in the legal proceedings at hand and had some foundation in the evidence or circumstances surrounding the case. It specified that the defendant had the *onus* of establishing that the statement was pertinent or germane. However, the defendant did not

54 1967 (2) S.A. 564 (A.D.).

55 1985 (1) S.A. 654 (A.D.). See Burchell & Dendy, *Law of Delict*, 1985 Ann. Surv. S. Afr. L. 179, 216-20; Schmidt, *The Sisyphean Burden of Proof*, (1985) 102 S.A.L.J. 579.

have the *onus* of establishing the statement's foundation in the evidence or surrounding circumstances. This position was required, in the court's opinion, by the principle of public policy stated in *Findlay v. Knight*:

> the welfare of society demands that an advocate or attorney who pleads the cause of his client should have a large degree of freedom in laying his client's case before the Court, even though in so doing he defames the other party or even a third party . . . . To hamper his freedom in this respect would be to hamper the administration of justice . . . .[56]

It was for the plaintiff to prove that the defendant did not have "some foundation" for making the statement. However, there were other means of defeating counsel's plea of privilege. It was always open to the plaintiff to prove that the defendant was actuated by malice in the sense of an improper or indirect motive. This the plaintiff could do, for example, by proving that the defendant knew that his statement was false or that there was no evidence to substantiate it, or that the defendant made the statement on his own initiative without instructions and on the strength of untrustworthy information, or that the defendant's real motive was personal spite or ill will. Counsel's affirmative belief in the truth of his statement was not a requirement of the privilege. A showing that counsel did not subjectively believe that his statement was true did not defeat the privilege.

The privilege of the witness, like that of the advocate and attorney, was a qualified one.[57] In the present case, the relevant defamatory statements had been deposed to by a litigant in an affidavit to be used in legal proceedings. The Appellate Division decided that to establish the privilege the defendants were required to prove that the statements were relevant and germane to an issue in the case. The privilege would be defeated by proof that the deponent was actuated by malice. Alternatively, the plaintiff might succeed upon proof that the deponent had no reasonable grounds for believing

56 Findlay v. Knight, 1935 A.D. 58, 71 (Wessels, C.J., with whom Curlewis, J.A., concurred).

57 In this respect, South African law differs from the law in common law countries, where these privileges are absolute. See Clerk & Lindsell, paras. 20-70, 20-71; Fleming, 529-31; Prosser & Keeton, 816-20.

in the truth of the statements. Whether it was necessary to go further and prove that the statements were false and that the deponent did not believe them to be true was not decided, although the opinion was expressed that proof of falsity should be required.

The court held that with respect to privileges there was to be no difference between witnesses who deposed to an affidavit and witnesses who testified orally or between party and non-party oral witnesses, reserving only the question of whether an oral witness bore an *onus* of establishing the relevance of his statement to an issue in the legal proceedings. Arguably, it was "contrary to the interests of the due administration of justice to whittle away the wide protection afforded in the cases" to an oral witness by requiring him to prove that his answer was relevant to the questions asked rather than solely that he was testifying under oath when he made the statement in issue. The question was not necessary to decide in *Joubert v. Venter* and left open. Ultimately, the Appellate Division sustained the claim of privilege of all defendants involved in the case.

The Rhodesian Appellate Division's judgment in *Parsons v. Cooney*[58] is primarily concerned with a private citizen's privilege to make a defamatory communication about a public employee to his superiors. The defendant made an oral statement about the plaintiff, a municipal traffic supervisor. The defendant was asked to put the statement in writing, which he did in a letter to the officer-in-charge of traffic supervisors. The letter reported that the plaintiff had been sentenced to gaol five years earlier, had been "unable to hold down employment" at various hotels and night clubs, and had been dismissed for dishonesty by a shoe company. It expressed the belief that "municipal uniformed officials deserve better men" than the plaintiff.

The defendant claimed a privilege to make these statements on the basis that he was a ratepayer and had an interest or moral duty in putting these matters before the plaintiff's employers. The court did not make a definitive ruling on the point--the plaintiff's express malice defeated any privilege that may have existed--but found that "all the indicators" were that the occasion was not privileged. The case was not one in which an employer had requested information about an employee. The defendant was asked to put his oral statement in writing but in substance had volunteered the information given.

In the court's view, it might not be strictly necessary for a prior

58 1970 (2) R.L.R. 75 (A.D.), 1971 (1) S.A. 165 (R.A.D.).

request to be made in order for a statement to be privileged. An employer who dismissed a servant for dishonesty might, for example, have a moral duty and privilege to warn a person with whom the servant sought employment. But it was doubtful that the former employer would have a privilege once the servant had been in the other's employment for some time and had been rendering honest and faithful service therein. A moral duty to complain to the plaintiff's superiors would have existed if, say, he had been drunk in the course of his duties, abusive toward members of the public, or taking bribes not to issue parking tickets, but the defendant made no complaint about the plaintiff's service as a traffic supervisor. "[U]nless such an exigency can be said to exist which makes it a matter of urgency" a member of the public (be he a ratepayer or not) was not privileged to gratuitously give information about an employee who was already in the employment of the municipality and, apparently, carrying out his duties satisfactorily.

> The question of the fitness and suitability of people for such posts as traffic supervisors, in the light of their past record prior to entering such service, is entirely a matter for the internal administration of the municipality, and has nothing to do with the ratepayers at all. . . . [I]t is only where the employee in question, as a public officer, so conducts himself in his employment as such *vis-à-vis* the members of the public, or the complainant in particular, as to give rise to an interest and/or duty to report such misconduct or misbehaviour to his employer, that the qualified privilege in question arises.[59]

In *Jordaan v. van Biljon*,[60] a high school teacher complained of a petition which the defendant had circulated in the district and sent to the school committee. The petition protested the appointment of the plaintiff as English teacher in the high school on the grounds that his pupils' performance in English was declining daily and he showed no interest in their progress, making it necessary for them to seek extra classes from another teacher. It was signed by the defendant and twenty-seven other persons. All were parents of children who were in the plaintiff's class or soon would be, but two

59 *Ibid.*, 81, 170.

60 1962 (1) S.A. 286 (A.D.). See Boberg, *Animus Injuriandi, Privilege, and the Law of Defamation*, (1962) 79 S.A.L.J. 113.

were parents of children who were not yet in the plaintiff's high school.

The defendant defended on the ground of privilege: the petition was published in furtherance of the common interest he shared with other school parents in the progress of their children, in the manner in which they were taught, and in preventing the appointment or service of a teacher who was incapable of proper instruction or insufficiently interested in his pupils' progress. The defendant also asserted his own interest in communicating the matter and a duty to the other parents in communicating the matter to them in their interest. The plaintiff denied that there was a privilege. No reasonable person with the defendant's limited knowledge of the plaintiff's alleged shortcomings could regard it as his duty or in his interest to communicate the contents of this petition to anyone else. Also, it was unnecessary to the asserted duty or interest to publish the petition to all the persons to whom it was shown.

The Appellate Division sustained the claim of privilege. As a parent, the defendant had with other parents a common interest in the education the children received. Publication was made pursuant to that interest, which encompassed discussion of a teacher's competency, and it was not excessive. The defendant, in order to further his interest in the progress of his own child, could communicate with other parents who also had an interest in order to achieve better results with their support. This applied to the parents of a child who would be in the plaintiff's class the next year as well as parents of current pupils. The occasion was privileged and the plaintiff had failed to prove that the defendant had malice or did not believe the truth of the statements. The plaintiff, therefore, could not recover damages.

The court in *Informa Confidential Reports (Pty.) Ltd. v. Abro*[61] considered whether any privilege attaches to a publication that reports credit information to business concerns. The defendant sent to subscribers a weekly list of judgments, orders for liquidation and other proceedings bearing upon the creditworthiness of the persons involved. One issue reported that a judgment or provisional sentence had been granted against the plaintiff. The plaintiff claimed damages for defamation, the defendant's publication having reflected adversely on the plaintiff's ability or willingness to pay his debts.

The defendant was not protected by the privilege to report judicial proceedings because its report was incorrect. As an

61 1975 (2) S.A. 760 (T).

alternative, the defendant asserted a privilege based upon its contractual duty to publish the type of information it did and the six hundred subscribers' interest in receiving it, so that they could protect themselves against credit risks. The court, following a seventy-year-old decision in the Cape Province,[62] held that no such privilege existed. The court did not believe that the increase in the use of credit during the intervening seven decades was reason to depart from the decision. To the contrary, it believed that it was now necessary for persons in the defendant's position to exercise even greater care to avoid wrongfully impairing a person's reputation for credit-worthiness.

In *de Klerk v. Union Government*,[63] a publication of the South African government defamed a trade union official by associating her with Communism.[64] The government had published the defamatory article in a periodical published by the State Information Officer in London and distributed primarily in the United Kingdom. A small number of persons and libraries in South Africa also received the periodical. The article was intended to refute criticism of the South African government's actions under the Suppression of Communism Act[65] to remove Communists and Communist influence from trade unions. It included the statement that a secretary of the leatherworkers' union had been revealed as a Communist and forced to resign his post but control of the union "remained in the hands of men sympathetic to this former secretary"; an anti-Communist group was set up in the union and then registered as a second union in order "to overcome the difficulties of overthrowing the present executive". The plaintiff was a member of that executive.

The government submitted that the article was privileged because it served to defend the government against attacks upon and criticism of its actions concerning trade unions. The State Information Officer had the duty to reply to such attacks, many of which had been made in the United Kingdom, and correct erroneous impressions they had created. The government relied upon authority recognising a privilege for a person whose character or conduct had

62 Pickard v. S.A. Trade Protection Society, (1905) 22 S.C. 89.

63 1958 (4) S.A. 496 (T).

64 See p. 314, *supra*.

65 No. 44 of 1950, repealed, Internal Security Act, No. 74 of 1982, s. 73 (S. Afr.).

been attacked to defend himself by making a reply to the attack. It contended and the court agreed that this privilege was not limited to defamation of the person who made the attack. Defamation of independent third parties could be privileged.

The court held that the defamation of the plaintiff was not privileged because it did not meet what the court believed was an essential requirement of the "self-defence" privilege: that the statement be relevant and appropriate to the occasion. The statements concerning the plaintiff--the references to the executive council of her union--were not necessary to vindicate the government against criticism of its attitude toward trade unions and its naming of unionists as Communists. They went beyond what was germane and reasonably appropriate. The statements were outside the scope of the privilege on which the government relied.

The court held, alternatively, that the government was not protected by privilege because the statements complained of were made recklessly. Publication was reckless because the government's director of information in London had the article published without making any enquiries concerning the accuracy or sources of the information it contained. He took it for granted that the facts were correct and did not consider that any particular person was libelled as a Communist. The article had been written by another employee of the South African government, who did not give evidence.

FAIR COMMENT

In *Marais v. Botha*,[66] the court held that in order to succeed on a defence of fair comment, a defendant must prove that at the time he made the comment he was aware of the facts on which the comment was based. The court then held that the defendants had failed to make the required proof. The defendant who uttered the defamatory statement did not testify and there were no proven circumstances from which it could be inferred that he had the necessary knowledge.[67]

66 1973 (3) S.A. 952 (O), rev'd, 1974 (1) S.A. 44 (A.D.).

67 Compare Waring v. Mervis, 1969 (4) S.A. 542 (W), in which it was held that the defendant was not required to present evidence that his statement genuinely expressed his actual opinion, in the absence of any imputation of dishonesty or express malice. A plea of fair comment would be justified if the comment was such that an honest man could have made it. This was a

A second requirement, held the court, was proof that the defendants' audience had knowledge of the facts commented upon. The defendants had failed to meet this requirement, too. The facts were not contained in the published statement, they were not proved to have been known to the audience, and they were not of such moment and so notorious that the average informed citizen would have been aware of them and realised that the matter published was comment thereon.

A more extensive treatment of fair comment is found in *Marais v. Richard.*[68] The case was adjudicated on the basis of requirements which had been established in *Crawford v. Albu:*[69] (1) the allegation published by the defendant must amount to comment (opinion); (2) the comment must be fair; (3) the factual allegations on which the comment was made must be true; and (4) the comment must refer to a matter of public interest. The fourth requirement was not in issue and the court did not directly address the question of truth. After analysing particular passages in a newspaper's leading article, whose publication had given rise to the litigation, the Appellate Division concluded that the passages were comment and not unfair. The judgment definitely applies the "ordinary reader" standard to the question of whether a statement is comment: would the ordinary reader (with ordinary qualities of reasonableness) have understood it as comment or fact, in light of its contents, the context in which it was used and the circumstances known to the reader. The judgment is, however, ambiguous concerning the standard to be applied to the question of whether comment is fair. The standard might be that of honesty and relevance, or it might import (in addition or substitution) considerations of reasonableness.[70]

matter the court could decide without presentation of evidence by the defendant.

68 1981 (1) S.A. 1157 (A.D.), aff'g 1979 (1) S.A. 83 (T).

69 1917 A.D. 102.

70 See the analysis of the judgment in Burchell & Lewis, *Law of Delict*, 1981 Ann. Surv. S. Afr. L. 193, 228-32.

16

PRIVACY

In the United States, but not other common law jurisdictions, "invasion of privacy" is actionable in tort.[1] It appears that invasions of privacy are actionable in Southern Africa as an impairment of a person's *dignitas*. The invasions which are actionable may be those established in American law.[2] Few cases are directly in point and only two warrant consideration here. One case involves "appropriation of name or likeness".[3] The other involves "publicity given to private life".[4]

In *O'Keeffe v. Argus Printing and Publishing Co. Ltd.*[5] the plaintiff, a radio announcer and producer, had consented to be photographed at the second defendant's shooting range for the purpose of illustrating a news article in the first defendant's newspaper. The photograph then appeared, with text including the plaintiff's name, in an advertisement of the shooting range, guns and ammunition. The advertisement was placed in the first defendant's newspaper by the second defendant. The text had the instructor correcting the plaintiff's aim of a pistol. She claimed damages for the unauthorised

1 See Prosser & Keeton, 849-69; Restatement (Second) of Torts, ss. 652A-652I (1977).

2 See generally McQuoid-Mason, The Law of Privacy in South Africa (1978).

3 *Cf.* Restatement (Second) of Torts, s. 652C (1977).

4 *Cf.* Restatement (Second) of Torts, s. 652D (1977).

5 1954 (3) S.A. 244 (C).

use of her photograph and name for advertising purposes.

The court held that this could be actionable. The plaintiff having claimed a "violation of her dignity" the question was whether, in the light of modern conditions, the plaintiff could reasonably be held to have been subjected to "offensive, degrading or humiliating treatment". This question was answered in the affirmative. To use a person's photograph and name, without consent, for advertising purposes might constitute offensive conduct. The court referred to the position in the United States. There it was well established that the unauthorised publication of a person's photograph for advertising purposes was actionable. The court believed that the principle prevailing in the United States went much further, striking at all invasions of privacy which could reasonably be considered offensive to persons of ordinary sensibilities. The unauthorised use of a person's photograph for advertisement purposes was merely one instance of this.

Similar considerations must apply in South African law, the court thought. The unauthorised publication of a person's photograph and name for advertising purposes was capable of constituting "an aggression upon that person's *dignitas*"--an *injuria*. This was all it was necessary to decide at this stage of the proceedings. The court was not holding that such publication was always actionable. Much would depend upon the circumstances of each particular case, the nature of the photograph, the personality of the plaintiff, his station in life, his previous habits with reference to publicity and the like.

In *X. v. Rhodesia Printing and Publishing Co. Ltd.*,[6] the plaintiffs applied for an order barring publication of a news article in the defendant's newspaper. The plaintiffs had been married to each other in the United States. Each had children from prior marriages. American courts awarded custody of the children to the plaintiffs' former spouses. In violation of the custody orders, the plaintiffs removed the children from the United States to Rhodesia, taking great pains to conceal their whereabouts from the ex-spouses. Two years later, an American detective traced the family to a farm in Rhodesia. A daily newspaper in Rhodesia received details of this from the United States. It prepared an article on these events which identified the family's name and address. The plaintiffs contended that publication of this article would be an *injuria* to themselves and their children and asked that the court prevent it.

6 1975 (2) R.L.R. 281 (G.D.), 1974 (4) S.A. 508 (R), aff'd, 1974 (2) R.L.R. 207 (A.D.), *sub nom.* Rhodesian Printing & Publishing Co. Ltd. v. Duggan, 1975 (1) S.A. 590 (R.A.D.).

The plaintiffs did not explicitly assert that the facts contained in the article were private matters to which publicity could not lawfully be given. They argued that publication would be detrimental to the children as well as embarrassing to themselves. The children might be distressed by reaction to the article, particularly at their schools. The defendant contended that publication would be in the public interest and pointed out that the matter had received considerable public attention in the American city from which the plaintiffs had come.

The court quoted from the judgment in *O'Keeffe v. Argus Printing and Publishing Co. Ltd.* and from Section 867 of the first *Restatement of Torts*,[7] to which that judgment had referred with approval. This provided, "A person who unreasonbly and seriously interferes with another's interest in not having his affairs known to others or his likeness exhibited to the public is liable to the other." The commentary to the section declared:

> The rule stated in this Section gives protection to the interest which a person has in living with some privacy, but this protection is relative to the customs of the time and place and to the habits and occupation of the plaintiff . . . . One who unwillingly comes into the public eye because of his own fault, as in the case of a criminal, is subject to the same limitations upon his right to be let alone. Community custom achieves the same result with reference to one unjustly charged with crime or the subject of a striking catastrophe. Both groups of persons are the objects of legitimate public interest during a period of time after their conduct or misfortune has brought them to the public attention; until they have reverted to the lawful and unexciting life led by the great bulk of the community, they are subject to the privileges which publishers have to satisfy the curiosity of public as to their leaders, heroes, villains and victims.
>
> . . . [L]iability exists only if the defendant's conduct was such that he should have realized that it would be offensive to persons of ordinary sensibilities. It is only where the intrusion has gone beyond the limits of decency that liability accrues. These limits are exceeded where intimate details of the life of one who has never

7 Restatement of Torts, s. 867 (1939).

> manifested a desire to have publicity are exposed to the public, or where photographs of a person in an embarrassing pose are surreptitiously taken and published. On the other hand, there is no invasion of a right of privacy in the description of the ordinary goings and comings of a person or of weddings, even though intended to be entirely private, or of other publications to which people do not ordinarily seriously object. In determining liability, the knowledge and motives of the defendant, the sex, station in life, previous habits of the plaintiff with reference to publicity, and other similar matters are considered. A distinction can be made in favor of news items and against advertising use. It is only when the defendant should know that the plaintiff would be justified in feeling seriously hurt by the conduct that a cause of action exists.[8]

The court held that the principles set forth in the *Restatement of Torts* were applicable to Rhodesian law. There was a right of privacy whose nature and extent depended in each case upon the kind of factors referred to in the *Restatement*. Applying these principles, parties to a custody dispute and the children involved would usually have a right to object and prevent the publicising of that dispute. Custody disputes were essentially of a domestic nature. It would normally be an offensive invasion of privacy, going beyond the bounds of decency, for a newspaper to publish the details, or possibly even the facts, of such a dispute. This conduct would be regarded *prima facie* as an *injuria*, giving rise to an action for damages or, in appropriate cases, to a right to claim an interdict.[9]

The court considered that insofar as the plaintiffs sought to protect themselves from publicity, they had forfeited any right to such protection by their conduct. A person who acted contrary to a court order and surreptiously disappeared with the children must expect

8 Restatement of Torts, s. 867, comments *c*, *d* (1939). Copyright 1939 by the American Law Institute. Reprinted with the permission of the American Law Institute.

9 The court noted that the Rules of Court provided that a court might order child custody proceedings to be held *in camera*--a rule which would be applicable if the parents awarded custody in the United States came to the Rhodesian court to seek the return of the children to them. The court believed that this rule reflected the existence of a right to privacy in custody matters.

publicity to ensue. It was by means of publicity that the custodial parent could best expect to find the children's whereabouts. The children might be harmed by the publicity, but until they were located their right to privacy was subservient to the right of the custodial parent to trace them. Wide publicity as to their disappearance would not constitute an offensive invasion of their privacy going beyond the bounds of decency. Even after they were found, the absconding parent could not complain on his own behalf of continued publicity.

Once the children were found, however, the legal position with respect to them became completely different. The need for publicity disappeared. The public would have no legitimate interest in further news. The issue became entirely domestic. No harm would result to anyone, press or public, in "restoring or restraining the veil of privacy". On the other hand, publicity might well have a detrimental effect on the children--particularly children of an impressionable age, as were the children in the present case. Now that the children had been found, publicity was to the court's mind "offensive, uncalled for, and beyond the bounds of decency". Accordingly, the plaintiffs were entitled to succeed insofar as they applied for an interdict on behalf of the children. The identity of the children could not be disclosed by the defendant. In order to prevent disclosure, a somewhat wider preliminary order was confirmed.[10]

10 This result and the court's reasoning in reaching it were subsequently approved in the Rhodesian Appellate Division. Rhodesian Printing and Publishing Company Ltd. v. X., 1974 (2) R.L.R. 207 (A.D.), *sub nom.* Rhodesian Printing & Publishing Co. Ltd. v. Duggan, 1975 (1) S.A. 590 (R.A.D.).

BIBLIOGRAPHIC NOTE

Texts: The principal English-language works on Conflict of Laws and the law of Delict (Tort) in Southern Africa are listed in the table of principal works cited and abbreviations, marked with an asterisk (*). Relevant general works on the law and legal system of Southern Africa include H.R. Hahlo & E. Kahn, The Union of South Africa: The Development of its Laws and Constitution (London: Stevens, 1960); W.J. Hosten, A.B. Edwards, C. Nathan & F. Bosman, Introduction to South African Law and Legal Theory (rev. ed. Durban: Butterworths, 1980); R.W. Lee, An Introduction to Roman-Dutch Law (5th ed. Oxford: Clarendon Press, 1953); R.W. Lee & A.M. Honoré, The South African Law of Obligations (2d ed. Durban: Butterworths, 1978); A.F.S. Maasdorp, The Institutes of South African Law, Volume 4 (8th ed. Cape Town: Juta, 1972); G. Wille, Principles of South African Law (7th ed. Cape Town: Juta, 1977); and a multi-volume encyclopedia, The Law of South Africa (Durban: Butterworths, annual supplements).

Periodical literature: Southern African law journals cited in this book are listed in the table of principal works cited and abbreviations. Other contemporary journals include Codicillus, De Jure, Fakulteitslesings, Lesotho Law Journal, Meditationes Medii, Natal University Law and Society Review (successor to Natal University Law Review), Responsa Meridiana, Speculum Juris, Tydskrif vir Regswetenskap (Journal for Juridical Science), and Zimbabwe Law Review (successor to Zimbabwe Law Journal). Specialised journals include Industrial Law Journal, Modern Business Law, South African Company Law Journal, South African Journal of Criminal Law and Criminology, South African Journal on Human Rights, South African Tax Journal, South African Yearbook of International Law, and Taxpayer. Journal commentaries in English on the cases and statutes discussed in this book are cited in the footnotes. The citations can be located by use of the tables of cases and statutes.

Law Reports: Southern African law reports published since 1947 are listed in the table of principal works cited and abbreviations. The South

African Law Reports (established in 1947) contain reports from all Southern African countries except Botswana (formerly Bechuanaland), Lesotho (formerly Basutoland) and Swaziland. Many cases are reported in both the South African Law Reports and the reports of Zimbabwe (formerly Southern Rhodesia). Before 1947, there were separate reports for each division of the Supreme Court of South Africa. A full list of pre-1947 reports is set forth in Hosten, Edwards, Nathan & Bosman, Introduction to South African Law and Legal Theory 873-79 (rev. ed. 1980).

The Annual Survey of South African Law, published annually by Juta (Cape Town) since 1947, contains extensive listings of legal texts and periodical literature, organised by subject, as well as comprehensive analysis of cases reported in the South African Law Reports and significant South African legislation.

PRINCIPAL WORKS CITED AND ABBREVIATIONS

SOUTHERN AFRICAN LAW REPORTS (1947 TO PRESENT)

B.S.C.	Bophuthatswana Law Reports
B.L.R.	Botswana Law Reports
H.C.T.L.R.	High Commission Territories Law Reports
L.L.R.	Lesotho Law Reports
R. & N.C.A.	Rhodesia and Nyasaland Court of Appeal Decisions
R. & N.	Rhodesia and Nyasaland Law Reports
R.L.R.	Rhodesian Law Reports
S.A.	South African Law Reports
S.R.	Southern Rhodesia Law Reports
S.L.R.	Swaziland Law Reports
Z.L.R.	Zimbabwe Law Reports

SOUTHERN AFRICAN LEGAL PERIODICALS

Acta Juridica	Acta Juridica
Ann. Surv. S. Afr. L.	Annual Survey of South African Law
Businessman's Law	Businessman's Law
Butt. S. Afr. L. Rev.	Butterworths South African Law Review
Comm. & Muni. L. Rptr.	Commercial and Municipal Law Reporter
C.I.L.S.A.	Comparative and International Law Journal of Southern Africa
De Jure ac Legibus	De Jure ac Legibus
De Rebus	De Rebus
Obiter	Obiter
Rhod. L.J.	Rhodesian Law Journal
S. Afr. Ins. L.J.	South African Insurance Law Journal
S.A.L.J.	South African Law Journal

T.S.A.R.	Tydskrif vir die Suid-Afrikaanse Reg (Journal of South African Law)
T.H.R.-H.R.	Tydskrif vir Hedendaagse Romeins-Hollandse Reg (Journal of Contemporary Roman-Dutch Law)
Zimb. L.J.	Zimbabwe Law Journal

CONFLICT OF LAWS TEXTS

Anton	A.E. Anton, Private International Law (Edinburgh: Green, 1967)
1 Castel	J.-G. Castel, Canadian Conflict of Laws, Volume 1 (Toronto: Butterworths, 1975)
2 Castel	J.-G. Castel, Canadian Conflict of Laws, Volume 2 (Toronto: Butterworths, 1977)
Cheshire & North	G.C. Cheshire & P.M. North, Private International Law (10th ed. London: Butterworths, 1979)
Dicey & Morris	A.V. Dicey & J.H.C. Morris, The Conflict of Laws (10th ed. London: Stevens, 1980)
Forsyth	*C.F. Forsyth, Private International Law (Cape Town: Juta, 1981)
Graveson	R.H. Graveson, The Conflict of Laws (7th ed. London: Sweet & Maxwell, 1974)
Kahn, Domicile	*E. Kahn, The South African Law of Domicile of Natural Persons (Cape Town: Juta, 1972)
Kahn, *Husband and Wife*	*E. Kahn, *Jurisdiction and Conflict of Laws in the South African Law of Husband and Wife*, in H.R. Hahlo, The South African Law of Husband and Wife (4th ed. Cape Town: Juta, 1975)
Kahn, *Succession*	*E. Kahn, *The Conflict of Laws in the South African Law of Succession*, in M.M. Corbett, H.R. Hahlo & G. Hofmeyr, The Law of Succession in South Africa (Cape Town: Juta, 1980)
Leflar	R.A. Leflar, L.L. McDougal III & R.L. Felix, American Conflicts Law (4th ed. Charlottesville: Michie, 1986)
McLeod	J.G. McLeod, The Conflict of Laws (Calgary: Carswell, 1983)
Morris	J.H.C. Morris, The Conflict of Laws (3d ed. London: Stevens, 1984)
Nygh	P.E. Nygh, Conflict of Laws in Australia (4th ed. Sydney: Butterworths, 1984)

Scoles & Hay	E.F. Scoles & P. Hay, Conflict of Laws (St. Paul: West, 1982)
Silberberg	*H. Silberberg, The Recognition and Enforcement of Foreign Judgments in South Africa (Pretoria: U.N.I.S.A., 1977)
Sykes & Pryles	E.I. Sykes & M.C. Pryles, Australian Private International Law (Sydney: Law Book, 1979)

TORTS TEXTS

1 Boberg	*P.Q.R. Boberg, The Law of Delict, Volume 1 (Cape Town: Juta, 1984)
Clerk & Lindsell	J.F. Clerk & W.H.B. Lindsell, Torts (15th ed. London: Sweet & Maxwell, 1982)
Dias & Markesinis	R.W.M. Dias & B.S. Markesinis, Tort Law (Oxford: Oxford U., 1984)
Fleming	J.G. Fleming, The Law of Torts (6th ed. Sydney: Law Book, 1983)
Linden	A.M. Linden, Canadian Tort Law (3d ed. Toronto: Butterworths, 1982)
McKerron	*R.G. McKerron, The Law of Delict (7th ed. Cape Town: Juta, 1971)
Prosser & Keeton	W.L. Prosser & W.P. Keeton, The Law of Torts (5th ed. St. Paul: West, 1984)
Salmond & Heuston	J.W. Salmond & R.F.V. Heuston, The Law of Torts (18th ed. London: Sweet & Maxwell, 1981)
Street	H. Street, The Law of Torts (7th ed. London: Butterworths, 1983)
van der Walt	*J.C. van der Walt, Delict: Principles and Cases (Durban: Butterworths, 1979)
Winfield & Jolowicz	P.H. Winfield & J.A. Jolowicz, Tort (12th ed. London: Sweet & Maxwell, 1984)

*Texts on the law of Southern Africa.

TABLE OF STATUTES

TABLE OF CASES

CONFLICT OF LAWS INDEX

TORTS INDEX

About the Author

PETER B KUTNER is Professor of Law at the University of Oklahoma. He has published articles on torts, conflict of laws, and evidence, and is the author (with Osborne M. Reynolds, Jr.) of *Advanced Torts Cases and Materials* (forthcoming).

www.ingramcontent.com/pod-product-compliance
Ingram Content Group UK Ltd.
Pitfield, Milton Keynes, MK11 3LW, UK
UKHW020233290926
15470UKWH00002B/507

9 780313 262